The Tree of Life

The Tree of Life

The Form of Human Consciousness

STEPHEN B. MACHNIK

RESOURCE *Publications* · Eugene, Oregon

THE TREE OF LIFE
The Form of Human Consciousness

Cover: Etching on a metal plate by the author 15" x 27." *Tree of Life*, Green Olive, S. B. Machnik

Resource Publications
An Imprint of Wipf and Stock Publishers
199 W. 8th Ave., Suite 3
Eugene, OR 97401

www.wipfandstock.com

PAPERBACK ISBN: 978-1-7252-8554-5
HARDCOVER ISBN: 978-1-7252-8555-2
EBOOK ISBN: 978-1-7252-8556-9

03/17/21

Where there is no vision

the people perish[1]

PROV 29:18

---

1. Later translations are more in keeping with the sense of the verse. However, the traditional translation from the KJV reflects the intent of this book. Where there is no revelation, the people cast off restraint; But happy is he who keeps the law. NKJV

Contents

Illustrations | *ix*

List of Tables | *xi*

Preface | *xiii*

Acknowledgments | *xv*

Abbreviations | *xvii*

Introduction | *xix*

Chapter 1: Some Experiential Background | 1

Chapter 2: The Analytical Trail | 5

Chapter 3: Lonergan: A Conscious Operation | 7

Chapter 4: Between Soul and Spirit | 11

Chapter 5: Man Created in the Image of God Reflects a Symbolic
        Cosmology | 16

Chapter 6: The Symbolic Form of the Menorah | 20

Chapter 7: Feelings Related to Knowing | 23

Chapter 8: Anthropological Structures of the Imaginary | 34

Chapter 9: The Burning Bush | 41

Chapter 10: The Menorah and Its Elements | 52

Chapter 11: The Holy Grail | 66

Chapter 12: Chronology of the Shroud of Turin | 79

Chapter 13: The Celtic or High Cross | 93

Chapter 14: Glastonbury | 98

Chapter 15: The Tree of Life | 113

Chapter 16: Long Term Cycles | 130

Chapter 17: Green Olive Tree | 147

Chapter 18: The Battle of the Trees | 152

Chapter 19: The Book of Romans, a Similar Pattern | 159

Chapter 20: The Tree and Menorah in Revelation | 167

Chapter 21: Relationship between the Books of Daniel and
        Revelation | 190

Chapter 22: Moving Forward | 194

Chapter 23: The Function of the Eternal in the Temporal | 196

Chapter 24: Conclusion | 198

Notes on Drawing | 200

Appendix Overview | 203

Appendix 1: The Rosary-Cross | 205

Appendix 2: Genealogy of Jesus | 212

Appendix 3: Sacred history and its relationship to Glastonbury | 217

Appendix 4: Origins of Kings | 268

Appendix 5: Literary Origins of the Arthurian Legend | 275

Appendix 6: Word Origins of the Menorah and Oil of Anointing | 313

Appendix 7: Myvyrian Archaiology | 317

Appendix 8: Maps of Southwest Britain | 322

Bibliography | 333

Index | 341

Illustrations

Figure 1: Dynamics of knowing | 29

Figure 2: Dynamics of doing | 29

Figure 3: Deepak Chopra order of being | 31

Figure 4: The ten sefirot, illustration by author | 45

Figure 5: The Arch of Titus in Rome | 54

Figure 6: Salvia Palaestina | 54

Figure 7: Mural from a synagogue in Dura Europus 244 CE | 55

Figure 8: Architectural remnant from Kouyunjik | 56

Figure 9: Sketch of menorah elements by the author | 61

Figure 10: Image of the Menorah | 64

Figure 11: The Tassilo Chalice | 70

Figure 12: Monasterboice—Tall Cross (7m) east face, photo by
author | 94

Figure 13: Monasterboice—Tall Cross west face, photo by author | 95

Figure 14: Monasterboice—Muiredach's Cross east face, photo by
author | 96

Figure 15: Egyptian Coptic curtain fifth to sixth century | 97

Figure 16: Brass plate rubbing from Glastonbury by Sir Henry
Spelman | 107

Figure 17: Willis Plan of Abbey Church | 109

Figure 18: Coat of Arms Joseph of Arimathea | 110

Figure 19: Methuselah | 130

Figure 20: Fieldbrook Stump | 134

Figure 21: Photo by the author showing a portion of a 64" Douglas fir | 136

Figure 22: The Three Sisters | 149

Figure 23: Photo by Jasper Machnik | 150

Figure 24: Etching "Tree of Life—Green Olive" 2010, S.M. | 151

Figure 25: The River of Life; design by author | 202

Figure 26: Notre Dame des Victoires Church in Quebec City 1688 AD | 207

Figure 27: Prayer bead counter | 209

Figure 28: 153 as a triangle | 210

Figure 29: King Arthur's Inscription | 267

Figure 30: Roman Britain | 323

Figure 31: Saxon Britain | 324

Figure 32: Somerset west | 325

Figure 33: Somerset east | 326

Figure 34: Monmouth Wales | 327

Figure 35: Cornwall east | 328

Figure 36: Cornwall west | 329

Figure 37: Devon west | 330

Figure 38: Devon east | 331

List of Tables

Table 1: Pattern of relations between analytical, metaphysical and symbolic operators | xxi

Table 2: Relation between being, feeling, and cognition | 27

Table 3: Isotopic classification of images | 36

Table 4: Christian origins of the kings of Britain | 77

Table 5: Chronology of the Shroud of Turin and the Grail Legend | 79

Table 6. Kings and Queens of Jerusalem | 88

Table 7. Hungarian, Byzantine, and German owners | 89

Table 8. German and French Origins of the Shroud 12–14C | 90

Table 9: Partial List of Longest Living Individual Organisms | 131

Table 10: Tree ring measurements S.M. | 137

Table 11: The seven Churches of Revelation | 170

Table 12: Patterns of four's, three's, and seven's | 186

Table 13: Number 153 | 211

Table 14. Genealogy of Jesus | 213

Table 15: Family of Jesus | 216

Table 16. Chronology of legends and events related to Glastonbury Abbey (G.A.) | 217

Table 17: Joseph of Arimathea in the New Testament | 234

Table 18: Genealogy of Welsh Kings and associated tables BC—1100 AD | 268

Table 19. Word Roots | 313

Table 20. An abridged copy of the list of kings | 317

Preface

What if the literary form of the Bible derived its pattern from the elementary process of creation? And what if that pattern, which is basic to all organic life, is the underlying dynamic that defines the content and form of the book? It appears that, in a very concrete sense, the order of biblical books reveals an innate symbolic shape that corresponds to our organic development. The same development, which is played out individually, from the womb to fulfillment, to the grave and life beyond similarly defines the dynamic of the Bible. The process also appears to mirror the operations of human understanding, whereby we move from natural and supernatural experience to an enlightened conclusion.

In *A Dangerous Method* (Vintage 1994), John Kerr's story of Jung, Freud, and Sabina Spielrein, Kerr writes, "For Jung the method of analogy was the mode of operation for the symbolizing mind. That was what Jung had in mind when he talked of psychoanalysis as requiring the skills of a 'poet.'"[2] Kerr goes on to say, "while the conscious mind operated within the Kantian categories of time, space, causality, etc., the unconscious mind operated symbolically, forging its affective meanings through a logic uniquely its own." *The Tree of Life* is an attempt to analyze the symbolic form.

If we are made in the image of God, what are the implications? The image does not refer to the physical eye and to what it sees, but rather it refers to image in the sense of a spiritual state that perceives the unity and interrelatedness of similar natures. The process of coming to know things, each other, and who we are is related to our natural development that corresponds to our nature, which we have in common with the divine. I use Bernard Lonergan's *Insight* to illustrate the process and to suggest that the images acquired through spiritual perception correspond to elementary

2. Kerr, *A Dangerous Method*, 110–1.

symbolic forms that permeate and constitute foundational systems of the
Bible and similarly constitute our form of being.

The Tree of Life is an appreciation of this profoundly symbolic nature
and its relationship to our divine natures. The book illustrates the three-
part relationship of flower, bud, and bowl. The origin of the design comes
from the description of the menorah (מְנוֹרָה) in Exodus, which says: Three
bowls (גְבִעִים) shall be made like almond blossoms on one branch, with
an ornamental knob (כַּפְתֹּר) and a flower (פֶּרַח). (Exod 25:33a) Lastly,
the tree of life is the x of the unknown within the equation of our human
consciousness.

The book can also be compared symbolically to the action of Jacob's
dream; where there is an exchange between heaven and earth. "And he
dreamed that there was a ladder set up on the earth, the top of it reaching
to heaven; and the angels of God were ascending and descending on it."
(Gen 28:12) NRSV.

Acknowledgments

Dear Wendy. Thank you for your love, your support, your comradery, and your infinite patience. I am also grateful for Dr. Stanley Krippner's encouragement in 2016 when he read through the text. I met Krippner at the Maimonides Dream Telepathy Lab in Brooklyn, New York in the late 60s. Thank you also to Louise Beinhauer for her help in formatting and copy-editing and to the department of theology at Concordia University in Montreal, Doctors Pamela Bright, Christine Jamieson, and Marie-France Dion, who helped me articulate my theological thinking. I am grateful to Wipf and Stock for the opportunity to publish.

Abbreviations

AV/KJV	Authorized version or King James Version
BDB	Brown, Driver, Briggs, Hebrew and English Lexicon
JSNT	Journal for the Study of the New Testament
LXX	The Septuagint
NIV	New International Version
NKJV	New King James Version
NRSV	New Revised Standard Version
OED	Oxford English Dictionary
RSV	Revised Standard Version
S	Strong's Concordance
SBD	Smith's Bible Dictionary
TDOT	Theological Dictionary of the Old Testament
TWOT	Theological Wordbook of the Old Testament

Abbreviations

Introduction

Is it possible that the Bible's revelatory nature can be appreciated by understanding its symbolic form? It is a form that mirrors the divine in which we were created, an image which corresponds intimately to the I Am. I suggest that humanity's evolution of consciousness is a macro development and a manifestation of the daily micro-processes of human understanding. And that the macro process reflects the Bible's symbolic nature.

My study came out of a desire to understand Christian-Jewish relations. At the same time, Bernard Lonergan's *Insight, A study of human understanding*,[3] helped me to concretize the relationship between the cognitive process and the metaphysical. I compare the cognitive operations by which we come to know what is real, to the micro, and the metaphysical elements to the symbolic, to the macro. Differences in relations that were insurmountable on a rational level became accessible on a metaphorical level. Lonergan relates his cognitive operations to Aristotle's metaphysical terms and says that they are similar in form.[4] I concluded that the combined form of these processes characterized a unifying symbolic operation which I believe is a development within human consciousness, a primordial symbolic operating principle that harmonizes the process of human understanding.

From an artistic point of view, the Hebrew menorah, a principal liturgical symbol for the Jewish people, expresses through its elements, a portrayal of the evolution from an elementary organic dimension to a dimension that ultimately transcends to the non-material. The menorah visually transcends from the organism as a seed to the organism in a state of light. The main stem, branch, and flame components of the temple artifact incorporate a

---

3. Lonergan, *Insight* (1957, 1970). Pages from the later University of Toronto Press (1992) are numbered 23–24 pages higher. That is, p. 124 instead of p. 100.

4. They are isomorphic. Lonergan, *Insight*, Chapter XV

recurring motif of bud, bowl, and flower. Several authors[5] have also concluded that the menorah is a cultural and sacred representation of the tree of life. Although the tree is referred to several times in the Bible, such as in the book of Proverbs, it only appears in Genesis and Revelation. In a sense, the menorah carries on the memory of the tree of life throughout the intermediate period from Genesis to Revelation.

The real and symbolic import of the tree is to provide substance to a non-material dimension. The tree, as a symbol, acts as an agent of representation, which enables a movement between conscious states from the organic to the non-material. As a real entity, it prefigures an abundant life experience. Both the menorah and the tree of life provide an underlying symbolic framework within the Bible. We then understand the Old and New Testaments as a movement from an infinite dimension to a cultural human dimension in which our evolution of consciousness is embedded. The Bible reveals itself as having a supra-conscious form that interacts directly with our patterns of understanding and with our personal desire to know by which we come to an understanding.

Symbolic and organic patterns relating to the tree imply a promise of an event or a representation of recurring events, such as the seed of the woman, the oil of anointing, and the olive tree. Lastly, when the combination of the menorah/tree of life as a symbolic template is applied to the Book of Revelation, a more comprehensible pattern emerges.

In chapter fifteen of Insight on the elements of metaphysics, Lonergan is very explicit regarding the relationship of his cognitive operations to Aristotle's terms. This is important because, in my further development of symbolic metaphor and its relation to Aristotle, the agreement must compare not just imaginatively, but realistically, to the process within which we can come to an intelligent conclusion.

5. C. Meyers (1976) and J. Levenson (1985)

Table 1: Pattern of relations between analytical, metaphysical and symbolic operators[6]

Tree of Life (Transcends all operations)	The menorah and the three elements	Aristotle's metaphysical terms	Lonergan's conscious operations
	Flame / Flower	Act	Judgment Decision Transcendent values
	Bowl	Form	Understanding
	Bud / Seed	Potency	Experience

It is my suggestion that there is a symbolic correspondence between the elements of the menorah, the tree of life, and the operations of knowing and being. When we see the Bible through the eye of transcendent being, through the eye of the heart, we grasp the unity of form, the immediacy of its potency, and the possibilities inherent in our transcendent relationship to the divine.

Recent research describes the nature of the human being as an electric body.[7] Although it is not my purpose in this book to investigate the electrical nature of consciousness, I want to consider that there is a correlation between the metaphysical elements and an electric circuit. I suggest that the metaphysical elements of potency, form, and act, compare to the resistive (-ᴡᴡ-), capacitive (-ǁ-), and inductive (-ᴇᴇᴇ-) elements of a circuit. Or similarly, that the seed is a resistor, the bowl is a capacitor, and the flame is an inductor. And that our being is both grounded (⏚) and has a capacity for induction. As humans, as humanity, we are an electrical-magnetic, transmitting-receiving being. To be able to imagine human consciousness as a form of electric energy facilitates the dynamic of our human knowing.

6. The pattern of understanding generally begins from the level of our experience and moves in an upward direction to an appreciative decision culminating in a heightened consciousness. There can also be revelatory insights flooding our consciousness from (a so-called) up to down movement.

7. Dispenza, *Becoming Supernatural.* Lipton, *The Biology of Belief.* Ober, *Earthing.* Scott, *The Electric Sky.* And many others.

Chapter 1

Some Experiential Background

In the sixties, at the Ecole des Beaux Arts in Montreal, Quebec, I had the opportunity to read Richard Maurice Bucke's *Cosmic Consciousness*.[1][2] Bucke graduated from McGill's School of Medicine in 1862. The book had a profound, experiential impact on me. I call it experiential because, although my understanding of the experience of self merging with the infinite remained in my psyche, I did not act on the experience with conscious intelligence. The idea of cosmic consciousness remained in the back of my mind. It probably motivated me to investigate more mystical avenues of thought, to go through an eastern meditation experience, and start a (short-lived) synectics-based organization to research methods of alternate consciousness and problem-solving methods for business. In retrospect, I believe if I had used a more conscious intelligent approach, I might have researched the biographies of the individuals listed by Bucke as having had a cosmic experience and possibly tried to understand whether there was a process involved in coming to that experience.

From my reading of Bucke's *Cosmic Consciousness,* a person may or may not identify with a supreme being. In my own experience, I have had "intimations," as Wordsworth would say, of cosmic experience. In 1964, I had a sense of connectedness to God, which I expressed in a poem, *The End.*

1. Thanks to Timothy Elliot a fellow art student from Hudson, QC.

2. The film *Beautiful Dreamers* (Colm Feore, NFB 1990), dramatizes Bucke's work at the asylum in London, Ontario and his relationship to the poet Walt Whitman.

In *Cosmic Consciousness*, Bucke defines three levels of consciousness. First: A simple consciousness which most humans and animals possess of the sensate world around them. Second: a self-consciousness in which humans are aware of themselves as distinct from their surroundings and can "identify their mental states as objects of consciousness." Third: A cosmic consciousness in which we have a consciousness "of the life and order of the universe." Bucke also identifies an associated "intellectual illumination—enlightenment," a "moral exaltation, a feeling of joy." There is also a "sense of immortality, a consciousness of eternal life," not as some future event but something that is immediately possessed. He believed that cosmic consciousness is a natural evolutionary step. Bucke also describes stages of consciousness similar to Lonergan's cognitive operations as described later.

> Thus, we have four stages of intellect, all abundantly illustrated in the animal and human worlds about us—all equally illustrated in the individual growth of the cosmic conscious mind and all four existing together in that mind as the first three exist together in the ordinary human mind. These four stages are, first, the perceptual mind—the mind made up of percepts or sense impressions; second, the mind made up of these and recepts—the so called receptual mind, or in other words the mind of simple consciousness; third, we have the mind made up of percepts, recepts and concepts, called sometimes the conceptual mind or otherwise the self conscious mind—the mind of self consciousness; and fourth, and last, we have the intuitional mind—the mind whose highest element is not a recept or a concept but an intuition. This is the mind in which sensation, simple consciousness and self consciousness are supplemented and crowned with cosmic consciousness.[3]

The intuitional mind! Many of us are familiar with and enchanted by the tales of Sherlock Holmes. But not many realize that the key to Sir Arthur Conan Doyle's character was inspired by Dr. Joseph Bell under whom Doyle served as a clerk. Bell was renowned for his ability to diagnose and describe the ailments, occupation, and activities of a stranger as a lesson in clinical observation. He was a forerunner in forensic science. The scientific mind wants to follow the evidentiary trail. However, it seems we miss the capacity for an intuitive grasp. That moment of insight that can see the forest in its completeness and not as the sum of its trees. "(T)he evidence of things not seen." (Heb 11:1b).

3. Bucke, *Cosmic Consciousness*, 13.

Bucke describes his own experience of cosmic consciousness as follows (~1872). (Note: 'he' Bucke speaks in the third person):

> He had finished reading Wordsworth, Shelley, Keats, Browning and Whitman with friends and was on his way home at midnight. He was in a state of quiet almost passive enjoyment. All at once, without warning of any kind, he found himself wrapped around as it were by a flame colored cloud. For an instant he thought of fire, some sudden conflagration in the great city (London, England), the next he knew that the light was within himself. Directly afterwards came upon him a sense of exaltation, of immense joyousness accompanied or immediately followed by an intellectual illumination quite impossible to describe. Into his brain streamed one momentary lightening-flash of the Brahmic Splendor which has ever since lightened his life; upon his heart fell one drop of Brahmic Bliss, leaving thenceforward for always an aftertaste of heaven. Among other things he did not come to believe, he saw and knew that the Cosmos is not dead matter but a living Presence, that the soul of man is immortal, that the universe is so built and ordered that without any peradventure all things work together for the good of each and all, that the foundation principle of the world is what we call love and that the happiness of everyone is in the long run absolutely certain. He claims that he learned more within the few seconds during which the illumination lasted than in previous months or even years of study, and that he learned much that no study could ever have taught.[4]

Bucke's experience resembles the experiences of the fifty or so individuals he has described in his book. A similarly insightful book, describing experiences of cosmic consciousness is Yogananda's *Autobiography of a Yogi*. A book that Steve Jobs of Apple kept on his desk.

I include the reference to Bucke to suggest that there is a manifest experience of the world of spirit, not exclusive to our notion of a "holy people," which implies a transcendent ground to our consciousness of being. Perhaps if children were taught by adults who acknowledged the domain of transcendent consciousness, we would not be so fragmented in our humanity. Or perhaps if children taught adults . . .

In the next chapter, I show that there is a correspondence between conscious intelligence and being. There is a progression towards a transcendent (or cosmic) consciousness, parallel to our intelligent processes, which are reflected in the symbolic patterns of the Bible. I hope to illustrate through

---

4. Bucke, *Cosmic Consciousness*, 8.

Bernard Lonergan's operations that we move through experience towards a transcendent state and that these states are reflected symbolically in the tree and the menorah, the relationship of which will be developed later. The following section departs from biblical symbolism to focus on the stages of development in being.

Chapter 2

The Analytical Trail

When I was 18 in 1965, I tried to express my general distress through poetry and by reading the dictionary. I felt I had achieved something until I
read an abridged version of Lonergan's *Insight*. He had condensed a basic
understanding of knowing into three simple words. It took a while for me
to recover my poetic sensibilities and to reconcile the work of scientific
method with my subjective, feeling-oriented universe. The blunt analytic
process described by Lonergan affected me in such a way that I could no
longer write poetry within the same stream of consciousness. It became a
necessary journey to frame the symbolic form within the cognitive process.
In the same way that laws govern our attachment to earth, other laws govern
our maturation and process of growth. I learned by questioning, by attempt-
ing to follow my intuitive drive, through a lengthy process that involved
much research, some understanding and a gradual process of maturation.
If you become disconcerted, I am asking you to bear with me through the
tangle of analytical thought and the symbolic underpinnings of psychological drives. The exercise is required to situate the act of knowing and the dynamics of behavior onto a generic footing that can be applied by any person
of any religion, creed or lack thereof. I suggest in the introduction that the
symbolic form of the Bible has a relationship to human consciousness. I
hope to show the nature of the relationship. At the same time, the relationship to the analytic process makes it accessible to anyone who attempts to
understand it. If the Hebrew bothers you, please skip over it. The intention
was to ground the word origins.

Lonergan uses the term judgment, and decision. The term is used in the sense of comparing possibilities, rather than impugning a person's character.

Chapter 3

Lonergan: A Conscious Operation

> While teaching theology at the Collegium Christi Regis, now Regis College federated with the University of Toronto, Lonergan wrote *Insight: A Study of Human Understanding*, inaugurating the generalized empirical method (GEM). GEM belongs to the movement of "transcendental Thomism" inaugurated by Joseph Maréchal. This method begins with an analysis of human knowing as divided into three levels—experience, understanding, and judgment—and, by stressing the objectivity of judgment more than Kant had done, develops a Thomistic vision of Being as the goal of the dynamic openness of the human spirit.[1]

I met Bernard Lonergan while taking night classes at the Thomas More Institute in Montreal in my late teens. My father, Stan Machnik, had asked Lonergan to be his spiritual advisor during a retreat in Oka, Quebec, in the early forties.[2] My inexperienced reading of *Insight* at that time had a definite impact on me. However, it wasn't until I pursued my master's in theology

---

1. http://en.wikipedia.org/wiki/Bernard_Lonergan (accessed Jan 5, 2010)

2. My parents Stan and Roberta (Soden) Machnik were two of the founders of the Thomas More Inst., in Montreal QC, in 1945 and remained in a leadership position until their early nineties. They believed that education was crucial to social progress. In the 1940s they sold the Canadian edition of Dorothy Day's the Catholic Worker journal for a penny. Roberta was the first female school commissioner in Quebec for a major school board.

(2006) that I was able to get a better grasp of the subject and incorporate his method as part of my search for meaning.

Lonergan's major work *Insight: A Study of Human Understanding*, is a 700-page opus that addresses our understanding of knowing, challenges its historical conceptions and helps to facilitate the individual need to transcend beyond the limitations of our personal experience and identify that desire which is unique to who we are meant to be. As he says: "Thoroughly understand what it is to understand, and not only will you understand the broad lines of all there is to be understood but also you will possess a fixed base, an invariant pattern, opening upon all further developments of understanding."[3]

Lonergan's theory of conscious operations relates the cognitive functions to our state of being. I hope to compare the symbolic form of the Bible to the stages of being, and by extrapolation to our process of knowing.

How do we know what is real? Lonergan defines an ongoing process of experience, understanding, and judgment, whereby we confirm to ourselves that what we have experienced, we come to understand and based on what is understood, we make decisions. Our decisions, of course, are always being weighed against the broader experience and so we are compelled to re-evaluate our understanding of our basic experience. Our understanding of reality is gradually being tested, and we are, hopefully, continually positioning ourselves along a path that is a closer approximation of what is true and real. The sum of our experience, understanding, and judgment is our being. And Lonergan concludes, "(T)he real is being."[4]

For Lonergan, the cognitive process is equal in form or is isomorphic with our metaphysical elements as defined by Aristotle. Our form of being is said to be defined by potency, form, and act.[5] Experience corresponds to potency, understanding corresponds to form and judgment corresponds to act.

Chapter xv of *Insight* on the Elements of Metaphysics describes the relationship between the cognitive operations and Aristotle's terms. I understand proportionate being to be being which is in proportion to the levels of operations and in relation to the metaphysical elements. That is, an experienced person may be very experienced but lacking in understanding or is indecisive and is disproportionate. Or, a very decisive, a purpose-oriented person, may lack experience and understanding. An empathetic person might lack purpose.

3. Lonergan, *Insight*, xxviii.

4. Lonergan, *Insight*, 482.

5. Aristotle, *Metaphysics*, Theta, 6, 1048. Also, Aquinas; In IX Metsphys., lect. 5, # 1828 ff. *Insight*; p. 432 (1957) gives the basis for the generality of the terms; potency, form, act. *Method in Theology*; p.95.

Proportionate being is what is to be known by experience, intelligent grasp, and reasonable affirmation. The integral heuristic structure of proportionate being is the structure of what is to be known when proportionate being is explained completely. But in that explanatory knowledge there will be affirmation, there will be understanding, and there will be experience of the empirical residue. Let 'act' denote what is known inasmuch as one affirms; let 'form' denote what is known inasmuch one understands; let 'potency' denote what is known inasmuch one experiences the empirical residue. From the distinction, relations, and unity of experienced, intelligible, and affirmed contents, there follow the distinction, relations, and unity of potency, form, and act. From the different modes of understanding concrete things and abstract laws, there follows the distinction between central and conjugate forms and, as a corollary, the distinctions between central and conjugate potency and between central and conjugate acts. From the structural unification of the methods by generalized emergent probability, there follow the structural account of the explanatory genera and species and the immanent order of the universe of proportionate being. Such are the elements of metaphysics.[6]

The essential value of Lonergan's theory is to provide a systematic method of understanding whereby an individual can identify within themselves a conscious operation, the process by which we can come to a sound decision. Since he compares the process of knowing to our state of being, ideas and values which might be treated as subjective and anecdotal within a scientific setting, can be critically evaluated even though they do not consist of measurable data as is common to science. Things that are of personal, cultural and religious value can be evaluated similarly, though perhaps not as specifically as temperature, density, and time.

Conversely, things that create bias and obstruct our understanding of the truth, can be seen for what they are. Lonergan places the study of theology on a generic footing, a footing grounded in the human experience and directed towards the transcendent.[7] The process of trying to come to terms with Lonergan's *Insight* helped in some way to resolve the gap in my thinking between literal reality and symbolic or spiritual realities.

6. Lonergan, *Insight*, 486.

7. A fellow graduate student at Concordia, an orthodox rabbi taught young ultraorthodox Hebrew students using Lonergan's *Method in Theology* at a local yeshiva. When I mentioned this to Fr. Robert Doran, an associate of Lonergan, he said that L. would have been happy knowing that his Method was being applied beyond the Christian context.

In the process of understanding—understanding,[8] Lonergan makes an important distinction that we do not see something as it is perceived, which I understand is the philosophy of Aristotle, but that we arrive at understanding through comparison and knowing things in relationship to similar things. However, in the realm of the metaphysical, the world of the psyche, the process is related to the symbolic and the imaginative, so there is an aspect of seeing things imaginatively. The cognitive operations work hand-in-hand with the metaphysical elements. The analytic self-conscious reflects on its experience and understands. It puts things in perspective, it assembles events in order of time, and it understands the individual relationships of one event to another. It compares the value of each understanding and eventually makes judgments about their value. However, there is another faculty that responds subjectively, not as a disinterested observer, but with the feeling that we are an intimately linked organism vitally dependent on the cosmos for our sustainability.

An example of this difference of cognitive or lack of cognitive understanding, is the account by Dr. Jill Taylor in her *My Stroke of Insight*.[9] Dr. Taylor is an analytical, accomplished neuroscientist who has a cerebral stroke that incapacitates her left-brain function. Her ability to recognize numbers, understand time, and dial a telephone becomes practically impossible. Eventually, a colleague at work recognizes her gibberish on the telephone, and she is rescued. Taylor is thrust from her world of system and routine into a world where she feels at one and at peace with the universe. She wants to stay where she is but recognizes that her health is at risk and that she needs to connect with the operational world. I would suggest that when her stroke short-circuited Dr. Taylor's cognitive sense, she became present to her metaphysical reality, and as a result, more in touch with her organic life. Many will argue for or against the right brain or left brain as related to a metaphysical vs. logical state, this remains, however, an open question.

In the following section, I hope to make a distinction between the metaphysical being as spirit and our psychological understanding of the psyche; this is necessary to make sense of the relationship between our psychological processes and our spirit being.

8. Not a repeated word. Lonergan is making sense of understanding.
9. Taylor, *My Stroke of Insight*, 2009.

Chapter 4

Between Soul and Spirit

Robert Doran in his *Theology and the Dialectics of History* makes the distinction between psyche and spirit. The psyche is the "sensitive stream of consciousness."[1]

Doran goes on to distinguish between the psyche and the life of the spirit. The life of the spirit consists of "questions for intelligibility or meaning." The "discovery of these objectives through insight," develops "questions for and affirmations of truth." There is "the inexorable drive for the unconditioned," we want to know what "is so," and do our insights "hold up against the evidence." The life of the spirit consists also in our "questions for deliberation, for value, for what is truly good."

Doran makes a clear distinction between the values of depth psychology and the life of the spirit.

> Psychology must unpack our intimations that there is a direction to be found in the movement of life, and that our lives are given significance to the extent that we find that direction and keep to it, and lose their significance to the extent that we either fail to find the direction or, once having found it, lose it. The process that leads to interiorly differentiated consciousness can raise these intimations out of the obscurity into which they are always in danger of being cast by the distortions that affect the dialectical processes of history. This process is a journey through our spiritual and psychic interiority, to rediscover the

1. Doran, *Theology,* 219.

entire domain of orientation: through the *operations* by which the search for direction is conducted, and through the *psychic states* in which the movement of life is itself experienced and the elemental *symbols* released by the energic compositions and distributions of which these psychic states are composed. Depth psychology's contribution to the inner journey aids the second dimension in particular. But it also complements and to an extent qualifies the first dimension; and it can be accurately understood only if depth psychology itself is reoriented on the basis of the first dimension of the journey, so that it becomes an integral partner with intentionality analysis in the exploration of the primal core of all human experience.[2]

Doran argues that there is a dynamic, a trajectory, a purpose to life which requires an understanding of the relationship between our psychic state and our purposeful orientation. This relationship is expressed as soul and spirit.

The relationship between soul (psyche) and spirit has been addressed in the Bible, whether explicitly or implicitly. The soul appears to be associated with emotions. The spirit, which suggests a relationship to the universal, appears to relate more to judgment, to decisions, and to what is right. It facilitates the skill of discernment required to orient ourselves on the right path:

> My soul yearns for you in the night, my spirit within me earnestly seeks you. For when your judgments are in the earth, the inhabitants of the world learn righteousness. (Isa 26:9) NRSV.

> And so it is written, the first man Adam was made a living soul; the last Adam was made a quickening spirit. (1 Col 15:45) KJV.

> Behold! My Servant whom I have chosen, My Beloved in whom My soul is well pleased! I will put My Spirit upon Him, And He will declare justice to the Gentiles. (Matt 12:18) NKJV.

From these readings, the soul appears to abhor judgment, whereas the spirit facilitates its exercise:

> And if you despise My statutes, or if your soul abhors My judgments, so that you do not perform all My commandments, but break My covenant. (Lev 26:15) NKJV.

> I will put my spirit within you, and make you follow my statutes and be careful to observe my ordinances. (Ezek 36:27) NRSV.

2. Doran, *Theology,* 219.

The relationship has certain parallels to C.S. Lewis' retelling of the Greek myth, Amor and Psyche,[3] which illustrates the tension between the analytical self and the self in relationship, in a state of grace.

To connect in a common-sense manner to soul and spirit, I felt that the prayers, the Our Father and the Hail Mary expressed that distinction. The Lord's Prayer communicates His will, His Spirit established in the earth. In the Hail Mary, the Son is conceived by the Spirit, and in response to Elizabeth, Mary says, "My soul magnifies the Lord, and my spirit rejoices in God my Savior." (Luke 1:46–47) RSV. In Glenda Green's, *Keys of Jeshua*, Jesus says that "prayer connects us with the Creator," whereas meditation "connects us with the Holy Spirit."[4]

TYPES OF PRAYER

Different types of prayer help to orient our spirits towards the divine and sensitize our innate godlike character to the ultimate nature of God. The active spiritual nature acts like and is analogous to passing a magnet over iron filings. Our physical nature—the iron filings become aligned with the infinite. There are organizations available for those who would prefer to remain unaffiliated to a religious denomination. Organizations such as Heart Math's, Global Coherence Initiative,[5] provides a web forum for those who want to meditate for peace. There are also prayer groups, rosary groups, and Taize.[6] The following are several methods:

1. Basic breathing exercises that help to regulate stress, slow the heart rate, and mentally focus on our physical nature and its relation to spirit. The focus on breathing helps to step back from cyclic mental patterns that consume our attention. In my own experience, when I am angry, I find it harder to meditate and more profitable to pray directly for the problem.

2. Reciting prayers such as the Our Father, the Rosary, that focus our attention on God.

3. Interceding for and asking for specific intervention in our lives, our loved ones, and those that offend us. "Love your enemy," in Luke 6, is not an easy task.

4. Have fun, sing.

3. Lewis, *Till We Have Faces*.
4. Green, *Keys of Jeshua*, 254.
5. https://www.heartmath.org/gci/
6. https://www.taize.fr/en

THE NAME REFLECTS THE BEING

Metaphysical reality is a process of being which has its own operative nature. It may be better expressed through poetry, music, and song because it involves rhythm and feelings and similes that bring together the essential and heartfelt qualities of a subject. It is not something to be rationalized, it is something to be appreciated. It reflects our innate organic quality in its potency through the form of its beauty, and by ultimately acting out, it fulfills its purpose to regenerate life in abundance.

The personal act of revelation, the conscious act of the self, which reflects on its own ability to reflect, is similar to the name of the Godhead. The Name—*I Am That I Am*—is the objective self, reflecting on subjective being in a condition of action. An example of this distinction is illustrated by Umberto Cassuto's analysis of Exodus 3:14.[7]

> When the Lord [YHWH] saw that he turned aside to see, God ['Elohim] called to him out of the bush. The sudden change of Divine name—YHWH in the first clause and 'Elohim in the second—which is difficult to explain by the mechanical division of the text between different sources,[8] is easily explicable in the light of what we have stated above, at the end of our commentary to chapter i. The children of Israel, including hitherto even Moses, forgot in the land of their exile the direct knowledge of YHWH, the God of their ancestors, and retained only a general and vague understanding of the concept "Elohim". Now Moses is vouchsafed a special revelation that elevates him to that knowledge of YHWH to which the patriarchs of the nation had attained. Consequently, the Divine names change in these verses, which precede the revelation of the Tetragrammaton to Moses, in accordance with the following principles: whenever the Lord is spoken of objectively, the name YHWH occurs; but when the reference is to what Moses saw or heard or felt subjectively, the name 'Elohim is used. Here in v. 4 the text has, When YHWH saw, because an objective statement concerning what the Lord saw is intended; but Scripture says, 'Elohim called to him, because the call heard by Moses appeared to him at the moment as

7. אֶהְיֶה אֲשֶׁר אֶהְיֶה Westminster Leningrad Codex. *I Am That I Am*, KJV. *Ego sum qui sum*, Vg. *I Am Who I Am*, ESV, NKJV, RSV, NRSV. *Je Suis Celui Qui Est* BJ. (Exodus 3:14)

8. Note: Cassuto is questioning the Literary Criticism approach which suggests that the Pentateuch was composed of four major documents J, E, D, P.

the voice of 'Elohim. He learns only subsequently that it is the voice of YHWH. Exodus III 2[9]

Cassuto understands that the name of God as perceived by the subject (Moses) and objectively (as God acting) establishes a key insight both in the understanding of the nature of God and in the nature of our perception. ''Elohim' defines the name as expressed by man and is the name which we commonly translate as God. YHWH is unique as "the Name" and reflects the divine character. The first defines the generic title of a supreme being, whereas "the Name" defines the qualities of the Divine in action, in place, and in a relationship.

The interplay between observation and reflection, external fact and subjective response, externality and interiority, presence to the universe of being and presence to self is at the heart of the dynamic of being. The dynamic reveals the interaction between my desire to know, which analyses my experience, my understanding and formulates judgments, and is, to some extent, independent—depending on my psychological makeup—of the potency, form, and acts which are the elements of my being. The process of coming to an understanding helps us to understand our being, and our becoming reflects the divine process of being. (Isa 1:18 "Come now, and let us reason together" Says the LORD, NKJV, or "let us argue it out," NRSV).

Lonergan quotes Thomas Aquinas, saying: "The human soul understands itself by its understanding, which is its proper act, perfectly demonstrating its power and its nature."[10]

Professors Christine Jamieson (Lonergan and Ethics) and Marie-France Dion (Biblical Hebrew) of Concordia University, Montreal have suggested that the Hebrew word שכל, shkl, which is translated as to prosper or to have success, as in "turn not from it (the law) to the right hand or to the left, that you may have good success wherever you go." (Josh 1:7b) RSV, might be better understood by "that you may have *insight* wherever you go."

9. Cassuto, *Exodus*, 32.

10 Lonergan, *Collected Works*, Vol 4. 175.

Chapter 5

Man Created in the Image of God Reflects a Symbolic Cosmology

To what extent did man's revelatory understanding of God and his own act of becoming influence the account of creation in the Biblical text? And, to what extent does the Mind of God in the moment of Creation, reflect the form of creation and does that form reflect the soul of man which was made in the image of God? These are two possible views that may reveal a metaphysical association between the understanding of being and the form of creation as it is and as it is understood in the Bible, the outline of the present book. The first is defined by the elements of metaphysics, originally described by Aristotle as potency, form, and act—the elementary processes of being. Secondly, there is the symbolic form of the biblical account of creation, which I believe reflects the nature of creation itself. In this book, I compare the metaphysical elements to the following biblical elements:

Potency: The tree of life / the Seed of the woman (as latent potency)

Form: The cycle of seasons / Days of worship / the Sabbath / who we are

Act: The Covenants: Jerusalem / the Seed of the woman (as manifest potency) / the New Jerusalem / the Bride of the Lamb and Revelation / the tree of life as manifest potency / our response to the divine

I also conclude that our state of being as defined by potency, form, and act is symbolized by the elements of the menorah, namely; the bud, the bowl, and the flower.

Secondly, the Bible, that is the Old and the New Testaments, begins and ends with the tree of life and the river of life which I believe reveals the symbolic dimension of the Bible.[123]

Genesis: The garden, the two trees and the river with four river heads

Revelation: The pure river with the water of life, proceeding from the throne of God and the Lamb. On either side of the river was the tree of life yielding fruit every month for the healing of nations.

When we consider the symbolic relationship between: a) the metaphysical elements (potency, form, and act) and; b) the tree–Seed, the cycles of life and covenants, the dynamic between potency, form, and act, reveals a similar dynamism within the elements of the Bible. The story begins with the loss of opportunity for eternal life (our exclusion from the tree of life),

---

1. Gen 2:8–15 The LORD God planted a garden eastward in Eden (pleasure), and there He put the man whom He had formed. And out of the ground the LORD God made every tree grow that is pleasant to the sight and good for food. The tree of life was also in the midst of the garden, and the tree of the knowledge of good and evil. Now a river went out of Eden to water the garden, and from there it parted and became four riverheads. The name of the first is Pishon (increase); it is the one which skirts the whole land of Havilah (circle), where there is gold. And the gold of that land is good. Bdellium and the onyx stone are there. The name of the second river is Gihon (bursting forth); it is the one which goes around the whole land of Cush (black). The name of the third river is Hiddekel (rapid); it is the one which goes toward the east of Assyria (a step). The fourth river is the Euphrates (fruitfulness). Then the LORD God took the man and put him in the garden of Eden to tend and keep it. NKJV.

2. Josephus: Now the garden was watered by one river, which ran round about the whole earth, and was parted into four parts. And Phison, which denotes a multitude, running into India, makes its exit into the sea, and is by the Greeks called Ganges. Euphrates also, as well as Tigris, goes down into the Red Sea. Now the name Euphrates, or Phrath, denotes either a dispersion, or a flower: by Tiris, or Diglath, is signified what is swift, with narrowness; and Geon runs through Egypt, and denotes what arises from the east, which the Greeks call Nile. *Antiquities of the Jews*—Book I. Chapter 1.3

3. Rev 22:1–3 And he showed me a pure river of water of life, clear as crystal, proceeding from the throne of God and of the Lamb. In the middle of its street, and on either side of the river, was the tree of life, which bore twelve fruits, each tree yielding its fruit every month. The leaves of the tree were for the healing of the nations. And there shall be no more curse, but the throne of God and of the Lamb shall be in it, and His servants shall serve Him. NKJV.

but we are promised a Seed who and which would prevail and eventually overcome.

The original Seed (potency) sustains the hope of the promise. The promise (potency defined by act) sustains the life of the people who recreate according to the cycle of life (the form, which in the temporal is lunar-based) the substitution of the ram or lamb, the rescue from destruction, the giving of the Torah, the atonement, and the indwelling. The following are the primary feasts which usually correspond to a sabbatical cycle.

Passover:	release from exile on the 14th of Nisan (March/April)
Unleavened Bread:	On the 15th, on this same day I will have brought you out of Egypt
First Fruits:	Come into the land, the 16th of Nisan
Shavuot/ Pentecost:	Seven Sabbaths shall be completed
Rosh Hashanah:	In the 7th month a Sabbath rest
Yom Kippur:	Day of Atonement, 10th of the 7th month
Succoth:	The Feast of Tabernacles, 15th of the 7th month for seven days
The Sabbath Year of Jubilee:	Conclusion of seven sabbatical years (Lev 25:10)

The Seed/promise/potency continues within the structure of the form and is foundational to and sustains each phase of the form. In the Passover (as one phase) we are continually reminded that the "I AM," the ultimate expression of potency, form, and act, is responsible for the deliverance of the people from endless servitude. The form represents a different dynamic to that of potency, but either one sustains the other, and form becomes a repository for memory generated by potency.

The condition of servitude (practically a human norm) of the Israelites under the Egyptians, which had been preceded by Abraham's act of faith, recalls a covenant agreement, an act, which leads to decision and specification and ultimately to place and the Land of Promise. The exclamation which completes the Passover account "next year in Jerusalem" exemplifies that expression.

In as much as potency, form, and act define the metaphysical elements of being and the dynamic of our becoming, so also do the tree, the cycles, and the covenants define a multi-millennial dynamic within the biblical text which helps to understand the organic process of the book as a whole. It is more than a historical narrative; it is the account of an ongoing regenerative relationship between God and man which historically reasserts itself as a literary organism. The Bible, as word of life, as an organism, is continually responsive to our humanity through the ages in our search for becoming. It is the book of Being, a literary preview of our relationship to the One who incorporated Himself as original potency, the Seed, whose generations prevailed until the ultimate Act of Redemption. John expresses our ultimate connection to God in Revelation as "I, John, saw the holy city, New Jerusalem, coming down out of heaven from God, prepared as a bride adorned for her husband."[4]

The Seed of the Woman eventually manifests itself in the personification of God's ultimate sacrifice and love for all humanity. For Christians it is fulfilled in the person of Jesus Christ. For Jewish people it will be fulfilled by the coming Messiah. The fulfillment is defined by specific acts and covenant agreements through history. For example, the agreement by Ruth the Moabite to follow her Israeli mother-in-law Naomi back to the land of Israel, where she eventually marries Boaz. Ruth is the great-grandmother of King David. It was Abraham who first responded by faith, and so, as the story unfolds, God is known as the God of Abraham, Isaac, and Jacob. There is a covenant agreement. The original potency, as symbolized by the tree of life, takes on a specific form in its actualization and traces its lineage through particular persons. This, I believe, is the meaning behind the symbolism of the regenerative component of the flower element. A similar sentiment is expressed in the Song of Solomon: "My lover has gone down to his garden, to the bed of spices, to browse in the gardens and to gather lilies. I am my lover's and my lover is mine; he browses among the lilies." (Song 6:2–3) NIV.

The following compares the form of the menorah to the form of being.

4. Rev 21:2.

Chapter 6

The Symbolic Form of the Menorah

In the following paragraphs and the chapter on the menorah, I am suggesting that there is a relationship between the elementary design of the menorah and the process of creation, which reflects our activity of knowing. This is an exercise in symbolic representation which may or may not have been in the mind of the author of Exodus originally. "See to it that you make them (the temple artifacts) according to the pattern which was shown you on the mountain." (Exod 25:40) NKJV.

> You shall also make a lampstand of pure gold; the lampstand shall be of hammered work. Its shaft, its branches, its bowls, its [ornamental] knobs, and flowers shall be [of one piece]. And six branches shall come out of its sides: three branches of the lampstand out of one side, and three branches of the lampstand out of the other side. Three bowls [shall be] made like almond [blossoms] on one branch, [with] an [ornamental] knob and a flower, and three bowls made like almond [blossoms] on the other branch, [with] an [ornamental] knob and a flower — and so for the six branches that come out of the lampstand. On the lampstand itself four bowls [shall be] made like almond [blossoms, each with] its [ornamental] knob and flower. And [there shall be] a knob under the [first] two branches of the same, a knob under the [second] two branches of the same, and a knob under the [third] two branches of the same, according to the six branches that extend from the lampstand. Their knobs and their branches [shall be of one piece]; all of it [shall be] one

hammered piece of pure gold. You shall make seven lamps for
it, and they shall arrange its lamps so that they give light in
front of it. (Exod 25:31–37) NKJV.

The bud (knob, calyx) traces the symbolic development and the primordial character of the tree of life through the Bible. Although human beings were separated from the tree initially, the tree is subsumed symbolically
within the Bible and potentially within all life. It is fragmented beyond normal recognition by man's sense of separateness from the divine. The Bible
records symbolic references to the Roots and Branch. These are manifested
fully in the conclusion, in Revelation, as the tree of life.

Secondly, the bowl (cup) traces the liturgical symbolism of the menorah in the cycle of the feast days of the Lord. The bowl exemplifies the form
of the cycle. The menorah is revealed as a flame that will not die, a burning
tree that is not consumed, which becomes the manifestation of the Churches
in Revelation. The bowl is both a vessel of offering and intercession as well
as a container for the accumulated bitterness, a normal response, by which
we have responded to our human condition. In the end, the bowl is poured
out, revealing our history which we can only Pass-through depending on
His mercy.

Thirdly, the flower (petals and flame) represent the Covenant acts as
well as the Songs (aspirations) of Zion, presumably songs in which God delights. As a God of love, He delights in the particularities of every member
of His creation. He has also said, "I am zealous for Zion with great zeal,"
and, if we are to make sense of the biblical narrative, the question should be,
what is so compelling that God would singularly identify with a place and
a people? To avoid such a question would be to deny the great mystery that
is God's choice.

What becomes apparent is that the symbolic order of the Bible reveals
an underlying cohesion that is elementary and beyond the scope of any one
author. During the last several hundred years, many questions have been
raised regarding the authorship of individual books, the period of publication, and whether events did or did not occur and at what dates. However,
when we consider the symbolic language of the bible, as Paul said, "for Jews
demand signs and Greeks desire wisdom" (1Col 1:22), the symbols reveal
themselves as an integral unifying order. The symbolic order reveals a god
of fusion, of an immensely comprehensive singular focus, rather than a god
of fission.

The order of the bud, bowl, and flower compares with the elements of
metaphysics as defined by the elements of potency, form, and act. The metaphysical elements reveal the structural relationship of the flower, bud, and

bowl. The bud contains the potential for all life as it was originally intended. The bowl illustrates the formal character of life in its cyclic and seasonal progression from birth to death. And act (in the expression of the flower and flame) is the present and ongoing outworking of a historic covenant relationship. It is the ultimate and unconditioned realization of what it means for man to come into "the manifestation as sons of God." (Rom. 8:19) AV.

Chapter 7

Feelings Related to Knowing

A SHORT ESSAY ON FEELING

I had always appreciated Lonergan's analysis of the process of human understanding. However, I also felt that feeling, although alluded to, was never very explicit until Lonergan's *Method in Theology*. I believe that feelings could and should mature and develop in conjunction with our experience, understanding, and judgment. Symbolism, especially as related to personal and spiritual values and ideas, carries with it many associated feelings and, to understand their symbolic function, it is important to grasp the relationship of feeling to thinking and being. Dr. Carol Meyers says of the association between emotion and symbol:

> This power to arouse us, this emotional impact, represents what Goodenough calls the "meaning" or "value" of a symbol. This characteristic of symbols is of central concern from the standpoint of studying symbols in ancient art. Historically, it is obvious that certain symbols can be found in many cultures. Where these cultures are contiguous in space and/or time, the appearance of the same symbols is hardly accidental. The fact that a symbol can make the transition from one culture to the next is a result of the continuity of value inherent in symbols.
>
> This migration of symbols is predicated upon the fact that all symbols arise from a universal inner need of man, namely, his need to respond to the conditions of life by the symbolization of experience. Thus the "perennity of symbols, which survive their

various and passing explanations, is conditioned by the peren-
nity of man's condition." "Inasmuch as symbols arise from man's
confrontation with reality, they can neither be invented nor
abolished. This retention of value, of emotional clout, is what
enables symbols to be transferred from one religion to the next;
it is the continuity of value in a symbol that makes it "live," or
"active," in the terminology of Goodenough."[1]

The symbolic form is appropriated on the level of an emotional connection, a feeling. Without the ability to identify with the inherent meaning
of the symbol, there will be no understanding. I hope to illustrate the relationship of the symbolic form to our emotional lives and to situate feeling
within the cognitive process.

Lonergan's Position on Feelings Progresses From:

(I)t will not be amiss to assert emphatically that the identifica-
tion of being and the common good by-passes human feelings
and sentiments to take its stand exclusively upon intelligible
order and rational value.[2]

To the following (1972):

Intermediate between judgments of fact and judgments in value
lie apprehensions of value. Such apprehensions are given of
feelings.[34]

And there are:

(F)eelings that have been snapped off by repression . . . But there
are in full consciousness feelings so deep and strong, especially
when deliberately reinforced, that they channel attention, shape
one's horizon, direct one's life. Here the supreme illustration is
loving.[5]

---

1. Meyers, The Tabernacle Menorah, 7.

2. Lonergan, Insight, 606.

3. In a discussion with Fr. Louis Roy O.P., Lonergan corrected his statement as follows: "Intermediate between judgments of fact and judgments of value lie apprehensions of value. Such apprehensions are given in feelings." Email from Fr. Roy February
28th, 2011 (Collège Universitaire Dominicain; Ottawa ON).

4. Lonergan, Method in Theology, (1972) 37.

5. Lonergan, Method in Theology, (1972) 32.

RELATIONSHIP BETWEEN BEING AND KNOWING

Feelings are elementary and operate as intermediaries between being and knowing. There are implications from the study of Lonergan that feelings are only related to experience. Or that they are part of the fourth level of decision, such as love. However, unless feelings were effectively integrated within the whole structure of knowing, a basic dynamism would be missing from our knowing being.

If the "apprehensions of value" which are "intermediate between judgments of value" (being) and "judgments of fact" (knowing) and those apprehensions are given in feelings, then we might conclude that our feelings are intermediaries between our being and our knowing. The apprehension, which consists in the feeling, is also an active condition of experience, understanding, and resolve.

It would also appear that a similar condition exists in understanding. I understand the relationship of the various parts. In the process, a sense of empathy, compassion, sympathy, or understanding (Lonergan: fellow-feeling) acts as an intermediary between the understanding and the form (person or thing) to be understood. As feelings work between knowing and being, so also they facilitate our understanding. Similarly, feeling operates on the level of experience. We feel the dynamic potency of the experience which senses the direction of movement.

Lonergan's Definition of Knowing

> Where knowing is a structure, knowing knowing must be a re-duplication of the structure. Thus, if knowing is just looking, then knowing knowing will be looking at looking. But if knowing is a conjunction of experience, understanding, and judging, then knowing knowing has to be a conjunction of (1) experiencing experience, understanding and judging, (2) understanding one's experience of experience, understanding and judging, and (3) judging one's understanding of experience, understanding and judging to be correct.[6]

The cognitive operations of experience, understanding, and judgment mirror and reflect the comparable operations within the experiencing, understanding, judging, and existential being. In chapter twelve on the "Notion of Being" Lonergan says:

6. Lonergan. *Collected Works*, Vol. 4, 208. A similar expression is found in Lonergan, *Method in Theology*, 14.

Being Then Is the Objective of the Pure Desire to Know

By the desire to know is meant the dynamic orientation manifested in questions for intelligence and for reflection. It is not
the verbal utterance of questions. It is not the conceptual for-
mulation of questions. It is not any insight or thought. It is not
any reflective grasp or judgment. It is the prior and enveloping
drive that carries cognitional process from sense and imagination to understanding, from understanding to judgment, from
judgment to the complete context of correct judgments that is
named knowledge. The desire to know, then, is simply the inquiring and critical spirit of man.[7]

The Pure Desire to Know Is Identified As:

1. A dynamic orientation
2. The prior and enveloping drive
3. The inquiring and critical spirit of man

It would seem from these definitions that feelings are closely affiliated with
the dynamic of the pure desire to know. Lonergan has concluded that they
are intermediate between judgments of fact and judgments of value. I would
also suggest that feelings are intermediate between "understanding, understanding," and "experiencing, experience."[8]

7. Lonergan. *Insight*. 348.

8. Note: I am not an expert on psychological definitions of behavior. I am propos-
ing that there is a development in the nature and complexity of feelings, which anyone
is welcome to re-evaluate.

Relationship between Being, Feeling, and Cognition

Table 2: Relation between being, feeling, and cognition

Values	Feelings	Operations
Being (Metaphysical)		Cognitive
Being is the objective	of the pure desire	to know"
	As expressed in feeling	
Experience (of value)	Is sensitive to is affected, pained, energized, touched by	Experience (actual)
Understanding (of value)	Is sympathetic to is compassionate, empathetic, affectionate of, intuitive, comforted, encouraged, receptive, anxious, isolated by, is distraught by	Understanding (of facts)
Judgments (of value)	Are appreciative /discerning of discriminating, hopeful, affirming, approving, yearning, alienated by, despairing, rejected by, harbor a ressentiment, (a root of bitterness) of, by . . .	Judgment (of facts)
Decisions (of value)	Become resolute loving, hateful, ecstatic, joyful, ardent, bonded, desirous, worshipful, zealous, self-hating, dreading, deny the person exists, rage, shamed, suicidal based on	Decisions (in fact)

Beginning with the cognitive operations, it can be said:

Cognitive	Feelings	Being	Metaphysical elements
Experiencing	feelings	of the experience	arising from potency
Understanding	relating to and sympathetic with	what is understood	defining form
Judging	formulates a critical appreciation	of judgments	leading to act
Decisions	are resolved	from our deciding	leading to a transcendent being

Each of these operations, sentiments, and states are interdependent upon each other, and the omission of any of these would result in poverty of being or a deficiency in knowing. As Lonergan says in the following on moral development, "When knowledge is deficient, then fine feelings are apt to be expressed in what is called moral idealism."[9]

In correspondence[10] with Dr. Philip McShane, a Lonergan scholar, he proposed that my diagram did not reflect the "what to do" dynamic and referred me to two drawings from Lonergan delivered at University College, Dublin, 1961.[11]

9. Lonergan. *Method in Theology*, 38.

10. Email: Friday, April 23, 2010.

11. Lonergan, *Collected Works*, Vol. 18, 322–23.

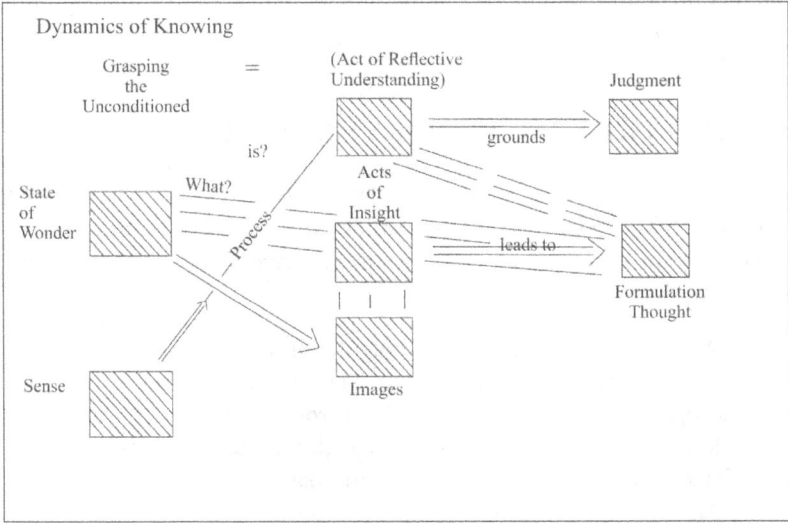

Figure 1: Dynamics of knowing

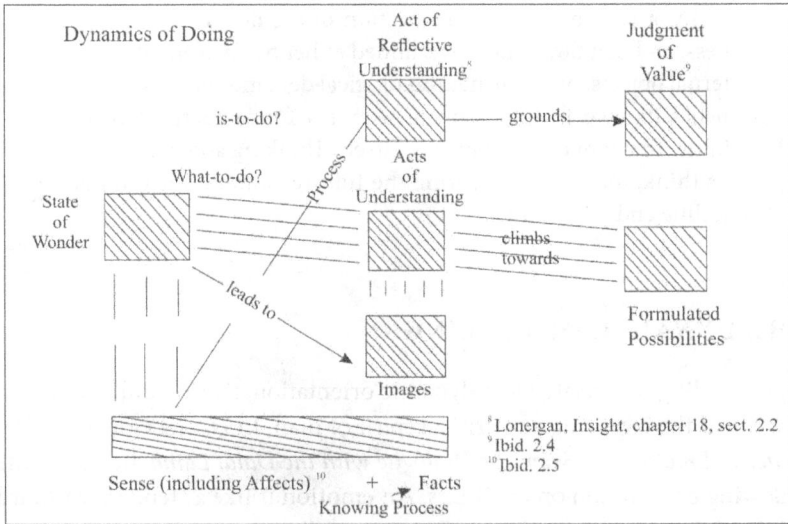

Figure 2: Dynamics of doing

Compared to my schematic, Lonergan's drawing illustrates the dynamic towards doing; however, I believe that my integration of feelings on multiple levels (other than sense) allows for their inclusion within the levels of the knowing process. Secondly, the position of the "images," which influence insight, illustrates the influence of symbols on understanding, which is at the heart of my thesis.[12]

ART AND THE FREEDOM OF THE SUBJECT

In the Collected Works of Bernard Lonergan, *Topics in Education*, Lonergan argues that philosophy has alienated man from himself, that despite our ability to rationalize the known universe, we have disassociated ourselves from being.

> (A)rt is an exploration of the potentialities of concrete living. That exploration is extremely important in our age, when philosophers for at least two centuries, through doctrines on politics, economics, education, and through ever further doctrines, have been trying to remake man, and have done not a little to make human life unlivable. The great task that is demanded if we are to make it livable again is the re-creation of the liberty of the subject, the recognition of the freedom of consciousness. Normally, we think of freedom as freedom of the will, as something that happens within consciousness. But the freedom of the will is a control over the orientation of the flow of consciousness, and that flow is not determined either by environment, external objects, or by the neurobiological demands of the subject. It has its own free component. Art is a fundamental element in the freedom of consciousness itself. Thinking about art helps us think, too, about exploring the full freedom of our ways of feeling and perceiving.[13]

THE DYNAMIC OF FEELING

Again, feelings are related to a dynamic orientation, a prior and enveloping drive, and the inquiring and critical spirit of man. In Daniel Goleman's *Destructive Emotions; A Scientific Dialogue with the Dalai Lama*, he makes the following observation on emotions. An emotion is like a "tendency toward motion," the perception, "is already intrinsically emotionally shaped."[14]

In Deepak Chopra's PBS (Public Broadcasting Service) special, he proposes that: 1. Being, 2. Feeling, 3. Thinking, and 4. Doing, radiate as

12. Lonergan, *Collected Works*, (author's redrawing of schematic). Vol. 18, 322–3.
13. Lonergan, *Collected Works*, Vol. 10, 232.
14. Goleman, *Destructive Emotions*, 323.

concentric circles from the core of being. Chopra's analogy relates to Lonergan's parallel forms of metaphysical and cognitive processes. Doing is concentric and in line with the heart of our being and is a development from our thoughts and feelings. Our being is our primary self.

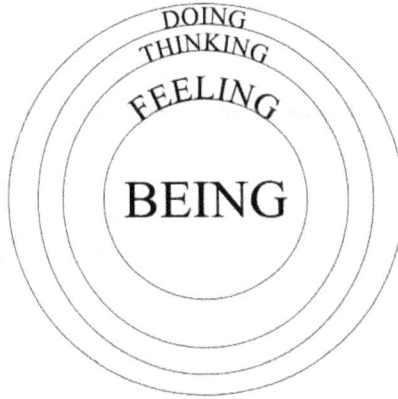

Figure 3: Deepak Chopra order of being

Chopra's diagram (which I redrew from a PBS presentation) is a valuable reminder that our value is not so much in our doing but in our being. And the centrality of being aligns with Exodus 3:14, "I Am That I Am," and John 8:58, "Before Abraham was, I am." At the same time, the Judeo-Christian tradition is also concerned with the implementation of institutional structures for the benefit of all. There is an understanding of a redeemed humanity. How do we move from what can be an unfortunate monotony of doing, to the blessing of being? How do we move from oppressive structures, to institutions that will facilitate the common good and which will provide a forum for a dynamic exchange on the possibilities of our ultimate coexistence?

Lonergan defines structures of the human good[15] and functional specialties.[16] His outlines provide a systematic understanding of the progress from our individual and our particular goods and needs, to our cooperative integration within a community, to our transcendent values and the realization of what is truly good. Similarly, his development of functional specialties identifies the process by which any enterprise can work cooperatively to bring about the facilitation of common needs and the reconciliation of

15. Lonergan, *Method*, 47–55.
16. Lonergan, *Method*, 125–368.

diverse ideologies. This process Lonergan defines as: a. research, b. interpretation, c. history, and d. dialectic. And their corresponding disciplines implemented as d'. foundations, c'. doctrines, b'. systematics, and a'. communications. The Christian message becomes "not disruptive of the culture . . . but a line of development within the culture."[17]

Societies evolve. A very conservative government in the United States might consider Canada's Medicare system, a form of socialism. Canadian Medicare was initiated in the 1960s by Tommy Douglas (1904–1986), a former Baptist pastor and Premier of Saskatchewan. The Hôtel-Dieu (House of God) hospital, the oldest in North America, was founded by Jeanne Mance on October 8, 1645, with the assistance of the sisters of the Religious Hospitallers of St. Joseph. The Jewish General Hospital in Montreal was founded in 1934 and is open to all patients regardless of race, religion, language, or ethnic background.[18] The hospital was founded by the comparatively small Jewish community of Montreal.

We still have a long way to go. As a comparison, would the people of Hong Kong, which was a former British colony, prefer to live in a society with "freedom of assembly, free press, and (an) independent judiciary," (CBC News, June 14, 2019) or its alternative?

FACTS VS. VALUES HISTORICALLY

It is essential to realize that facts and values have been separated historically, as James Sauer mentions in his commentary on *Method in Theology*.

> In Western culture, since David Hume, facts and values have been separated. They form two distinct spheres of inquiry. Facts are what are empirically verifiable. They are 'sure' and objective. Values, on the other hand, are regarded (in general) as subjective (individual tastes or preferences). Since values represent personal preference, verification is either (1) the personal preferences of individuals or (2) the aggregate preference of groups. (1) leads to either moral egoism or moral subjectivism and (2) leads to either moral conventionalism or moral relativism. (1) And (2) taken together lead toward utilitarianism.
> The 'fact-value' debate has had enormous influence in ethics, value theory, and everyday practice. For example, there is a wide accepted dictum that science is (or ought to be) a

---

17. Lonergan, *Method*, 362.

18. It was also founded because Jewish doctors were unable to get accreditation from McGill's medical department.

'value-free' inquiry. Any introduction of values taints objectivity. Thus, in this section, L. has to show that this position is not sustainable.[19][20]

I suggest that there is a hyper-rational ceiling in academia that inhibits a movement beyond our current understanding of life, and which restricts our understanding of a dimension that has yet to be defined. If the underlying ground is tied to the "repression of sexuality or death as the primary truth," to quote Doran, or it is a very intellectualized and depersonalized philosophy of life, then we have no framework to articulate our experience beyond the material universe. In Carl Jung's *Man and his Symbols*, he says, "modern man does not understand how much his 'rationalism' (which has destroyed his capacity to respond to numinous symbols and ideas) has put him at the mercy of the psychic 'underworld.' He has freed himself from 'superstition' (or so he believes), but in the process he has lost his spiritual values to a positively dangerous degree. His moral and spiritual tradition has disintegrated, and he is now paying the price for this break-up in worldwide disorientation and dissociation."[21]

19. Sauer, *Commentary on Lonergan*, 63.
20. Sauer, *Commentary on Lonergan*, 36–41.
21. Jung, *Man and his Symbols*, 94.

Chapter 8

Anthropological Structures of the Imaginary

THE ISOTOPIC CLASSIFICATION OF IMAGES

It may seem that the tree and the menorah have been lost in some philosophical exercise. It was necessary to show the relationship of form and symbol to being and knowing and, in the following, to show that symbolism is very much a part of our psychological framework. The elements of the menorah—the bud, flower, and bowl—are part of our subconscious symbolic process.

Gilbert Durand proposes three primary psychological drives that characterize fundamental behaviors. He identifies these as standing/uprightness, swallowing food, and mating. The three classes are subsumed under Carl Jung's basic personality types. Extroversion represents daytime and standing, whereas introversion represents the night, swallowing, and mating. The relevance of this categorization is to show that primary psychological responses, which typify patterns of behavior, can be shown to be represented historically in symbolic form. The image of St. George and the dragon depicts the character of uprightness dominating the engulfing dragon. Jonah and the whale illustrate the reverse. Lonergan writes that symbols "obey laws not of logic but of image and feeling."[1] The exodus of the

---

1. Lonergan, *Method*, 66.

Israelites from Egypt contains a combination of swallowing, standing, and a nighttime commission.

> Then they shall eat the flesh on that night; roasted in fire, with unleavened bread and with bitter herbs they shall eat it. Do not eat it raw, nor boiled at all with water, but roasted in fire—its head with its legs and its entrails. And thus, you shall eat it: with a belt on your waist, your sandals on your feet, and your staff in your hand. So you shall eat it in haste. It is the LORD'S Passover. (Exod 12:8–11) NKJV.

The three reflexes can be compared to the form of Aristotle's elements; standing implies act, swallowing coincides with form, and mating to potency. Durand further compares these archetypical structures to "schizomorphic, mystical, and synthetic structures of the imaginary," and says that the imaginary reality is a secondary level of meaning which we apply to our perceived reality." "It means outlining a philosophy of the imagination that might be called the *transcendental fantastic*, as Novalis suggests."[2]

In his very comprehensive catalog of symbols, Durand describes a history of psychological imagery which he believes relates to common underlying impulses. I suggest that this is important to show that the images with which we are concerned describe fundamental drives within our human awareness or subconscious, which evolve through our transition to a more enlightened consciousness. The following is a chart of Durand's symbolic structure in which the elemental images correspond to psychic drives.

---

2. Durand, *Anthropological Structures*, 364.

DURAND—ISOTOPIC CLASSIFICATION OF IMAGES[3]

Table 3: Isotopic classification of images

Orders or Polarities	Diurnal	Nocturnal	
Structures	Schizomorphic (or Heroic)	Synthetic (or Dramatic)	Mystical (or Antiphrastic)
Justificatory Principles or Logics	Objectively heterogenising (antithesis) and subjectively homogenising (autism) representation.	Diachronic representation which links contradictions through the time factor.	Objectively homogenising (perseveration) and subjectively heterogenising (antiphrastic effort) representation.
	The Principles of Exclusion, Contradiction and Identity are fully operative.	The Principles of Causality, in all its forms (spec. Final and Efficient), is fully operative	The Principles of Analogy and Similitude are fully operative.
Dominant Reflexes	Postural dominant with its manual derivatives and the support of sensations at a distant (sight, hearing).	Copulative dominant with its rhythmical motor derivatives and its sensorial supports (kinetic, rhythmo-musical etc.).	Digestive dominant with its coenaesthetic and thermic supports and its tactile, olfactory and gustatory derivatives.

	East		Centre		West
Verbal Schemata	Distinguish		Link		Mix
	Separate ≠ Mingle	Rise ≠ Fall	Mature Progress	Return	Descend Possess Penetrate
Epithet Archetypes	Pure ≠ Sullied Bright ≠ Dark	High ≠ Low	Forwards Future	Backwards Past	Deep Calm Warm Intimate Hidden
Tarot	Sword	Sceptre	Baton	Denary	Cup

3. Durand, *Anthropological Structures*, 416.

Substantive Archetypes	Light ≠ Dark-ness Air ≠ Miasma Heroic Weapon ≠ Bond Baptism ≠ Stain	Summit ≠ Abyss Heaven ≠ Hell Chief ≠ Subaltern Hero ≠ Monster Angel ≠ Animal Wing ≠ Reptile	Fire-Flame Son Tree Seed	Wheel Cross Moon Androgyne Plural God	Micro-cosm Child Tom Thumb Animals-within-animals Color Night Mother Receptacle	Dwelling Place Centre Flower Woman Food Sub-stance
From Symbols to Synthemes	Sun Azure Eye of the Father Runes Mantra Weapons Closure Circumcision Tonsure	Ladder Staircase Bethel Steeple Ziggurat Eagle Lark Dove Jupiter	Initiation "Twice born" Orgy Philosopher's Stone Music	Sacrifice Dragon Spiral Snail Bear Lamb. Hare Spinning Wheel Tinder box Churn	Stomach Swallowers and Swallowed Kobolds, Dactyls Osiris Dyes Crystals Melusine Veil Coat Cup Cauldron	Tomb Cradle Chrysalid Island Cave Mandala Boat Basket, Sack Egg Milk, Honey Wine Gold

Compared to cognitive operations:

Act—Judgment	Potency—Experience	Form—Understanding

Compared to the elements of the menorah:

Flower	Bud	Bowl

So, for our own purposes and to compare Durand's elements to the elements of the menorah and Aristotle's metaphysics: 1) The diurnal, upright, schizomorphic drive expressed by images of light, heaven, hell, eye, ladder, etc., corresponds to the flower/flame of the menorah and the act of decision.

2) The nocturnal, synthetic, rhythmical, mating drive with images of son, tree, seed, wheel, music, spiral, etc., corresponds to the bud of the menorah, the operation of experience, and the element of potency. 3) The nocturnal, mystical, digestive drive with images of child, mother, night, stomach, cup, cauldron, dwelling place, food, substance, cave, etc. corresponds to the metaphysical element of form, the conscious process of understanding and the symbolism of the bowl in the menorah. These drives work in dynamic relationship with one another.

In *The Voice of Rolling Thunder*, the Native American psychologist Dr. Leslie Gray talks about the place of the West (right column) which corresponds to Durand's mystical structure:

> The direction West on the Native American medicine wheel is called the "Looks-Within Place." It is the place of dreams and daydreams. It is the dark cave. It is the place Bear goes to sleep in order to survive the harshest season. So, the healing power of West is that we do not know. Surely that is one place we can dwell in honesty. By selecting and trusting answers from the Looks-Within Place, I have personally arrived at ways to turn apparently hopeless situations around while operating from what seems to be a powerless position.[4]

We could compare Durand's classification to the character of the prophet Elijah who challenges the prophets of Baal and Asherah to call down fire from heaven and light the sacrifice on Mount Carmel. Elijah is successful, the prophets of Baal are not. Several days later, Elijah is threatened by Jezebel: he "runs for his life" and "prays that he might die." An angel of the Lord comes to him and feeds him a "cake baked on coals and a jar of water." On the strength of the meal, he flees to Mount Horeb, a forty-day journey to the opposite end of Israel from where he began at Mount Carmel. He hides in a cave. When the Lord appears, Elijah complains that "they have killed your prophets, and I alone am left." The Lord reveals to him that He is not in the wind, the earthquake, or the fire, but in the still small voice. He then instructs Elijah on his future assignments. The cup of Elijah is put out at every Passover service, and the door is opened in anticipation of the messiah.

The story portrays two opposed character traits. First, Elijah is a confident, prophet of God who can stand up to hundreds of false prophets and who calls down fire from heaven. Secondly, he is shown as someone who is intimidated by the queen and who hides in a cave. The story reflects the diurnal and nocturnal dimensions of Elijah's character.[5]

4. Jones and Krippner, *Rolling Thunder*, 39.
5. I Kings 18 and 19.

A comparable definition related to a person's vocation might be illustrated by the following. A ruler (someone with executive qualities) who can distinguish priorities. A farmer-sower is someone who facilitates production and industry, an entrepreneur. A priest/pastor or listener-counselor is someone with a heart who can understand relationships.

The three-part characterization compares to the persons of the Holy Trinity. The Father personifies judgment/decision, and the Son is the Seed. Jesus illustrates potency. The Spirit corresponds to understanding, as described in John 14:16 as the Comforter (KJV), the Helper (NKJV), or the Advocate (NRSV).

On the web site for the teachings of Yogananda, he compares the Hindu understanding of the three-part nature of God to the Christian:

> "Aum-Tat-Sat" is the triple designation of Brahman (God). By this power were created, in the beginning, the Brahmins (knowers of Brahman), the Vedas, and the sacrificial rites. — The Bhagavad Gita XVII: 23
>
> In the Christian Bible, Sat-Tat-Aum is spoken of as the Father, Son, and Holy Ghost. Aum (the "Word" of the Bible) is God the Holy Ghost, Invisible Vibratory Power, the direct creator and activator of all creation. Tat ("That") is God the Son, the Christ or Kutastha, the Cosmic Intelligence actively present in all creation. Sat ("Being, Truth") is God the Father, beyond creation, existing in vibration-less unchangeability.[6]

The Hindu understanding of the trinity appears to correspond closely, although a Christian believes that God the Son is the Word. In the Druidic tradition, there is the concept of the Awen, the /|\, which is defined as 'flowing spirit.' I have also heard it interpreted as the shadows cast by the morning, noon, and evening sun. It appears to represent the past, present, and future as a trinitarian symbol. There is a tradition that suggests that the Druidic godhead was, or is, trinitarian and is identified as Bel, Taranis, and Yesu, a prefiguration of Jesus? Many authors suggest this tradition is documented by Procopius, but I am unable to locate the reference.

Recently I created an abacus-rosary[7] which had three rows with ten (Hail Mary's), five (the Lord's Prayer), and three beads (for the Apostles Creed). This made a multiple of 150. The fifty times three Hail Mary's were meant to remind us of the Psalms of David, the proclamations of which were incarnated and fulfilled in the life of Christ. While praying the Rosary,

6. https://yogananda.com.au/gita/gita17230m.html accessed October 25, 2017.
7. Canada patent application, 3,077,788.

a Christian is expected to meditate on the events in the life of Christ, that is the joyful, sorrowful, and glorious mysteries.

The three experiences reflected the psychological aspects of Gilbert Durand's dynamic. The Joyful represents the incarnation of the Divine, the indwelling of the Seed, and the I AM in which we were created. The Suffering represents the mystical, the aspect of understanding and the compassion of Christ by which He, and we, identify with our humanity. The Glorious represents the ultimate victory of the transcendent Self, as fulfilled by Jesus' death and resurrection and as realized by our selves as we appropriate our divine purpose.

The Sorrowful mysteries teach us compassion for our fellow man. The Joyful mysteries help us to understand that we are made in the image and likeness of the I AM. The Glorious mysteries inspire us, in that we are ultimately capable of transcending whatever is detrimental to our true purpose.

Dr. Stephen Porges' *Polyvagal Theory*[8] also appears to correspond with Durand's *Classification of Images*. As I understand it, and I apologize for any misinterpretation, the parasympathetic, dorsal vagus nerve, with its low metabolism, low oxygen, low heart rate, and low blood pressure, which goes into the gut, corresponds to Durand's digestive, or homogenising principle, and by extension, Lonergan's operation of understanding. The parasympathetic, ventral vagus nerve corresponds to Durand's synthesizing principle, with its attributes of social engagement, breathing, listening, and facial expression. The ventral vagus nerve moderates between: 1. the more intense sympathetic nervous system, Durand's heterogenising principle, with its attributes of healthy aggression, fight/flight, get up, walk, exercise, and chores, and 2. the dorsal vagus nerve, with its attributes of low metabolism, low oxygen, low heart rate, low blood pressure, and the digestive system.[9]

---

8. Dr. Stephen Porges: *What is the Polyvagal Theory,* https://www.youtube.com/watch?v=ec3AUMDjtKQ Posted Apr 23, 2018, accessed March 14, 2020. 4 min.

9. Porges, *The Polyvagal Theory,* 2011.

Chapter 9

The Burning Bush

The burning bush on Mount Horeb in Exodus 3:2–4 is a manifestation of the tree of life. A bush that burns but is not consumed. In a sense, the event marks a transitional point between the original tree of life in Genesis as a primeval organism and the revelation of the menorah as temple artifact during the exodus (which is approximately a year after the burning bush event). The design of the menorah was given to Moses "after the pattern for them, which is being shown you on the mountain." (Exod 25:40) RSV.

> And the Angel of the LORD appeared to him in a flame of fire from the midst of a bush. So he looked, and behold, the bush was burning with fire, but the bush was not consumed. Then Moses said, "I will now turn aside and see this great sight, why the bush does not burn." So when the LORD saw that he turned aside to look, God called to him from the midst of the bush and said, "Moses, Moses!" And he said, "Here I am." (Exod 3:2) NKJV.

The indwelling (*shekhinah*) of the glory of the Lord, which was manifest in the thorn bush and its centrality to the tabernacle experience, as well as its inclusion as the root of the term tabernacle (*mishkan*), reveals how central to temple worship the burning bush experience is. The tabernacle, *mishkan* combines the root *shakan* with the prefix *m* for *in*.

> And Moses was not able to enter the tabernacle[1] of meeting, because the cloud rested (שָׁכַן—*shakan*) above it, and the glory

[1] אֹהֶל מוֹעֵד literally tent of appointment.

41

(כָּבוֹד—*kevod*) of the LORD filled the tabernacle (מִשְׁכָּן—*mish-kan*). (Exod 40:35) NKJV.

In the only other description in the Old Testament of the burning bush, in Deuteronomy 33:16, the author describes the presence of the Lord as the indwelling, the *shekhinah* glory. Deuteronomy associates the indwelling of God with "the favor of Him who dwelt (שֹׁכְנִי) in the bush." The term "in the midst of" in Exodus becomes personified in the "dwelt." It is later remembered and experienced in the feast of Succoth, the Feast of Tabernacles, on the fifteenth day of the seventh month. "You shall dwell in booths for seven days. All who are native Israelites shall dwell in booths, 'that your generations may know that I made the children of Israel dwell in booths when I brought them out of the land of Egypt: I am the LORD your God.'" (Lev. 23:42, 43) NKJV.

Jesus comments on the appearance of God to Moses in the burning bush in Mark 12:26 ("have you not read in the book of Moses, in the passage about the bush"), and Luke 20:37. Luke also mentions it in Acts 7:30–35, as an angel of the Lord. These passages are told in the context of the resurrection of the dead and whether there is marriage in heaven. "But in the account of the bush, even Moses showed that the dead rise, for he calls the Lord 'the God of Abraham, and the God of Isaac, and the God of Jacob.' He is not the God of the dead, but of the living, for to Him all are alive." (Luke 20:37, 38) NIV. The passages affirm the resurrection of the dead and give a sense of the historical work of God in man.

THE FEMININE SIDE

There is a similarity to the Arabic *sakīnah,* translated as *tranquility* from the root *sakana, to be quiet, to abate* and *to dwell.* "The sign of his kingship is that the Ark will come to you in which there is *tranquility* from your Lord and a relic from the family of Moses and the family of Aaron, borne by the angels. In this is a sign for you if you are true believers." (Quran 2:248) *Sakinah* is a feminine singular noun.

The Shekhinah is also an alternate term for Malchut, the bottommost emanation of the ten sefirot of the Kabbalist's tree of life and is female. (See figure following):

> In the imagery of the Kabbalah, the shekhinah is the most overtly female sefirah, the last of the ten sefirot, referred to imaginatively as 'the daughter of God.' . . . The harmonious relationship between the female shekhinah and the six sefirot,

which precede her causes the world itself to be sustained by the flow of divine energy. She is like the moon reflecting the divine light into the world.[2]

Similarly, in Gershom Scholem's, *Trends in Jewish Mysticism,* he says that in the "Talmud and the Midrashim . . . there is no hint that it represents a feminine element in God." . . . "The introduction of this idea (the feminine) was one of the most important and lasting innovations of Kabbalism. The fact that it obtained recognition . . . is proof that it responded to a deep-seated religious need.[3]

In Reverend Symon Patrick's commentary on the Song of Solomon, he compares the Malchut the bride, to the groom (Christ), referencing the passage from Matthew 22, which is in the same context as Christ's reference to the burning bush (Mark 12:26).

> But, for the fuller Explication of this, it may be fit to note, that the profoundest of the Hebrew Divines, whom they now call Cabbalists, having such a Notion as this among them, that sensible things are but an Imitation of things above, conceived from thence, that there was (for instance) an original Pattern of that Love and Union, which is between a Man and his Wife here in this World. This they expressed by the Kindness of Tipheret to Malcuth: which are the Names they give unto the invisible Bridegroom and Bride in the upper World. And this Tipheret (i.e. Beauty or Ornament) they call also by the Name of the Adam on high, and the great Adam, in Opposition to the terrestrial or little Adam here below. As Malcuth (i.e. Kingdom) they call also by the Name of Cheneseth Israel, i.e. Congregation of Israel; who is united, they say, to that Celestial Adam as Eve was to the terrestrial. Which heavenly Adam, or Tipheret, they call likewise the Sun, and Malcuth the Moon: and make the former an active Principle, the latter passive; or as their Phrase is, Tipheret is but the masculine Power which influences Malcuth; who is but recipient of those Influences. So that, in sum, they seem to say the same that the Apostle St. Paul doth, when he tells us, that Marriage is a great mystery; but he speaks concerning Christ and his church, Ephe V. 32. For the Marriage of Tipheret and Malcuth (or Cheneseth Israel) is the Marriage of Christ, the Lord, from Heaven, with his Spouse the Church, which is the whole Congregation of Christian People. Which was represented in the Conjunction of Adam and Eve, and of all other Men and

2. Unterman, *Dictionary of Jewish Lore,* 181.
3. Scholem, *Trends in Jewish Mysticism,* 229.

women descended from them, when they are joined together in holy Matrimony; insomuch that those Divines, called Cabbalists, have formed this Maxim about this matter; that wheresoever in the holy Scripture we read the Love of Man and Wife, there is mystically designed the Conjunction of Tipheret and Cheneseth Israel. Now this Notion (of which the Learned Dr. Cudworth hath long ago wrote a peculiar Discourse) was so ancient among those Doctors, that they had it before the times of Christ; it gives the plainest Account, why John the Baptist uses the Word Christ and Bridegroom, as if they were in a manner synonymous, and of the same Import, John. III. 28, 29. And why Christ himself compares the whole Business of his heavenly Kingdom (called by the People in St. Mark XI. 10. The Kingdom of our Father David) to a Marriage, or Marriage-feast, which a King made for his Son, Matt. XXII. 2. &c.[4]

The ten sefirot are the emanations of the divine in Jewish mysticism.

The first three Sefirot, Keter, Hokmah, and Binah, form a unity among themselves; that is, knowledge, the knower, and the known are in God identical, and thus the world is only the expression of the ideas or the absolute forms of intelligence. Thus the identity of thinking and being, or of the real and ideal, is taught in the Cabala in the same way as in Hegel. Thought in its threefold manifestation again produces contrasting principles; namely Hesed (חסד = "mercy"), the masculine, active principle, and Din (דין = "justice"), the feminine, passive principle, also called Pahad (פחד = "awe") and Geburah (גבורה = "might"), which combine in a common principle, Tiferet (תפארת = "beauty"). The concepts justice and mercy, however, must not be taken in their literal sense, but as symbolic designations for expansion and contraction of the will; the sum of both, the moral order, appears as beauty. The last-named trinity of the Sefirot represents dynamic nature, namely, the masculine Nezah (נצח "triumph"); and the feminine Hod (הוד = "glory"); the former standing for increase, and the latter for the force from which proceed all the forces produced in the universe. Nezah and Hod unite to produce Yesod (יסוד = "foundation"), the reproductive element, the root of all existence.[5]

Referenced to Strong's Concordance and Brown, Driver, Briggs.[6]

4. Patrick, *Song of Solomon*, 500.

5. *Jewish Encyclopedia*, Vol. III, 474–5.

6. S:BDB: 1. 3804:509d. n.m. 2. 2451:315b. n.f. 3. 995:106c. vb., 998:108a. n.f. 4.

1
כתר
keter
Crown

3
בין
bineh
Understanding

2
חכמה
hochmah
Wisdom

5
גבורה
givorah
Severity

6
תפארת
tipheret
Beauty

4
חסד
hesed
Kindness

8
הוד
hod
Splendour

7
נצח
netzach
Eternity

9
יסד
yesod
Foundation

10
מלכות
malchut
Kingship

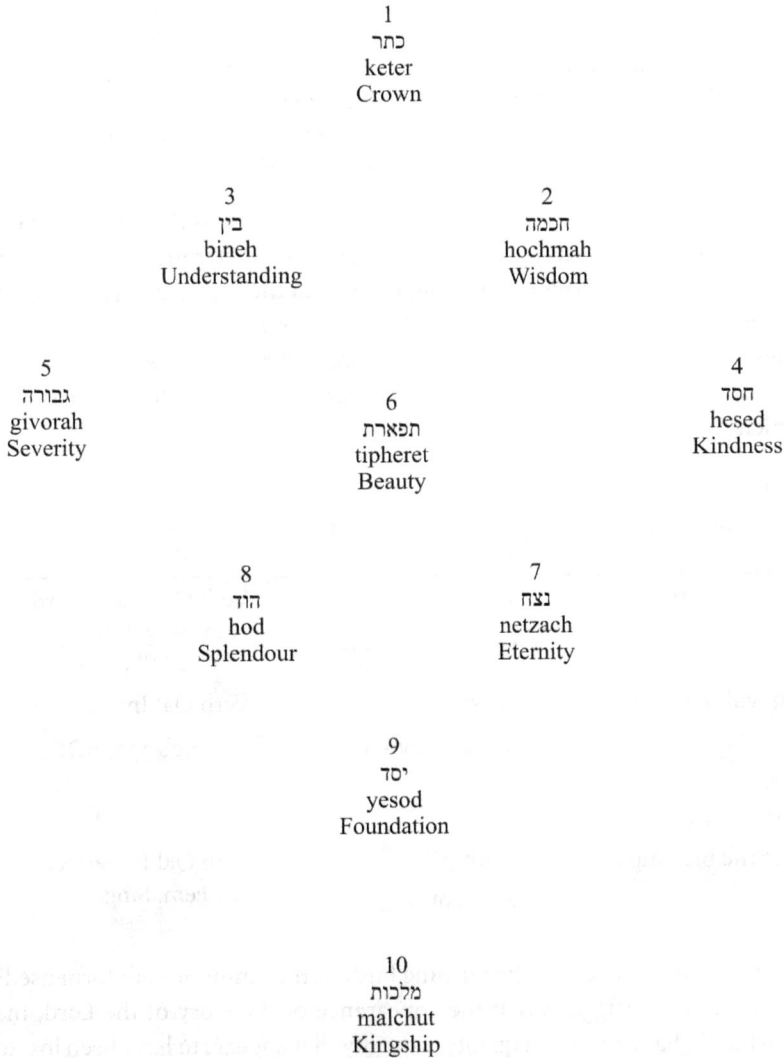

Figure 4: The ten sefirot, illustration by author

In a similar vein, several authors have pointed out that the masculine form in Isaiah 51:9, 10 is feminine and is an allusion to the pillar of fire residing among the exiles in the desert. There is probably much grammatical evidence that there is a feminine side to the godhead, which has been whitewashed by the notion that God can only be masculine.

2617:338c. n.m. 5. 1369:150b. n.f. 6. 8597:802c. n.f. 7. 5331:664b. n.m. 8. 1935:217a. n.m. 9. 3245:413d. vb. 414b. n.f. 10. 4438:574d. n.f.

> Awake, awake, put on strength, O arm of the LORD! Awake as in the ancient days, in the generations of old. Are You (הִיא, she)[7] not the arm that cut Rahab apart, and wounded the serpent? Are You (הִיא, she) not the One who dried up the sea, The waters of the great deep; That made the depths of the sea a road For the redeemed to cross over? (Isa 51:9–10) NKJV.

The preceding reveals that there is much more to the nature of God than the overtly masculine. In the passage from Deuteronomy 33 which is analyzed by Labuschagne following, it refers to the blessing of Joseph from "Him who dwelt in the thorn bush." Isaiah 10 refers to the Light of Israel, who will burn and devour the thorns and briers of the Assyrians—two similar lights, two bushes. In both instances, the fire has a feminine aspect, which is not evident in most translations.

Isaiah 10:17

Common translation	Hebrew and literal translation	Verb form
It will burn	וּבָעֲרָה and she consumes	Verb Qal Perfect 3rd Fem. Sing. (Strong's 1197, BDB p.129)
(it will) devour	וְאָכְלָה and she devours	Verb Qal Imperative (Strong's 398, BDB p.97)

Deut. 33:16

Let the blessing come	תְּבוֹאָתָה She shall come	Verb Qal Imperfect 3rd Fem. Sing.

Why, in both instances of the burning bush, is the feminine verb form used? The translation suggests that the appearance of the glory of the Lord, the Shekhinah, has a feminine quality, a quality that appears to have been lost to the minds of the translators. Umberto Cassuto describes Joseph's blessing, as the "most comprehensive and most solemn." He says that we "must avoid the temptation to emend the text to make it agree with that in Genesis, even when there is no need for such emendations, as there is a tendency to do to-day." However, Cassuto goes on to suggest that the feminine form is corrupt:

> תבואתה is a difficult form; nay more, it is really impossible. Undoubtedly the text here is corrupt; but it is not easy to

---

7. BDB: 214.

determine what the original reading was, or to explain the cause of the corruption.[8]

Did Cassuto miss an opportunity to understand the nature of the Shekhinah? It is possible that the biblical tendency to acknowledge God as the Father has overlooked a feminine quality of the divine, which is possibly the nature of the Holy Spirit.

THE BURNING BUSH AND THE MENORAH, LABUSCHAGNE

Casper Labuschagne, whose work on word patterns is referenced in the Word Bible Commentary[9] series, very explicitly shows that the form of the poetic text is comparable to the form of the menorah and proposes that the centrality of the "dwelt in the bush" verse relates to the centerpiece of the lamp (Deut 33).

> In terms of the 324 words of the poem as a whole, its arithmetic centre is constituted by the two words שֹׁכְנִיסְנֶה, 'the One Dwelling in a Bush," in v. 16b (161 + 2 + 161). The meaningfulness of the middle words lies in the fact that they focus specifically on YHWH as the source of all the blessings. The word סְנֶה, 'bush', was obviously chosen to allude to the burning bush, where Moses met YHWH, but it was also meant to pun upon סִינַי, 'Sinai', in order to call the attention back to the Sinai event where Moses proclaimed the law (note the reference to the law in v. 4).
>
> The two meaningful middle words fall within the middle verse line (16a–b) of the poem as a whole (45 = 22 + 1 + 22), which may be considered its larger meaningful centre:
>
> וּמִמֶּגֶד אֶרֶץ וּמְלֹאָהּ Yes, with the bounty of the earth and its fullness
>
> וּרְצוֹן שֹׁכְנִי סְנֶה And the favour of the One Dwelling in a Bush.
>
> The central verse line falls within the blessing for Joseph (vs. 13–17), where it forms the culmination of the *seven* bounties of the land of Joseph, which are complemented by the personal favor of the God of Moses. The *seven* bounties, with which YHWH blesses the land, are arranged in a menorah pattern, to which the favor of YHWH is added as an extra, most bounteous blessing.[10]

8. Cassuto, *Oriental Studies*, 70.

9. Christensen, *Deuteronomy* Vol.2, 848.

10. Labuschagne, http://www.labuschagne.nl, 7.

Labuschagne[11] illustrates the menorah pattern related to the blessing of the twelve tribes as:

A Reuben and Judah

  B Levi, with first apostrophe (and Simeon?)

    C Benjamin

      X Joseph (Ephraim and Manasseh)

    C' Zebulon and Issachar

  B' Gad and second apostrophe (Moses as leader)

A' Dan, Naphtali and Asher

In Labuschagne's article *The Blessing of Moses*, he breaks down the blessings of Joseph within the twelve tribal blessings into a similar form:

1. With the bounty of the heavens in the form of dew

  2. And with that from the deep, lying beneath

    3. And with the bounty of the crop of the sun

      4. And with the bounty of the yield of the months

    5. And with that from the top of the ancient mountains

  6. And with the bounty of the everlasting hills

7a. And with the bounty of the earth and its fullness

7b. And the favour of the One Dwelling in a Bush.[12]

My basic thesis does not focus on the microcosmic structure of word analysis, but more generally on the macrocosmic relationship of elementary biblical forms. However, I believe that Labuschagne's work, which reveals a relationship to the shape of the menorah on a textual level, confirms my associations on a macro level, the association of the menorah to the burning bush, to the tree of life and the overall form of the text. In a similar pattern, I suggest that the two lampstands (menorah) and the two witnesses in Revelation 11 are located at the textual midpoint of Revelation.[13]

The word μονή, *mone*, is unique to John 14:2, 23, translated as many *mansions*, or the Father and I will "make our *home* (or *abode*) with him." (14:23) A similar word μονίμων, is used and reinforces again the centrality of the blessing of Jacob to Joseph in Genesis 49:26 and is translated as "the blessings of the *eternal* mountains." (RSV, LXX)

11. Christensen, *Deuteronomy* Vol.2, 845.

12. Labuschagne, http://www.labuschagne.nl, 8.

13. *Tree of Life*, chapter, Revelation.

Isaiah 10:17 is similar to Deuteronomy 33; "so the Light of Israel will be for a fire, And his Holy One for a flame; It will burn and devour His thorns and his briers in one day." The same fire as existing in "the favor of Him who dwelt in the bush." (Deut 33:16b) In Isaiah, however, it is a reverse analogy, the thorns represent arrogance, and the 'Light' will devour. Within the context of Isaiah chapters 10 and 11 and the fire which consumes the thorns, Isaiah goes on to say that the "Branch shall grow out of his roots." The Branch is situated shortly after the devouring fire. I show in the chapter on Romans that Paul is associating the olive tree metaphor to this passage in Isaiah.

HITLAHAVUT

Hitlahavut was a Hasidic expression for passion or ardor. The term is used in Psalm 29:7:

> The voice of the Lord flashes forth flames of fire (NRSV)
> The voice of the Lord divides the flames of fire (NKJV)
> לַהֲבוֹתאֵשׁ *lehavut-aesh* flames of fire

בְּלַבֹּתאֵשׁ *belabot-aesh* is the term which expresses the appearance of the messenger of Yahweh with "the heart on fire" in the thorn bush (Exod 3:2). In the *Evolving Symbolism of the Burning Bush*, Professor Etan Levine of the University of Haifa writes that "the flame is essential, for *hitlahavut* unlocks the meaning of life; without it, even heaven has no meaning."[14] God chooses the "lowliest bush" to "convey intimacy." He is both "transcendent and immanent." "Just as the bush is the lowest of trees, so had Israel been reduced to the lowest of conditions, and (God) went down to rescue them from the land of Egypt." In the *Aesthetics of Renewal*, and in the chapter on the *Phenomenology of Hasidic Mysticism*, Professor Martina Urban writes:

> Buber regards hitlahavut as "the primal principle [Urprinzip] of Hasidic life" (9L29/F40). Ekstase, Wonne ('bliss'), and Inbrunst ('fervor,' 'ardour') are synonyms employed to translate the term hitlahavut. Indeed, the words derived from the Hebrew root l-h-v (burning flame, to be inflamed) evoke several of the features attributed to Hasidic mysticism. Although hitlahavut 'is the burning,' it is not to be confined to the ardour of ecstasy, but is the value denoting the enthusiasm that 'unlocks the meaning of life.'" (L2/F7)[15]

---

14. Levine, *Symbolism*, 191.
15. Urban, *Aesthetics of Renewal*, 125.

In Hasidism Buber writes, there are four forms of life or life forces—
"*hitlahavut* (ardour), '*avodah* (service), *kawwanah* (mystical intention), and
shiflut (humility)." (P.117)

In Rashi's commentary on Exodus 3, he suggests that the "flame of fire"
is in the "very heart of" (לב). He says:

> We are "not to be puzzled by the ה, although the ordinary word
> for heart, לב, does not require the ה in the construct form, be-
> cause we have another example of this form, viz., (Ezek XVI:30)
> "how weak is thy heart (לִבָּתֵךְ)."[1617]

The two terms לַהַב flaming and לֵב heart, are closely related and appear to be interchangeable with the appearance of the angel in the bush.
The heart of the angel was on fire, and the bush was burning but was not
consumed. The Theological Wordbook of the Old Testament also points out
the parallel between flame and blade: "The overlap between the meanings
'blade' and 'flame' raises the possibility that at some point the image of the
voice as a flame of fire (#Ps 29:7) and the image of the tongue as a sword
(#Rev 19:15) were originally the same image."[18] The "two-edged sword" is a
quality of the word of God in Hebrews and of the Son of Man (Rev 1:13) and
the Faithful and True (19:15) in Revelation. The sword which went out of
His mouth. A word that is capable of "dividing between soul and spirit" and
discerning "the thoughts and intents of the heart." (Heb 4:12) The conclusion is that the appearance of the angel of the Lord in the burning bush with
the heart on fire becomes a core symbolic affirmation. It is also reminiscent
of the disciples on the road to Emmaus, whose "hearts burned within them."
(Luke 24:32)

The experience of Moses and the burning bush has some similarities
to the phenomena experienced by R.M. Bucke, as mentioned previously, as
well as to the vision of the Son of Man among the lampstands in Revelation. In Martin Buber's *Legends of the Baal Shem*, he describes the nature of
hitlahavut. It is "the burning," the ardor of ecstasy. "A fiery sword guards the
way to the tree of life." "*Hitlahavut* unlocks the meaning of life."[19]

In Glenda Green's very unusual yet credible book describing her encounter with Jesus she quotes:

> In the depths of your being is your own sacred center. It is the
> still, quiet chamber wherein you are one with God. Your own

16. Rashi, *Commentary on Exodus*, BS 1221–1934 V2.

17. Pentateuch, Vol. 2.

18. TWOT, 1077b.

19. Buber, *Legend of the Baal Shem*, 3.

indigenous power is held in place through this connection. Therefore, you cannot underestimate the value that conscious participation may bring. Knowledge of the heart is priceless to your life. The heart is a place where you must be alone, for it is your sacred ground. The very act of being there is the essence of prayer.[20]

Green was an art history teacher and guest artist at the University of Oklahoma. She is a prominent portrait painter with many works displayed in museums worldwide, including the Smithsonian, the Louvre, and the British Museum. Her most famous work is a portrait of Jesus titled *The Lamb and the Lion*.[21]

The next chapter is an analysis of the principle iconic elements of the menorah and is provided as background information to the understanding of their symbolic form.

20. Green, *Love Without End*, 172.
21. http://www.lovewithoutend.com/Miracle_Story_Lamb_Lion.htm

Chapter 10

The Menorah and Its Elements

> Three bowls shall be made like almond blossoms on one branch, with an ornamental knob and a flower, and three bowls made like almond blossoms on the other branch, with an ornamental knob and a flower—and so for the six branches that come out of the lampstand. (Exod 25:33) NKJV.[1]
>
> Three cups shaped like almond blossoms, each with calyx and petals, on one branch, and three cups shaped like almond blossoms, each with calyx and petals, on the other branch—so for the six branches going out of the lampstand. NRSV

The following are the principal iconic elements associated with the menorah, as well as elements from the root of Jesse and the symbols of wrath in Revelation. This chapter is not written to be a stumbling block for want of Hebrew, but only to give some background into the word meanings.

1. THE MENORAH

> The word for "Lampstand" in the Hebrew Bible is מנורה (English "candlestick" in the AV and RV is anachronistic), a nominal form from the common root, ניר:נור = nyr (nur). This is a good Semitic word which probably meant, originally, "to flame."

---

1. Menorah: BDB 633. Root: BDB 632 / S 4501. Bowls: BDB 149 / S 1375. Knob: BDB 499 / S 3730. Flower: BDB 827, V. 826 / S 6525.

It can be compared with the Ugaritic *nyr* and Accadian *nuru*,
both of which have celestial associations; Arabic and Aramaic
traditions are similar. The Lampstand is thus, with the mem-
preformative added to the verbal stem, the repository or support of the lamp, the latter object being the thing which flames.
An interesting and perhaps parallel development is the related
mnhrt, or "torch," in Minaen."[2]

The minaret, the Muslim prayer tower, also comes from the root *nar*
meaning flame, suggesting that a common Semitic root is found in the derivative. (OED)

In Umberto Cassuto's *Commentary on the Book of Exodus*, he gives the
following description.

> The general shape imitates a natural object: the stem or stalk of
> a plant with paired branches at the sides, which are all turned
> upwards. The ornamentation is also of floral design. This
> is how they are described: three גְּבִיעִים gebhi'im—three
> decorations in the form of a cup or beaker (Gen. xliv 2 ff.)—
> מְשֻׁקָּדִים mešuqqadhim—shaped like an almond-blossom—shall
> be made on one branch, and every cup shall consist of two parts:
> (a) a knob, that is, the receptacle at the base of the almond-
> blossom, which contains the ovary (the word כַּפְתֹּר kaphtor
> ['knob'] is an expansion of the word כֶּתֶר kether ['crown'], which
> denotes in general anything round); (b) and a flower—in the
> restricted sense of the term; what is called 'corolla'. The same
> shall be made on the other branches: and three cups made like
> almond-blossoms on the other branch, a knob and a flower; so
> for the six branches going out of the lampstand.[3]

Cassuto also stresses the importance of the number seven within the
description of the Menorah:

> The number seven is placed at the end for emphasis, נֵרֹתֶיהָ שִׁבְעָה
> nerotheha šibh'a, which is contrary to the usual construction,
> שִׁבְעָה נֵרֹתֶיהָ šibh'a nerotheha or שִׁבְעַת נֵרֹתֶיהָ šibh'ath nerotheha
> ['its seven lamps']

The following images depict the menorah in different contexts. In Israel's Biblical Gardens *Neot Kedumim*, there is a species of a bush called Moriah
(*salvia palaestina*), which resembles the menorah.[4] The salvia has gallnuts

2. Meyers, *The Tabernacle Menorah*, 18.

3. Cassuto, *Book of Exodus*.

4. http://www.neot-kedumim.org.il/ Neot Kedumim, Kiryat Ono, Israel.

that grow from the stem with white flowers and a green stalk. The Arch of Titus in Rome shows Roman soldiers with the captured menorah following the siege of Jerusalem in 70 CE. It is a well-worn 2000-year-old mural. The following three images are pencil drawings by the author of the images.

Figure 5: The Arch of Titus in Rome

Figure 6: Salvia Palaestina

This mural from a synagogue in Dura Europus (244 CE) illustrates the primary symbolic elements of Jewish history. The menorah, the temple, the altar of sacrifice on Moriah with ram's horn, the hand of God, Sarah in the tent, Abraham with his knife, and the ram in the bush.

Figure 7: Mural from a synagogue in Dura Europus 244 CE

2. THE KNOB, BUD OR CALYX

Caphtor (כפתר). This occurs in the description of the candlestick of the sacred tent in, {#Ex 25:31–36} and, {#Ex 37:17–22} the two passages being identical. The knops are here distinguished from the shaft, branches, bowls, and flowers of the candlestick; but the knop and the flower go together, and seem intended to imitate the produce of an almond-tree. In another part of the work they appear to form a boss, from which the branches are to spring out from the main stem. In {#Am 9:1} the same word is rendered, with doubtful accuracy, "lintel." The same rendering is used in, {#Zep 2:14} where the reference is to some part of the palaces of Nineveh, to be exposed when the wooden upper story—the "cedar work"—was destroyed. The Hebrew word seems to contain the sense of "covering" and "crowning" (Gesenius, Thes. 709). Josephus's description (Ant. iii. 6, 7) names both balls (σφαιρια) and pomegranates (ροισκοι), either of

which may be the caphtor. The Targum {a} agrees with the latter,
the LXX (σφαιρωτηρες) with the former. [Lintel][5]

Umberto Cassuto also suggests that the knop relates to the crown, as
in his previous quotation.

The knob (old English 'knop'), bud or calyx, conveys multiple meanings, first in the sense of something round which has a plant origin, but
which eventually developed into an architectural form and served to
strengthen the capital or lintel, the point between the column and the roof.
The floral design from Kouyunjik (Ninevah) illustrates the combination of
floral design and architectural support. The design alternates between the
bud and flower with the sixteen-segment circle on the upper layer, possibly
reflecting the number of open petals on the bottom layer.

Figure 8: Architectural remnant from Kouyunjik

There may also be a second metaphorical meaning, which alludes to
the notion of covering as Gesenius proposes. The word כַּפְתֹּר *kaphtor* relates
to the root כִּפֻּרִים *kippur(im) translated* covering or shelter as in *yom kippur*
the "Day of Atonement" (Lev 23:28). The bud acts as the covering to the
flower until it is mature. The Day of Atonement following the seven sabbatical years becomes the year of Jubilee, on which the slaves are released, and
possessions returned.

Words related to kaphtor

כַּפְתֹּר   *Kaphtor* (bud)

כִּפֻּרִים   *Kippur(im)* plural (covering) also 'to cover over sin' Lev 23:28
         and Yom Kippur (Day of Atonement)

---

5. Smith's Bible Dictionary, *Knop.*

כֶּתֶר   *Keter* (crown) Esther 2:17. Job 36:2 "Bear with me" a little.

כַּפֹּרֶת   *Kapporet* (the covering of the ark or 'mercy seat') Exod 25:17

The three elements, bud, bowl, and flower appear very much interrelated in form and meaning. The flower can also be translated as bud as in "the staff of Aaron for the house of Levi had sprouted (פֶּרַח). It put forth buds (פֶּרַח), produced blossoms, and bore ripe almonds." (Num 17:8) The use of the term calyx to translate knob or bud is also the root of chalice or cup. The *kaphtor* translated as lintel (Am 9:1) also has a more functional use, which is suggestive of the bowl as compared to a bud. The word bowl גְּבִיעַ *gebiya* has the same root as hill גִּבְעָה *gibah*, an upside-down bowl and the name of a town—Gibeah, a hilltop. If the bowl of the menorah were turned upside down, like a hill, then the bud would serve as the crown. Also, the term גִּבְעֹל *gibol* translates as bud—'the flax was in bud.' (Exod 9:31).

The various meanings of the three elements illustrate the complex interrelation of organic identities. It evokes a very dynamic and fluid condition as opposed to a static independent state, not unlike a quality of being.

In the last chapter, I suggest that the seal of Revelation corresponds to the bud of the menorah. The symbolism of the seal implies a covering, a binding agreement, a bond which secures until the appointed time, something which is of tremendous value.

3. BOWLS AND CUPS

Dr. Carol Meyers points out that the word גְּבִיעַ that is "bowls" used for the menorah is translated variously as in the story of Joseph and the silver cup as "drinking vessel" and in the Rechabite section of Jeremiah as "earthen vessel."

> The locus classicus of this word is the Black Obelisk of Shalmaneser III. The caption to the relief depicting Jehu's homage contains a list of the golden vessels, among which are the *gabuati hurasi*, offered as tribute by the Israelite king.
>
> The AV rendition "bowl" is perhaps to be preferred for גְּבִיעַ insofar as "cup" (RSV) gives the impression that the Hebrew word is כּוֹס. גְּבִיעַ undoubtedly was a vessel of somewhat different shape from כּוֹס used in wine consumption. That it was broader and more bowl shaped may be inferred by noting that the corresponding feature on the Lampstand of Zachariah 4 is גלה. This word can be related to Accadian *gullatu*, which means "ewer" or,

probably in a derivative sense, some sort of architectural feature of a column such as its base, volutes, astragal, or bowl-shaped capital.[6]

The symbolism of the Bowl related to an architectural device corresponds similarly to the knob as a possible lintel or capital again revealing the interplay between the various elements and their corresponding vegetal and structural themes.

4. THE SHAFT

The shaft of the menorah is translated as "thigh" as in "*table leg*" which describes the supporting structure of the table. In the KJV it is translated as in the following: thigh 21, side 7, shaft 3, loins 2, and body 1. The thigh describes the strongest point of the man from which issue his offspring. As Abraham said to his servant:

> Please, put your hand under my thigh, (יְרֵךְ yarek) and I will make you swear by the LORD, the God of heaven and the God of the earth, that you will not take a wife for my son from the daughters of the Canaanites, among whom I dwell (Gen 24:2b,3) NKJV.

5. THE BRANCH

The image of the Branch from Isaiah 11 is an archetypical messianic metaphor. The meaning is implied in Zechariah 3:8, "I will bring forth my servant the Branch."

The use of the branch symbol has other implications such as Jesus' "I am the vine you are the branches." Paul, in Romans 11, says that gentiles are grafted into the branches of the olive tree. The branch also reminds us of the rod of Aaron which budded, and which was housed (sealed) in the Ark of the Covenant (Numbers 17) as well as the staff of Moses, which turned into a serpent. Tamar asks Judah for his staff, his signet ring, and bracelets as a sign to acknowledge having had intercourse with her. The signet ring and staff (branch) seal the vow. The Branch can also imply descendants such as "Ben Hur of the tribe (branch) of Judah." (Exod 31:2) The branch of the menorah, the term is probably derived from the hollow reed of the Nile, is translated as reed, branch, calamus, cane, stalk, balance, bone, and

---

6. Meyers, *Tabernacle Menorah*, 23.

spearmen. The branch can also have a secondary association as a time marker using the word "bone." The word bone *otzem* is derived from the root of the word tree, *etz*. Exodus 12:17 says; "on this very day (בְּעֶצֶם הַיּוֹם *botzem hyom, 'bone day'*) I have brought you out of the land of Egypt." The rod, reed or branches have several symbolic meanings including their use as measuring instruments for the dimensions of the temple (Ezekiel 40 and Revelation 11).

> This noun apparently denotes the Persian reed Arundo donax. However, vS. AkkH II, pp. 897–98 notes this root represents several reed-like plants in Akkadian. From the primary denotation derives the second meaning, that which is shaped like a reed, i.e. a stalk, bone, {only #Job 31:22} balance part. {#Isa 46:6, lever} This word also represents anaromatic spice used in sacred ministration (cannot be 'calamus,' according to KD, Isaiah, II, p. 199, n.1). Our word occurs sixty-two times. It is to be distinguished from *gome'* (Cypenus Papyrus), *sûp* (an Egyptian loanword meaning rushes in general), *'ahû* (marsh plant), and *yaraq* (green plant). Cf. *qanâ*, I, 'get, acquire, create.'[7]

6. FLOWER

> פרח likewise represents a vegetative form translated into architectural design. That it denotes the "lily" seems most likely. The Targum, Peshitta, and Vulgate all take it as such. The Septuagint renders it κρινον, which can have the general meaning of "flowers." However, κρινον is also the word employed to translate שושן or its variants wherever they occur in the Bible. Both κρινον and שושן are in fact words as general as the English word "lily," which is applied to flowers of a number of various gena of the botanical order *liliaceae* as well as to some not of that order.[8]

The quotation from I Kings illustrates the use of the various terms in building design and shows the relation between the capital (a.k.a. bud) and the floral design of the column. The "capitals were in the shape of lilies."

> Then he made two capitals (כֹתָרֹת) of cast bronze, to set on the tops of the pillars (הָעַמּוּדִים). The height of one capital was five cubits, and the height of the other capital was five cubits. He made a lattice network, with wreaths of chainwork (שְׂבָכָה),

---

7. TWOT, 2040a.

8. Meyers, *Tabernacle Menorah*, 24.

for the capitals which were on top of the pillars: seven chains for one capital and seven for the other capital. So he made the pillars, and two rows of pomegranates above the network all around to cover the capitals that were on top; and thus he did for the other capital. The capitals which were on top of the pillars in the hall were in the shape of lilies (שׁוּשָׁן), four cubits. (I Kgs 7:16–19) NKJV.

The word for lily *shushn,* appears to be an Egyptian loan word (Gesenius) *sssn, sosen* also describing a lily. The city of Susa in Persia (Book of Esther) is written שׁוּשָׁן *Shushān.* "King Ahasuerus sat on the throne of his kingdom which was in Shushan the palace." (Esth 1:1) KJV. The modern Iranian town of Shush is located at the site of ancient Susa. The Hebrew word שׂוּשׂ "to be elated" or to "rejoice" appears to have a similar root. The Wikimedia entry for the girl's name Susan (Shoshana in the Hebrew) says:

> Susan is a feminine given name, a form of Susanna, deriving originally from Middle Egyptian "*sšn*" (lotus flower), first reported on an 11th Dynasty sarcophagus dating from approximately 2000 BC. However, the Hebrew root for the name for the lily, שׁוּשָׁן is derived from the root שׂוּשׂ or שׂשׂ, meaning "to be joyful, bright, or cheerful," which is the basis for the word and name שׂשׂוֹן Sasson, meaning "joy of life." The Persian name for lily is سوسن *sousan,* Susan.[9]

7. ALMOND BLOSSOMS

The three bowls which were made like "almond blossoms" שׁקדים comes from the root "almond tree" or "almond nut" שָׁקֵד which comes from the root שׁקד to be alert or watchful. The almond was the first to sprout in spring. The lamp of the Lord is watchful and alert. It recalls the rod of Aaron, which budded. In dealing with the multitude of complaints, the Lord said that whoever had the rod which budded would act as a testimony against the rebellious of Israel. The rod along with the pot of manna and the tablets of the law were kept in the Ark of the Covenant.

> "And it shall be that the rod of the man whom I choose will blossom; thus I will rid Myself of the complaints of the children of Israel, which they make against you." So, Moses spoke to the children of Israel, and each of their leaders gave him a rod

9. Originally quoted from Wikimedia but which is no longer available. A similar entry is at https://en.wikipedia.org/wiki/Susana_%28given_name%29 accessed July 2020.

apiece, for each leader according to their fathers' houses, twelve rods; and the rod of Aaron was among their rods. And Moses placed the rods before the LORD in the tabernacle of witness. Now it came to pass on the next day that Moses went into the tabernacle of witness, and behold, the rod of Aaron, of the house of Levi, had sprouted and put forth buds, had produced blossoms and yielded ripe almonds (שְׁקֵדִים). Then Moses brought out all the rods from before the LORD to all the children of Israel; and they looked, and each man took his rod. (Num 17:5–9) NKJV.

In the following sketch by the author, the bud, the bottom element, is meant to illustrate a budding almond, whereas the cup incorporates the shape of the almond blossom and the function of the bowl. The flame is meant to illustrate a lily pad.

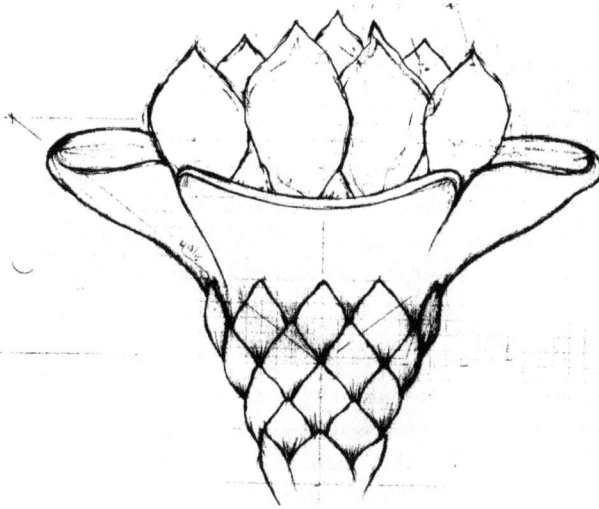

Figure 9: Sketch of menorah elements by the author

8. THE ANOINTING OIL

I include the anointing oil and the incense in this section because they are a part of the symbolic process.

Also take for yourself quality spices—five hundred shekels of liquid myrrh, half as much sweet-smelling cinnamon (two hundred and fifty shekels), two hundred and fifty shekels of sweet-smelling cane, five hundred shekels of cassia, according to the shekel of the sanctuary, and a hin of olive oil. And you shall make from these a holy anointing oil, an ointment compounded according to the art of the perfumer. It shall be a holy anointing oil. With it you shall anoint the tabernacle of meeting and the ark of the Testimony. (Exod 30:23–27) NKJV.

Appendix 6 contains the word origins and meanings for the foregoing chapter.

9. THE INCENSE

And the LORD said to Moses: "Take sweet spices, stacte and onycha and galbanum, and pure frankincense with these sweet spices; there shall be equal amounts of each. You shall make of these an incense, a compound according to the art of the perfumer, salted, pure, and holy." (Exod 30:34) NKJV.

JOSEPHUS AND THE MENORAH

Josephus describes the temple ornaments in detail, which gives us another perspective on the symbolic meaning. His analysis may be colored by a philosophical view that is more cosmic than the original revelation as understood by Moses; however, it makes for interesting reading. He compares the seven lamps to the seven planets, the seven days of creation, and says that they "represented the dignity of the number seven among the Jews."

> Now here one may wonder at the ill-will which men bear to us, and which they profess to bear on account of our despising that Deity which they pretend to honor; for if anyone do but consider the fabric of the tabernacle, and take a view of the garments of the high priest, and of those vessels which we make use of in our sacred ministration, he will find that our legislator was a divine man, and that we are unjustly reproached by others; for if anyone do without prejudice, and with judgment, look upon these things, he will find they were everyone made in way of imitation and representation of the universe. When Moses distinguished the tabernacle into three parts, and allowed two of them to the priests, as a place accessible and common, he denoted the land and the sea, these being of general access to all; but he set apart the third division for God, because heaven is inaccessible to men. And when he ordered twelve loaves to be set on the table, he denoted the year, as distinguished into

so many months. By branching out the candlestick into seventy parts, he secretly intimated the Decani, or seventy divisions of the planets; and as to the seven lamps upon the candlesticks, they referred to the course of the planets of which that is the number. The veils, too, which were composed of four things, they declared the four elements; for the fine linen was proper to signify the earth, because the flax grows out of the earth; the purple signified the sea, because that color is dyed by the blood of a sea shell-fish; the blue is fit to signify the air; and the scarlet will naturally be an indication of fire. Now the vestment of the high priest being made of linen, signified the earth; the blue denoted the sky, being like lightning in its pomegranates, and in the noise of the bells resembling thunder. And for the ephod, it showed that God had made the universe of four elements; and as for the gold interwoven, I suppose it related to the splendor by which all things are enlightened. He also appointed the breastplate to be placed in the middle of the ephod, to resemble the earth, for that has the very middle place of the world. And the girdle which encompassed the high priest round, signified the ocean, for that goes round about and includes the universe. Each of the sardonyxes declares to us the sun and the moon; those, I mean, that were in the nature of buttons on the high priest's shoulders. And for the twelve stones, whether we understand by them the months, or whether we understand the like number of the signs of that circle which the Greeks call the Zodiac, we shall not be mistaken in their meaning. And for the mitre, which was of a blue color, it seems to me to mean heaven; for how otherwise could the name of God be inscribed upon it? That it was also illustrated with a crown, and that of gold also, is because of that splendor with which God is pleased. Let this explication suffice at present, since the course of my narration will often, and on many occasions, afford me the opportunity of enlarging upon the virtue of our legislator.[10]

The following is my drawing of the menorah.

---

10. Josephus, *Antiquities,* Book III Chapter 7.7.

Figure 10: Image of the Menorah

The following chapters depart from a philosophical, psychological, and symbolic route to analyze the symbolic as it is embedded in our sacred history. Our history reveals essential values that, in a sense, can be described as images buried in our consciousness. I have tried to give a sense of sacred history, as a somewhat romanticized legend, of which the Holy Grail and the Shroud of Turin[11] are two principle icons. I included my understanding of the chronology in the appendix.

11. *The Catholic Talk Show* hosts provide a very thorough description of the Shroud's antiquity and reverential relevance at: https://catholictalkshow.com/10-mindblowing-facts-about-the-shroud-of-turin/ "The most important artefact in all of creation, in all of history."

The Knights of the Round Table was a very popular legend in the 1960s. It was made more popular by Terence H. White's (b. 1906) *A Once and Future King*, and later a Broadway adaptation of the same, titled *Camelot*. Another White, Theodore H. (b. 1915), a political journalist and historian, interviewed Jacqueline Bouvier Kennedy, following the assassination of her husband President John F. Kennedy, November 22, 1963. In the interview, *For President Kennedy, An Epilogue*,[12] Mrs. Kennedy compares her husband's presidency to the lines from Camelot, "Don't let it be forgot, that once there was a spot, for one brief, shining moment that was known as Camelot." It is hard to communicate the sense of loss following that time, which had been preceded by tremendous hope. It felt like Camelot. Later the assassinations of his brother Robert, and two months earlier that of Martin Luther King (April 4, 1968) compounded a nations tragedy. I met Robert Kennedy at the World's Fair in Montreal in 1967, while I was working as a sculptor at the Youth Pavilion. Five minutes was all I needed to feel humbled by the charisma of the man. In the article by T. H. White, Mrs. Kennedy asks us to remember John as, "history made Jack what he was," "think of him as this little boy," "reading the Knights of the Round Table."

These legends are indelibly engraved in the hearts of many in the English-speaking world. The legends reach even further back, suggesting that Joseph of Arimathea visited Britain with the youth Jesus. That is the allegory hinted at in Blake's *Jerusalem* (1804). It is also possible that the origins of the Shroud of Turin became enmeshed with the tales of the Holy Grail. The symbolic forms, the tree of life, the burial shroud, the cup of remembrance, the flame of the lantern, and the soldier's lance continue their journey to the western isles. There is a continuity to sacred history.

12. *An Epilogue*, LIFE, Dec 6, 1963, pp.158–9.

Chapter 11

The Holy Grail

There are obvious actual and symbolic connections between the cup of the Last Supper, the designs of the chalice, and the cup icon in the menorah. There are also symbolic associations with the vision of Zechariah of the two olive trees that pour oil through the golden pipes to the golden bowl. The Arthurian legend, which describes the quest for the Holy Grail, contains many of the principle symbols related to this present research and provides a mythic and imaginative context for a modern appreciation of symbolic continuity.

You are probably wondering why I would depart from an essentially abstract understanding of the form of consciousness, into a more specific historic development. The principle symbol, the menorah, which had been localized in the temple at Jerusalem, held pre-eminence until it was carried off by Titus to Rome in 70 CE, after the conquest of Jerusalem on Tisha B'Av. It's interesting that the British government, in a sense a part of the Roman legacy, gifted the Israeli Knesset with a very artistic and substantial four-ton bronze menorah on April 15, 1956, the eighth anniversary of Israel's founding. Following the destruction of the temple, and towards the end of the first century, John in his Revelation carries forward the image of the seven churches as a menorah to go into all the world. The symbol is engraved in the hearts of men and women to bear witness to Christ's sacrifice. It is no longer localized but has become incorporated into the feelings and the lives of the faithful. The legend of the Holy Grail is one expression of that continuity. The temple artefact is now carried on the wings of the Holy Spirit.

If we read history as a series of events, as cause and effect, as this nation against that, we miss out on the sacred initiative that motivated many of the Christian kingdoms following the ascension of Christ. That initiative was the desire to carry forward the new revelation, the revelation that we are made in the image of God and that we are intimately connected. I am suggesting that we can trace a symbolic trail through the lives and actions of the saints which underlies the everyday goings-on of individuals and nations. Besides the fractured ascendancy of the mighty, there was also a cooperative spirit of nation states to find equanimity. I am suggesting an alternate view of history, a view that finds evidence in Christian legend, and which is more fully documented as historical record in the appendix.

The first account of the grail is told in Chretien de Troyes *Perceval, the Story of the Grail*, written between 1181 and 1190. Robert de Boron (late 12th and early 13th centuries) in *Joseph d'Arimathe* further suggests that the cup of the Last Supper was the bowl used by Joseph of Arimathea to capture the blood of Jesus on the cross which ultimately came to Avalon as the Holy Grail. There is also Nennius' account in his *History of the Britons* (c. 830) that "Arthur bore the image of the Holy Virgin, mother of God, upon his shoulders, and through the power of our Lord Jesus Christ, and the holy Mary, put the Saxons to flight."[1]

The primary elements are the sword Caliburn (or Excalibur), Arthur's shield on which he has painted Mary, the mother of Jesus, and the sacred cup of the Last Supper. The legend also tells of the lance of Longinus "one of the soldiers who pierced His side" (John 19:34), and the candelabra (a menorah?) carried before the Fisher King. The original legend, as narrated by Chretien de Troyes, is an obvious Christian legend imbued with Christian symbolism. Percival arrives at Arthur's court on the feast of Pentecost. There are many instances of Christian observances in the tale, such as the honor and respect for women required of the knight. Nineteenth and twentieth century authors such as Jessie Weston have attempted to show a relationship to more primitive vegetation worship. I am grateful for Professor Monica Brzezinski Potkay's audio series entitled the *Eternal Chalice*,[2] to help sort out the multitude of esoteric associations related to grail legend, including the more recent attempts by Jessie Weston, Marion Zimmer Bradley, Michael Baigent, Richard Leigh, Henry Lincoln, and Dan Brown, the readings of which can lead to no end of fanciful speculation. As an example, in T.S.

1. Nennius, *History of the Britons*, 29.
2. Potkay, *Eternal Chalice*.

Eliot's poem *The Waste Land*, he gives credit to Jessie Weston's *From Ritual to Romance*.[3]

In Chretien de Troyes, *The Story of the Grail*,[4] editor Robert White Linker[5] suggests four origins of the Grail legend. A Byzantine theory, a Ritual or Vegetation theory, a Celtic theory, and the Judaeo-Christian theory.

THE SECRET OF THE GRAIL AS ASSOCIATED WITH THE LOVE OF GOD

In the legends of the grail, Jesus tells Joseph of Arimathea there must be a "table" for the grail, a type of mass. The table brings "joy and delight," which is reminiscent of the joy felt in the Garden of Eden. The grail represents a "piece of heaven." De Boron claims that even reading about the grail will bring joy like that experienced in heaven. Joseph of Arimathea entrusts the grail to a brother-in-law, Bron or Hebron, later known as the Fisher King. Bron lives for ages because of the grail. He entrusts it to his son Alain le Gros (a nephew of Arimathea) who carries it to the isle of Avalon, the location of King Arthur's final resting place. Alain becomes the father of Percival. Percival supposedly meets Bron, his grandfather at the Fisher King's castle. In de Troyes's account, Percival keeps silent, whereas, in the De Boron account, Percival asks the Fisher King the purpose of these things. The asking and answering of the question cures the Fisher King, and he dies three days later. Percival becomes the Fisher King.

THE CHALICE

The Chalice or cup of wine which Jesus instituted at His Last Supper for His remembrance has generated a very romantic history, not the least of which is the legend of the Holy Grail. Alternatively, the Catholic Encyclopedia gives the following accounts of possible but questionable artifacts. "In the sixth and seventh centuries pilgrims to Jerusalem were led to believe that the actual chalice was still venerated in the church of the Holy Sepulchre." Later, Adamnan, describes it as a "silver cup holding the measure of a Gallic sextarius and with two opposite handles." The Encyclopaedia also mentions, the *sacro catino* of Genoa, "made of green glass," and another, at Valencia in Spain, "is a cup of agate." "The fact is that the whole tradition is

3. Eliot, *The Waste Land*, 44.
4. De Troyes, *The Story of the Grail*.
5. De Troyes, *The Story of the Grail*, trans. Linker.

untrustworthy and of late date. It will be referred to further under the article Grail."[6]

In my research on the origins of the chalice, I could find no comment suggesting a relationship to the design elements of the menorah. The design of the chalice of the Last Supper appears out of nowhere without reference to its Jewish heritage. However, further investigation reveals its symbolic origins. The obvious knob at the base of the cup (as in the following image), which is a common element in chalice design, is said to facilitate its grasp. This functional explanation for the knob and cup ignores the relationship to the design elements (the knob at the base of the bowl) of the menorah. Similarly, in the Middle Ages, the communicants drank from the cup through a pipe or reed known in Latin as a *canna* or *calamus*. Again, this is an element represented in the menorah design. The reed and its Latin root *canna* are the translations for the branch *qane* of the menorah and are reminiscent of the reeds that fed the menorah from the olive trees in the vision of Zechariah. Today at the papal high mass, the pope drinks from the chalice through a golden reed. There is an obvious connection with the vision of Zechariah, where the prophet says to the angel, "What are these two branches of the olive trees, which are beside the two golden pipes from which the oil is poured out?" (Zech 4:12) RSV. The olive trees symbolize the "two anointed ones," and again, reinforce the symbolic link.

The following image of the Tassilo Chalice which I redrew to accentuate the design elements, is interesting because it highlights the centrality of the menorah (the four cupped branches) to the Christ and as well as the beginning and the end, the alpha and omega, of His ministry. The menorah design is not as apparent in the photos and I only noticed it while I was drawing. The Tassilo Chalice was created for "Tassilo's wedding with the Longobard Princess Liutpirc (around 763)."[7] It also incorporates Celtic design elements in the filigree, and the rose motif compares to the design of the Coptic cross in the following chapter.

If we see the design of the chalice as a symbol of the sacrifice of the Messiah instituted at the Last Supper and as a representation of the menorah which in turn is representative of the tree of life, on which the person of Christ was hung the following day—the chalice as symbol becomes much more meaningful historically.

6. Catholic Encyclopedia (1908): *Chalice*.

7. https://stift-kremsmuenster.net/2014/07/08/tassilokelch-auf-auslandsreise/

Figure 11: The Tassilo Chalice

A RE-EVALUATION OF WELSH HISTORY

The historians Alan Wilson and Baram Blackett, who are generally at odds with academia, claim that there is a wealth of ancient literature, such as *The Myvyrian Archaiology of Wales* which attests to the legends of Arthur. In the *Transactions of the Honourable Society of Cymmrodorion 1948*, P. C. Bartrum, in his article *Some Studies in Early Welsh History* proposes a lineage of Arthur I as a son of Magnus Maximus and a later Arthur II, a grandson of Tewdrig who presumably fought the battle of Baedon. Bartrum interprets dates by using approximate lifetimes. I have recompiled the ancestry chart from Bartrum's *A Welsh Classical Dictionary* in the table following as well as using the lineage from *The Holy Kingdom* by Adrian Gilbert, Alan Wilson, and Baram Blackett and comparing the results if possible to www.geni.org. Wilson suggests that the notion that Arthur was buried at Glastonbury was a ploy by the abbey for popularity, rather that he is buried in Wales in Caer Caradoc. This is possible. However, his dismissal of Glastonbury's history is difficult to accept since there are so many other attestations. Such as the royal charters of kings Ina, AD 688 (Bede), Cuthred, 745 AD and Edmund I, 944 AD. There is also the entry in the Doomsday Book AD 1086 and the Ecclesiastical Councils affirmation of Glastonbury's antiquity in 1409, 1417, 1418, 1424 and 1434 AD. Joseph of Arimathea's tin would have been exported out of Cornwall, the center of tin mining and not Wales, which establishes the original history. This does not invalidate a Welsh Arthurian dynasty and the incredible historical trajectory of the sacred incorporating itself in the life of man.

The chart following shows the ancestry of King Arviragus, the king who befriends Joseph of Arimathea and who may have married a grand-niece or cousin of the Virgin Mary.[8] Linus, the son of Caradoc, is the first bishop of Rome. Caradoc's daughter Claudia marries Rufus Pudens, a son of Quintus Cornelius Pudens, and the half-brother of Paul the Apostle by Priscilla. The names Claudia, Rufus, and Linus are mentioned together in scripture as well as in the poems of the Roman poet Martial, who writes that Claudia (nee Gladys) was a Briton.[9] "Greet Rufus, chosen in the Lord, and his (Paul's) mother and mine." (Rom 16:13) NKJV. "Do your utmost to come before winter. Eubulus greets you, as well as Pudens, Linus, Claudia, and all the brethren." (2 Tim 4:21) NKJV. These three relations are well documented. There are probably historical errors in my interpretation of the line of kings, and I apologize for them, however, I believe it provides a discussion point for the early history of Britain. There is also in the *Apostolic Constitutions* an entry by Saint Peter regarding the ordination of bishops. "Of the church of Rome, Linus, the son of Claudia, was the first, by Paul, and Clement, after Linus's death, the second, by me, Peter." However, I am not clear on the origins of the *Constitutions*.[10]

In a second table in the appendix, I traced the genealogical tree backward from the present. This table shows the ancestry of the house of Spencer—Diana Spencer, the present Prince Charles' first wife, to the house of Gamage of Coity, where presumably the artifacts of the Arthurian Kingdom

8. See the quote from the Harlean MS 3859 in my Appendix: The Genealogy of Jesus.

9. Martial, *Epigrams*, xi: liii. *On Claudia Rufina*. And iv: xiii. *To Rufus, on a Happy Marriage*. "Claudia Peregrina, Rufus, is about to be married to my friend Pudens."

10. Peter, *Constitutions*, Book I Chapter 46.

are buried. This ancestry links directly to Iestyn ap Gwrgan (1040–93), a prominent Welsh king, and to Athrwys ap Tewdrig (b.540) the possible King Arthur. The genealogical site geni.org suggests that unlike my table following, "Athrwys ap Meurig died without issue and should not be conflated with his uncle, Arthwys ap Tewdrig through whom the Gwent line carried."[11]

Noel Currer-Briggs in his *The Shroud and the Grail* (1987) traces a separate tradition to King Abgar V of Edessa, who communicated by letter to Jesus Christ requesting healing. A napkin with the face of Christ was sent to the king. There appear to be several shrouds or napkins in antiquity such as the Shroud of Turin, the Mandylion, Veronica's veil, and the Cloth of Oviedo, and these articles were presumably stained with the blood of Christ. Both the Shroud of Turin in Italy and the Cloth of Oviedo in Spain have multiple (15+) bloodstain patterns that match their comparable positions, and both AB blood types are the least common type. According to standard forensic analysis this match constitutes an authentic link. As an aside, the AB type can accommodate any other donor. The image on the Shroud also compares forensically to icons of the Christ, at least to the fifth century. The Cloth of Oviedo is described by Eusebius.[12]

The legend of King Arthur's Grail may have been unintentionally conflated with the sacred grill, which was the lattice-work box that covered the Shroud during its earliest history. The latticework is seen on paintings from the Early Middle Ages illustrating the Shroud of Turin. The sacred grill, the etymological origins of which in the Oxford English Dictionary are from the Old French *gril, grail, greil,* becomes the Sainte Greil, which houses the bloodied shroud and has similar word origins to the legend of the cup of the Last Supper. The holy grill, or Sainte Greil compares to the Holy Grail, which is derived from the Old French *graal, grael, greel, greil,* from medieval Latin *gradalis* 'dish' (OED). Chretien de Troyes, whose benefactor was Philip of Flanders, the nephew of King Amalric I of Jerusalem, may have unintentionally conflated the two legends of the Holy Grail and the Sainte Greil. Philip of Flanders and King Amalric I were probably both knowledgeable regarding the Shroud of Turin.

---

11. https://www.geni.com/people/Athrwys-ap-Tewdrig-King-of-Glywyssing-Gwent /6000000005598120039

12. Eusebius. Bk I, Ch XIII. You have written evidence of these things taken from the archives of Edessa, which was at that time a royal city. For in the public registers there, which contain accounts of ancient times and the acts of Abgarus, these things have been found preserved down to the present time. But there is no better way than to hear the epistles themselves which we have taken from the archives and have literally translated from the Syriac language in the following manner.

Both the sacred grill and the sacred cup are repositories for the Blood of Christ. The question in Grail literature has always been 'whom does the Grail serve?'

> Whom does the Grail serve? The grail serves to cloth the mortal remains of the Lord. The One who came to serve us all and by Whom we come to know our service. And then the King is healed.

There is a loss of continuity in Welsh history and an understanding of the Christian origins of Britain for several reasons. The Saxons dealt the Welsh a serious blow at the so-called peace conference of 466 AD, where most Welsh rulers were killed—except for King Teithfallt. A later event, as evidenced by the vitrification of the uppermost layers of stone turrets, suggests that a sizable meteor struck the southwest corner of Britain, destroying much of its civilization in 540 AD.

In what appears to be a private paper published by Michael G. L. Baillie, Professor Emeritus of Palaeoecology at Queen's University of Belfast,[13] he suggests that the dates 3195 BC, 2345 BC, 1628 BC, 1159 BC, 207 BC, and 540 AD were times of severe impact to earth's atmosphere far beyond the destructive effects of a volcanic eruption. (Baillie and Munro 1988). He suggests that the date 540 AD coincided with Irish mythic references to a solar entity not unlike a comet in appearance. The Welsh dragon may have been a dramatization of a comet. The suggestion is that at the time of the Saxon raids, further upheaval to Britain's already difficult way of life was exacerbated by the comet's destructive force.

Genealogical data for the kings was compiled by me, the author, and from *The Holy Kingdom* by Adrian Gilbert, Alan Wilson, and Baram Blackett, 1988. (Ref. as THK p.#) and www.geni.org. Also, from P.C. Bartrum's *Some Studies in Early Welsh History* and *A Welsh Classical Dictionary*.

History is the mast of the ship of state, which supports its direction of travel. If our history is based on vague mythology rather than real data, we are left rudderless. We have lost the heartfelt respect for the intentionality and desire for a better life, which was the purpose of Christian kingdoms, however imperfect such as Camelot. The notion of Arthur as mere legend or myth is prevalent even today from what I understood from friends in Montreal of Welsh origin.

The following table represents the Christian origins of the Kings of Britain. In the appendix, I developed more extensive tables illustrating, two parallel and alternate genealogical tables, which include the ancestry

13. https://www.celt.dias.ie/publications/tionol/baillie02.pdf Accessed October 20, 2019.

of King Arthur. In the chapter following I included genealogical tables which attempt to trace the families associated with the Shroud of Turin and a chronology of the Shroud's movements. Also, in the appendix, there is an abridged version of the *Myvyrian Archaiology* which traces the Kings of Wales and a description of their character. There are probably many discrepancies, which at a later date more experienced genealogists will sort out. I am using the following descriptors to denote relations or origins:

- *map, ap* or *ab* is the Welsh for the 'son of'
- *ferch, merch,* or *verch* is the Welsh for the 'daughter of'
- the order of names generally represents the direct descendant
- the *underline* with the bar | represents a direct descendant
- the equal sign = represents a married relation or a partner
- (1) represents the first marriage and (2) the second
- *b.* born, *d.* died, *r.* reign, *c.* circa.
- If the born-reign date ends in the reign it implies that the person died in office.
- *sib(s).* siblings, *dau.* daughter, *bro.* brother.
- *SatG.* represents *The Shroud and the Grail.*
- *THK.* represents *The Holy Kingdom*

GENEALOGIES OF THE BRITISH SAINTS.[1415]

1. Bran the Blessed, the son of Llyr Llediaith, was the first of the Welsh nation who was converted to the Christian faith; and his lineage was one of the three families of British Saints.

2. Saint Cyndav, an Israelite, who came to Britain with Bran the Blessed, the son of Llyr Llediaith.

3. Saint Hid, an Israelite, came to Britain with Bran the Blessed; and his church is Llanilid in Gwent.

---

14. Williams, *Iolo Manuscripts*, 495. With footnote citing the following.

15. From the Book of Thomas Hopkin of Coychurch, which was one of the MSS. of Thomas ap Evan of Trebryn, in the same parish; and was transcribed by him about the year 1670.

4. Saint Lucius, descended from Bran the Blessed, king of the Island of Britain; who was also called Lleuver, the son of Coel, the son of Cyllin, and Lles, the son of Coel, the son of Cyllin. His church was Llandaff; being the first that he erected; and, in fact, it was the first that was ever built there. Llanleirwg[16] in Morganwg, is another church dedicated to him.

5. Saint Dyvan, who came to Britain in the time of Saint Lucius, to administer baptism to the Cymry; for, previously, no one of that nation had ever been baptized. His church is Merthyr Dyvan, in Morganwg.

6. Saint Fagan, who came at the same time to Britain; having been deputed by Pope Eleutherius, at the request of Saint Lucius, to confer baptism on the nation of the Cymry. His church is Saint Fagan's, in Gwent.

7. Saint Medwy, whose church is Llanvedwy, in Morganwg. He lived in the time of Saint Lucius.

Footnotes to Table 4 following

1. 2 Tim 4:21 Gwladys, aka. Claudia. Adopted by Claudius I. THK p.299

2. First bishop of Rome

3. Rom 16:13, Half-brother of Paul the Apostle by Priscilla. A son of Quintus Cornelius Pudens and aide de camp for Aulus Plautius

4. First Christian King of Britain

5. Gwrgan Mawr-Aurelian the Great, father of Onbrawst

6. Cousin of the Virgin Mary

7. Assassinated by Vortigern

8. Possibly Sir Gawain THK p.201

9. Fausta. Daughter of Maximus Galerius Daia

10. Arthur II who fought at Mount Baedon. He is either Athrwys ap Meurig or Athrwys ap Tewdrig

The chapter following the origins of the Christian kings traces the origins of the Shroud of Turin and some of its parallels to the Holy Grail. Despite what some scientists have concluded, probably from evidence taken from a repaired section of the cloth, the Shroud is the most tangible and incredible photographic witness to an event, which records the light transfiguration of a dead being. Other evidence records coins, *leptons*, placed on the

16. The church of Lleurwg or Lucius, now called St. Melon's, near Cardiff.

eyes of the deceased, from the time of Pilate, as well as pollen impregnated in the textile from the area of Jerusalem. In terms of the symbolic origins of the Tree of Life, there is no more revelatory witness than that a being incorporated within Himself, life's ultimate potential.[17]

Both the Shroud, as the alleged burial cloth of Christ, and the Holy Grail, the legendary cup of the Last Supper, are related to Joseph of Arimathea. This in itself is unusual. The forensic trail becomes more pronounced. Chapter 12 traces the origins of the Shroud of Turin and is not essential to the development of the symbolic form of the Bible. It is a complex genealogical overview. If you choose to omit it, it will not take away from developing an understanding of symbolic form.

17. Wilson and Schwortz, *The Turin Shroud*.

Table 4: Christian origins of the kings of Britain

Beli Mawr

Caswallan Cassivellaunos ap Beli	Lludd Llaw Ereint ap Beli Mawr	Afallach
Llŷr Llediaith = Penardim	Tasciovanus ap Llud	(King of
Brân ap Llyr Lleddiarth (the	Cunobelinus Cynvelin ap	Sarras?)
Blessed)	Tasciovanus	
Caradog ap Bran	Arviragus Gweirdd ap Cunobelin =	
	Genuissa or Anna[6]	

Eurgen =	Claudia[1][2][3]	Linus	Guid Gen	Meurig ap Gweirydd (d.125)
Salog	= Rufus	Lleyn [1][2]	ap Caradoc	Coel ap Meurig King of Britain
	| Pudens			Lucius Lleuver Mawr[4] = Gwladys
| saints				| (Gwladys verch Eurgen)
Timotheus	Novatus		Praxedes	Gwladys of Britain (d.222) = Cadfan of Britain
	and Pudentia			

(2) Theodora = Constantinus I Chlorus (d. 306) = (1) Helena merch Cadfan

			(Helen of the Cross)
Dalmatius	Julius	Hannabalian	Constantia

____(1) Minervia =   Constantine the Great (2) = Fausta

Flavius Julius Crispus Caesar (d. 326)	Constantine II	Constantius	Constans
| = Fausta[9]			

(1) Ceindrech ferch Rheiden = Magnus Maximus (Macsen Wledig d. 388) (2) = Helen

			(St. Helen of Caernarfon) |	
Arthur I (Andragathius)	Owain Vindu[8]	Victor	Constantine	Servilla =
Tathal	Eugene, Eidinet	Augustus	Fyn	Vortigern
Teithrin	Tutagual			
Teithfallt (EmRhys Wledig)	Dinacat	Constantine III the Blessed[7]	Vortimer
Tewdrig	Senill	Meneduc = King Pebiau	

Gwerla	Marchell	Meurig ap T.	Cinust	Cynfyn	Guidci
= Bicanys	= Brychan	= Onbrawst[5]			
|	|	|		Gwrgan Mawr[5] = St. Ninoca
St. Illtyd	Merthyr Tydfil	|		

Athrwys II[10]	Madoc	Ffriog	Idnerth	Pawl	Anna
|		|			|
Morgan Mwynfawr	Ithael I				St. Samson of Dol
Gwaidnerth (Caswallon)	Ithael II (b.675)				

BY WAY OF THE LAND LAID WASTE

Whither to the wasteland comes
the sacred cup
the world undone.
Guided by hearts ablaze
what to make
of the dreadful maze
only to set sight
on an unearthly vector

What can passion have to do
within the confines
where the waters move
spiraling ever downward
except to steer
by that unseen star
guided by faith and fate
to Avalon's bar

All we are left
with a ruddy cup
a distant image
of the Saviour's last sup
clinging to scant hope
from endless strife
the otherworldly intrudes
within our earthen life.
S.M.
September 30, 2015

Chapter 12

Chronology of the Shroud of Turin

Table 5: Chronology of the Shroud of Turin and the Grail Legend

30 AD	Abgar V of Edessa King of Osroene (4–50) Mannos VI King of Osrhoene King Abgar VI of Osrhoene (AD 45–90)	The first instance of a cloth facsimile of the face of Jesus Eusebius. Bk I, Ch XIII. Narrative Concerning the Prince of the Edessences. Also, mentioned in the Doctrine of Addai, a Syriac Christian text written around 400 AD which recites the Legend of the Image of Edessa in Parthia. Shroud of Turin 172" x 43.7" (437 cm x 111 cm)
500	Battle of Baedon Hill. King Arthur	
540	Possible comet strike, southwest Britain	
544	Persians attack Edessa	King Chosroes I (501–79) of Persia attacks Edessa. According to legend, the people's faith is restored in the image of Christ and they are able to repel the Persian advance.
544	The Mandylion, the face of Christ imprinted on cloth and given to Abgar of Edessa.	The Mandylion is found in a niche in the walls of Edessa. It has imprinted itself onto a tile

570	Sudarium of Oviedo or Cloth of Oviedo (33" x 21")	Said to be the sweat cloth wrapped around the face of Christ. The bloodstains align with the stains of the Shroud of Turin and the AB blood type is comparable. The earliest literature suggests that it was present in Jerusalem in 570 AD.
614	Persians capture Jerusalem	Chosroes II (r. 590–628) of Persia occupies Jerusalem.
	Precious relics, such as the Cloth of Oviedo are taken out of the capital ahead of the Persian army. The Cloth eventually arrives in Toledo, Spain where it remains until 718. During the invasion of the Moors, the Cloth is moved to Oviedo, Spain.	
639	Edessa captured by Muslims	
648	Muslims capture Jerusalem	Christian sites are destroyed. Pilgrims are persecuted, robbed.
944	Mandylion arrives in Constantinople (Aug 5, 944)	Emperor Constantine ransoms the Mandylion from the Muslim ruler of Edessa and commissions study of Mandylion (SatG p.58) Aug 5, 945
1025	Byzantine coin with the face of the Shroud	Coins from Constantinople depicting Shroud face
1050	Welsh *Peredur*, part of *Mabinogion*. Written between 1050–1250	
1075	Mar 14, 1075 The Cloth of Oviedo. The ark with the Cloth is opened before King Alfonso VI of Spain, various bishops and El Cid. There is an official record of the event	
1089	Foulques V Comte de Anjou et Roi de Jérusalem (1089–r.1131/1143) d. Acre	The Shroud has been the private heirloom of one, or several families descended from or linked with Fulk of Anjou. It was never the property of church or state. (SatG p. 34)
1096	The founding of Oxford University. The motto; "The Lord is my Light"	
1096–99 First Crusade		Raymond IV, Count of Toulouse, of Saint Gilles captures the city of Jerusalem July 15, 1099.

1118	The founding of the Knights Templar aka. The Poor Fellow-Soldiers of Christ and of the Temple of Solomon. Hugues de Payns and Godefroi de St. Omer. Bernard of Clairvaux draws up rules. According to Noel Currer Briggs, the Templars were not affiliated with the Freemasons or the Rosicrucians. (SatG p. 109)	
1147–49 Second Crusade		
1170	Finding of King Arthurs tomb at Glastonbury	Gerald of Wales 1146–1223. *Liber de Principis Instructione*
1171	King Amalric I of Jer. visits his father-in-law Emperor Komnenus of Constantinople.	All the sacred objects were exposed. The cross, nails, lance, reed, the crown of thorns, sindon (Shroud) and sandals. (SatG p.120) William, Archbishop of Tyre chronicles the events. He later informs Walter Map, the chronicler for Henry II of England at the Second Lateran Council 1179–80
1180	Chretien de Troyes	Conte del Graal
1188~	Walter Map c. 1140–1210	*Quest of the Holy Grail, Merlin, Launcelot* and *the Death of King Arthur.* SatG p. 7
1190	Teutonic Knights. Est. at Acre, Holy Land. The Order of Brothers of the German House of Saint Mary in Jerusalem. Formed to aid Christians pilgrims in the Holy Land and to establish hospitals.	
1191	Philip of Flanders whose uncle is King Amalric I of Jerusalem sponsors Chretien de Troies	Philip of Alsace Count of Flanders (d.1191) commissions Chretien de Troies for the *Conte del Graal*
1189–92 Third Crusade		
1200	Robert de Boron	*Joseph d'Arimathe, Merlin, Lesser Holy Grail, and* Did. Mod *Perceval.*
1204	The fourth Crusade	The sack of the eastern orthodox kingdom of Constantinople during the 4th Crusade Apr 12, 1204, by Boniface of Montferrat, Baldwin of Flanders, Geoffrey de Villehardouin of Champagne and Enrico Dandolo Doge of Venice.

1204	Robert de Clari, a soldier in the Crusade recounts his visit Apr 23, and describes the Shroud.	De Clari visits the Good Friday mass of the Soudarion (Shroud). Boniface of Montferrat and Mary Margaret leave Constantinople with the Shroud
1205	Theodore Ducas Comnenus Angelos writes to Pope Innocent III	Angelos complains to the Pope that the "sacred linen in which our Lord was wrapped" has been taken to Athens
1206	Perlesvaus	Written anonymously between 1206–1212. Knights wear white with red crosses as do the Templars
1205–08	Parzival	Wolfram von Eschenbach. Fighting men (Templiesen, Templars?) dwell at Munsalvaesche (Montsegur?). Grail=*lapsit exillis*, (stone, jasper)
1208	1208–1343 Church at Besancon	A copy of the Shroud is in Besancon, France
1209	Walter Map is chronicler for Henry II	Map (c. 1140–1210) Dedicates Grail books to Henry II (SatG p.7–8)
1214	Louis IX King (Saint) of France.	(Apr 25, 1214–Aug 25, 1270) Acquired many relics from the Holy Land.
1214	St. Dominic receives the form of the Rosary	
1215	Magna Carta	
1217–21 Fifth Crusade		King Andrew II of Hungary and Leopold VI, Duke of Austria
1228 Sixth Crusade		Frederick II, Holy Roman Emperor and Roi de Jérusalem
1228–54 Seventh Crusade		Led by Louis IX of France from 1248 to 1254
1270–72	Eighth Crusade Louis IX of France	Against the city of Tunis in 1270 and ninth Crusade

1271	Prince Edward (King Edward I) of England went to the Holy Land. E. Waterton's *Pietas Mariana Britannica* p. 86	"A piece of linen cloth which touched the Shroud of Christ." Comment in the Wardrobe Books referring to Edward I in The Holy Land, venerating the Shroud and leading a raid on Acre with Templars and Hospitallers. He also befriends Hugh of Lusignan, King of Jerusalem.
1274	Possible exhibition of the Shroud at a Templar chapter in Lyons by G.M. Guillaume de Beaujeu. "By now I felt sure that the Templars 'idol' was none other than the Shroud of Turin, and that it had been kept in a reliquary which might have been the Holy Grail. It had been produced on occasions of great solemnity." (SatG p.98)	
1291	Fall of Acre.	Templars lose control of the Holy Land. Grand Master Guillaume de Beaujeu killed at the siege of Acre.
1307	Dissolution of Templars. Shroud is moved from Voulaine to Charny	Most of the Templars are arrested on Friday, Oct.13.1307 by Philip IV of France. Many are executed numbering in the 100's or 1000's.
1314	Execution of the leadership of the Templars. Girard de Villiers escapes.	Execution of Jacques de Molay (1244–Mar 18, 1314) who was the 23rd and last Grand Master of the Knights Templar, by Philip IV of France. Along with Geoffroi de Charney, Master of Normandy and Hugues de Peraud, Visitor of France.
1349	The church at Besancon burns to the ground	Besancon is the curator for the Shroud copy.
1353	Shroud exhibited at church in Lirey	The church at Lirey is founded by Geoffrey de Charny where the Shroud is located

1356	Geoffrey de Charny I Sr. de Savoisy, Lirey et Montfort. (1300–Sep 19, 1356) killed at the Battle of Poitiers protecting King Jean II of France = Jeanne de Vergy	He is the Porte (carrier) Oriflamme, the standard of the crown of France. https://www.geni.com/people/Geoffroi-de-Charny-true-and-perfect-Knight/600000016555500567 = Jeanne de Vergy. Jeanne marries (2) Aymon de Geneve (uncle of Pope Clement VII). Geoffrey (Geoffroi) is the nephew of the Templar Master of Normandy
1367 Joseph of Arimathea's body 'found' at Glastonbury		
1389	The second exhibition of the Shroud.	Bishop d'Arcis complains that it is a forgery
1398	Geoffroi de Charny first known owner of the Shroud in the 14th C. (1352–1398). Daughter Marguerite inherits the Shroud and the land.	Margaret de Charny, dame de Lirey, Comtesse de Villersexel (c. 1390–Oct 7, 1460) = (1) Jean de Beauffremont and (2) Humbert de la Roche-St. Hippolyte (d.1437) Marguerite de Charny acquires S of T from her father Geoffroi.
1418	Shroud moved to Montfort Jul 6, 1418.	Husband of Marguerite (Humbert) moves Shroud to Montfort for safekeeping after husband 1 (Jean de B.) is killed at Agincourt. Then moved to St. Hippolyte sur Doubs for 34 years (1452)
1453	Shroud moved to House of Savoy in 1453 until 1983	Margaret de Charney donates shroud to the Duke of Savoy and Anne of Lusignan
1517	October 31st Martin Luther's 95 theses, Wittenberg	
1531	Our Lady of Guadalupe	
1532	Fire at Chambery, December 1532 near French Alps	
1571	Battle of Lepanto, Oct 7th. Naval battle between the fleet of the Ottoman empire and the allied Christian forces of the Holy League.	It was a major defeat for the Ottoman's and was credited by Pope Pius V to the saying of the Rosary. Miguel de Cervantes, the author of Don Quixote was a sailor in the Spanish fleet.
1578	Shroud moved to Turin from Chambery	

1683	Battle of Vienna, Sep 11, 1683	History of 9/11. The Islamic Ottoman Empire is turned back at the gates of Vienna
1737	Exposition of the Shroud in Turin	Marks the marriage of Duke Charles of Savoy
1898	First photograph May 25, 1898	Secondo Pia (1855–1941). The first photograph showing the image as negative.
1902	Paul Vignon and Yves Delage—'Vignon markings'	Vignon identifies 15 forensic facial markers that can be cross identified to other 1st millennial icons
1917	Russian Revolution. From Feb. to March	
1917	Apparition at Fatima May 13 to October 13, 1917.	October 13. The spinning sun is witnessed by 70,000 people. Mankind is exhorted to pray the rosary and for the conversion of Russia.
1917	Balfour Declaration Nov. 2nd	
1917	Battle for Jerusalem. November 17 to December 30, 1917.	General Allenby enters Jerusalem on foot, December 11th, at the head of the British Empire's XX Corps, XXI Corps, and the Desert Mounted Corps.
1973	Nov 22, 1973.	Shroud is televised by Cardinal Pellegrino of Turin.
1978	STURP team examines Shroud	Composed mostly of NASA scientists
1997	Major fire at the Turin cathedral, Apr 11, 1997.	
1983	Shroud bequeathed to Pope John Paul II	
1988	Carbon 14 dating of Shroud (~1260–1390)	Two theories suggest that the Carbon 14 date is compromised. (1) The sample is taken from a fourteenth century cotton (not linen) repair. (2) The radioactive characteristic of the image affects the properties of the carbon. (Robert A. Rucker)
1998	Sermon by Pope John Paul II on Shroud. https://w2.vatican.va/content/john-paul-ii/en/travels/1998/documents/hf_jp-ii_spe_24051998_sindone.html	

"The Shroud is a challenge to our intelligence. It first of all requires of every person, particularly the researcher, that he humbly grasp the profound message it sends to his reason and his life. . . .The Church urges that the Shroud be studied without pre-established positions that take for granted results that are not such; she invites them to act with interior freedom and attentive respect for both scientific methodology and the sensibilities of believers."

KINGS OR FAMILIES ASSOCIATED WITH THE SHROUD OF TURIN

A. The image of the Shroud has been replicated, according to forensic analysis, in many icons of Jesus prior to its first report in Constantinople by William, Archbishop of Tyre, the soldier Robert de Clari, and King Amalric.

B. King Amalric marries Maria Komnene in 1167 and visits the palace of his father-in-law Manuel I Komnenos (1118–1180), the Byzantine Emperor.[1] He reports that all the sacred objects including the Shroud, were on display. (B. Table 6)

C. The Shroud is in the possession of Isaac II Angelos (1156–1204), Byzantine Emperor and his wife, Margaret Maria Árpád, Princess of Hungary (1175–1240). (C. Table 7)

D. The sack of the eastern orthodox kingdom of Constantinople during the 4th Crusade April 12, 1204, is led by Boniface of Montferrat. Isaac II dies, Boniface marries Margaret Maria and acquires the Shroud. (D. Table 7)

E. It is possible that Konrad I von Hohenlohe-Brauneck (1195–1249) who was with Frederick II, the Holy Roman Emperor while in Jerusalem in 1228 acquired the Shroud. It may have passed from the Templar to the custody of the Teutonic knights. (E. Table 8)

F. Persons related to, or colleagues of, Konrad I von Hohenlohe may have been responsible for the Shroud during the early to mid-1200s. Otto I von Henneberg (1186–1244) marries Beatrix de Courtenay (1176–1245) (F. Table 7) and Konrad's sister Kunigunde Hohenlohe (b. 1198), marries Hans von Weinsberg, possibly known as Jean de Charny. (G. Table 8)

---

1. Note, there is some confusion between (1) Maria Komnene (1154–1217), Queen of Jerusalem dau. of John Doukas Komnenos and (2) Maria of Byzantium (1152–82), dau. of Manuel I Komnenos, Emperor of Byzantium. I am referencing Noel Currer-Briggs, *The Shroud and the Grail*, which I understand draws upon the notes of William, Archbishop of Tyre (1130–1186), *Receuil des Histoires des Croisades*, (Paris, 1844–95).

G. Kunigunde Hohenlohe's marriage transfers the ownership back into the hands of the Knights Templar through a possible marriage to Jean de Charny. It is reported to be displayed at a Templar gathering in 1274 and is in the possession of Geoffrey de Charny (1251–1314), the Templar Master of Normandy. (G. Table 8)

H. The Shroud remains in the de Charny family's possession until Margaret de Charny, dame de Lirey, (c. 1390–1460) bequeaths it to the family of Savoy. (H.I. Tables 6, 8)

I. The Shroud is in the possession of the family of Savoy. Anne of Lusignan of Savoy (1418–1462) is the descendent of Isabella II, Reine de Jerusalem (b.1212) (I. Tables 6, 8)

J. The Shroud is bequeathed to Pope John Paul II in 1983.

Table 6. Kings and Queens of Jerusalem

1. Godfrey (Protector of the Holy Sepulcher) (c. 1060 r. 1099–1100)
2. Baldwin (Baudouin) I (1100–1118)
3. Baldwin II (1060–r.1118/1131)
4. Mélisende d'Édesse, Reine de Jerusalem (1105–r.1131/1153–d.1161) = Foulques V Comte d'Anjou et Roi de Jérusalem (1089–r.1131/1143)
5. Baudouin III, Roi de Jérusalem (r.1143–1163)
[B] 6. King Amalric I Roi de Jérusalem, (of Anjou Flanders) (b.1136–r.1163–1174) = (1) Agnès de Courtenay (dau. of Joscelin III Count of Edessa) and = (2) Maria Komnene.
7. Baldwin IV Roi de Jérusalem (r.1174–85) (son of Amalric)
   8. Baldwin V (r.1192/1197) + (r.1183/86)
9. Sibylla Reine de Jerusalem (dau. of Amalric) (r. 1186 to 1190) =
= (1) Guillame de Montferrat of Jaffa and Ascalon
= (2) Guy de Lusignan Roi de J. (r.1186/1190 d.Jul.18.1194)
Sibylla (9) and Isabella I (10) are cousins of Philip of Flanders (d.1191)
(Philip is the benefactor for Chretien de Troyes)   Maria of M. = Jean I de Brienne, Roi de Jérusalem (r.1210/1212–d.1237)
12. Frederick II (1194–r.1225/1228 d.1250)= Isabella II, aka. Yolande (dau of Jean I) Reine de Jérusalem (b. r. 1212–1228)
                                                        (Holy Roman Emperor and Roi de Jérusalem)

Fall of Jer. 1187–Saladin   13. Conrad II Roi de Jérusalem, Hohenstaufen (b. r. 1228–1254) = Elisabeth of Bavaria
Mamluks capture Acre in 1291   14. Conrad III Roi de Jérusalem, Hohenstaufen (1252–r.1254/1268) son of Conrad II
[I] Anne Lusignan = Duke Louis of Savoy (Owners of the Shroud from 1453)

Foulques (Fulk) d'Anjou (1043–Apr.14.1109) of France (father of Mélisende d'Édesse)
John II Komnenos (1087–1143), Byzantine emperor = Árpád(házi) Piroska (and his son) Manuel I Komnenos (1118–1180), Byzantine Emperor
6. Almalric = (2) Maria Komnene, Reine de Jer. (dau. of Manuel I Komnenos) (and her dau.)
10. Isabella I of Jerusalem (1172–r.1190/1205): reigns with (a, b, c) = a. Conrad I
10a. Conrad I of Montferrat (1192) (bro. Boniface)
10b. Henry I of Champagne
10c. Amalric II of Lusignan (r.1198/1205)
11. Maria of Montferrat, Reine de Jerusalem (1192–r.1205/1221) (dau. of Isabella I)

Table 7. Hungarian, Byzantine, and German owners

From the preceding table: Relation to the Kings of England

Foulques V Comte de Anjou et Roi de Jérusalem (1089–r.1131/1143) d. Acre, the Holy Land   Henry I, King of England =
= (1) Ermengarde, countess of Maine and = (2) Mélisende d'Édesse (dau of Henry I)   Matilda of Scotland
Geoffroy V, Count of Anjou (1113–1151) son of Fulk V = Empress Matilda, dau of Henry I.
Henry II, King of Eng. (1133–1189) = Eleanor d'Aquitaine (H. is the patron of Walter Map. E. sponsors Chretien de Troyes)

Árpád(házi) III. Béla Király, King of Hungary & Croatia (1148–1196)   Berthold IV von Andechs
    Berthold III (IV) von Andechs-Meranien (1159–1204)

siblings:
Sophie von Andechs (d.1218) (son Otto)
Berthold von Andechs, V (1175–1251)
Hedwig von Andechs of Silesia
    Patron Saint of Silesia (1170–1243)

[C] Margaret Maria Árpád(házi)   Árpád(házi) András (Andrew) II
Princess of Hungary (1175–1240)   = Gertrud of Hungary von Andechs
[C] = (1) Isaac II Angelos, Byzantine Emperor (1156–1204)
[D] = (2) Boniface I, Marquess of Montferrat (1150–1207)
    (leader of the Fourth Crusade)
= (3) Nicolas de Saint-Omer, Seigneur de Böotien

Origins of the Henneberg family
Joscelin III de Courtenay, Count of Edessa = Beatrice de Courtenay (of Saone)

Joscelin IV de Courtenay = Agnes de Milly   Agnès de Courtenay
    Agnès = King Amalric I Roi de Jérusalem

Poppo VI Graf von Henneberg (1140–90)
= Sophie von Andechs (1150–1218)

[F] (2) Otto I von Henneberg (1186–1244) = Beatrix de Courtenay (1176–1245) = (1) Guillaume de Lusignan (d.1208)
Otto is buried at Kloster Frauenroth, Frauenroth, Bad Kissingen Deutschland with Beatrix de C.

Table 8. German and French Origins of the Shroud 12–14C

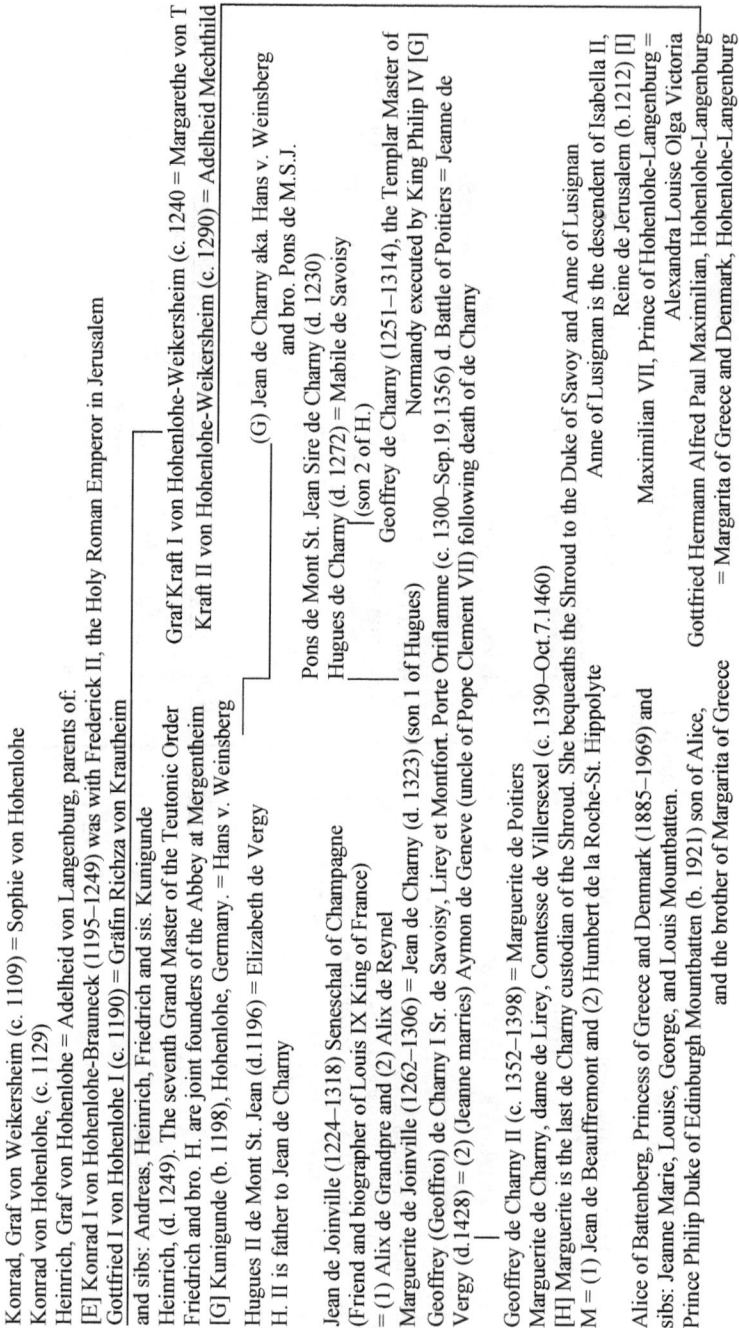

Konrad, Graf von Weikersheim (c. 1109) = Sophie von Hohenlohe

Konrad von Hohenlohe, (c. 1129)

Heinrich, Graf von Hohenlohe = Adelheid von Langenburg, parents of:

[E] Konrad I von Hohenlohe-Brauneck (1195–1249) was with Frederick II, the Holy Roman Emperor in Jerusalem

Gottfried I von Hohenlohe I (c. 1190) = Gräfin Richza von Krautheim

and sibs: Andreas, Heinrich, Friedrich and sis. Kunigunde

Heinrich, (d. 1249). The seventh Grand Master of the Teutonic Order

Friedrich and bro. H. are joint founders of the Abbey at Mergentheim

[G] Kunigunde (b. 1198), Hohenlohe, Germany. = Hans v. Weinsberg

Graf Kraft I von Hohenlohe-Weikersheim (c. 1240 = Margarethe von T

Kraft II von Hohenlohe-Weikersheim (c. 1290) = Adelheid Mechthild

(G) Jean de Charny aka. Hans v. Weinsberg and bro. Pons de M.S.J.

Hugues II de Mont St. Jean (d.1196) = Elizabeth de Vergy

H. II is father to Jean de Charny

Pons de Mont St. Jean Sire de Charny (d. 1230)

Hugues de Charny (d. 1272) = Mabile de Savoisy [son 2 of H.]

Geoffrey de Charny (1251–1314), the Templar Master of Normandy executed by King Philip IV [G]

Jean de Joinville (1224–1318) Seneschal of Champagne
(Friend and biographer of Louis IX King of France)
= (1) Alix de Grandpre and (2) Alix de Reynel

Marguerite de Joinville (1262–1306) = Jean de Charny (d. 1323) (son 1 of Hugues)

Geoffrey (Geoffroi) de Charny I Sr. de Savoisy, Lirey et Montfort. Porte Oriflamme (c. 1300–Sep.19.1356) d. Battle of Poitiers = Jeanne de Vergy (d.1428) = (2) (Jeanne marries) Aymon de Geneve (uncle of Pope Clement VII) following death of de Charny

Geoffrey de Charny II (c. 1352–1398) = Marguerite de Poitiers

Marguerite de Charny, dame de Lirey, Comtesse de Villersexel (c. 1390–Oct.7.1460)

[H] Marguerite is the last de Charny custodian of the Shroud. She bequeaths the Shroud to the Duke of Savoy and Anne of Lusignan

M = (1) Jean de Beauffremont and (2) Humbert de la Roche-St. Hippolyte

Anne of Lusignan is the descendent of Isabella II, Reine de Jerusalem (b.1212) [I]

Maximilian VII, Prince of Hohenlohe-Langenburg = Alexandra Louise Olga Victoria

Gottfried Hermann Alfred Paul Maximilian, Hohenlohe-Langenburg = Margarita of Greece and Denmark, Hohenlohe-Langenburg

Alice of Battenberg, Princess of Greece and Denmark (1885–1969) and

sibs: Jeanne Marie, Louise, George, and Louis Mountbatten.

Prince Philip Duke of Edinburgh Mountbatten (b. 1921) son of Alice, and the brother of Margarita of Greece

Table 7 traces the Hungarian, German and Byzantine origins of the Shroud. The Byzantine Emperor Issac Angelos is married to Margaret Mary Arpad of Hungary. In 1204 at the sack of Constantinople, Angelos dies and Boniface I, the leader of the fourth Crusade marries Margaret Mary. They leave Constantinople with the Shroud and are in Athens in 1205. The Shroud is believed to have been brought to Germany.

Otto I von Henneberg, the son of Sophie von Andechs marries Beatrix de Courtenay, the daughter of Joscelin IV de Courtenay-Edessa and the niece of Agnes de Courtenay who is the wife of King Amalric I of Jerusalem. Otto's mother Sophie is the sister-in-law of King Andrew II of Hungary, whose sister Mary Margaret is the last known recipient of the Shroud. Otto and Beatrix are buried in the chapel at Frauenroth. The church at Frauenroth, which was founded by the Henneberg family and is also their resting place, was home to a von Weinsberg family. The chapel wall is decorated with the arms of the von Weinsberg's and they are the same arms as the de Charny's (gules three escutcheons argent). Hans von Weinsberg (a.k.a. Jean de Charny) marries Kunigunde von Hohenlohe. Many of the descendants of the von Hohenlohe family are monks, nuns, and Teutonic Knights, suggesting the possible influence and sacred responsibility entrusted to the family of the Shroud. Heinrich and Freidrich von Hohenlohe join the Teutonic Order (the German equivalent to the Templars) and are founders of Mergentheim Abbey. The town of Mergentheim, Germany was the capital for the Teutonic Order from 1526 until 1809 prior to its move to Vienna, Austria where it stands currently. Hans von Weinsberg (Jean de Charny) is the most likely owner of the Shroud in the mid-1200s and possibly carried it to France to be held by the Templars and the de Charny family whose descendant is the Templar Master of Normandy. The Shroud is mentioned in a Templar meeting in 1274 prior to the dissolution of the Order in 1307, at which time (1314) the officers of the order (among them Geoffrey de Charny) are executed by Philip IV. The Shroud is passed on to his nephew Geoffrey de Charny I, who is killed at the battle of Poitiers (1356) and is later exhibited by his son Geoffrey de Charny II in the church in Lirey in 1353. His daughter Margaret is the last of the de Charny's and she bequeaths the Shroud to the House of Savoy in 1453.

The ownership of the Shroud is difficult to confirm from the time that it was held by Margaret Mary Arpad of Hungary (1205) to the time of the de Charny's and the Templars (1274). During the sixth crusade (1228–1229) which was led by Frederick II Hohenstaufen, the Holy Roman Emperor (1194–1250), there was friction between Frederick's Teutonic knights and the Templars, possibly because Frederick had excluded Templar land when he arranged a peace treaty with al-Kamil, the sultan of Egypt, and also because Frederick and the Pope (to whom the Templar's owed allegiance) were in conflict. The Shroud may have been acquired by Konrad I Hohenlohe, one of Frederick's major supporters. The Hohenlohe family is unusual as mentioned previously because Konrad's brothers Heinrich and Freidrich von Hohenlohe are founders of Mergentheim Abbey, the Seat of the Teutonic knights. And their sister Kunigunde may be the wife of von Weinsberg or de Charny. The burden of trust which was obviously the sacred responsibility of any individual who was entrusted with the Shroud affected many of the family members of the Hohenlohe, Henneberg, and de Charny families, possibly continuing to this day. Prince Philip, the Duke of Edinburgh's sister is Margarita of Greece and Denmark, Princess zu Hohenlohe-Langenburg. Margarita's and Philip's mother is Princess Alice of Battenberg who founded the Orthodox nursing order of nuns known as the Christian Sisterhood of Martha and Mary. During WWII Alice sheltered Jewish refugees in Athens for which she is recognized by the holocaust memorial center, Yad Vashem. She is buried in the Convent of Saint Mary Magdalene in Gethsemane on the Mount of Olives in Jerusalem. Table 8 traces the genealogy from the time of Konrad I in Germany to the present. The de Charny's are the keepers of the Shroud from c.1274–1453.

Chapter 13

The Celtic or High Cross

Dr. Pamela Bright, the former chair of theology at Concordia University in Montreal, and Sara Terreault associate professor completed an online course on Celtic Christianity for the department just months prior to Professor Bright's death (November 16, 2012). Dr. Bright showed that the Egyptian Coptic motif of the cross, compared the crucifix to the tree of life (see figure 15). It included a circular wreath-like form with flowers as in the following photos, which conveyed to the believer the notion that Christ's death had more to do with life than execution. That imagery migrated from Egypt to the Emerald Isles where the present-day Celtic cross with its circular form remains a vivid communicator of that pattern.

Beginning in the early 1500s, Martin Luther developed his doctrine of "justification by faith alone" which was written as a necessary response to the Catholic church's doctrine that salvation could be achieved, and sin absolved by good works. The doctrine of the Reformation was based on a literal interpretation of the Scriptures, the translation into the vernacular and a renunciation of images and icons. Reformists were concerned that churches and monasteries were using questionable relics as sacred objects to lure a gullible congregation. However, elaborate sculptures, such as the Ruthwell Cross[1] in the southwest of Scotland which were created to illustrate to an illiterate public the message of the Bible, were destroyed by Cromwell's Roundhead's in the 1640s.

1. https://www.historicenvironment.scot/visit-a-place/places/ruthwell-cross. Parts of the poem 'The Dream of the Rood' are from the design of the cross

I was fortunate to have the acquaintance of Father Eoin de Bhald-raithe from Bolton Abbey in Moone, County Kildare, Ireland who interpreted the high crosses in Moone and Castledermot.[2] Many of the images show continuity among the crosses; the crucifixion, the nativity, the three children in the furnace and Saint Anthony in the desert. In the local cemetery, Father de Bhaldraithe pointed out the use of the cross on the Catholic headstone and its omission on the Protestant headstone, within the same family, within the same plot, as recently as the early 1900s. The action reflects the comment by Bishop Goodman of Gloucester "harmless Crosses were demolished." (next chapter)

I used the photos from the two crosses in Monasterboice in County Louth because the imagery was more spectacular in detail. There is a wealth of un-interpreted or difficult to interpret imagery especially in the Book of Kells which may eventually serve as a road map to understanding the development of theology through the Dark Ages. The iconography might help us understand the transition between the visionary mindfulness of the early saints to the beginnings of the era of publication.

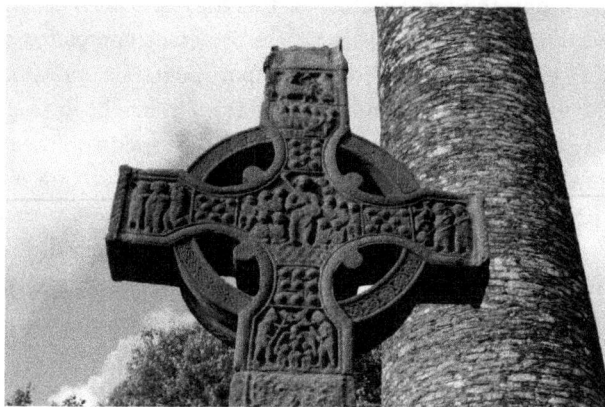

Figure 12: Monasterboice—Tall Cross (7m) east face, photo by author

On the horizontal arm from left to right: the temptation of St. Anthony, Joshua crossing the Jordan, the fall of Simon Magus. On the vertical arm from top to bottom: Manasseh, Christ saves Peter from the waves, Joshua, the three children in the fiery furnace.[3] Peter Harbison in his *Irish High Crosses* suggested that the Muiredach cross (images following) was probably

2. de Bhaldraithe, *The High Crosses of Moone and Castledermot.*

3. Harbison, *Irish High Crosses.* The interpretations of the cross imagery are derived from Harbison's book as well as their seemingly obvious meaning.

erected during the time of Abbott Muiredach who reigned from 887 to 924. I am relying on Harbison's description for an interpretation. As for the topmost image, I can only assume that the interpretation of the bull comes from the blessing of Moses to Joseph which includes his two sons, the tribes of Ephraim and Manasseh: "His glory is like a firstborn bull, And his horns like the horns of the wild ox." (Deut 33:17a) NKJV. The focus of the imagery is also on Saint Anthony, the hermit of the desert as compared to the order of Saint Benedict. The Ruthwell cross also depicts Saints Anthony and Paul with the inscription "*Sanctus Paulus et Antonius duo eremitae fregerunt panem in deserto*." The difference between Anthony's solitary life, a life which according to legend Anthony is fed by a raven and the order of Benedict is the difference between a life in nature and an institutional life. The order of Benedict is sustained by ritual, monastic walls, and community observance.

In a recent PBS documentary on The *Mysteries of the Jesus Prayer* an icon of Anthony is shown with the inscription: "Fight the battle for your own heart," an appropriate message in an age where we can be caught up in the tribalism of what appears to be the idealism of our own system of belief.

Figure 13: Monasterboice—Tall Cross west face, photo by author

On the horizontal arm from left to right: Christ is mocked, the crucifixion, flanked by the denial of Peter, the arrest of Christ. On the vertical arm from top to bottom: Pilate washes his hands, Peter with sword, the Crucifixion, soldiers.

Figure 14: Monasterboice—Muiredach's Cross east face, photo by author

On the horizontal arm: The Last Judgment. On the vertical arm from top to bottom: beehive structure covering saints Paul and Anthony, Christ in majesty, the Last Judgment, Saint Michael weighs a soul, the adoration of the Magi.

The following is a Coptic curtain redrawn by the author. The tapestry is light beige with rose and yellow flowers, brown outlines, and with bluegreen squares.[4] The curtain shows the influence of Egyptian design which eventually migrated to Ireland and the Celtic cross.

4. The Minneapolis Institute of Art. The Centennial Fund: Aimee Mott Butler Charitable Trust, Mr. and Mrs. John F. Donovan, Estate of Margaret B. Hawks, Eleanor Weld Reid (1.4 m x 69.9 cm).

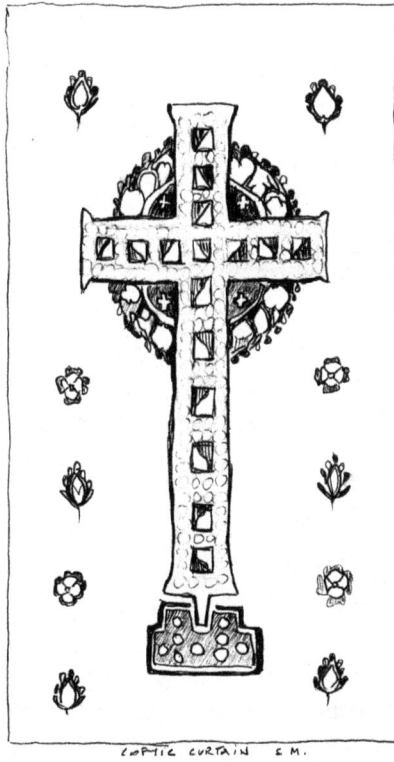

COPTIC CURTAIN E M.

Figure 15: Egyptian Coptic curtain fifth to sixth century

Chapter 14

Glastonbury

The legends and records of Glastonbury in county Somerset, England are a natural and symbolic development from the ancient arboreal past. The legend provides a mystic continuity for the sacred evolution of the messianic Branch. The most dramatic legend suggests that Joseph of Arimathea, the member of the Sanhedrin who was responsible for Jesus' burial,[1] and who had been exporting Cornish tin into the land of Judah arrived shortly after the crucifixion, planted his staff on Wirral Hill in Glastonbury and that the rod continues to bloom to this day.

In the *Biographia Britannica* of 1747 under the entry for Arthur (King of the Britons) the following argument is made regarding the listing of persons such as Arthur whose existence is, even at that time, legendary. The case for documenting what is known is just as important, if not more so than the documents of Greek and Latin mythological heroes.

> After allowing that nothing can be more dubious than the history of Arthur is generally esteemed, some readers may think his life might be as well omitted. Now as the same objection may be made to several other articles taken from our ancient history; it will be proper to return an answer once for all. In the first place then, one can see no reason, why we should be at so much pains, to read and to understand the fabulous history of other nations, and yet absolutely reject our own. What pains have the

1. O.T. And they made His grave with the wicked — But with the rich at His death. (Isa 53:9) N.T.: Matt 27:57, Mark 15:43, Luke 23:51, John 19:38

learned taken with the fables both of Greeks and Latins; and with what solemnity of late years, especially, have we seen the oriental romances, which in their kind exceed all others, commented upon, and thereby rendered useful to the judicious reader. By what figure in rhetoric shall we distinguish between the wisdom shown in these labours, and the folly of dwelling on the less credible history of this island If under the former there may remain truths of great importance, why may not something of the same kind be buried under the latter but farther still, what if the understanding these fables contribute not a little to the understanding of true history. For how fabulous forever a story may be, yet if once it gain credit, and pass in the opinion of men for undoubted truth, it's circumstances will in time become so intermixed, even with the most authentic relations, that without a thorough understanding the one, there will be no such thing as coming at the true sense of the other. On this account therefore the reading of fabulous history is necessary to avoid the believing fables; since if we should once grow so nice, as to think it not worth our while to peruse anything branded with the name of fiction, it might become the means of our receiving, under the name of true history, the meanest and most absurd fictions for want of knowing their origin. Add to all this, that as in the case of all extremes, so here excessive incredulity becomes credulity itself. For if from an apprehension of being thought less critical in taste than others, we should reject the authority of all authors whose credit have been questioned, or resolve to give up all facts, with respect to which there have been any doubts, we evidently embrace the error we endeavour to shun, and by affecting criticism lose all the advantages deducible from that kind of knowledge ; let us therefore be content, especially in such a work as this, to hear whatever our forefathers thought worth the leaving; to examine fairly both sides of the question, and then decide freely as the weight of evidence inclines us. It is indeed one great use of a dictionary like this, that it assembles in little room a multitude of passages relating to the same matter, and yet lying scattered in a variety of authors, whereby the reader in a few minutes becomes possessed of that knowledge, which cost the author much pains and time to acquire.[2]

Jerome[3] in his Vulgate refers to Joseph of Arimathea as *nobilus decurio*. The term has a different sense than the Greek ευσχημων βουλευτης

---

2. *Biographia Britannica.* 1747. Vol. I, No. 17, 197.

3. Jerome, Vulgate. Mark 15:43. Venit Ioseph ab Arimathia nobilis decurion.

which means an honorable counselor. The *nobilus decurio* was a Latin term signifying a position of responsibility, such as a superintendent of mines under Caesar. It apparently carried more weight than a senator. His position in the metal trade (as well as his possible relationship as Mary's uncle) would have given him authority with Pilate and added import to his request for the removal of Jesus' body which would have otherwise been consigned to a grave with common criminals.

GLASTONBURY IN HISTORY

According to legend Joseph of Arimathea is said to have been the great-uncle of Jesus and that Jesus accompanied him during His early years by boat to Cornwall. After Joseph had buried the body of Christ, he is said to have journeyed back to Avalon where he planted his hawthorn staff on Wirral Hill[4]—a staff that continues to bloom to this day—in the last year of Tiberius in 36 AD. He also carried with him two cruets containing the blood and sweat of Jesus. In keeping with the symbolic development of this book, the symbolism of the tree (Joseph's staff which budded—representative of the tree of life) and the cup (the two cruets of blood and sweat)[5] reinstates the symbolic journey during a period we consider the beginning of the Dark Ages. The legend (or fact) suggests that the Gospel of Peace, within a world at war, had found a land whose government, during the reign of King Arviragus, was receptive to the notion that there was one God, that He had incarnated in the person of Jesus Christ and that humanity had a common bond. Modern history and the history of the Reformation continue to ridicule the legitimacy of the event, however, the abundance of records early and late testifying to the actuality of the legend cannot be dismissed. There are a multitude of reasons why the history of Glastonbury has been ignored.

- The mission of Saint Augustine of Canterbury, the envoy of Pope Gregory the Great in AD 596 marked the beginning of the Roman Catholic establishment of Christianity in Britain and took precedence over earlier accounts

- The Venerable Bede (672–735) a reliable historian, does not record Joseph of Arimathea. There might be an excuse for his omission; however, he also does not mention Saint Patrick, St. David (of Wales) or King Arthur who quite possibly lived in the previous century. Is Bede

---

4. Wirral Hill is approximately 500 m southwest of the Abbey. The name is derived from Weary All.

5. For the life of the flesh is in the blood. (Lev 17:11a)

biased against the Celtic church? Bede mentions Vortigern and Vortimer, the alleged predecessors of Arthur. (Bk, I Ch 14–15)

- Bede uses the term England (as of Anglo-Saxon) whereas Cressy, Camden, Gildas, Geoffrey of Monmouth and Spelman use the term Britain (Britannia)

- "The hostile attacks of the Danes and the Normans" against the abbey (*The Chronicle of Glastonbury Abbey*. 1985 p.199) destroyed valuable documentation. Figure twelve of the Irish Celtic cross in the previous chapter shows the approximate 90-foot tower built by monks as a protection against Viking raids

- The fire in 1184 AD destroyed most of the abbey records

- The Reformation finished what remained of the abbey. Also, the execution of Richard Whiting the last Abbot of Glastonbury by Henry VIII, the murder of the monks, the destruction of the Thorn of Glastonbury (Joseph's staff)[6] and the use of parchment records for cannon charges guaranteed a break in continuity.

- The advent of the Age of Reason ridiculed any manifestation of the mystical

The authentication of the record of Glastonbury remains a serious possibility.

- Metal analysis confirms the trading of tin and lead between Cornwall and the Middle East during the late Bronze Age

- There are extensive records throughout history testifying to Glastonbury's legitimacy and these records warrant a serious investigation to separate fact from fiction

- The antiquity of the British church was affirmed by Ecclesiastical Councils five times. The Council of Pisa (1409), the Council of Constance (1417), the Council of Sens (1418), the Council of Sienna (1424) and the Council of Basil (1434). It was stated that the British church took precedence over all other churches, as it was founded by Joseph of Arimathea, immediately after the Passion of Christ

- There are records in the Vatican Library as alluded to by Cardinal Baronius in the sixteenth century testifying to correspondence between Britain and Rome and earlier accounts of the Apostles landing at Marseilles, some of whom continue to Britain

6. The tree continues to bloom because individuals have taken care to replant the shoots.

- According to the *London Morning Post*, March 27, 1931, Pope Pius XI recognized the settlement of Christianity in England 200 years before Augustine in an address to English Roman Catholic Mayors of Bath, Colchester, and Dorchester

- There is the possibility that records exist in Germany which were appropriated at the time of the Reformation since the new Church of England considered them valueless

The problem of succession begins early, possibly with the Celtic bishops who were agreeable to a Christian accommodation but unwilling to submit all authority to Rome under Augustine.[7] Later during the Reformation, the Catholic Godfrey Goodman, the Bishop of Gloucester wrote to Oliver Cromwell in 1652 lamenting the destruction of sacred relics and observances:

> I finde that the Fonts where we are baptized, and make profession of the Trinity, and the Incarnation, they are generally pulled down. I finde that the solemnity and joy at Christs Nativity, was forbidden; that Fasting in Lent, and sorrow at Christs Passion, were by publick Order neglected; I found that all the Memorials of Christs Passion, the harmless Crosses were demolished; I found no honor was given to the Name of Jesus, no setled form of Prayer, but every one left to his own inventions; nor was there any time appointed for prayers, but onely a little preparation for preaching; I found that in very many Parishes the Church-doors were locked up, and there was not so much as any publick Meeting, the Churches generally decaying, and never repaired.[89]

More ancient testimony to the mystic Christian past recounts that Joseph of Arimathea's staff, which he had inserted into the ground upon his arrival, revived and budded twice a year. It also was cut down by the Reformists.

> That St. Joseph of Arimathæa landed not far from the Town, at a Place, where there was an Oak planted in memory of his landing, called the Oak of Avalon: That he and his Companions march'd thence to a Hill, near a Mile on the South side of the

7. The meeting took place under a tree later given the name "Augustine's Oak," probably around the present-day boundary between Somerset and Gloucestershire. Was Augustine's Oak the same as the Oak of Avalon? http://www.unitythroughdiversity.org/gog—magog.html

8. Goodman, *The Two Great Mysteries of Christian Religion*, Reprinted in:

9. Hearne, *Antiquities of Glastonbury*, 301.

Town, and there being weary rested themselves, which gave the Hill the Name of *Weary all Hill*: That St. Joseph stuck on the Hill his Staff, being a dry Hawthorn Stick, which grew and constantly budded and blow'd upon Christmas Day, but, in the time of the Civil Warrs, that Thorn was grubb'd up; however, there were in the Town and Neighbourhood several Trees raised from the Thorn, which yearly budded and blow'd upon Christmas Day, as the old Root did.[10]

Goodman also describes the destruction of the Holy Thorn following his petition to Cromwell:

And I will insist in one particular, the White-thorn at Glastenbury, which did usually blossom on Christmas day, was cut down, yet I did not hear that the party was punished; certainly the Thorn was very extraordinary, for at my being there, I did consider the place, how it was sheltred, I did consider the soyle, and all other circumstances, yet I could finde no Naturall cause; this I know, that God first appeared to Moses in a bramble bush; and that Aarons Rod being dried and withered did budde; and these were Gods actions, and his first actions; and truly Glastenbury was a place noted for holinesse, and the first Religious Foundation in England, and in effect it was the first dissolved, and therein was such a Barbarous inhumanity, as Aegypt never heard of the like; it may well be that this White thorn did then spring, and began to blossom upon Christmas day, to give a Testimony to Religion, that it might flourish in persecution, as the Thorn did blossom in the coldest time of Winter (though the Sun in so great a distance might seem to want heat to bring forth the sap) so Religion should stand, or rather rise up, though Religious houses were pull'd down. I never heard nor read, that any Ancient Author did mention this Thorn, which certainly they had not omitted, if there had been any such thing; and by the growth of the Thorn, truly I did judge the age thereof to be much about the time of the dissolution of that Abbey.[11]

Bishop Goodman, in the seventeenth century, reminds us of the symbolic continuity of the burning bush, Aaron's rod, and Joseph's staff. In 1965, Queen Elizabeth II in recognition of the seemingly miraculous event, erected a cross with the following inscription: "The cross, the symbol of our faith, the gift of Queen Elizabeth II, marks a Christian sanctuary so ancient that only legend can record its origin."

10. Hearne, *Antiquities of Glastonbury*, 2.
11. Goodman, *The Two Great Mysteries of Christian Religion*, 301.

The earliest known official account according to historians is recorded by the Venerable Bede who describes the reign of Ina:

> A. 688. This year Ina succeeded to the kingdom of the West-Saxons, and held it thirty-seven years; and he built the minster at Glastonbury; and he afterwards went to Rome, and there dwelt to the end of his days: and the same year Caedwalla went to Rome, and received baptism from the pope, and the pope named him Peter; and in about seven days he died. Now Ina was the son of Cenred, Cenred of Ceolwald, Ceolwald was Cynegil's brother, and they were sons of Cuthwine the son of Ceawlin, Ceawlin of Cynric, Cynric of Cerdic.[12]

APOSTOLIC SUCCESSION

From my understanding, the following are a list of the Christian churches that have a direct link to apostolic succession. The original "laying on of hands"[13] is directly attributed to an apostle or a successor of the primitive church and is a vital sacramental function sensitizing and incorporating the body of Christ within the body of humanity. The church of Glastonbury, it seems, should be similarly commemorated and much of the evidence points in that direction. The anointing is born out of the desire of the people comingling with the work of the Holy Spirit.

A list of churches which acknowledge apostolic origins:

- Alexandria: The Patriarch of Alexandria (Saint Mark the Evangelist)

- Antioch: The Patriarchate of Antioch (Saint Peter, St. Ignatius of Antioch)

- Armenia: the Armenian Apostolic Church (Apostles Bartholomew and Thaddeus)

- Assyria: the Assyrian Church of the East, the Ancient Church of the East and the Chaldean Catholic Church. (Thomas the Apostle, Bartholomew the Apostle, Thaddeus of Edessa and Saint Mari)

- Constantinople: The Ecumenical Patriarchate of Constantinople (Apostle Andrew)

- Cyprus: The Orthodox Church of Cyprus (Barnabas the Apostle)

---

12. Bede, *Ecclesiastical History of England*, 330.

13. Do not neglect the gift that is in you, which was given to you by prophecy with the laying on of the hands of the eldership. 1 Tim 4:14

- Ethiopia: The Ethiopian Orthodox (St. Frumentius)

- France: St. Denis (Dionysius) Bishop of Paris

- Georgia: The Orthodox Church of Georgia (Saint Andrew, Saint Nino, Mirian III)

- India: the Syro-Malabar Catholic Church, the Syro-Malankara Catholic Church, the Jacobite Syrian Christian Church, the Malankara Orthodox Syrian Church and the Mar Thoma Syrian Church (Thomas the Apostle)

- Jerusalem: The Eastern Orthodox Patriarchate of Jerusalem (Composed of the Greek Orthodox from the first century AD, the Armenian Patriarch from 638 AD, the Latin Patriarch of Jerusalem, from 1099 AD and a Melkite Patriarch of Antioch). There is also an Anglican Church of St. George in Jerusalem from 1841 AD though not considered a patriarch.

- Rome: The Roman Catholic Church (St. Peter)

- Russia: the Russian Orthodox Church (Apostle Andrew, Vladimir the Great 988 AD)

- Spain: the pilgrim's Way of the Camino de Santiago (the Peregrinatio Compostellana) and the shrine of St. James the Great in the Cathedral of Santiago de Compostela

It is unfortunate that with such an abundance of testimony that the Celtic Church has not been given an ear for its own very significant place in Christian history. According to the website Historic UK, there is an argument for replacing St. George as patron saint, (a foreigner who it seems never set foot in England) with St. Edmund, a person who was born in England and as a Christian and king defended his faith against the pagan Vikings and was subsequently beheaded for his stand.[14] Although according to legend Joseph of Arimathea entrusted the symbol of the cross of St. George to Arviragus. In 944 AD King Edmund's Charter affirmed the historic right of Glastonbury as the first establishment of Christianity in Britain. Historians during the Reformation seemed to have difficulty corroborating Biblical history and the early first century with the legends originating in Avalon.

14. http://www.historic-uk.com/HistoryUK/HistoryofEngland/Edmund-original
-patron-saint-of-England

WITNESSES TO GLASTONBURY

Sir Henry Spelman (1564–1641) recorded the existence of a brass plate at Glastonbury testifying to the original church. Archbishop James Ussher also refers to the same plate. The plate can no longer be found but Spelman made a rubbing of it at that time. The drawing is recorded in his *Concilia* published in 1639 on page nine. Spelman himself is incredulous of the provenance of the plate. The Benedictine monk and historian R.F.S. Cressy quotes Spelman saying that it is a "thing borrowed from fabulous Legends," Spelman "doubts whether any Christian Churches at all were erected so early," (the churches) "were not encompassed with ground for buriall," that churches were "against the Rite of Consecrating Churches mention'd in this Inscription, which he thinks to be of a far later date." "Lastly that which most displeases Sir Henry Spelman (according to Cressy) is the Dedication of this Church to the Honour of the Blessed Virgin: A Devotion he thinks not in use till severall ages following." Cressy rebuts Spelman's arguments showing lastly, that "even in this very age this was not the only Example of such a Veneration exhibited to the most Holy Virgin Mother of our Lord, the ancient Churches of Spain will assure us, which by a Tradition universally received among them, attested in all their Liturgies & severall of their Councils, relate that there were even from the first entrance of Christianity into that Kingdom several Churches erected to her honour."[15]

---

15. Cressy, *Church-History of Brittany*, Book 2. Chap VIII.

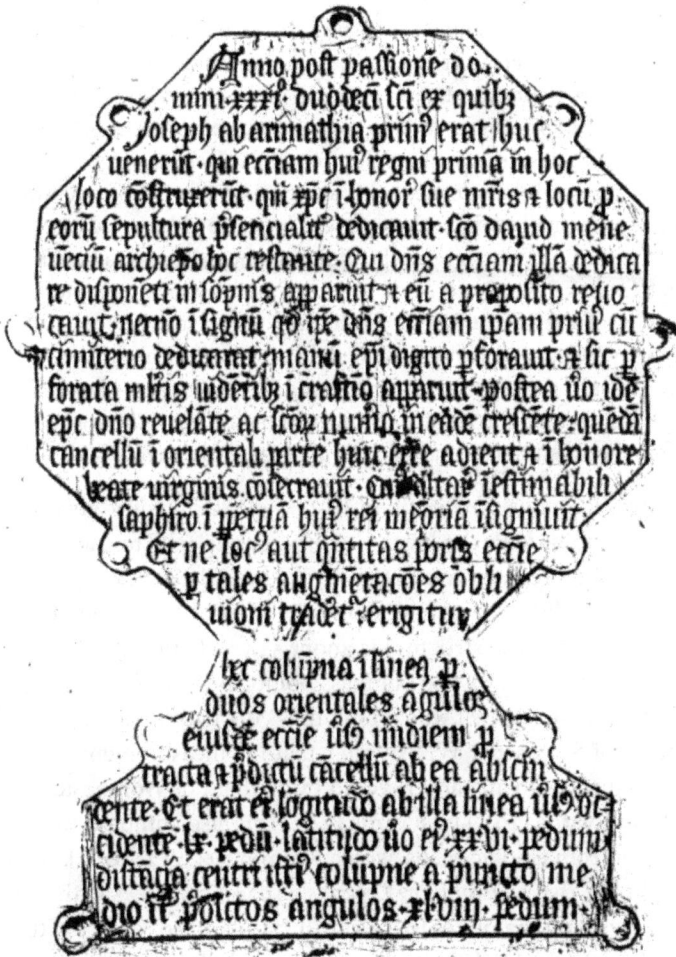

Figure 16: Brass plate rubbing from Glastonbury by Sir Henry Spelman[16]

The following translation was provided by Cressy.

In the one and thirtieth year after the Passion of our Lord twelve Holy men, among whom Ioseph of Arimathea was Cheif, came to this place: and here built the first Church of this Kingdom: Which Christ, in the honour of his Mother, himselfe dedicated, together with a place for their buriall: as S. David Bishop of Menevia testified, who having an intention to consecrate it, our Lord appearing in a vision by night to him, forbad him: And moreover for a sign that our Lord himselfe had formerly

16. Spelman, *Concilia*, 9.

dedicated the Church together with the Church-yard, he with his finger bored through the Bishops hand, which was next day seen by many persons so peirced. Afterward the same Bishop by Divine Revelation, and upon occasion of the encreasing number of Holy persons there, added a Chappell to the East-side of this Church, and consecrated it in honour of the Blessed Virgin: The Altar of which he adorned with a Saphir of inestimable valew, for a perpetuall Memory hereof. And least the place or quantity of the former Church by such Additions should come to be forgotten, this Pillar was erected in a line drawn by the two Eastern angles of the sayd Church southward, which line divides the foresayd Chappell from it. Now the Length of it from the sayd line toward the West was sixty feet, the Breadth twenty-six: And the distance of the Center of the sayd Pillar from the middle point between the foresayd angles contained forty-eight feet.[17][18]

In Revd. R. Willis' *Architectural History of Glastonbury Abbey* (1866), he identifies a point with the letter *k* which corresponds to the location of the 'Pillar' in the previous translation by Cressy. The following engraving is taken from Willis' *History* and shows the plan of the Abbey Church.[19] The overall length of the structure is about 514 feet and the width is 88. I inserted the measurements and compass points to the illustration. There is some disagreement between which building is the Lady's Chapel and which is the chapel of St. Joseph. Willis writes that his measurement of 109 feet by 24 feet compares to an earlier record by William of Worchester in 1478 which gives 34 yards (102') by 8 yards (24'). This also compares to my own measurement from Google Maps, which was 109 feet by 22 feet. J. Armitage Robinson in his *Two Glastonbury Legends*, (1926), disagrees with the location of *k*, suggesting that it lies to the north.[20] Willis also refers to Stukeley's *Itinerary*, (1723) which labels the western most building as "the chapel of Saint Joseph of Arimathea, the patron and asserted founder of the whole." The site may have originally been the site of the original *Olde Churche*, or wicker church, or *vetusta ecclesia*, which was dedicated to Mary. The following print is a copy of Willis' plan of the Abbey church.

17. Cressy, *Church–History of Brittany*, Book 2. Chap VIII. Similarly:

18. John of Glastonbury, *The Chronicle of Glastonbury Abbey*, 29–31.

19. Willis, *History of Glastonbury Abbey*, frontispiece, Plate 1.

20. Robinson, *Two Glastonbury Legends*, 56.

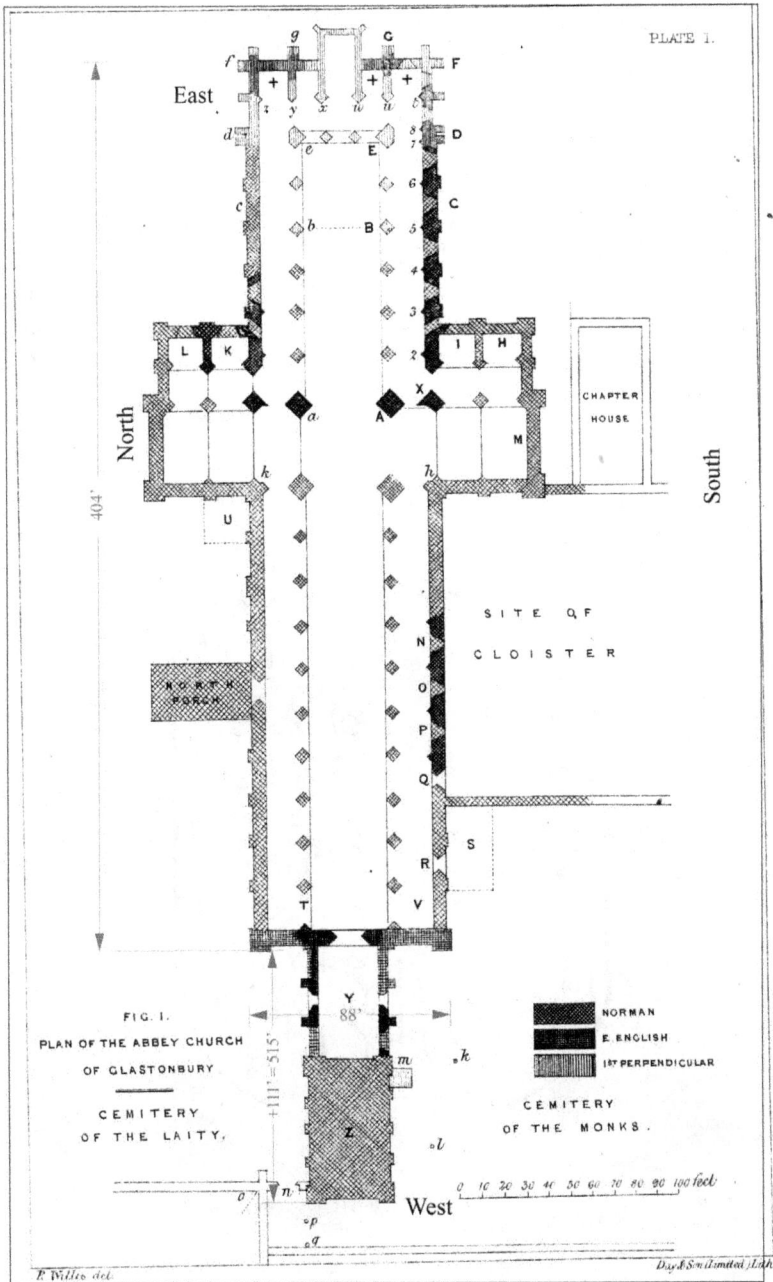

Figure 17: Willis Plan of Abbey Church

The name Avalon is possibly from the early Welsh *afel* meaning apple. The island was also called Yniswitrine meaning island of glass, from the Latin *insula*, island and *vitri*, glass. Also, from the later French *vitrine*, a *glass showcase* or *window*. Is T.S. Eliot referring to the origins of Druidic history when he talks about the apple tree or to the children in the Garden of Eden, or both? (*Little Gidding*)

One of the first books printed in England is *The Lyfe of Joseph of Armathy*. It was "Printed at London in Fletestrete at the sygne of the George by Richard Pynson printer vnto the kinges noble grace Anno domini. MCCCCCXX" (1520). The book contains a drawing of Joseph's coat of arms and I am quoting Cressy's description of the icons. The coat of arms shows the thorn cross, two cruets with the blood and sweat of Christ, and the background with droplets of blood.

¶ Here begynneth the lyfe of Jo-
feph of Armathia.

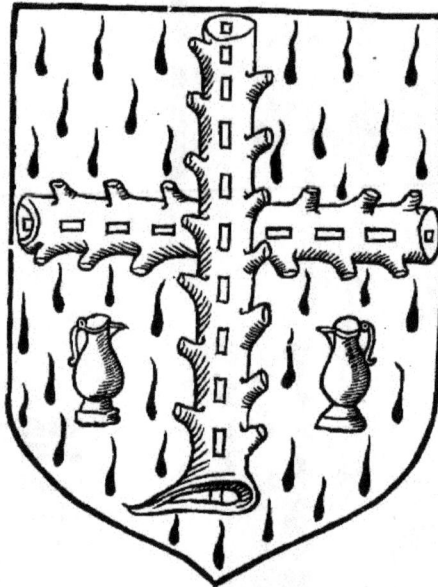

[Reprinted from the black-letter copy printed
by Richard Pynson, A.D. 1520.]

Figure 18: Coat of Arms Joseph of Arimathea

On the out-side of the wall of this Chappell erected to the honour of the most blessed Virgin were ingraven in a stone in most
ancient Characters these two words, IESUS, MARIA. These
things are likewise confirm'd by the ancient Arms of the same
Monastery, which are a white Scutcheon upon which is erected
straight downwards the stock of a Crosse, green and knotted:
and from side to side are the arms of the Crosse of the same
colour: There are likewise sprinkled all over the field drops of
blood: and on both sides of the stock under the wings of the
crosse are placed two viols gilded. These were always call'd the
Badges of St. Ioseph, who is piously beleived to have dwelt, and
peradventure been buried there.[21]

There is no mention of Joseph of Arimathea or Nicodemus in the *Encyclopaedia Judaica* although they are mentioned in the *Jewish Encyclopedia*.
There are entries for Joseph Caiaphas, Caiaphas' father-in-law Anan son
of Seth, the Annas of John 18:13, Paul of Tarsus, Jesus, but no mention of
Joseph, a 'respected' member of the council of the Sanhedrin. He is briefly
mentioned under the heading British Israelites. The argument against the
British Israelites is important because they advocate for the supremacy
of the British people over the Jews. It is a theology of supersessionism or
replacement theology which suggests that the Abrahamic Covenant and
the descendants of Abraham have been superseded by the church, the
New Covenant and British elitism. The exiled tribes of the Israelites in the
eighth century BCE are more likely to have been driven east by the Assyrians as evidenced by the Jewish cemetery in Herat Afghanistan.[22] There
are also the Jews of Nanking, of Ethiopia, of Burma, (Myanmar) and of
Bombay (Mumbai) as discovered by Benjamin of Tudelo to mention a few.
There is also evidence as researched by Alan Wilson, a British historian,
that some of the tribes (Israelites as opposed to Judaites?) may have migrated to Britain. The Jews were exiled from England in 1290 so obviously,
the history has a more complex journey than the ten tribes ending up in
Britain. Wilson has also shown that the Welsh Coelbren alphabet can be
used to translate the text of Etruscan and Egyptian tablets, and possibly
the Qumran copper scroll.

However, to include Joseph in the same paragraph as the "ten lost
tribes" of Britain would be a disservice to actual history since his position

21. Cressy, *Church-History of Brittany,* Book 2. Chap XIII.

22. http://www.iajgsjewishcemeteryproject.org/afghanistan/herat.html Also: http://www.
reuters.com/article/us-afghanistan-synagogue-idUSTRE55N01P20090624 (Accessed
April 18, 2017)

in the Sanhedrin, his sizable tin trade from Cornwall and his influence, he went "boldly to Pilate," suggest a more authoritative role.

In Glenda Green's *Love Without End*, (as she described in her book regarding the many conversations with Jesus), she asks regarding His early years.

> In my boyhood and for a year after my Bar Mitzvah, I worked with my father as a carpenter. When I was fourteen, I had an opportunity to return to Egypt with my uncle Joseph. My parents encouraged it for my education as well as to get me out of harm's way with increasing turmoil in our homeland. After that sojourn, I continued to work with my uncle, who was getting on in years, and tended his extensive trading business, which stretched from the Himalayan foothills to what is now known as England.
>
> My years of travel also provided an occasion to become familiar with many other cultures and customs. This deeply strengthened my vision of world unity far beyond the political recovery of Israel. These varied experiences gave me rich opportunities to prepare for my destiny, in addition to finding relocation points ready for Jewish refugees in the coming years.[23]

Green continues to write in *Love Without End*. Jesus says that He "consecrated (Mary Magdalene) as an apostle to women," and that she had a daughter named Sarah.[24] This compares to the legend of the church of Saintes Maries de la Mer in the region of Camargue west of Marseille. There is a legend in the history of the church that the Mary's and a Sarah landed there from Jerusalem after being cast adrift in a boat without oars. There is an annual pilgrimage by the Romani people to honor Sarah. He also said that there was a change in His DNA that would have resulted in a change in the species. It was "not my desire or covenant to start a new race of humans in the biological sense."

---

23. Green, *Love Without End*, xiii. (Note: The preface is not available in the first edition)

24. Green, *Love Without End*, xvii. (2019)

Chapter 15

The Tree of Life

"ON EITHER SIDE OF THE RIVER IS THE TREE OF LIFE" (REV 22:2) NKJV.

The tree of life represents the known unknown in the transcendent universe. It is the x of the equation towards which the menorah, the temple icon of the tree, points. Why did the author of the book of Revelation use the singular form to describe what according to nature would require two trees? Since most of the Book of Revelation is written in a symbolic language it is quite probable that a symbolic meaning was intended. The language is not a grammatical inconsistency but rather a key to the revelatory nature of the book. Edmondo Lupieri says of Revelation 22:2:

> I am not comfortable with the theory that John is unaware of the inconsistency and prefer instead to see this as another example of the mystical geography of the sacred which we have seen in the previous visions of the throne of God. I think that John was trying to communicate something mystical and made a deliberate choice about how to do so.[1]

It would appear that John[2] intended a symbolic meaning.

---

1. Lupieri, *Commentary on the Apocalypse*, 354.

2. There is some discussion regarding authorship, however since the author uses John, I will use John.

On a symbolic level and possibly on an actual level—that is on a level that we can appropriate within our own experience—the tree of life represents the key to eternity. If a man ate from the tree, he would "live forever." (Gen 3:22) The character of the tree of life is eternal. There is only one tree.

It is possible to conclude then that there is only one tree of life because the tree that was in the Garden of Eden did not reproduce itself. There is no other reference to it as a unique entity until envisioned by the author in Revelation.[3] The original tree had not disappeared. It is always the same tree of life as described in Genesis and as described in the book of Revelation. This is probably the reason for the use of the singular by John. It is a symbolic representation on an organic level that reflects the state of the uncreated in the divine. It reflects the statement by Jesus who said in Rev 1:8a "I am the Alpha and the Omega, the Beginning and the End."

The tree represents, in an organic form, the notion of something that will live forever, or for eons as the Hebrew *olam* suggests. The tree appears as a unique entity in only two places. It appears at the beginning of the Bible or literally "in beginning" in Genesis (Gen 2:9, 3:22, 24, three times) and at the end of the Bible in Revelation (Rev 2:7, 22:2, 14, three times). It is referred to four times in Proverbs as a reference to a quality of life (Prov 3:18, 11:30, 13:12, and 15:4), but not as an actual entity. It is also alluded to in Ezekiel and Daniel. The one tree appears as a beginning and an end. It serves as a marker, to transition from the created to the uncreated and provides a symbolic frame of reference to allow us, as humans, to understand that all of creation can be contained as an integral whole in eternity. All of creation can be symbolically contained in the one symbolic form.

The tree in Revelation 2:7 related to the churches, as well as the symbolism of the tree on either side of the river, represent:

1. The tree in Genesis and the same tree in Revelation, symbolically affirming the position of the tree as a beginning and an end.

2. The tree in Revelation 2:7 illustrates its symbolic relationship to the menorah

3. The Messiah standing in "the midst of the lampstands" relates the Seed of the Woman, to the menorah, to the tree.

4. The two witnesses of Revelation 11 directly connect the symbolism of the lampstands to the menorah and to the two olive trees from the vision of Zechariah. The vision of Revelation 11 is the midpoint of the

3. The references in Proverbs (Pro 3:18, 11:30, 13:12, and 15:4) are to the qualities of the tree of life and although the tree of life is not mentioned per se in Ezekiel 47:12 'the fresh fruit every month . . . and their leaves for healing' it is directly related to Rev 22:2.

book possibly alluding to the centrality of the menorah as a temple artifact and as the symbolic centerpiece. The lampstands and olive trees
represent the original tree.

5. The tree of life is referred to twice in Revelation (chapters 2 and 22)
corresponding to its position in the Bible in Genesis and Revelation.

It could be said that the author of Genesis wrote about a tree of life
and the author of Revelation wrote about a similar tree—although it had
not been specifically identified for at least several millennia. From a natural
perspective, there appear to be two trees. From a supernatural perspective
or from the perspective of eternity there is only one tree. The vision in Revelation of the one tree on either side of the river lends weight to the notion
of a singular entity that is witnessed twice. The corresponding visions of the
olive trees in Zechariah and Revelation 11 also suggest a two-tree, singular-
function nature.

The "river of life" (Rev 22) possibly represents the continuum of creation which is delineated by the tree of life. It is the one tree that exists on
either side of the river simultaneously. The relationship to creation's boundaries, while appearing to have a beginning and an end, is a relationship to
the one tree of life which represents the source of life from which all things
were generated.

There appear to be two operations at work. One is the action of the
transcendent symbolic as it compares to our natural understanding of life
as we know it. It is the action of the symbolic which transforms our natural
thought process and helps us to understand life in its unfolding dynamic.
This action begins with our understanding of the known and directs us towards a grasp of the unknown. The symbolic helps to frame or contextualize
what is unknown.

The second is the process whereby several key symbols are generated
from the notion of a tree of life. This is a historical and actual development
that reveals the out-workings of organically related elements and individuals to the tree of life.

This chapter will attempt to understand the two operations and their
interaction.

THE TRANSCENDENT SYMBOLIC ENABLES
A GRASP OF THE KNOWN UNKNOWN

Bernard Lonergan distinguishes between image, symbol, and sign.

> The image as image is the sensible content as operative on the sensitive level; it is the image inasmuch as it functions within the psychic syndrome of associations, affects, exclamations, and articulated speech and actions. The image as symbol or as sign is the image as standing in correspondence with activities or elements on the intellectual level. But as symbol, the image is linked simply with the paradoxical 'known unknown'. As a sign, the image is linked with some interpretation that offers to indicate the import of the image.[4]

The symbol of the tree of life facilitates an intelligent grasp of the known unknown.

Carol Meyers in *The Tabernacle Menorah* says that the power of certain symbols precludes a wealth of associated textual material since the emotional value of the symbol is personally and immediately apparent and does not require explanation. The following quotation is in reference to the tabernacle menorah but serves to illustrate the elusive nature of the tree of life.

> (B)y their very nature, the tabernacle texts in which the graphic tradition of our artifact is conveyed in no way addresses itself to the ideational tradition lying behind a cultic symbol. For after all, the mark of a live symbol is its ability to carry a message on a non-verbal, emotional level; any explanations which theoretically might attach themselves are therefore subsidiary to the immediate impact of the symbol and cannot truly present the full range of associations carried by the symbol at its primary sensate level. In some sense, the existence of a potent symbol precludes the existence of an accurate and contemporary commentary thereon.[5]

Both the menorah and the tree of life have very little by way of description in the Bible to help encourage our imagination. Yet both are very symbolically profound in terms of emotional impact. The former is the emblem of the state of Israel.

The fact that the tree of life occurs at the very beginning of the Bible, and then is practically non-existent over the centuries, transiting multiple writers, only to occur at the very end of the Bible, is both perplexing and revealing. It is perplexing because it survives and, although not referred to directly, resurfaces in Revelation, and revealing because it operates outside of time, but is latent within the entire biblical message. This reveals its latent potency and its transcendent function, transcending the historic

---

4. Lonergan, *Insight*, 533.

5. Meyers, *The Tabernacle Menorah*, 134.

and temporal character of the Bible. To use Goodenough's expression, it was "live and active" for the duration from Genesis, but it is also strangely quiescent because for whatever reason mankind has felt separated from its elemental potency.

It is revelatory by its absence. Therefore, when it is present it provides an intelligible clue and an intellectual grasp of the unknown which suggests that the eternal is a basic invisible function which is essential to, but which for now is seemingly independent of the operation of creation.

When Lonergan describes the unconditional nature of God, he describes the idea of a perfect primary being which is similar in nature to the tree of life.

> (B)ecause man develops, every additional element of understanding and affirming and willing is a further act and reality in him. But the perfect primary being does not develop, for it is without defect or lack or impaction; and so the unrestricted act understands and affirms and wills contingent beings to be without any increment or change in its reality.[6]

There is no development because the nature of the tree is substantial and sustainable within itself. Whether it represents an actual element or whether it represents a transcendent function of the eternal within creation is open for question. The fact is the symbolic notion of the tree acts as an intellectual function to suggest that embodied within our created reality is an element that does not deteriorate, that has the capacity to be for eons, and which functions to transform what is to what can be. By extension or by extrapolation, since the understanding of reality is what can be experienced, understood, judged, and reasonably acted upon then that understanding of the eternal which may be incorporated within our intellectual faculty can be used as a reference point to say that there is a transcendent element, which has been understood from within our primordial consciousness which is unchangeable. It is life-giving and is a functional part of our created reality. That reference point may be considered operative within our conscious functionality and may facilitate our grasp of the unknown. It can be experienced, understood, evaluated, and reasonably, and rationally acted upon. Paul Tillich says of symbol, "Man's ultimate concern must be expressed symbolically, because symbolic action alone is able to express the ultimate."[7]

Thomas Aquinas responds to the argument that the tree of life "could not act beyond its own species," that it would have been a "natural

---

6. Lonergan, *Insight*, 661.

7. Tillich, *Dynamics*, 47.

immortality" and that the mythic notion of a plant giving immortality to the gods was "ridiculous."

> The tree of life in a certain degree was the cause of immortality, but not absolutely. To understand this, we must observe that in the primitive state man possessed, for the preservation of life, two remedies, against two defects. One of these defects was the loss of humidity by the action of natural heat, which acts as the soul's instrument: as a remedy against such loss man was provided with food, taken from the other trees of paradise, as now we are provided with the food, which we take for the same purpose. The second defect, as the Philosopher says (De Gener. i, 5), arises from the fact that the humor which is caused from extraneous sources, being added to the humor already existing, lessens the specific active power: as water added to wine takes at first the taste of wine, then, as more water is added, the strength of the wine is diminished, till the wine becomes watery. In like manner, we may observe that at first the active force of the species is so strong that it is able to transform so much of the food as is required to replace the lost tissue, as well as what suffices for growth; later on, however, the assimilated food does not suffice for growth, but only replaces what is lost. Last of all, in old age, it does not suffice even for this purpose; whereupon the body declines, and finally dies from natural causes. Against this defect man was provided with a remedy in the tree of life; for its effect was to strengthen the force of the species against the weakness resulting from the admixture of extraneous nutriment. Wherefore Augustine says (De Civ. Dei xiv, 26): "Man had food to appease his hunger, drink to slake his thirst; and the tree of life to banish the breaking up of old age"; and (QQ. Vet. et Nov. Test. qu. 19 [*Work of an anonymous author, among the supposititious works of St. Augustine] "The tree of life, like a drug, warded off all bodily corruption." Yet it did not absolutely cause immortality; for neither was the soul's intrinsic power of preserving the body due to the tree of life, nor was it of such efficiency as to give the body a disposition to immortality, whereby it might become indissoluble; which is clear from the fact that every bodily power is finite; so, the power of the tree of life could not go so far as to give the body the prerogative of living for an infinite time, but only for a definite time. For it is manifest that the greater a force is, the more durable is its effect; therefore, since the power of the tree of life was finite, man's life was to be preserved for a definite time by partaking of it once; and when that time had elapsed, man was to be either

transferred to a spiritual life, or had need to eat once more of the tree of life. From this, the replies to the objections clearly appear. For the first proves that the tree of life did not absolutely cause immortality; while the others show that it caused incorruption by warding off corruption, according to the explanation above given.[8]

I would suggest from my understanding of Aquinas' statement that on the level of natural cause the tree would support the restoration of the human body. However, there is also a spiritual component intrinsic to the tree, a component of spiritual desire, that helps us to transcend from our limited physical nature to the realm of the infinite. "The dynamic orientation, a prior and enveloping drive and the inquiring and critical spirit of man." We embody within ourselves the nature which caused the tree to burn without being consumed.

ELEMENTS PROCEEDING FROM THE TREE OF LIFE

There are other elements and persons who work in parallel or as an extension of the unchangeable nature of the tree of life. These are elements that proceed from the notion of an unchangeable nature and are distinct from, but are related functionally or symbolically, to the tree.

1. The Tree of Life (Gen 2:9)

The tree of life is a generic organic symbol related to humankind in general as a symbol of life and hope and is independent of national identity. It occurs at the very beginning and the very end of the Bible. It remains somewhat indistinct within our imagination. It appears to be beyond our grasp because we seem to have lost access to it. It is referred to briefly in biblical literature and occasionally is identified with the qualities of wisdom (Prov 3:18), the fruit of the righteous (Prov 11:30), desire (Prov 13:12), a wholesome tongue (Prov 15:4) and he who overcomes (Rev 2:7). The Torah is similarly associated saying it is "a fountain of life" (Prov 13:14) or the Bible is a "book of life" (Rev 22:19). The tree of life is indirectly associated with the olive and the almond tree. It is also alluded to in Ezekiel 17:22–24, 47:12 and Daniel 4:10–12. It is described in Revelation (Rev 2:7, 22:2, 14). There is

8. Aquinas, *Summa Theologica*, Vol. 1, Part 1, Question 97 Article 4. See also web references: http://dhspriory.org/thomas/english/Metaphysics.htm
http://www.basilica.org/pages/ebooks/St.%20Thomas%20Aquinas-Summa%20Theologica.pdf

also a symbolic similarity to the vision of Daniel in chapter 12 which refers
to the end times.

> Then I Daniel looked, and behold, two others stood, one on this
> bank of the stream and one on that bank of the stream. And I
> said to the man clothed in linen, who was above the waters of
> the stream, "How long shall it be till the end of these wonders?"
> The man clothed in linen, who was above the waters of the
> stream, raised his right hand and his left hand toward heaven;
> and I heard him swear by him who lives for ever that it would be
> for a time, two times, and half a time; and that when the shat-
> tering of the power of the holy people comes to an end all these
> things would be accomplished. (Dan 12:5–7) NKJV.

2. The Seed of the Woman the Promise of a Messiah

The Seed of the woman relates figuratively to the tree of life. ("trees bearing
fruit in which is their seed" Gen 1:11b). The Seed is a unique seed among
all seeds as is the tree a unique tree among all trees. Like the tree of life, the
Seed of the woman begins as a somewhat generic organic symbol. It runs
continuously from the very beginning to the very end of the Bible (from
Gen 3:15 to Rev 22:14) but, contrary to the concept of the tree of life, it
becomes specifically more identifiable through time as it is associated with
historical figures. Its DNA becomes more singular. "I am the God of your father—the God of Abraham, the God of Isaac, and the God of Jacob." (Exod
3:6a) NKJV. The Seed represents Life in the particular as active potency.

3. The Burning Bush

As has been mentioned previously, the burning bush is a type of tree of life
and a preview of the menorah. In the quotation by Levenson in section five
following (The Menorah Symbolic of a Tree), we see how the symbolism of
the tree, the bush, and the menorah are related.

4. The Oil of Anointing and the Anointed One

The Seed of the woman and the oil of anointing are related both by symbolic
meaning and by practical function. The function of anointing the anointed
is done using the olive oil which is derived from the flesh (the *mesocarp*) of
the seed. The oil of the olive is the instrument for the consecration of those

who are set aside for a specific purpose such as but not limited to, a priest or a king. (For example; Isa 45:1 "Thus says the Lord to his anointed, to Cyrus.") The flesh of the olive seed is used to consecrate the human seed. The Anointed One is the final expression of the identity of the Seed of the woman. The anointed one both symbolizes and is the actual representation of the original Seed, who has been identified through history as the generation of, the son of, and in the literal Hebrew "the seed of."

> Know therefore and understand, That from the going forth of the command To restore and build Jerusalem until Messiah (the anointed one) the Prince, There shall be seven weeks and sixty-two weeks; The street shall be built again, and the wall, even in troublesome times. (Dan 9:25) NKJV. The NRSV reads 'an anointed prince').

The identity of the seed is either general as in: "Did you not, O our God, drive out the inhabitants of this land before your people Israel, and give it forever to the descendants (KJV *the seed*) of your friend Abraham?" (2 Chr 20:7) NRSV. Or very specific as in: "Listen to her voice; for in Isaac your seed shall be called." (Gen 21:12b) NKJV.

The identity of the anointed one completes a unique organic continuum beginning with the tree of life, the Seed of the woman, the continuity of seeds, and the setting apart or consecration by means of the anointing (smearing on) of the oil from the flesh of the seed. The anointed one is also compared symbolically and functionally to the parts of a tree. In Isaiah 11:1 "A shoot shall come out from the stump of Jesse, and a branch shall grow out of his roots." (NRSV)[9]

5. The Menorah as Symbolic of a Tree

The design of the menorah[10] was meant to evoke the tree. In Jon Levenson's *Sinai and Zion*, the author makes a very compelling argument showing the relationship between the burning bush, the menorah and the tree of life.

> In the encounter of Moses and the burning bush, two of YHWH's emblems—tree and fire—clash, and neither overpowers the other. The two will appear in tandem in the menorah, the Tabernacle candelabrum which is actually a stylized tree, complete with "branches," "almond-shaped cups," "calyces," and

---

9. Shoot: חֹטֶר (branch, twig), Stump: גֵּזַע (stock, stem), Branch: נֵצֶר (scion), Roots: שֹׁרֶשׁ.

10. Exodus 25, Zech 4 and Rev 1 & 11.

"petals." (Exodus 25:31–39)[11] This arborescent lampstand appears not only in the Tabernacle which served as Israel's central sanctuary in the period of wandering in the wilderness, but also in the Temple that was to be built by Solomon in the early monarchal era (1 Kgs 7:49). The Temple at Jerusalem was lit by the fires of the burning tree.[12]

The menorah is fed by the same oil of anointing, the olive oil which is used to consecrate the anointed ones. Both the menorah in Zechariah and the lampstand in Revelation are said to represent the two anointed ones (Zech 4) and the two witnesses (Rev 11). The fuel oil of the lamp would appear to represent the action, the lighting up by the Holy Spirit which is a witness to the Anointed One, and the action of igniting the tree of life.

> Turning now to the mystic imagery of Zechariah (Zech iv: 3, 11–14), and of St. John in the Apocalypse (Rev xi: 3, 4), we find the olive-tree used, in both cases, in a very remarkable way. We cannot enter into any explanation of "the two olive-trees . . . the two olive-branches . . . the two anointed ones that stand by the Lord of the whole earth" (Zech.); or of "the two witnesses . . . the two olive-trees standing before the God of the earth" (Rev.): but we may remark that we have here a very expressive link between the prophecies of the O. T. and the N. T.[13]

The Greek for lampstand in Revelation λυχνια, *luchnia* is the same term used for the menorah in the Greek Septuagint of Exodus twenty-five. The seven churches which are the seven lampstands are the one menorah or the burning tree. This links the seven churches of Revelation to the original tree. The seven lampstands or menorah are the seven witnesses to the original Seed which is the first witness to the prophesied Anointed One. The menorah, and by extension the seven churches, reflect a design of the original tree and are fueled by the flesh of the seed—the olive oil—testifying to the One Seed, the One who incorporated Himself into the sacred history of earth.

---

11. In the footnote in Levenson's *Sinai* he makes the following reference. On the symbolism of the tree in biblical Israel, see C. L. Meyers, *The Tabernacle Menorah*, ASOR Diss Series 2 (Missoula: Scholars, 1976), 143–56.

12. Levenson, *Sinai and Zion*, 20.

13. Smith's Revised Bible Dictionary, *Olive*.

6. The Olive and Almond as symbolic of the Tree of life

The following quote from *Encyclopaedia Judaica* gives a very dramatic account of the relation between a tree of oil and the tree of life.

> Oil of Life: There appears to have been a tradition in certain circles according to which the tree of life in the Garden of Eden was an olive tree (a tradition which is not found in Talmud or Midrash, cf. Ber. 40a; Gen. R. 15:7). As a result, there emerged the belief that immortality is gained by anointing with oil. According to Apocalypsis Mosis 9:3, 13:1–2, when Adam fell ill Seth went to the garden to request "the oil of mercy" with which to anoint Adam and restore his health. His entreaty was refused, but the angel Michael promised that oil would be granted to the righteous at the end of days. In the parallel passage in the Latin *Vitae Adae* the oil is referred to as "the tree of mercy from which the oil of life flows" (ch. 36, cf. 40, 41). The same tradition is to be found in the Acts of Pilate (Gospel of Nicodemus III (XIX). This oil is perhaps to be identified with the heavenly oil with which Enoch is anointed and which transforms him into a heavenly being. Called "the good oil," it is shining and fragrant (II En. 9 = 22:8–9, cf. 14 = 56:2). A further reference to the tree of life in the Garden of Eden as an oil-yielding tree may be found in IV Ezra 2:12—"*lignum vitae erit in illis in odorem unguenti*"—and this idea is also perhaps to be discerned in the Acts of Thomas §157. The furthest circulation of this concept is to be observed in Pseudo-Clement, Recognitiones 1:45 which again refers explicitly to the oil of the tree of life. The legend of Seth's quest for the oil had various later developments and acquired considerable importance in Christian legend and art.[14][15]

The almond tree has also been suggested as a tree of life by Leon Yarden in *The Tree of Light*, a study of the menorah, the seven-branched lampstand. Yarden shows that the design of the flowers on the menorah is derived from an almond. Aaron's rod that budded also produced almonds and buds. (Num 17:1–13)

> That the almond was originally conceived as a tree of life, indeed most probably the mythological Paradise Tree itself, is clear from the circumstance that Aaron's master scepter, also referred to as the 'rod of God', is likewise described as a branch

14. Encyclopaedia Judaica, 'Oil of Life', Vol. 15, n. 11618. 394.

15. Bibliography: Ginzberg, *Legends*, 5 (1925), 119; E.M.C. Quinn, *Quest of Seth for the Oil of Life* (1962). [Michael E. Stone]

of almond: And . . . Moses went into the tent of testimony; and behold, the rod of Aaron . . . had sprouted, and put forth buds, and produced blossoms, and it bore ripe almonds.[16]

The tree's etymology is no less fascinating. Firstly, its archaic, by all accounts Semitic name Amygdala, still its botanical name (*Amygdalus communis*), means conceivably Great Mother (אמ גדלה)—a prototypal, apparently Mesopotamian fertility goddess and image of All Living (at times also of All-Father and Child) that later, inter alia, was identified in Phrygia with Cybele and known at Rome, where the cult was adopted in 204 BC, as Mater Magna.[17]

7. The Hebrew People and the Tree of life

The Hebrew people as a nation are distinct from most others. The comment in I Samuel 8 reveals that, while other nations had been building up their monarchies, the Hebrew people had so far been guided by prophets, judges, and seers. In *The Tabernacle Menorah*, Carol Meyers writes that:

> The locus classicus for the portrayal of Israel as a tree upon God's holy mountain is the Song of the Sea in Exodus 15, a lengthy poetic section rivaling if not surpassing the blessings of Jacob and Moses in archaism and antiquity. . . .
>
> The verb נטע, used to describe the establishment of Israel at the mountain, is a clear agricultural term, used especially to convey the notion of planting trees or vines. It is the word used in the episode mentioned above (p. 140), in which Abraham plants a tamarisk at Beersheba. Thus, in the Song of the Sea, Israel becomes metaphorically a vine or a tree.[18]

The people of Israel have as their primary focus the return of the Messiah (the Seed of the woman) to the specific locale of Jerusalem wherein they as a living tree will be reunited. Ultimately, humanity, presumably those who are written into the Book of Life,[19] will be grafted into the tree as Paul writes in Romans 11:17.

---

16. Yarden, *Tree of Light*, 40.
17. Yarden, *Tree of Light*, 41.
18. Meyers, *Tabernacle Menorah*, 148.
19. Philippians 4 and Revelation 3, 13, 17, 20, 21, 22.

8. The Bible as a tree of life

The Torah is said to be "a fountain of life." (Prov 13:14)

9. Gentiles Grafted into the tree of life

The metaphor of the olive tree in Romans 11 extends the analogy of the original tree in Genesis and concludes that mankind can be grafted in by faith into the original line of the Seed of the woman, including (with respect) certain covenant agreements established between God and the Hebrew people.[20][21]

10. Many cultures have incorporated a tree of life symbol

In the HBO (Home Box Office) film *Bury My Heart at Wounded Knee,* James McLaughlin, the Indian agent in charge of the Standing Rock Reservation asks Chief Sitting Bull what he is making. Sitting Bull is whittling away at a short branch. The chief finally replies, "This is what is left of the great tree that was my people. Take it and you will have it all." There is also Yggdrasil, the Nordic tree of life, as well as Chinese, Egyptian, and Mayan myths.

ELEMENTS CONTRARY TO THE TREE

The following section contrasts the central tree symbolism, rooted in Hebraic consciousness, with contrary notions that arise from within the nation from a desire to be like other nations. What becomes obvious is that the primary underlying modus vivendi of the people was associated more with a pastoral lifestyle. The religion was not interested in building huge monuments to a majestic god, but in understanding the immanence of the divine within His creation as in Deuteronomy 30:12–15.

> It is not in heaven, that you should say, 'Who will ascend into heaven for us and bring it to us that we may hear it and do it?' Nor is it beyond the sea, that you should say, 'Who will go over the sea for us and bring it to us that we may hear it and do it?'

20. https://genographic.nationalgeographic.com/genographic/index.html

21. It is interesting that the company Family Tree DNA, which is the testing partner for the National Geographic Genographic Project and which is also the company with the largest database of YDna and MtDna profiles (over 2,000,000 records, 2019), was originally founded to reconnect with Jewish relatives http://www.familytreedna.com/

> But the word is very near you, in your mouth and in your heart, that you may do it. See, I have set before you today life and good, death and evil.

The following three events contrast a common olive/fig/vine association with a desire to "be like others" or else to a specific individual who has risen to impose his own lordship, or when the Jews were subjugated by war. The fourth instance is the ultimate redemption by way of the tree of the cross.

1. The Trees Went Forth to Anoint a King

In Judges 9:8, Abimelech "hired worthless and reckless men" and killed the 70 sons of Jerubbaal. Jotham the youngest son of Jerubbaal, was left and when he addresses the people he speaks to the nation as follows, asking if they would forego their prosperity and fruitfulness to side with Abimelech. He addresses the nation saying; "the trees once went out to anoint a king over themselves." The trees respond as follows saying they would not forego their oil, sweetness, and cheer to rule and eventually the people settle for the bramble. And for the bramble, this is an interesting turn of events because it is the Lord Himself who had previously identified with the thorn bush. However, the bramble, in this case, is a lesser choice, not a redemptive choice.

1. Olive: will not forego its oil to honor God and man

2. Fig: will not forego its sweetness

3. Vine: will not forego its cheer to rule over the people

2. Give Us a King

Several generations later the people of Israel, represented by their elders, come before Samuel:

> Then all the elders of Israel gathered together and came to Samuel at Ramah, and said to him, "Look, you are old, and your sons do not walk in your ways. Now make us a king to judge us like all the nations." But the thing displeased Samuel when they said, "Give us a king to judge us." So Samuel prayed to the LORD. And the LORD said to Samuel, "Heed the voice of the people in all that they say to you; for they have not rejected you, but they have rejected Me, that I should not reign over them." (I Samuel 8:4–7) NKJV.

Samuel warns the people saying, "a king will take:"

1. Your sons for war

2. Daughters for servants

3. Your vineyards and olive groves

4. You will become his slaves

3. In Wrath Remember Mercy

In Habakkuk, chapter three, just prior to the exile to Babylon, Habakkuk pleads with God saying, "in wrath remember mercy." Even so, despite the calamitous situation, Habakkuk says, "I will rejoice in the Lord" though:

1. The fig does not blossom

2. There is no fruit on the vine

3. And olive's labour fails (Hab 3:17)

According to Jewish teaching, the olive, fig, vine trilogy is part of the eight species as listed in Deuteronomy: "A land of wheat, and barley, and vines, and fig trees, and pomegranates; a land of oil olive, and honey." (Deut 8:8) AV.

It would appear that a primary theological message of the Bible is associated with the tree of life or Book of Life (Rev 22:19). In the instances given above, the nation of Israel is contrasted against other nations as a type of agrarian nation symbolized by the olive, fig, and vine metaphors. However, the people desire to become more like other nations and are subjugated and lose their fruitfulness. They become increasingly distanced from the original notion of the tree of life.

4. Cursed Is Anyone Who Hangs on a Tree

In the New Testament, the person of the Messiah is the one who is most closely associated with the original notion of Life as represented by the tree, vine, bread, and water. He is the one who addresses the curse associated with the loss of the original tree of life by revoking the curse of the "one who hangs on a tree." (Gal 3:13, Deut 21:2–23)

Christ has redeemed us from the curse of the law, having become a curse for us (for it is written, "cursed is everyone who
hangs on a tree").[22] (Gal 3:13) NKJV.

The following words are from Glenda Green's encounter with the apparition of Jesus describing the origins of Eden. He gives a very credible
picture.

The tree in the center of the garden was a tithing tree. It was a
community symbol of charity, gratitude and faith. Its generous,
untouched bounty united the community in their reverence
for life and their assurance of continued supply. In the Genesis
story, Eve's transgression was that of violating a sacred area of
open beneficence and consuming its fruit for personal gratifi-
cation. To put it in modern terms, she had just authorized the
building of an oil refinery in a sacred wildlife refuge or bought
a yacht with corporate retirement funds. The 'Tree of Life' was a
preserved area that symbolized abundance beyond expectation.
Man can only hope to connect with the highest level of creativity
and true replenishment through such reverence and respect.[23]

In Saint Louis de Montfort's *The Secret of the Rosary*, he also describes the
Rosary as a mystical rose tree.

Good and devout souls, who walk in the light of the Holy Spirit:
I do not think that you will mind my giving you this little mystical rose tree which comes straight from heaven and which is to
be planted in the garden of your soul. It cannot possibly harm
the sweet-smelling flowers of your contemplations; for it is a
heavenly tree and its scent is beautiful. It will not in the least in-
terfere with your carefully planned flower beds; for, being itself
all pure and well-ordered, it inclines all to order and purity. If
it is carefully watered and properly attended to every day it will
grow to such a marvelous height and its branches will have such
a wide span that, far from hindering your other devotions, it will
maintain and perfect them.

Of course you understand what I mean since you are
spiritually-minded; this mystical rose tree is Jesus and Mary in
life, death and eternity; its green leaves are the Joyous Mysteries, the thorns the Sorrowful ones and the flowers, the Glorious

22. Deut 21:2–23: If a man has committed a sin deserving of death, and he is put to
death, and you hang him on a tree, his body shall not remain overnight on the tree, but
you shall surely bury him that day, so that you do not defile the land which the LORD
your God is giving you as an inheritance; for he who is hanged is accursed of God.

23. Green, *Keys of Jeshua*, 199.

Mysteries of Jesus and Mary. The buds are the childhood of Jesus and Mary, and the open blooms show us both of them in their sufferings, and the full-blown roses symbolize Jesus and Mary in their triumph and glory.[24]

In the following chapter I depart momentarily from the symbolic and spiritual to the notion that God works through His creation. All "creation groans." (Rom 8:22) His work surrounds us. Dr. Larry Crabb, the psychologist and Christian counselor, writes concerning the "two-book view of revelation."[25] God has written the Bible, and He is also found in creation. Christian students in whichever discipline they pursue, rely on one or the other, or both, for their authoritative guidance. I suggest in the following that we have much to learn from creation. Lonergan's statement "men are apt to judge the universe by anthropomorphic standards," at the end of the chapter, keeps things in perspective.

> The nature of our world in all its compartments is a testimony, that we have fully shared His profoundest and kindest deliberations; and is a pledge, that what He has so curiously and so benevolently planned and framed, will never be unnoticed or uncared for by Him. It is on these principles that the Sacred History of Man is founded. They assure us that there must be a sacred history attached to his existence, and that his race has been always living under the development and conduct of it. It is a difficult subject for us to discover the Divine system which has been pursuing thro it; but not more difficult than that of material nature has been found to be. As already intimated, I do not presume to be able to accomplish more, than to place my foot upon the threshold of the sacred building which I admire, and to glance upon the awful interior and the grand avenues connected with it.[26]

24. Montfort, *Secret of the Rosary*, 13.
25. Crabb, *Understanding People*, 37.
26. Turner, *Sacred History*, 37.

Chapter 16

Long Term Cycles

Figure 19: Methuselah

This is a sketch of a possible photo of Methuselah, a 4,846-year-old Bristle-cone Pine in the White Mountains of California which remains unidentified for security reasons. The rotation of the tree is probably from the effects of the wind. However, it also suggests that the rotation of the earth may have influenced its growth.

Long-term cycles or longitudinal studies provide a rare glimpse into our historic place within the earth. When we, as common humanity, can identify with the incredible age of the universe and begin to understand the solar and seasonal cycles within which we are encompassed, we will have the perspective necessary to understand our future possibilities. Creation acts as a creative transformer within which we, as humans understand our place as a part of infinity, as part of the tree of life. The following is a partial list of ancient organisms.

Table 9: Partial List of Longest Living Individual Organisms

Age years	Species	Location	Notes
5064	Great Basin bristlecone pine. *Pinus longaeva*	White Mountains, California, United States	The oldest known currently living tree. Tree cored by Edmund Schulman, the age determined by Tom Harlan.
Methuselah			
4846	Great Basin bristlecone pine	Inyo County, California, United States	Rocky Mountain Tree Ring Research, Edmund Schulman, Tom Harlan
The President			
3200	Giant sequoia	Sierra Nevada, California, United States *Sequoia dendron giganteum*	
Jaya Sri Maha Bodhi			
2302	Sacred fig *Ficus religiosa*	Anuradhapura, North Central Province, Sri Lanka	A sapling from the historical Bodhi tree under which the Buddha became enlightened. It was planted in 288 BC and is the oldest living human-planted tree in the world with a known planting date.
1941	Subalpine Larch	Kananaskis, Alberta, Canada *Larix lyallii*	
FL117			

1676	Northern Whitecedar	Ontario, Canada	*Thuja occidentalis*
Llangernyw Yew			
4000–5000	Common Yew *Taxus baccata*	Llangernyw, Conwy, North Wales	A girth of 10.75m. Situated in the churchyard of St. Dygain's. Church in Llangernyw village. One of the 50 Great British Trees
3500	Olive	Olive tree of Ano Vouves, Crete.	One of the oldest olive trees. It still produces oil and its branches were used as wreaths during the recent Olympics. Dia. 4.6 m.
Oliveira de Santa Iria de Azóia			
2850	Olive *Olea europaea*	Santa Iria de Azóia, Portugal	Magnific Olive tree, probably the last one from a large olive grove. Studied by UTAD University and now classified "Public interest tree" by the Portuguese National Forest Authority.
	Olive	Gethsemane, Jerusalem, Israel 4–meter girth. *Olea europaea.*	
Fieldbrook Stump			
4000	Sequoia *semper-virens*	Fieldbrook California, USA	Said to have been cut down in 1890 for the Astor family to compete in a wager. Image page following. 33' or 10 m Dia.

Footnotes applicable to table references:[1][2][3].

CLONAL TREE SYSTEMS

Clonal organisms can have a multi-millennial root system although the perceivable growth is relatively new. These systems may be coral, sponges, trees, microorganisms, etc. The following are some examples:

1. Larson, *Canadian Journal of Botany* 69 (7): 1628–1636. doi:10.1139/b91–206

2. http://en.wikipedia.org/wiki/List_of_oldest_trees#cite_note-RMTRR-6

3. http://wayback.archive.org/web/20120326162609/ http://www.afn.min-agricultura.pt/portal/ArvoresFicha?Processo=KNJ1/601&Concelho=&Freguesia=&Distrito=

Pando is a *Populus tremuloides* (Quaking Aspen) tree or clonal colony that has been estimated at 80,000 years old. Unlike many other clonal "colonies," the above-ground trunks remain connected to each other via a single massive subterranean root system. Whether it is to be considered a single tree is disputed, as it depends on one's definition of an individual tree.[4]

The Jurupa Oak colony is estimated to be at least thirteen millennia old, with other estimates ranging from five to thirty millennia. Old Tjikko, a Norway Spruce in Sweden, is a tree on top of roots that have been carbon-dated to 9,550 years old. The tree is part of a clonal colony that was established at the end of the last ice age. Discovered by Professor Leif Kullman, at Umea University, the tree is in the county of Dalarna in Sweden. Old Tjikko is small, only 5 meters (16 ft) in height.[567]8

Ancient Trees

The Dawn Redwood, *Metasequoia glyptostroboides* is unique because it is a deciduous tree. From the Save the Redwoods website:

> The dawn redwood was once one of the most widespread tree species in the Northern Hemisphere (during the Tertiary period). Scientists had identified fossil remains of this redwood in North America, Asia and Greenland and had concluded that it must have been extinct for millions of years. However, in 1944, a Chinese forester found an enormous dawn redwood in the Sichuan province of China.[9]

When we consider the evolution of intelligence we tend to think of artificial intelligence. How far can machines take us? The conventional evolutionary paradigm suggests that we evolve from ape to man to robot. However, there is already an innate biological intelligence that is even more developed and underrated. We are intimate biological beings attracted to other very like-minded biological beings. Books by Diana Beresford-Kroeger such as *The*

---

4. Quaking Aspen. http://www.nps.gov/brca/naturescience/quakingaspen.htm

5. Swedish Research Council, http://www.idw-online.de/pages/de/news255795

6. Reuters, http://www.reuters.com/article/2008/04/11/us-sweden-tree-idUSL1190 625120080411

7. National Geographic News, http://news.nationalgeographic.com/news/2008/04/080414-oldest-tree.html

8. http://www.rmtrr.org/oldlist.htm

9. http://www.savetheredwoods.org/redwoods/dawn-redwoods/ accessed 09_2015.

Sweetness of a Simple Life, The Global Forest: Forty Ways Trees Can Save Us and *Arboretum America: A Philosophy of the Forest,* as well as Mary Reynolds' *The Garden Awakening: Designs to Nurture Our Land and Ourselves,* help us understand our relationship to nature. Diana Beresford-Kroeger is or was an advisor to David Milarch's Archangel Ancient Tree Archive.[10] The understanding of our relationship to nature can help restore our humanity.

Figure 20: Fieldbrook Stump[11]

The sketch above was made of a photo taken by Augustus (Gus) William Ericson (1848–1927) and archived at the Humboldt State University Library in Arcata, California. It shows the relative size of the Fieldbrook Redwood which had a trunk diameter of approximately 32 feet.

The apparent age of the universe can be difficult to imagine especially for most of us who are not involved in scientific research. However, it is possible to go to a local museum such as the Redpath at McGill University in Montreal, Quebec, and get a sense of the immensity of the time scale. For my own satisfaction and to get perspective on the global warming or freezing debate, I measured the tree rings of a five-hundred-year-old Douglas fir at the museum. Within the context of this book, that is within the context

10. https://www.ancienttreearchive.org

11. The Fieldbrook Stump was said to be cut down by John Jacob Astor in the late 1800s. It had a diameter of approximately 32 feet. In an email from Tim Crauford, the Lead Ranger at the National Trust, Cliveden Estate Office, in Taplow, England he suggested that a slice of the trunk remained on the estate. "The tree ring is a near perfect circle, measuring between 4.2m (14 feet) and (15 feet) 4.6m in diameter. It has a thickness of between 0.56 and 0.63m." He said that it cannot be fully confirmed that it came from the Fieldbrook stump. Email Nov 29, 2019.

of the meaning of the tree of life, it becomes evident that trees, whether ancient or new, are a very real witness to the seeming vagaries of our existence. The trees speak to us from hundreds to thousands of years prior to the present. The following table includes my measurements for tree ring growth over a 535-year period, showing an average growth of 1.5 mm per year and varying from 0.6 mm to 2.4 mm depending on solar activity. The earth is heating up because of the unusually high concentrations of carbon dioxide in the atmosphere. Inuit natives who live near Cabot Square in Montreal, Quebec will testify that their elders witnessed a much different Arctic than today. And conversely a decrease in solar activity can cause a cooling spell as Dr. John Casey writes in his book *Dark Winter.* (2014)[12] From our current viewpoint, there are obvious arctic warming conditions unlike our recent pre-history; however, at the same time we are possibly on the verge of a mini ice age such as the Maunder Minimum (1645–1715) which caused severe cold spells possibly precipitating the civil strife of the late 1700s. Nasa has suggested that there is no impending 'mini ice age' and that the impact on climate from fossil fuel is more significant than the sun's temperature swings. I am not sure how they have arrived at this long-term conclusion.[13] We will not be properly forewarned unless we consider both sides of the debate.

Captain Sir John Franklin, who had departed England in 1845 to search for the Arctic Northwest Passage aboard H.M.S. Erebus and H.M.S. Terror, was not seen again. Parks Canada recently located Erebus west of O'Reilly Island on September 9, 2014 and two years later, the wreck of Terror was found south of King William Island (68° 54' 13" N, 98° 56' 18" W) by the Arctic Research Foundation. A scientist on the Nova film *Arctic Passage,* documenting the disappearance noted that an unusual cold spell very likely trapped the unsuspecting Franklin for several years in an icebound summer condition.

Narrator: "Dated 1848—more than a year after the original note was written, Francis Crozier, the captain of the Terror added in the margin that the ships were still trapped in the ice in the same location. They hadn't moved in nearly two years. . . . No previous polar expedition had ever reported a summer so cold that the ice didn't break up." Polar scientist Roy Koerner's examination of the ice core showed that this period of extreme cold likely lasted for five long years.[14]

12. Casey, *Dark Winter.*

13. https://climate.nasa.gov/blog/2953/there-is-no-impending-mini-ice-age/ Posted, February 13, 2020.

14. *Arctic Passage,* © 2006 WGBH Educational Foundation

My own measurement in the figure following shows an extreme dip in temperature/tree-ring growth at the 1840 mark, adding authenticity to the record of the climatic condition at the time. The photo has the date 1469 at the 22-cm mark of the radius. It shows the variation in ring size.

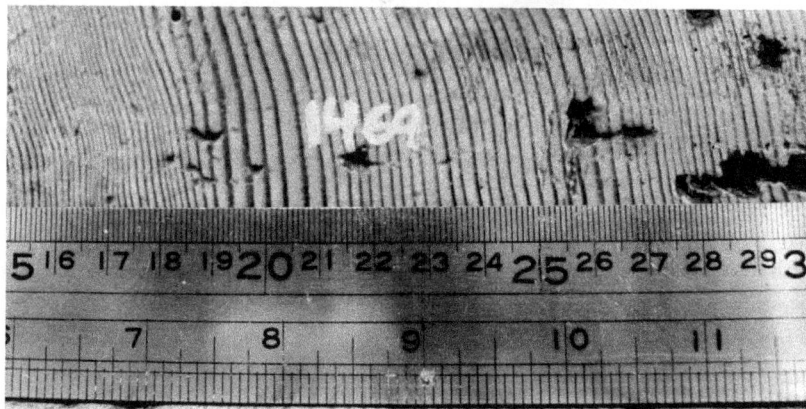

Figure 21: Photo by the author showing a portion of a 64" Douglas fir

Table 10: Tree ring measurements S.M.[15]

mm per decade 1360 - 1880 (avg 1.5 mm /year ~ 535 years)

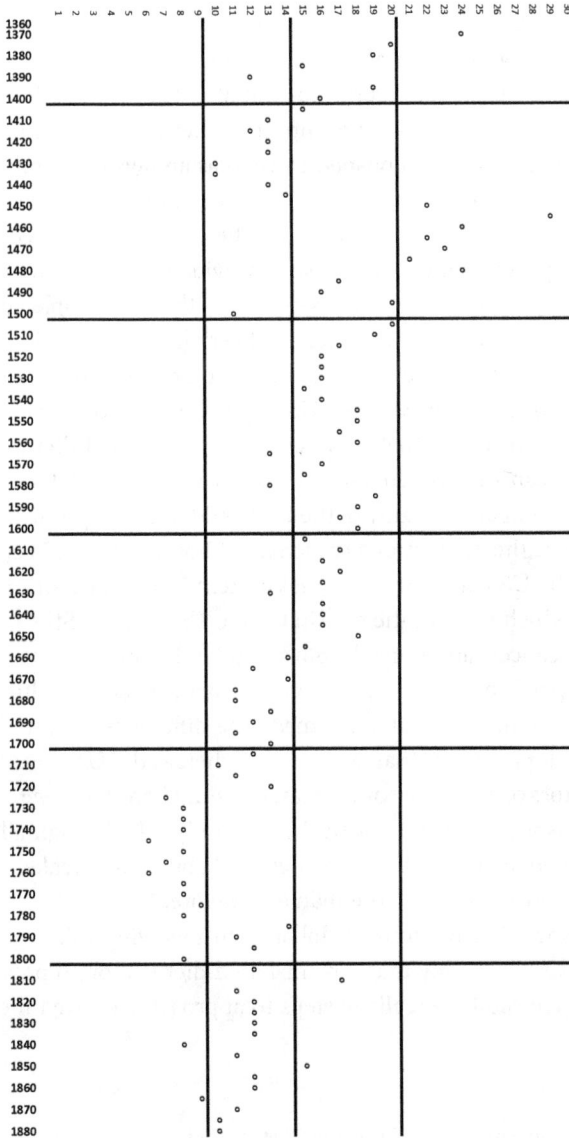

1360	
1370	
1380	
1390	
1400	
1410	
1420	
1430	
1440	
1450	
1460	
1470	
1480	
1490	
1500	
1510	
1520	
1530	
1540	
1550	
1560	
1570	
1580	
1590	
1600	
1610	
1620	
1630	
1640	
1650	
1660	
1670	
1680	
1690	
1700	
1710	
1720	
1730	
1740	
1750	
1760	
1770	
1780	
1790	
1800	
1810	
1820	
1830	
1840	
1850	
1860	
1870	
1880	

15. The Maunder Minimum is the name used for the period starting in about 1645 and continuing to about 1715 when sunspots became exceedingly rare, as noted by solar observers of the time. It would seem from the above tree ring data that there is a several decades delay between the decreased energy transmitted to earth and the resulting decrease in growth.

LONG TERM EPIDEMIOLOGICAL STUDIES

In the early 1970s when Premier Chou En Lai of China was dying of cancer, he called for a large-scale study of population mortality rates to study the disease. The study involved 650,000 Chinese workers who tabulated the rates for twelve different cancers affecting a population of 880 million people.[16] In the 1980s a subsequent study was initiated because of Chinese American cooperation to evaluate the impact of diet on disease known as *The China Study*. It was first published in 1990 as an 896-page monograph.[17][18] It used the results of the Atlas of Cancer Mortality as a reference. The *New York Times* said that the China Study can be considered the "Grand Prix of Epidemiology." The study tested 6,500 individuals in 24 provinces for 367 variables. Most of the population is known as the Han people and the wide range of results indicated that cancer had very little to do with genetics and more to do with diet. The average Chinese worker consumed ten percent of animal protein as compared to the US population. The diet in China ranged from a rich plant-based diet to a very rich plant-based diet as compared to the American diet which ranged from a rich meat diet to a very rich meat diet. A comparable study in the US would not have produced the same results because the population is much more homogeneous. Even a vegetarian diet in the US can contain animal protein in the form of milk, cheese, and yogurt which was not the case in China. The results of the China Study showed that cancer rates ranged from several individuals to several hundred individuals per 100,000 of population and that the rate was directly attributed to the amount of meat consumed. The differences in the data results varied by factors of more than a hundred, whereas the U.S. results varied at most by factors of 2 or 3. In some areas, no animal products were consumed at all and this was reflected positively. The study, which originally involved millions of people, is a statistically high probability. It revealed that we are inherently more of an herbivore than a carnivore.[19]

After spending millions of dollars and involving millions of people, we can say very probably that a plant-based diet is more representative of our nature. We can take realistic steps to approach who we inherently are.

16. Li Jun-Yao, Llu Be-Al, T Li Guang-Yi et al.: *Cancer Mortality, International Journal of Epidemiology.* 10 (1981) 127–133.

17. Chen J, Campbell TC, Li J, et al. *Mortality in China.*

18. Campbell TC, Parpia B, and Chen J. *Etiology of Coronary Artery Disease,* 1998; 82:18T–21T

19. Campbell TC, Campbell Thomas M.; *The China Study.*

A more recent study of 3,100 foods shows that a plant-based diet "protects against chronic oxidative stress-related diseases"[20]

However

More recently the evidence for a ketogenic diet seems to weigh in favor of burning fats rather than carbs. Carbohydrates and sugars have been identified as the cause of weight gain and as possible cancer-causing agents. Dr. Thomas N. Seyfried,[21] who teaches at Boston College, advocates for diet changes in his *Keto for Cancer: Ketogenic Metabolic Therapy as a Targeted Nutritional Strategy*. Miriam Kalamian has a similar study in, *Cancer as a Metabolic Disease,* as well as Dr. Annette Bosworth's *Anyway You Can*. In a recent Youtube discussion, Dr. Mark Hyman and Nina Teicholz[22] suggest that our science has been determined by a prior agenda rather than an analysis of evidence in the field of nutrition. The answer at this point is very problematic because the science has been biased by the demands of the food industries.[23] So, there can be misleading and contradictory statements. The medium answer may probably lie in a diet that has very reduced carbohydrates/cereals, some grass-fed meat, or fish, or protein, more fat, and many more vegetables? Or, according to the keto diet, approximately: 70 percent fat, 25 percent protein, and 5 percent carbs.

EMERGENT PROBABILITY

I tend to be technologically inclined. I purchased my first computer in 1980, a Timex Sinclair with 16k of ram and a Basic operating system. I typed out a program to calculate Pi and after two days the TV screen filled up with numbers. Many of us believe that technology will solve our problems: global warming, violence/security, transportation, relationships, etc. What can I say? Technology has its place, even our local rooftop farm, Lufa Farms, considers their operation to be data-driven.[24] As of 2020 Lufa Farms will

---

20. The total antioxidant content of more than 3,100 foods, beverages, spices, herbs and supplements used worldwide Carlsen et al; licensee BioMed Central Ltd. 2010 https://nutritionj.biomedcentral.com/articles/10.1186/1475-2891-9-3

21. https://www.bc.edu/bc-web/schools/mcas/departments/biology/people/faculty-directory/thomas-seyfried.html

22. https://www.youtube.com/watch?v=Zc_e5ME_5Cg

23. That is why it is crucial that government health departments and nutritional analysis be independent of food group financing.

24. http://lufa.com/en/our-story.html

have the largest greenhouse structure to date —163,800 square feet. It will be their "most efficient greenhouse in terms of energy and water consumption." Electric transportation will reduce our dependence on fossil fuels, especially in Quebec where our electricity is derived primarily from hydroelectric resources, and walking may even make a comeback. The debate over technological solutions can be acrimonious. How much money to spend on a given solution? The following excerpt from Lonergan's chapter xv.5 on metaphysics and finality helped me to keep in mind that we are not an isolated intelligence trying to apply solutions, but we are an intelligent organism within an already complex and evolving intelligence. Our sustainability will be determined by our ability to live in a dynamic relationship with life as it is, as it evolves. The tree of life is immanent and real within the whole of creation.

> (The) directed dynamism is realistic. It results from the classical laws that rest on forms, from the statistical laws that rest on acts, from the emergent process that rests on potency. It is not a contrivance added to an incompetent universe to make it work but an unfolding of its immanent implications that is bound to work. Men are apt to judge the universe by anthropomorphic standards. They look for the efficiency of their machines, the economy of their use of materials and power, the security of their comprehensive plans, the absence of disease and death, of violence and pain, of abuse and repression that reflects the desires and the aspirations of their hearts. But human utopias are paper schemes. They postulate in the universe more perfect materials than those with which it builds. They suppose that the building can be some extrinsic activity apart from the universe itself. They forget that they themselves and all their great achievements and all their still greater hopes and dreams are but by-products of the universe in its proper expansion in accord with its proper intelligibility.[25]

In contrast to Lonergan's very realistic description of our evolving universe, C.S. Lewis' description of the body of Christ gives us a much more intimate preview of our spiritual potential.

> When (Christians) speak about being in Christ or of Christ being "in them," this is not simply a way of saying that they are thinking about Christ or copying Him. They mean that Christ is actually operating through them; that the whole mass of Christians are the physical organism through which Christ acts—that

25. Lonergan, *Insight,* 448.

we are His fingers and muscles, the cells of His body. And perhaps that explains one or two things. It explains why this new
life is spread not only by purely mental acts like belief, but by
bodily acts like baptism and Holy Communion. It is not merely
the spreading of an idea; it is more like evolution—a biological
or superbiological fact.[26]

EARTH'S BIODIVERSITY

The intention of this chapter has been to appreciate the nature of very long-
term cycles and our relationship to them. Like an ocean wave compared to
a babbling brook, we are a part of eternity in its many manifestations. Jon
Luoma's, *The Hidden Forest,* helped me to understand the complexities and
diversity of the forest. A cup of "real" soil contains millions of organisms
without which reforestation and forest life cannot thrive. The science of tree
harvesting needs to be thought of in terms of eighty-year and not twenty-
year cycles.

> Scientists now believe that somewhere around 40 percent of the
> total photosynthate made by the leaves of trees actually does
> not feed the plant at all but rather seeps out of the roots to feed
> mychorrhizal fungi and the rest of the ecosystem that thrives
> in a special region just a fraction of an inch beyond the roots, a
> biologically teeming zone called the rhizospere. Here, according
> to Amaranthus, "a single gram of forest soil . . . about a thimble-
> ful may contain a hundred million bacteria, and several miles of
> fungal hyphae."[27]

In another experiment in Oregon, scientists studied a site that had
been leveled by loggers and had been "replanted four times without success." The scientists removed soil from the root zones of healthy trees from
a nearby forest, an amount of 150 milliliters of healthy soil per seedling to
inoculate the fifth round of planting. In the first year "seedling growth and
survival increased by half." In the third year "only seedlings that had been
inoculated with soil from the healthy, still intact site survived."

Julia Hill's 738-day encampment atop a 200-foot redwood was very
inspirational and touched me deeply as it showed the determination that
some humans have, to protect our old-growth. It was just as troubling to find
out that after the group had negotiated a settlement with Pacific Lumber/

---

26. Lewis, *Mere Christianity*, 63–64.

27. Luoma, *Hidden Forest*, 123.

Maxxam to protect the tree (named Luna) vandals cut a huge slice through the trunk.[28] David Milarch's story and his program to clone the most ancient trees are told in *The Man Who Planted Trees*.[29] Milarch's experience transcends the real to the mystical.[30]

Naomi Klein's *This Changes Every Thing* shows that we are so entrenched within a capitalist system that it is incredibly difficult to facilitate worthwhile change because the structure of commerce is so dependent on an unsustainable resource-based economy. In her analysis of extractivism, Klein shows how we have separated ourselves from nature.

> Extractivism is a nonreciprocal, dominance-based relationship with the earth, one purely of taking. It is the opposite of stewardship, which involves taking but also taking care that regeneration and future life continue. Extractivism is the mentality of the mountaintop remover and the old-growth clear-cutter. It is the reduction of life into objects for the use of others, giving them no integrity or value of their own—turning living complex ecosystems into "natural resources," mountains into "overburden" (as the mining industry terms the forests, rocks, and streams that get in the way of its bulldozers). It is also the reduction of human beings either into labor to be brutally extracted, pushed beyond limits, or, alternatively, into social burden, problems to be locked out at borders and locked away in prisons or reservations. In an extractivist economy, the interconnections among these various objectified components of life are ignored; the consequences of severing them are of no concern.[31][32]

> Within groups, selfish individuals win. However, groups of altruistic individuals always beat groups of selfish individuals. E. O. Wilson. *Of Ants and Men*. PBS Special 2015.

Films such as *Seed: The Untold Story*[33] broadcast on PBS by Independent Lens, reveal how tenuous our grasp of nature is because of our reliance

28. Hill, *Legacy of Luna.*

29. Robbins, *The Man who Planted Trees.*

30. https://www.ancienttreearchive.org

31. Klein, *This Changes Every Thing*, 169.

32. In Glenda Green's *Keys of Jeshua*, a similar statement is made by Jesus. "Only as you shift your thinking from objects to relationships will you conquer separation and harvest the power of life. To know this power is to know the experience of caring. Just as you care for yourself, without reservation or enforcement to do so, when you extend that sense of caring to include all others, you will know the full measure of being alive." (p.45)

33. http://www.pbs.org/independentlens/films/seed-the-untold-story/

on industrialization. We are responsible for our children's heritage and their sustenance. If we forfeit our rights to seed ownership and diversity, we have forfeited our claim to the land. The story of Seed is our story of creation. Some of the quotes from the film are deeply meaningful to this present symbolic understanding. "All these seeds have a memory," "all the seed banks, are arks," Hopi saying; "carry on the way of the corn," "a seed is a time capsule, preserving things from the past, also things for the future," "seed saving is all about sex," "seeds embody a sense of hope." There are also the films *Percy* (2020), recounting the events of farmer Percy Schmeiser's trials with Monsanto, and *Seeds*[34], a play, also on the same subject. Some of the seed banks mentioned:

- Hawaii Seed, Kauai, Hawaii, USA

- Mohawk Sierra Seeds, North San Juan, CA, USA

- Native Seeds Search, Tucson, AZ, USA

- Navdanya Seed Bank, India

- Rocky Mountain Seed Alliance, Idaho, USA (and search function for local U.S. resources)

- Scatter Seed Project, Maine, USA

- Svalbard Global Seed Vault, Norway

- Tesuque Pueblo Seed Bank, New Mexico, USA

- Vavilov Research Institute, Saint Petersburg, Russia

In Canada, I have purchased from Mumm's Sprouting Seed, Parkside, SK, Canada.

The experiments with the South American tea known as ayahuasca are also evidence of an herbal extract providing awareness of our relationship to the natural and spiritual universe. It has been beneficial in "psychotherapy and treatment of post-traumatic stress disorder (PTSD), anxiety, depression, pain, abuse, and other destructive behaviors, as well as in the treatment of terminal cancer patients."[35][36]

It might seem that in this chapter on nature, I have departed from my theological bent and drifted off at right angles. I can only say that it is only by understanding the immediate worlds around us and the miracle of their infinite complexities, that we will be able to ground our understanding of

---

34. *Seeds*. Annabel Soutar, documentary playwright and theatre director.

35. Kjellgren and Norlander, *Encounters with Ayahuasca*, 309–315. See also:

36. Harris, *Listening to Ayahuasca*.

the infinite in the very tangible appreciation of a concrete creation. Creation acts as a transformer to sensitize our spirit to the one spirit. The alternative is an abstract appreciation of a world that is immediate, but which is separated by an intellectual function that literalizes every event through a perceived sense of what is supposed to be, rather than what is. In my introduction, I suggested that "the literary form of the Bible derive its pattern from the elementary process of creation." If the form of the Bible is intimately linked to creation, then the study of creation should reveal within itself the form of the sacred and conversely the study of the sacred should reveal itself in creation.

To paraphrase Deuteronomy 30:

> For this commandment which I command you this day is not too hard for you, neither is it far off. The (tree of life) is not in heaven, that you should say, 'Who will ascend into heaven for us and bring it to us, that we may hear it and do it?' Nor is the (tree of life) beyond the sea, that you should say, 'Who will go over the sea for us and bring it to us, that we may (see) it and do it?' But the (tree of life) is very near you, in your mouth and in your heart, that you may do it. See, I have set before you today life and good, death and evil.

THE TIME OF CREATION

In a recent Netflix documentary *Is Genesis History*,[37] the evidence as illustrated by the creationist scientists shows that there were earth-wide catastrophic events as revealed in the strata which indicated that contrary to the evolutionist's theory—that changes were caused over millions of years—the changes in the strata happened in an alarmingly short period of time. There was also evidence of cellular development beginning at the level of our DNA showing four dimensions of interdependent cellular functions that could not have evolved linearly, that is one proceeding from the other. The fourth level had to have been present for the first level to occur. This is all amazing science which contradicts the current paradigm that, given a million years, anything can happen. However, I have difficulty with the creationist notion of a 24-hour day for creation. In the documentary, the argument for a literal seven-day creation rests on the understanding that the term *day* as translated throughout the Bible means a 24-hour day. My suggestion is that there are other meanings for the term. In 2 Peter 3, Peter addresses the skepticism of

37. https://isgenesishistory.com/ directed by Thomas Purifoy, 2017.

those who do not believe there was a flood. This is a controversy not unlike today's polarization between evolutionists and creationists. In 2 Peter 3:8, he says "But, beloved, do not forget this one thing, that with the Lord one day is as a thousand years and a thousand years as one day." The term *day* in the Greek is ἡμέρα, *hemera*. In the creation account of Genesis 1:5a it says, "God called the light Day." In the Greek Septuagint which was translated from the Hebrew in the third century BCE, the translators used the term ἡμέρα for the 11 instances of the word *day* in Genesis 1. Genesis 1:5a reads "καὶ ἐκάλεσεν ὁ θεὸς τὸ φῶς ἡμέραν." According to the apostle Peter's interpretation, the word is not a closed 24-hour period but an open-ended thousand-year possibility.

Secondly, the actual creation of an earth day occurs on day four of the Biblical account.

1. God created the heavens and the earth and said, "Let there be light."

2. God created the firmament to divide the waters, to make Heaven, Earth and Seas.

3. God created grass, herbs and fruit trees bearing fruit of its kind.

. . . So far there is no chronological time (or solar rotation) as we know it.

4. God created the lights in the heavens to divide day and night, and for signs and seasons and days and years. Then God created the greater light (the sun) to rule the day and the lesser light (the moon) to rule the night.

5. Following the creation of a possible 24-hour day God created the creatures of the sea and the birds of the air.

6. God said, "Let Us make man in Our image, according to Our likeness." Let them have dominion over all of creation on the face of the earth.

7. God rested.

So, the actual creation of a solar day is not until day four. Creation is much longer than what is understood by a literal seven-day view of creation. There were long periods of times and very accelerated times and there were very catastrophic events within short time periods. As Christians, we tend to box ourselves into a literal understanding which shouldn't be defended for the sake of arriving at an intelligent reading of the Bible.

The following records are taken from the National Ice Core Laboratory (NICL), which is in Denver, Colorado.[38] NICL is the primary repository in the United States and is managed by the United States Geological Survey (USGS). The NICL currently houses ~17,000 m of ice cores collected from

38. https://icecores.org/

Greenland and Antarctica. The oldest continuous ice core records extend to 130,000 years in Greenland, and 800,000 years in Antarctica. The West Antarctic Ice Sheet (WAIS) project reached its final depth goal of 3,405 meters on December 31, 2011, completing the longest U.S. ice core ever recovered from the polar regions. Over 400,000 years, levels of carbon dioxide (CO_2) have risen and fallen from about 180 parts per million to 280. Today, however, for the first time in more than 400,000 years, CO_2 is at 390 parts per million and continuing to rise at 2 parts per million (ppm) per year.

Chapter 17

Green Olive Tree

The oil was expressed to the last drop
and Tree stood parched and bare
her leaves had sheltered generations
who now were beyond her care

The vegetation was uprooted and burned
when the Roman roads cut through
yet Olive had clung to the side of the slope
for the sake of friends she once knew

Her fingers tore through the limestone bed
to squeeze every drop from the ground
she was keeping alive a memory
when Father's tears touched her gown

There was also—in the long distant past
her sister Terebinth told
three humans—indescribable
who sheltered under her fold

They appeared in an instant as if through a door
and suppered on wheatcakes on the soft desert floor
while the lady could be heard
laughing softly to herself in the distance

In another instance but difficult to place
when late an elusive soul
had turned up the soil at Olive's feet
and buried shards of an alabaster bowl

She remembered it well as a time out of time
being so perpetually perpendicular
a rush of human emotions had overwhelmed
so beyond her she no longer could care

Later that Man came around
at least in essence a man
it seemed he had passed through Olive's press[1]
and poured out his blood on the sand

The blood carried the scent of Nard
made you want to turn inside out
mixed with an anguished beauty
night collapsed under Sick Man's rout

Later the Romans salted the ground
which made for a very lean year
so she turned on her back away from the blast
and stretched leaves toward her distant-most care

She was waiting for the Man to come back again
but felt she would probably die in the interim

S.M. 01/31/2008
(Gen 18, Ps 52:8, Jer 11:16, Rom 11:17)

---

1. Gethsemane: of Aramaic origin, גת שמני = "an oil press"

The following photo is of my wife Wendy crawling out of the root system of one of the Three Sisters, three giant cedars located on the west coast of Vancouver Island. The three cedars are located several hundred feet from the Red Creek Fir, the largest known Douglas Fir in terms of board feet although there are taller Douglas Firs in other locations. The Red Creek Fir measures 4.2m in diameter and 73.8m in height and is more than 1,000 years old.

Figure 22: The Three Sisters

I drove my 2015 Chevy Volt in the 2019 Montreal St. Patrick's Day Parade representing AVEQ, the Association des Véhicules Électriques du Québec. Until March 2020 and Covid-19, the parade would have been, at 197 years, the longest consecutive running parade in North America. My car had signs like:

My Car Is Brown, But Her Heart Is Green
1L OF GAS = 0.75 KG = 2.4 KG OF CO2
Real IRISH Drive GREEN (Or Walk!)[2]

2. An American gallon, which is 3.8 litres, weighs 6.3 pounds. When combined with the oxygen in the air it creates 20 pounds of CO2, transferring billions of tons of carbon from under the earth into the atmosphere, all this within the last 100 years.

Figure 23: Photo by Jasper Machnik

The following chapter is a poem by Taliesin, the sixth century Welsh bard, *The Battle of the Trees*. it is also known as *The Battle of Godeu*.[3] It provides an imaginative description of a tree battle. The poem is taken from *The Four Ancient Books of Wales*, Volume I, published in English in 1868.[4]

3. *Book of Taliessin* viii. vol. ii. p. 137. Notes, vol ii. p. 399.
4. Skene, *The Four Ancient Books of Wales*, 276–84.

Figure 24: Etching "Tree of Life—Green Olive" 2010, S.M.

Chapter 18

The Battle of the Trees

I HAVE been in a multitude of shapes,
Before I assumed a consistent form.
I have been a sword, narrow, variegated,
I will believe when it is apparent.
I have been a tear in the air,
I have been the dullest of stars.
I have been a word among letters,
I have been a book in the origin.
I have been the light of lanterns,
A year and a half
I have been a continuing bridge,
Over three score Abers.
I have been a course, I have been an eagle.
I have been a coracle in the seas:
I have been compliant in the banquet.
I have been a drop in a shower;
I have been a sword in the grasp of the hand:
I have been a shield in battle.
I have been a string in a harp,
20 Disguised for nine years.
In water, in foam.
I have been sponge in the fire,
I have been wood in the covert.
I am not he who will not sing of

A combat though small,
The conflict in the battle of Godeu of sprigs.
Against the Guledig of Prydain,
There passed central horses,
Fleets full of riches.
There passed an animal with wide jaws,
On it there were a hundred heads.
And a battle was contested
Under the root of his tongue;
And another battle there is
In his *occiput*.
A black sprawling toad.
With a hundred claws on it.
A snake speckled, crested.
A hundred souls through sin
40 Shall be tormented in its flesh.
I have been in Caer Vevenir,
Thither hastened grass and trees,
Minstrels were singing,
Warrior-bands were wondering,
At the exaltation of the Brython,
That Gwydyon effected.
There was a calling on the Creator,
Upon Christ for causes,
Until when the Eternal
Should deliver those whom he had made.
The Lord answered them,
Through language and elements:
Take the forms of the principal trees.
Arranging yourselves in battle array,
And restraining the public.
Inexperienced in battle hand to hand.
When the trees were enchanted,
In the expectation of not being trees,
The trees uttered their voices
60 From strings of harmony,
The disputes ceased.
Let us cut short heavy days,
A female restrained the din.
She came forth altogether lovely.
The head of the line, the head was a female.
The advantage of a sleepless cow
Would not make us give way.
The blood of men up to our thighs,

The greatest of importunate mental exertions
Sported in the world.
And one has ended
From considering the deluge,
And Christ crucified,
And the day of judgment near at hand.
The alder-trees, the head of the line,
Formed the van.
The willows and quicken-trees
Came late to the army.
Plum-trees, that are scarce,
80 Unlonged for of men.
The elaborate medlar-trees,
The objects of contention.
The prickly rose-bushes,
Against a host of giants,
The raspberry brake did
What is better failed
For the security of life.
Privet and woodbine
And ivy on its front,
Like furze to the combat
The cherry-tree was provoked.
The birch, notwithstanding his high mind,
Was late before he was arrayed.
Not because of his cowardice,
But on account of his greatness.
The laburnum held in mind.
That your wild nature was foreign.
Pine-trees in the porch,
The chair of disputation,
100 By me greatly exalted,
In the presence of kings.
The elm with his retinue,
Did not go aside a foot ;
He would fight with the centre.
And the flanks, and the rear.
Hazel-trees, it was judged
That ample was thy mental exertion.
The privet, happy his lot.
The bull of battle, the lord of the world.
Morawg and Morydd
Were made prosperous in pines.
Holly, it was tinted with green,

He was the hero.
The hawthorn, surrounded by prickles,
With pain at his hand.
The aspen-wood has been topped,
It was topped in battle.
The fern that was plundered.
The broom, in the van of the army,
120 In the trenches he was hurt.
The gorse did not do well,
Notwithstanding let it overspread.
The heath was victorious, keeping off on all sides.
The common people were charmed.
During the proceeding of the men.
The oak, quickly moving,
Before him, tremble heaven and earth.
A valiant door-keeper against an enemy,
His name is considered.
The blue-bells combined,
And caused a consternation.
In rejecting, were rejected.
Others, that were perforated.
Pear-trees, the best intruders
In the conflict of the plain.
A very wrathful wood,
The chestnut is bashful,
The opponent of happiness,
The jet has become black,
140 The mountain has become crooked,
The woods have become a kiln,
Existing formerly in the great seas,
Since was heard the shout: —
The tops of the birch covered us with leaves,
And transformed us, and changed our faded state.
The branches of the oak have ensnared us
From the Gwarchan of Maelderw.
Laughing on the side of the rock,
The lord is not of an ardent nature.
Not of mother and father,
When I was made.
Did my Creator create me.
Of nine-formed faculties.
Of the fruit of fruits,
Of the fruit of the primordial God,
Of primroses and blossoms of the hill,

Of the flowers of trees and shrubs.
Of earth, of an earthly course,
When I was formed.
160 Of the flower of nettles,
Of the water of the ninth wave.
I was enchanted by Math,
Before I became immortal,
I was enchanted by Gwydyon
The great purifier of the Brython,
Of Eurwys, of Euron,
Of Euron, of Modron.
Of five battalions of scientific ones,
Teachers, children of Math.
When the removal occurred,
I was enchanted by the Guledig.
When he was half-burnt,
I was enchanted by the sage
Of sages, in the primitive world.
When I had a being;
When the host of the world was in dignity,
The bard was accustomed to benefits.
To the song of praise I am inclined, which the tongue recites.
I played in the twilight,
180 I slept in purple;
I was truly in the enchantment
With Dylan, the son of the wave.
In the circumference, in the middle,
Between the knees of kings,
Scattering spears not keen,
From heaven when came,
To the great deep, floods,
In the battle there will be
Four score hundreds,
That will divide according to their will.
They are neither older nor younger,
Than myself in their divisions.
A wonder, Canhwr are born, every one of nine hundred.
He was with me also.
With my sword spotted with blood.
Honour was allotted to me
By the Lord, and protection (was) where he was.
If I come to where the boar was killed,
He will compose, he will decompose,
200 He will form languages.

The strong-handed gleamer, his name.
With a gleam he rules his numbers.
They would spread out in a flame,
When I shall go on high.
I have been a speckled snake on the hill,
I have been a viper in the Llyn.
I have been a bill-hook crooked that cuts,
I have been a ferocious spear
With my chasuble and bowl
I will prophesy not badly,
Four score smokes
On every one what will bring.
Five battalions of arms
Will be caught by my knife.
Six steeds of yellow hue
A hundred times better is
My cream-coloured steed,
Swift as the sea-mew
Which will not pass
220 Between the sea and the shore.
Am I not pre-eminent in the field of blood?
Over it are a hundred chieftains.
Crimson (is) the gem of my belt,
Gold my shield border.
There has not been born, in the gap,
That has been visiting me,
Except Goronwy,
From the dales of Edrywy.
Long white my fingers,
It is long since I have been a herdsman.
I travelled in the earth,
Before I was a proficient in learning.
I travelled, I made a circuit,
I slept in a hundred islands.
A hundred Caers I have dwelt in.
Ye intelligent Druids,
Declare to Arthur,
What is there more early
Than I that they sing of.
240 And one is come
From considering the deluge,
And Christ crucified,
And the day of future doom.
A golden gem in a golden jewel.

I am splendid
And shall be wanton
From the oppression of the metal-workers.

Taliesin, sixth century.

There is an interesting reference in the poem to the *occiput*, italicized in the original, at line 35, which is considered an energy center where dreams enter. What was Taliesin imagining with his "black sprawling toad, with a hundred claws on it." The OED defines occiput as the base of the skull. Its earliest reference is to a 1398 phrase, "Trevisa, the nolle, is the hynder parte of the heed."

In William Skene's, *The Four Ancient Books of Wales*, volume II, he analyses the use of the word *occiput* as:

> This poem has been considered in Chapter xi. It is classed with the poems relating to the Gwyddyl of Gwydyon ap Don. They are described in lines 28 to 38 under various figures. The reference in lines 32 and 34 to a combat at the root of the tongue, and to another in the *occiput*, I cannot help suspecting refers to the most striking difference between the Cymric and Gaelic—viz. the interchange of gutturals and labials, which might be called a combat at the root of the tongue; and it is remarkable that in the *crania* found within the limits of ancient Manau there is an artificial compression in the *occiput*. Godeu was certainly the name of a district, but the word also means trees, and the subject of the poem soon passes over into a symbolical battle of trees. It seems also to have a philological meaning, as in lines 51, 52, 53, 54—
> "The Lord answered them
> Through language and elements:
> Take the forms of the principal trees.
> Arranging yourselves in battle-array."

And in lines 199 and 200— "

> "He will compose, he will decompose,
> He will form languages."[1]

---

1. Skene, *Four Ancient Books of Wales*, 399–400.

Chapter 19

The Book of Romans, a Similar Pattern

The book of Romans appears to contain a symbolic form similar to the previously described elements. The book begins with the "seed of David" and concludes the organic metaphor with the olive tree in chapter 11. The olive tree represents the engrafting into our spiritual origins and ties our redemption to a historical process, a process linked to "all of creation."

1. Paul outlines his primary theme, the Messiah as the son of David. "Born of the seed of David according to the flesh." (Rom 1:3b)

2. The original tree of life reappears metaphorically in the longing by all of creation. "Creation eagerly waits for the revealing of the sons of God." (Rom 8:19b).

3. The singular identity of the Seed. "In Isaac your seed shall be called." (Rom 9:7b)

4. There is a faith community that comprised those who believed in the promise of the Seed of the woman. "Isaiah also cries out concerning Israel: "Though the number of the children of Israel be as the sand of the sea, the remnant will be saved." (Rom 9:27)

5. The olive tree represents the integration of the tree of life with the seed of the woman as identified by the Branch. The gentiles "became a partaker of the root and fatness of the olive tree."[1] (Rom 11:17b) NKJV.

1. I used the NKJV because it uses the more literal 'seed' rather than 'descendants' i.e. NRSV.

1. BORN OF THE SEED OF DAVID

In his first paragraph, Paul specifically identifies the outline of the book as being the fulfillment of the promise, a promise which was originally made to Eve, but which has evolved to represent the regal authority as identified by the "son of David." The promise has been made incarnate "according to the flesh."

2. THE LONGING OF CREATION

Romans 8:19–26 outlines a three-part gestational development beginning with creation, followed by the redemption of mankind and thirdly the intercessory action of the Holy Spirit. What began with a primeval organism as symbolized by the tree of life in Genesis takes on a dynamic interrelationship between all of creation, a redeemed mankind and the Holy Spirit. Creation and mankind appear to be undergoing a transformative outworking from innermost being to the rebirth of a new engagement. All three entities are undergoing birth pangs resulting in a new creation, possibly a creation which results in the formation of a new "species of man," (a son of man?) more profoundly developed than the sum of its three parts. It is an emergent probability.

a) Creation

We know that the whole creation groans (*sustenazo*) and labors (*sunodino*) with birth pangs together until now. (Rom 8:22) NKJV.

b) Mankind

Not only that, but we also who have the firstfruits of the Spirit, even we ourselves groan (*stenazo*) within ourselves, eagerly waiting for the adoption, the redemption of our body. (Rom 8:23) NKJV.

c) Holy Spirit

Likewise, the Spirit also helps in our weaknesses. For we do not know what we should pray for as we ought, but the Spirit Himself makes intercession for us with groanings (*stenagmos*) which cannot be uttered. (Rom 8:26) NKJV. "Too deep for words." RSV.

The three-part groaning and birthing reveal that the redeemed body of mankind involves all of creation and suggests that the whole will be transformed into a new relationship. We are transformed from the inside out. Paul appears to suggest that the "one new man" will not be determined by our sense of a physically finite independent self but will involve a radically new relationship with all aspects of creation, facilitated by the action of the Holy Spirit.

> So then, remember that at one time you Gentiles by birth, called "the uncircumcision" by those who are called "the circumcision"—a physical circumcision made in the flesh by human hands—remember that you were at that time without Christ, being aliens from the commonwealth of Israel, and strangers to the covenants of promise, having no hope and without God in the world. But now in Christ Jesus you who once were far off have been brought near by the blood of Christ. For he is our peace; in his flesh he has made both groups into one and has broken down the dividing wall, that is, the hostility between us. He has abolished the law with its commandments and ordinances, that he might create in himself one new humanity in place of the two, thus making peace, and might reconcile both groups to God in one body through the cross, thus putting to death that hostility through it. So he came and proclaimed peace to you who were far off and peace to those who were near; for through him both of us have access in one Spirit to the Father. So then you are no longer strangers and aliens, but you are citizens with the saints and also members of the household of God, built upon the foundation of the apostles and prophets, with Christ Jesus himself as the cornerstone. In him the whole structure is joined together and grows into a holy temple in the Lord; in whom you also are built together spiritually into a dwelling place for God. (Eph 2:11–22) NRSV.

The original notion of a tree of life symbolizing a unique foundation of immortality has been changed into a dynamic cooperative interaction with all of creation. It has evolved into a creative interrelated dynamic. Similar types of relationships have been described in the Bible, wherein different types of species and, ultimately, the human and the divine live together cooperatively.

> The wolf also shall dwell with the lamb, the leopard shall lie down with the young goat, the calf and the young lion and the fatling together; and a little child shall lead them." (Isa 11:6) NKJV.

"For we are members of His body, of His flesh and of His bones. For this reason, a man shall leave his father and mother and be joined to his wife, and the two shall become one flesh. This is a great mystery, but I speak concerning Christ and the church." (Eph 5:30–32) NKJV.

"Let us be glad and rejoice and give Him glory, for the marriage of the Lamb has come, and His wife has made herself ready." (Rev 19:7) NKJV.

"And I John saw the holy city, New Jerusalem, coming down from God out of heaven, prepared as a bride adorned for her husband." (Rev 21:2) AV.

3. THE SINGULAR IDENTITY OF THE SEED

Commentaries have generally shown Paul's argument to be a rhetorical or diatribe method, but some interpreters more recently have shown it to be a style of Midrash. Midrash uses conceptually interrelated word forms. The following quotation is taken from the NET Bible footnotes to Romans 9:1.[2]

> Rom 9:1–11:36. These three chapters are among the most difficult and disputed in Paul's Letter to the Romans. One area of difficulty is the relationship between Israel and the church, especially concerning the nature and extent of Israel's election. Many different models have been constructed to express this relationship. For a representative survey, see M. Barth, The People of God (JSNTSup), 22–27. The literary genre of these three chapters has been frequently identified as a diatribe, a philosophical discussion or conversation evolved by the Cynic and Stoic schools of philosophy as a means of popularizing their ideas (E. Käsemann, Romans, 261 and 267). But other recent scholars have challenged the idea that Rom 9–11 is characterized by diatribe. Scholars like R. Scroggs and E. E. Ellis have instead identified the material in question as Midrash. For a summary and discussion of the rabbinic connections, see W. R. Stegner, "Romans 9.6–29—A Midrash." JSNT 22 (1984): 37–52.

Midrash appears to relate to a form of writing that relies on a common (at that time) appreciation of major symbolic themes. These are symbolic themes as indicated by Meyers (p.134) which may contain little in the way

2. http://www.bible.org/netbible Footnote 1 for Romans 9:1.

of descriptive language but much to do with their emotional and historical import. The themes are the determining elements around which the arguments are assembled.

Stegner goes on to suggest that the word "seed" is the primary keyword that Paul is referencing in the text. (9:6–29) Stegner[3] quotes Earl Ellis to say that "Paul is writing Midrash in Romans 9–11." He proposes that "two elements of Paul's basic pattern are shared with the classical midrashim." "First, it shows how 'catchwords' or keywords are used to draw in other subordinate Old Testament quotations." "Secondly, it shows that a number (as opposed to one or two) of subordinate texts may be found in a Midrash." And thirdly "The conclusion is tied to the beginning of the paragraph by the keyword."

Stegner suggests that Paul's concluding quotation in 9:29 from Isaiah "Unless the LORD of Sabaoth had left us a seed" ties the composition to v.7 "In Isaac your seed shall be called." He points out that Kasemann was aware of this word usage. He suggests that the word 'son' in v.9 is derived from Hosea 1.10 in v. 26 and in Isaiah 10.22–23 in v. 27. He goes on to say that "most commentators have not noted the interplay of key words whereby the proof-texts are linked to one another."[4]

To reiterate, the book of Romans begins with the central notion that the Messiah is of the seed of David. Secondly, creation is vitally involved, combining the three groanings of all of creation, mankind, and the divine work of the Holy Spirit. Thirdly, the seed is unique in character and the functions of calling and faith are interrelated and tied to the seed.

4. THE ROLE OF THE REMNANT RELATED TO THE SEED

The remnant like the husk of the seed implies that within Israel there is a believing group of people who, like midwives, must ensure the safe delivery of the messiah. The identity of the "Seed of the woman's" progeny may not be immediately apparent as in the case of the Canaanite prostitute Rahab who was the great-great-grandmother of David (Matt 1:5, Heb 11:31). The survival of the seed and the remnant appears precarious but survives by the will of God. Paul quotes Isaiah:

> Though the number of the children of Israel be as the sand of
> the sea, The remnant will be saved. For He will finish the work

3. Stegner, Romans 9.6–29—A Midrash, 37–52

4. Stegner, *Romans*, 40.

and cut it short in righteousness, Because the LORD will make
a short work upon the earth. And as Isaiah said before: "Unless
the LORD of Sabaoth had left us a seed, We would have become
like Sodom, And we would have been made like Gomorrah."
(Rom 9:27–29 from Isa 10:22, 23 and 1:9)

The contrast between the remnant of the Israelites and the possibility
of violence and of extermination are represented in Romans 9:27, 29 and
11:5. The verse is a potent reminder of the holocaust. Both characteristics
are representative of the names of the sons of Isaiah.

Son 1: Isa 7:3 Shearjashuv שְׁאָר יָשׁוּב
    a remnant returns

Son 2: Isa 8:3 Mahershalalhashbaz מַהֵר שָׁלָל חָשׁ בַּז
    speed the spoil hasten the plunder

Isaiah symbolically identifies his two sons, one representing the fragile
remnant and the second representing swift and exacting judgment. In terms
of the metaphysical elements, it reveals the dynamic between the natures
of potency, the seed, and the remnant, and the nature of act and judgment.

While it seems that Paul is using the notion of seed in Romans nine, it
is also possible that he was similarly defining the section bracketed by 9:27
and 11:5 with the keyword "remnant." Verse 9:27 says "The remnant will be
saved" which is a quote from Isaiah 10:22,[5] the same verse that Paul is tying
to the word son/seed. The term remnant is also used as a concluding word
In Romans 11:5 where Paul says, "there is a remnant according to the election
of grace." There are two keywords, first, the word seed defining chapter nine
and secondly, the word remnant defining chapters ten and eleven. What is
interesting is that the Greek word seed in 9:29 can be used interchangeably
with the Hebrew word remnant depending on whether the Masoretic text is
referenced or whether Paul is quoting from the Greek Septuagint. In Isaiah
1:9 (from which Rom 9:29 is quoted) the Hebrew שריד remnant is translated
in the LXX as σπερμα or seed. The remnant/seed interpretation acts as a
coupling word between 9:27 and 9:29 linking the seed section to the remnant section. It reveals that in the Hebrew mind at that time, the symbols
"seed and remnant" were interchangeable or at least closely related. Dunn
has also identified a similar idea as to the one that I was intending with his
statement. The "seed" and "remnant" can be treated as closely correlated
concepts. Fitzmyer does not appear to have noticed the distinction.

---

5. Isa 10:22b (LXX): το καταλειμμα αυτων σωθησεται, a remnant of them shall be
preserved.

The quotation is in verbatim agreement with Isa 1:9 LXX, including LXX's use of σπερμα to translate שָׂרִיד:כִּמְעַט (a few survivors); see Cranfield. But the ideas of "seed" and "remnant" can be treated as closely correlated concepts (cf. Isa. 6:13; 37:3–4; CD 2.11–12; 1 Enoch 83.8 with 84.5; Zeller). Since so many of the themes in these closing verses pick up key motifs from the opening of the section (see 9:6–29 Form and Structure) it is more likely that Paul intends the σπερμα to recall the σπερμα of vv 7–8 (Barrett; against Cranfield). The language also points forward to 11:4–5 (καταλειπω . . . λειμμα) (Michel). Sodom and Gomorrah (Gen. 19) are used elsewhere as types of eschatological judgment (Deut 32:32–35; Jub. 16:5–6; Matt 10:15 par.: 11:23–24; Luke 17:28–30; 2 Pet 2:6; Jude 7; Rev 11:8; cf. Jer 23:14 and Ezek 16:46–49) (Wilckens). "The situation of Israel is such that Paul can mention Israel in the same breath as Sodom and Gomorrah" (Lubking, 76). Mayer (224) rightly notes that vv. 27–29 speak not only of the sovereign choice of God, but simply of the fact that at present only a remnant of Israel believe.[6]

The difference between the Masoretic and the LXX is as follows:

Isa 1:9 (LXX) και ει μη κυριος σαβαωθ εγκατελιπεν ημιν σπερμα
Unless the Lord of Hosts left us a seed
Isa 1:9 (Masoretic): לולי יהוה צבאות הותיר לנו שריד
Unless the Lord of Hosts left us a remnant

Paul concludes the remnant section with the illustration from Kings where Elijah, who having single-handedly outwitted the priests of Baal during the sacrifice on Mount Carmel, complains that he alone is left. In response, God says that He has reserved for Himself 7,000 who have not bowed the knee to Baal (Rom 11:4, I Kings 19:18). Paul concludes that "even so at this present time there is a remnant according to the election of grace." (Rom 11:5) The reserved and the remnant conclude the primary notion from 9:29 that "unless the LORD of Sabaoth had left us a seed, we would have become like Sodom." What is vital to the salvation of mankind is the survival of the seed, the remnant exists by the grace of God.

5. THE OLIVE TREE IN ROMANS 11

The olive tree is the primary symbol following the seed, remnant chapters. The tree provides an organic as well as a historical image by which and

6. Dunn, Romans, 574.

into which other symbols can be incorporated or related. The following are several examples:

- The Seed (Gen 3:15, 21:12; the Promised One)
- The root of Jesse (Isa 11:10; the Messiah)
- The Branch (Is 11:1, Zech 3:8, 6:12; the Messiah)
- The two anointed ones (Zech 4:3; represented by two olive trees)
- The roots (Rom 11:17; the patriarchs)
- The cultivated and wild branches (Rom 11:17; Jews and Gentiles)
- The two witnesses (Rev 11:4; represented by two olive trees).

Following the *remnant* section and continuing from Romans 11:5 to 11:17, Paul parallels Isaiah 10:22 to 11:1. Both sections are similar in length and appear to mirror each other. Romans 11:5 says, "there is a remnant according to the election of grace" which compares to Isaiah 10:22 "A remnant of them will return." Romans 11:17 says, "(you) became a partaker of the root and fatness of the olive tree," which compares to Isaiah 11:1 "There shall come forth a Rod from the stem of Jesse, and a Branch shall grow out of his roots." If we retrace our steps there is a good argument that Paul is relating the olive tree to the Messianic typology of the "Branch," to the "Rod," to the "roots," to the "remnant," to the "seed of Isaac," to the "Son of David" and ultimately to the tree of life.

Paul is not only using the olive tree as a metaphor for our (gentile) relationship to the patriarchs, but he is also using very specific messianic word images which would have been apparent to Jewish scholars at the time. The olive tree metaphor is a type of common contemporary form which links the new gentile believer to the Branch, to the seed of Isaac (the Abrahamic promise), to the Seed of the woman, and to the tree of life.

Chapter 20

The Tree and Menorah in Revelation

1. THE SEVEN LAMPSTANDS
REPRESENT THE MENORAH

The book of Revelation reveals a symbolic pattern that appears to follow the style of the menorah. The menorah as a stylized tree symbolizes the tree of life and, by extension, the Seed of the woman and the anointed one(s). Much of our attention is focused on the apocalyptic nature of the book. However, when we interpret the underlying pattern through its symbolic form, the dramatic imagery becomes comparatively more understandable. The seven churches are the seven-branched menorah. The menorah and the tree of life are symbolically interchangeable. And the tree of life appears at the beginning and end of Revelation which mirrors its placement in the Bible as situated in Genesis and Revelation.

2. OVERVIEW OF REVELATION

Primary Components	Components, related to the tree and the menorah
Chapters: 1–3 The Seven churches	The lampstand is mentioned (6x) Tree of life (2:7—1x)
Chapters: 4–16 The Seven Seals, Trumpets and Bowls	Seals, bowls, and trumpets compare to bud, bowl, and flame. The two witnesses are the two olive trees and the two lampstands before God (7th mention of the lampstand and the midpoint of Revelation) (11:3)
Chapters: 17–22 The end The woman and the beast	
The New Jerusalem The Bride of the Lamb	Tree of life (22:2,14—2x)

Chapters one to three reveal the relationship between the menorah as a tree of life and the seven churches. The seven lampstands are the menorah. As indicated previously, the Greek for lampstand in Revelation λυχνια, *luchnia* is the same term used for the menorah in the Greek Septuagint of Exodus 25. What John perceived was not seven individual lampstands but one menorah with seven lamps.

> Then I turned to see the voice that spoke with me. And having turned I saw seven golden lampstands, and in the midst of the seven lampstands One like the son of man. (Rev 1:12,13a)
> The mystery of the seven stars which you saw in my right hand, and the seven golden lampstands: the seven stars are the angels of the seven churches, and the seven lampstands which you saw are the seven churches. (Rev 1:20) NKJV.

The seven angels, symbolized by the seven stars, represent the purposes of the Godhead. The divine intentions are incorporated into the seven churches as symbolized by the menorah. Chapter one of the book of Revelation implies a beginning as divine intent.

After the first prophecy to the church of Ephesus, Jesus makes a general statement to the seven churches, "He who has an ear, let him hear what the Spirit says to the churches. To him who overcomes I will give to eat from the tree of life, which is in the midst of the Paradise of God." (Rev 2:7)

NKJV. The tree of life, located in the midst of the sacred universe, is the primary blessing to each of the seven churches as well as to the first-mentioned church of Ephesus.

The symbol of the menorah is the most prominent artifact in the first three chapters; it represents the seven churches. Whether that has any significance, it is mentioned six times and once in chapter eleven for a total of seven. The tree of life is the reward to the church of Ephesus as well as to the seven churches, which ties the menorah symbolism directly to the tree of life as it has been tied previously through the vision of the burning bush, as well as by various authors and possibly as a general association in the Hebraic consciousness.

As indicated in the first part of this book, the tree of life reveals itself in only two places in the Bible as an actual entity; in Genesis and in Revelation. In the book of Revelation, the tree is revealed similarly at the beginning and end of the book. It is first mentioned as a promise to those who overcome (chapter two) and in chapter twenty-two as present to John in a vision. Or it may be said to be offered as a possibility and then presented as a finished reality.

3. THE DESIGN OF THE MENORAH IN REVELATION

When the design of the menorah is superimposed upon the book of Revelation in template form, a pattern emerges. First, the seven churches are revealed as the seven lamps of the menorah. The Messiah stands in the middle of the lamps as the primary light giver. The church of Ephesus is cautioned that their lamp could be removed. Many of the qualities in the vision of the Messiah and the rewards to the churches, reflect the design of the menorah; the seven stars, the seven spirits, eyes like fire, feet like brass, the tree of life, a pillar in the temple. The beginning chapters situate the menorah as a symbolic cultural and institutional emblem to remote groups of Christians. The seven churches go into the world as a form of the menorah. The Son of Man is standing amid the lampstands. Symbolically, the tree of life has returned in the person of Christ, through the ministry of his Church.

Secondly, the three symbols indicated for the outpouring of destruction also seem to reflect the design of the menorah. The seven seals, trumpets, and bowls (3 x 7 = 21) pictorially compare to the repeated pattern of the bud, bowl, and flower on the menorah which are repeated three times for each branch plus one (3 x 7 + 1 = 22). There are four elements on the main stem compared to the three on each of the six branches. It resembles the 22 letters of the Hebrew alphabet.

4. THE SEVEN CHURCHES AS MENORAH

Table 11: The seven Churches of Revelation

> The Son of Man, Alpha and Omega, Beginning and End
> In the Midst of The Menorah
> Eyes Like Fire, Feet Like Brass, Mouth with Sword
> Seven Stars in His Right Hand
> Key of David, The Keys of Hades and of Death
> Voice Like Many Waters

The characteristics of the messiah and the attributes of those that overcome have similarities to the design of the menorah and suggest a symbolic form to the book. In the sections following I analyse the symbolic representations of the Messiah as described in the lampstands.[1]

---

1. Rev 1:8–20, 3:7.

	Ephesus	Smyrna	Pergamos	Thyatira	Sardis	Philadelphia	Laodicea
The character of the Messiah	7 Lampstands 7 Stars	The First and Last Who was dead and lives	Two-edged sword	Son of God Eyes of fire feet like brass	7 Spirits 7 Stars	Who Is Holy, True and the Beginning of creation. Key of David Opens and shuts	The Amen The Faithful and True witness Beginning of creation
	2:1	2:8	2:12	2:19	3:1	3:7	3:14
Character of the Church	Patience Perseverance Hated the Nicolaitans	Poverty and tribulation for 10 days	Hold fast to my name	Love, service faith, patience	A few have not defiled their garments	Kept my command to persevere	Neither hot nor cold but lukewarm
"I have this against you"	Left first love		Hold the doctrine of Balaam and Nicolaitans	Allowed Jezebel	You are dead		
Messiah will give the. . . to those that overcome	Tree of life 2:7	Crown of life	Hidden manna A white stone and a new name	Rod of iron over nations Morning star	White garments Book of life	Pillar in the temple Name of God New Jerusalem	Open the door I will dine Sit on the throne

a. The Rod of Iron

The 'rod of iron' is mentioned four times in the Bible. It is first mentioned in a quote from Psalm 2:9, a messianic psalm which says, "You are My Son, today I have begotten You. . .You shall break them with a rod of iron" (2:7). Secondly to the church of Thyratira (church # 4) which acts positionally as the centerpiece, the central shaft of the menorah in the placement of churches. The blessing to Thyratira promises that he who overcomes will "rule over (the nations) with a rod of iron," and is the second mention of the phrase, rod of iron, in the Bible. The third mention is at 12:5 where the woman clothed with the sun will bear "a male Child who was to rule all nations with a rod of iron." The position of the rod of iron at 12:5 is situated at the center point of the book, a reflection of its position as the center shaft of the menorah and it also associates the male Child with the Son of Man who stands in the midst of the lampstands and to "My Son," the messianic reference from Psalm 2. The fourth mention at 19:15 describes the final battle, the appearance of the messianic figure, the Faithful and True who "will rule over them with a rod of iron," which is also the character of the messiah of the right-hand branch represented by the church of Laodicea. The rod of iron relates the Son of Man, the male Child and the Faithful and True. The rod of iron symbolically demonstrates the central form of the menorah, central to the book of Revelation. Its image expresses great strength which the Hebrew root conveys for the term shaft, the shaft of the menorah which is derived from the word thigh. It evokes the strength of a behemoth:

> Look at Behemoth, which I made just as I made you; it eats grass like an ox. Its strength is in its loins, and its power in the muscles of its belly. It makes its tail stiff like a cedar; the sinews of its thighs are knit together. Its bones are tubes of bronze, its limbs like bars of iron. It is the first of the great acts of God— only its Maker can approach it with the sword. (Job 40:15–19) RSV.

The center shaft also reminds us of the apparition of the burning bush in Exodus, where the presence of the Lord dwelt "in the midst of the bush." And that the blessing of the indwelling was the blessing to Joseph which Labuschagne compares to the shape of a menorah.

b. The Faithful and True

The Faithful and True witness is mentioned three times in the whole of the Bible and only in the book of Revelation. First it is mentioned in Revelation 3:14 to the church of Laodicea (church # 7), secondly in 19:11, to the one who is Faithful and True and lastly at 22:6 which completes the description of the tree of life, the final blessing, that these words "are faithful and true."

c. The Tree of Life

As indicated previously, the phrase "tree of life" is mentioned 10 times in the Bible: three times in Genesis (2:9, 3:22, 24), four times in Proverbs (3:18, 11:30, 13:12, 15:4) and three times in Revelation (2:7, 22:2, 14). The tree of life reflects the symbolic form of the menorah as a left, right and center branch. The placement of the tree of life in Revelation, as a beginning and an end, also reflects its place in the Bible.

d. The Seven Golden Lampstands

The phrase "seven golden lampstands" is another phrase found only three times and only in the book of Revelation. The word lampstand(s)[2] is found seven times, six in the plural and once in the singular in reference to its removal from the church of Ephesus (church # 1). The phrase identifies the character of the book of Revelation with the menorah. (Rev 1:12, 20, 2:1) The two lampstands which are the two witnesses is in chapter 11. There is also the "seven lamps of fire were burning before the throne, which are the seven Spirits of God." (Rev 4:5) This also reinforces the image of the "eyes of the Lord" which "scan the earth." (Zech) The flames of the menorah, the seven spirits are the action of the divine in the earth.

e. The First and the Last

The "First and the Last" is another phrase found only in Revelation and is a reference to the messiah. It is found four times: twice as a characteristic of the messiah, the Son of Man, and the Alpha and Omega, (Rev 1:11, 17), thirdly in the address to the church of Smyrna (church # 2) in 2:8, and lastly in 22:13, "I am the Alpha and Omega, the beginning and the end, the first and the last," reiterating the beginning of chapter one and reflecting the symbolic function of the tree of life as a beginning and end and as a quality of the Messiah, "I am the life."

2. It is found approximately 54 times (42 OT, 12 NT).

f. The Two-Edged Sword

The "two-edged sword" phrase is mentioned five times in the Bible, twice in Revelation, first to the Son of Man (1:13) who "out of his mouth went a two-edged sword," and secondly to the church of Pergamos, the third church of the lampstand. The phase "out of His mouth" is expressive because the phrase is associated with the worship of the saints—"Let the high praises of God be in their mouth, and a two-edged sword in their hand." (Ps 149:6) Also the word of God is "living and powerful, and sharper than any two-edged sword." (Heb 4:12) It recalls the notion of the *hitlahavut*, the flames of fire, from the burning bush. The fifth mention is a negative connotation in Proverbs describing an immoral woman. (Prov 5:4)

g. Eyes like a Flame of Fire

The phrase "eyes like (a flame of) fire and feet like (fine) brass," another messianic symbol is found only three times in the Bible: once as a reference to the Son of Man (Rev 1:14–15) in John's first encounter; secondly as a description of the Son of God in a proclamation to the church of Thyratira (church # 4), and lastly; (19:16) the one who is Faithful and True has eyes which "were like a flame of fire, and on His head were many crowns." The eyes like fire are a reminder of Zechariah's vision of the menorah which associates the seven lights to the seven eyes "these seven rejoice to see . . .They are the eyes of the Lord, Which scan to and fro throughout the whole earth." The vision of Zechariah directly associates the seven flames of the menorah to the eyes of the messiah. (Zech 4:10) The vision of the menorah in Zechariah is important as will be seen later because the vision follows the vision of "My Servant the Branch" (Zech 3:8) and the stone which is laid at the feet of Joshua with seven eyes. The vision implies that the functions of the seven churches, like the seven lamps, are the eyes of the messiah in the earth. The Branch is a clear reminder of the messiah's relationship to the tree of life.

h. The Crown of Life

The phrase "crown of life" is mentioned twice in the Bible: once in Rev 2:10 to the church of Smyrna (church # 2) who will endure tribulation, and a similar meaning in James 1:12 as a blessing to those who "endure temptation." It has been translated as crown, compass (encompass), and suffer (bear with). The crown, כתר, *ktr*, is also the topmost element in the diagram of the ten sefirot of the tree of life diagram in the kabbalah. It represents the will of the Divine superconscious that is beyond conscious intellect.

i. The Book of Life

The phrase "book of life" is mentioned eight times in the Bible: once in Philippians 4:3 "whose names are written in the Book of Life," and seven times in Revelation. The first mention is to the church of Sardis, the fifth church whose names "I will not blot out . . . from the Book of Life." (Rev 3:5) NKJV. And lastly, in reference to those whose names are or are not written in the Book of Life. It is a Book of Remembrance.

j. The Son of Man

The phrase "Son of Man" is only mentioned twice in Revelation, although it is mentioned approximately 193 times throughout the Bible. In Numbers 23:19 it says: "God is not a man (אִישׁ—aish), that He should lie, nor a son of man (בֶּן אָדָם,—ben adam) that He should repent." There is a distinction between the male form aish and what is generally considered a generic term for humanity, ben adam or son of Adam, sometimes translated as human (although it doesn't seem gender-neutral). The two instances of its mention in Revelation are first, the Son of Man in the midst of the lampstands (1:13), in the midst of the churches and secondly, the Son of Man (14:14) who, in response to the angels' cry that the "harvest of the earth is ripe" thrusts in His sickle to reap. This event is a midpoint in the drama of Revelation and follows the Woman clothed with the sun, as well as the two outpourings of the trumpets and seals. A work has been completed in mankind. What follows are the outpourings of the seven bowls, the spiritual battle against Satan, the red woman and the red beast. The Son of Man is no longer mentioned subsequent to 14:14 possibly signifying a completion in the work of man.

The Son of Man in the midst of the lampstands also reminds us of the presence of the angel who dwelt in the midst of the burning bush. It is a vivid reminder that the menorah commemorates the experience of Moses with the Lord on Mount Horeb.

The three-fold pattern which appears for most phrases, portrays a form that is possibly unique to Revelation which corresponds to the form of the menorah (as a left-hand branch, a right-hand branch, and centerpiece and which is similarly duplicated in its place within the book). The tripartite quality suggests the beginnings of the Son of Man, the centrality of the male child and lastly, the one who is Faithful and True, the One who has completed the original mission, on whose thigh is written King of Kings and Lord of Lords (19:16). In Benjamin Blech's esoteric book, *The Secrets of Hebrew Words,* he proposes that the Hebrew letters of the word Adam אדם, *adm* represent the names of Adam, David, and Messiah.[3] The Son of Man in the person of Jesus is possibly a prototype of a spiritually evolved human who is divinely conscious of the unity and interdependency of all human beings.

5. THE SEVEN SEALS

Following chapters one to three which describe the seven churches, chapters four to sixteen describe the outpouring of God's wrath illustrated by the seven seals, trumpets, and bowls. There are intermediate periods between the 6th and 7th seals and the 6th and 7th trumpets as well as between the seventh trumpet and first bowl.

The seal σφραγις, *sfragidzo* which begins in Revelation five has as its most elementary meaning, the covering of the heart or that which is most precious, as expressed in Song of Solomon chapter eight.

> Who is that coming up from the wilderness, leaning upon her beloved? Under the apple tree I awakened you. There your mother was in labor with you; there she who bore you was in labor. Set me as a seal upon your heart, as a seal upon your arm; for love is strong as death, passion fierce as the grave. Its flashes are flashes of fire, a raging flame. (Song 8:5–6) NRSV.

The seal on the heart reflects the notion from Romans four—"He received the sign of circumcision as a seal of the righteousness that he had by faith"—which is of the heart (4:11) "real circumcision is a matter of the heart—it is spiritual and not literal." (Rom 2:29) Other notions of the seal relate to the signet inscription on the breastplate of judgment. Aaron bears the breastplate of the judgment of the children of Israel "over his heart" as he enters the temple. The engraving of the signet proclaims, "Holiness to the Lord." (Exod 28:36) Similarly in Zechariah 14:20 at the end of time "Holiness to the Lord" shall be engraved (sealed?) on the bells of the horses. Finally, in Revelation 4:8, the four creatures with the six wings proclaim "Holy, holy, holy . . . " to the one who opens the seven seals. In chapter 19, the one who is Faithful and True who is on the white horse has on His robe and on His thigh "King of King and Lord of Lords." The "holy, holy, holy" proclamation of the four creatures (lion, calf, man, and eagle) reminds us that what was sealed until the end was something of the utmost value and

---

3. Blech, *Secrets of Hebrew Word,* 145.

purity. It had been covered over, hidden until the time of Revelation. The seraphim are also symbolically suggestive of the menorah. The six wings remind us of the six branches with eyes flashing in all directions. The following are the outpourings from the seven seals:

- White Horse (with bow & crown) for conquest (6:1)
- Red Horse (sword for war) to remove peace
- Black Horse (scales) a famine of wheat and barley, do not touch the olive and vine
- Pale Horse (death) to kill by sword, famine, and plague
- Martyrs are slain for their testimony
- Great Earthquake, the sky recedes as a scroll
- Silence in heaven for a half-hour, and incense is hurled to the earth

The expression *four* or *fourth* is mentioned approximately seven times in the section on the seven seals, which is a high occurrence. There are the four living creatures, the four horsemen and the four angels standing at the four corners of the earth. The term "quart" for wheat and barley derives from the fourth part from the French *quatre* for four. "I heard what seemed to be a voice in the midst of the four living creatures saying, "A quart of wheat for a day's pay, and three quarts of barley for a day's pay, but do not damage the olive oil and the wine!" (Rev 6:6) Although the actual term χοῖνιξ—*coinix* means a measure, the one-part wheat, and three-parts barley equal four parts and so the symbolism of a quart is appropriate. The seven trumpets describe thirds and the seven bowls, sevens. The fourths, thirds, and sevens suggest a part of, or the completed seven, of the menorah. This is analysed in a later section.

6. THE SEVEN TRUMPETS

Chapters eight to twelve describe the seven trumpets and another outpouring of calamity. Like the passage on the seven seals, there is a pause between the sixth and seventh trumpets. Just prior to the sounding of the seventh trumpet the voice from heaven says, "Seal up the things which the seven thunders uttered, and do not write them." The first incident before trumpet seven describes the little book and the angel who stands on the sea and the earth. The trumpet is a time indicator, it expresses finality. It is a marker for a beginning and an end as well as suggesting the dynamic of an act, or judgment, or decision-making.

The seven trumpets σαλπιγξ, *salpinx* of Revelation eight reflect the trumpet which is sounded in the year of Jubilee. The foregoing expresses the release of the captives in Leviticus in contrast to the trumpets of Revelation as omens of destruction.

> You shall count off seven weeks of years, seven times seven years, so that the period of seven weeks of years gives forty-nine years. Then you shall have the trumpet sounded loud; on the tenth day of the seventh month—on the Day of Atonement—you shall have the trumpet sounded throughout all your land. And you shall hallow the fiftieth year and you shall proclaim liberty throughout the land to all its inhabitants. It shall be a jubilee for you: you shall return, every one of you, to your property and every one of you to your family. (Lev 25:8–10) NRSV.

The trumpet sounds the exultation in the year of liberty. It is reminiscent of the flower on the menorah, perhaps the lily, שוש which is derived from the root שוש or שש, meaning "to be joyful, bright, or cheerful" which is the root for the name ששון Sasson, meaning "joy of life" or Shoshana (female) שושנה.[4] The trumpet is used both to herald an announcement and to signal a battle. The blast (*teruah*) of the shofar signals both a war cry and a shout for joy. The sound *ruah* relates to the spirit (wind) *ruach* of Elohim which hovered over the waters (Gen 1:2) Both of the Hebraic terms that relate to trumpet, the words shofar and yobel (a root of jubilee) are derived from the root for the ram's horn. The trumpet symbolically incorporates the original sacrifice of the ram (see Dura-Europus), an original covenant (seal) which for Christians prefigures the sacrifice of the Messiah, as well as the blast of the wind of Elohim which renews all things as expressed in the regenerating symbol of the flower. The following are the outpourings from the seven trumpets:

- Hail, fire, and blood on the earth, a third of the earth, trees and grass burned (8:7)

- Mountain thrown into the sea, a third of sea creatures and ships destroyed

- Star fell from heaven—Wormwood a third of the rivers turn bitter

- A third of the sun, moon, and stars were struck, a third less light

- Star falls from heaven, the bottomless pit; Abyss (Abaddon) men suffered in agony

- A third of mankind killed by the four angels of the Euphrates

- The heavens are opened to reveal the ark in the temple (11:19)

---

4. See the description for flower in the chapter on menorah

Note: the term a *third* is repeated approximately fourteen times in the trumpet section, which is a high occurrence. Most of the calamities precipitated by the seven trumpets destroy a third of all things.

7. THE INTERVAL PERIODS

There are two minor interval periods between the sixth and seventh seal and the sixth and seventh trumpet and a major interval between the seventh trumpet and the first bowl or at the two-thirds point.

a. Minor Intervals

The first minor interval corresponds to the notion of sealing within the time of the seven seals. In Revelation 7:4, the 144,000 servants of God are sealed of the twelve tribes. Following the sealing of the tribes, a great multitude clothed in white robes appears from every nation, people, tribe, and tongue. These are also those who have come out of the great tribulation (like Smyrna) and have washed their robes (like Sardis) in the blood of the Lamb.

The second minor interval occurs between the sixth and seventh trumpets. This is an important vision that confirms the relationship between the lampstand and the menorah. The lampstands in chapter one could be said to relate as a translation of the word menorah in Exodus. However, the two parallel visions of John in Revelation and Zechariah in chapter four very specifically relate the vision of the lampstand in the Greek to the vision of the menorah in the Hebrew language confirming that the lampstand is, in fact, the menorah and confirms the symbolic importance of the menorah to the book of Revelation.

The vision in Revelation 11 describes the two witnesses who are symbolized by the two olive trees and the two lampstands (menorah). This vision is almost identical to the vision of Zechariah chapter four, and the vision of the two olive trees on either side which serve to fuel the single menorah. The identity of the two anointed ones as olive trees in Zechariah, relates directly to the two witnesses in Revelation. This vision further confirms the association between the oil of anointing as a primary symbol, and the role of the olive tree related to the menorah.

Zechariah 4	Revelation 11
Two olive trees (right and left of the)	Two olive trees
One lampstand (*menorah*)	Two lampstands (*luchnia*)
Two olive branches	
Two gold pipes with oil	
Two anointed ones	Two witnesses
	3½ years + 3½ days

The notion of the trumpet as time indicator and the notion of finality are further emphasized by the expression of a symbolic time. The time of the two witnesses is identified by a 1,260-day interval.

The two witnesses prophesy for 1,260 days (1,260/360 = 3½ years)

Gentiles tread the holy city underfoot for 42 months
(42/12 = 3½ years)

The witnesses are killed

After 3½ days the two witnesses are revived

Total = 7 a sabbatical time symbolizing the sacred period of the menorah

The time interval is a sacred period, 3½ years prior to and 3½ days subsequent to a witnessing period within which the menorah is the primary symbol. The years vs. the days difference may be an indication of an accelerated time following the initial revelation. After this, the seventh trumpet is sounded and there are loud voices saying, "The kingdoms of this world have become the kingdoms of our Lord and of His Christ."

b. The Major Interval

The beginning of chapter twelve represents the textual midpoint of the book of Revelation and is an interval between the seventh trumpet and the first bowl. Chapter twelve describes the woman clothed with the Sun who is with Child. The chapter is situated positionally at the juncture between the two, three and one-half year, or day periods. It is the position of the church of Thyatira, the Son of Man, the rod of iron, and the central shaft of the menorah. The dragon seeks to destroy the child as soon as it is born. There are a number of references to a three-and-a-half-year period. The Woman symbolizes the fulfillment of the original prophecy from Genesis 3:15 "And I will put enmity between you (the serpent) and the woman, and between your seed and her Seed."

The woman is in the wilderness 1,260 days
(1,260/360 = 3½ years)

She is nourished for a time, times and half a time
(1 + 2 + ½ = 3½)

The beast speaks blasphemies for forty-two months
(42/12 = 3½ years)

Note: both the "gentiles treading" and the "beast" (as destructive events) are identified by 42 months.

The period of the 3½ symbolic years suggests an intermediate time, a time of a pause before the final time. It is my sense that the interval time relates to the "fullness of time" when "God sent forth His Son, born of a woman, born under the law." (Gal 4:4) NKJV. I suggest that the interval between chapters 1–12 and 12–22 represents an interval between the Old Earth and the New Earth. It is a time for the gestation of the son of man who stands in the midst of the lampstands, the child with the rod of iron (12:5).

During these interval periods in Revelation, there are transformative events that I understand to be related to the tree of life working within us despite the enormity of violence on the earth.

The seals are unlocked by the Lion of Judah of the Root of David (4:5)

- The 144,000 of the tribes of the children of Israel are sealed (7:4)
- The little book is given (10:8)
- The temple of God is measured (11:1)
- The two witnesses prophecy (11:3)
- The Woman Clothed with the Sun who is with Child hides from the dragon (Ch 12)
- The earth swallows the flood spewed by the dragon (12:16)
- The Lamb on Mt. Zion with the 144,000 (Ch 14)

Chapter 13:18 mentions the number 666 which, besides being a reference to an individual, may refer to a life without the purposeful direction of the Holy Spirit. It is the idea of a life lived to excess, regardless of its own sustainability. In the same way, that cancer is a living thing, but the life of the tumor threatens the life of the body.

8. THE NUMERICAL CENTRE

The midpoint of Revelation, from chapters 10 to 14, is an important symbolic juncture. The predominant images from 10–14 are comparable to Labuschagne's textual analysis which situates the blessing of Joseph as the centerpiece, the shaft of the menorah within the twelve tribes, and as the son of Jacob who inherits the "favour of the One Dwelling in a Bush." Similarly, the midpoint of Revelation situates the Son of Man, as the center shaft who is "in the midst of the seven lampstands." The image of the Son of Man at the beginning of Revelation is the introductory vision describing the role of the churches (Rev 1:13). The position of the Son as the central entity of the menorah in chapter 14 situates the Son of Man as central to the book of Revelation. The imagery is a reminder of the angel who is "in the midst of the bush," (Exod 3:2) an event which the menorah alludes to.

The midpoint of Revelation is also replete with numerical symbols. Both the two witnesses of chapter 11 and the woman in the wilderness in chapter 12 have multiple references to 3½. To reiterate, the two witnesses prophesy for . . . , the holy city is trodden down for, the witnesses are revived after, the woman is in the wilderness for, she is nourished for and the beast blasphemes for, all instances of 3½. The 3½ is presumably one half of the seven-branched menorah and suggests that the chapters prior to chapter twelve and after chapter twelve are left and right sides of the menorah. As indicated in Table 16 following, there is also a pattern of 3's and 4's prior to the midpoint and a pattern of 7's after, which confirms the completion. In the days of the sounding of the seventh angel, "the mystery of God would be finished." (10:7) The event of the two witnesses in chapter 11 stands as a symbolic action illustrating the form of the book. The two witnesses are the two menorot, and as symbolic time, the witnesses are the sacred center of the numerical seven. The two witnesses prophesy for 3½ years (11:3), they are killed by the beast (11:7) and are revived after 3½ days (11:11). The temple is opened (11:19). These events are just prior to the textual midpoint (12:6–7). At this midpoint (12:5) the woman clothed with the sun bore "a male Child who was to rule all nations with a rod of iron." This is the same verse which is quoted in the blessing to the church of Thyatira, and is a quote from the messianic Psalm, "You shall break them with a rod of iron." (2:7) The positional center of Revelation at 12:5 is the "rod of iron." To further emphasize this imagery, the blessing to the church of Thyatira, the centerpiece church whose messianic descriptor is the 'Son of God' (2:18), will be given the power to rule with "a rod of iron." (2:27)

Some individuals who have suffered unduly under an abusive authority might take this symbol as the ultimate in unrestricted power. From my perspective, I see the 'rod of iron' as a sign of integrity. Jesus displayed these qualities in his respect for women (John 7:53–8:11), his challenge to the burdens of a heavy-handed authority (Matt 23:4), and his ultimate love for all mankind (Luke 23:34).

I would not presume that the symbolic form is a carefully assembled construction by the author. Rather, the author operates from a position of consciousness that assembles the symbolic form in a coherent order. To quote Tillich again, "Man's ultimate concern must be expressed symbolically because symbolic action alone is able to express the ultimate." Or to quote the poet Jessie Sampter, "simplicity is the peak of civilization."

The main point of my thesis is that the Bible despite its obvious historical, social, and legal content is a text written by prophets, seers, scribes, and judges from a revelatory position. The revelatory and symbolic nature of the writer's perspective acts to give coherence to a symbolic framework which in some books is more pronounced than others. Revelation begins with the churches as symbolized by the menorah. It centers the book with the two menorot and the numerous references to seven and its parts. The book of Revelation is also book-ended by the two trees of life which is a singularity, which is represented by the menorah and compares to the placement of the trees at the beginning and end of the Bible.

9. THE SEVEN BOWLS

Following the seven trumpets are the seven bowls of God's wrath (chapter 16). After the sixth bowl, the kings of the earth are gathered for the great day of the battle described as Armageddon. Following Armageddon,[5] the seventh angel pours out his bowl and a loud voice from heaven says, "it is done."

The bowl represents a container of mercy which carries the "prayers of the saints" as well as an offering for atonement. It also implies a time interval in the sense of a grace period, compared to the trumpet which is a time initiator. The seal might be a time capsule. Another aspect of looking at the symbolic relationship of elements is to suggest that they are related to electrical functions. The seal is resistive, the bowl is capacitive, and the trumpet is inductive. The butterfly in the cocoon is in a resistive state. When it has overcome the restrictions of the cocoon it develops the capacity and strength to fly.

These three electrical functions, when tuned together, create specific harmonic frequencies. We could compare the symbolic function to our own electrical state. Clinton Ober's work in *Earthing* shows that we are more of an electric body dependent on the earth's electrical nature than we had

5. *Har Megiddo,* The hill of Megiddo.

previously imagined. Since the advent of plastics, we have insulated ourselves from the natural healing ground which had previously tied us to
earth. From that time, there was a comparable increase in stress-related
and immune-related diseases compared to previous centuries which had
required the treatment of infectious and physical injuries.[6]

The idea that we as humans are electric bodies lines up with more
recent research such as Dr. Bruce Lipton's *The Biology of Belief*, Dr. Joe
Dispenza's *Becoming Supernatural*, Gregg Braden's *The Divine Matrix*, and
Eileen McKusick's work with tuning forks in *Tuning the Human Biofield*.
These examples of a conscious awareness that is mediated by our electric
body are very tangibly illustrated. Dispenza has suggested that thoughts are
electric, and feelings are magnetic,[7] an understanding which also appears
in *Christ Returns*, "the mental/electrical and emotional/magnetic fields."[8]
I was originally inspired by Dr. Stanley Krippner's, *Dream Telepathy* (in
1973).[9] The consciously aware electric body operates independently of the
constraints of a Newtonian cause and effect body.

The bowl has several interrelated meanings such as a cup of offering,
an intercessory vessel, the symbol of a city, the burden of the Redeemer.

Bowl as an intercessory instrument:

> So, Moses said to Aaron, "Take a censer and put fire in it from
> the altar, put incense on it, and take it quickly to the congrega-
> tion and make atonement for them; for wrath has gone out from
> the Lord. The plague has begun." (Num 16:46–48)

> Now when He had taken the scroll, the four living creatures and
> the twenty-four elders fell down before the Lamb, each having a
> harp, and golden bowls full of incense, which are the prayers of
> the saints. (Rev 5:8) NKJV.

Bowl as a city:

> I will make Jerusalem a cup of trembling unto all the people
> round about (Zech 12:2a)

Jesus is our intercessor:

> O My Father, if it is possible, let this cup pass from Me; never-
> theless, not as I will, but as you will. (Matt 26:38–39)

6. Ober, *Earthing*.

7. Dispenza, *Breaking the Habit*, 20.

8. Recorder, *Christ Returns*, 369.

9. Krippner was also kind enough to read my work in 2016 and encouraged me to
continue.

The outpourings of the seven bowls:

- Disease on those who bore the mark of the beast (16:1)
- Blood in the sea every living thing died
- Blood in the rivers
- Sun scorches men with fire
- Beast's kingdom turns to darkness
- Euphrates river dries up—preparation for Armageddon
- "It is done" a great earthquake like no other

10. THE PATTERN OF FOURS, THREES, AND SEVENS

The number seven is obviously a prominent number in Revelation because of the association with the seven churches. Secondly, the seven seals, bowls, and trumpets also emphasize its importance. It is a focus in chapters fifteen with the seven plagues, in chapter seventeen with the beast and the seven horns, and chapter twenty-one with "one of the seven angels who had the seven-bowls filled with the seven last plagues came to me and talked with me, saying, "Come, I will show you the bride, the Lamb's wife."

However, there is also a further pattern within the sevens. The four creatures (beasts) and the four horsemen in chapters four to eight emphasize a four-part. The three-part destruction of a third of all, by the angels of the seven trumpets, emphasizes a three-part. And lastly, the multiple uses of sevens by the angels of the seven plagues, suggest an overall numeric pattern to the outpouring of wrath. The partial (thirds or threes) and a partial (four, fourths, or quarts) are followed by a completion (seven). The fourths and the thirds are prior to the midpoint of chapter 12 which focuses on the time, times, and half-times (3½) which is also the midpoint of the seven times. It is the symbolic centerpiece and representative of the shaft of the menorah. Following the midpoint, and the second part of the 3½, the bowls, the form, describe the completion, the sevens. I suggested that the seal relates to the bud of the menorah like the hull of the seed which protects the life in the kernel and to the notion of potency from Aristotle. The four parts might relate to the elementary forces within the earth, to life. The three parts relate to the aspect of judgment, the pronouncement of the trumpets and the seventh is the completion, the understanding of the mystery of the work of the Lord as it is. This section is not meant to minimize the serious nature of the book, it is meant to show that there can be understanding from within the apocalyptic drama. "Because you have kept My command to persevere, I also will keep you from the hour of trial which shall come upon the whole world, to test those who dwell on the earth." (Rev 3:10)

Is it possible that the pattern of threes and fours is the intended representation on the floor of the church of Glastonbury?

> The very floor, inlaid with polished stone, and the sides of the altar and even the altar itself above and beneath are laden with the multitude of relics. Moreover, in the pavement may be remarked on every side stones designedly interlaid in triangles and squares, and figured with lead, under which if I believe some sacred enigma to be contained.[10]

It is interesting to compare the character of the Messiah with the legendary document ascribed to Jesus' communication with King Abgar of Edessa. The letter reads "I have sealed this letter with my own hand, and I have sealed the letter with seven seals, which are given below."

+ + Ψ E X P Y Δ."[11]

Table 12: Patterns of four's, three's, and seven's

	4s	3s	7s
	7 Seals (Ch 6:1–8:5)	7 Trumpets (Ch 8:6–9:21 and 11:15–19)	7 Bowls (Ch 15–16)
	The Four living creatures individually call out to the Four horsemen, "come."	The seven angels with trumpets	The seven angels with seven plagues. With the last, God's wrath is complete
1	White Horse (with bow & crown) for conquest (6:1)	Hail, fire, and blood on the earth, a Third of earth, trees and grass are burned (8:7)	Disease on those who bore the mark of the beast (16:1)
2	Red Horse (with a sword for war) to remove peace	Mountain is thrown into the sea, a Third of the sea turns to blood, a Third of creatures and ships destroyed	Blood in the sea every living thing died

10. Malmesbury, *Chronicle of the Kings*, 22.

11. Guscin, *Image of Edessa*, Footnote: The explanations (apart from the cross) all depend on the first letter of the relevant Greek word. See: εγώ χερουβείμ etc. p.123

3	Black Horse (with scales) a famine of (1 Quart) of wheat and (3 Quarts) barley for a day's wages, do not touch the olive and vine	Star fell from heaven—Wormwood. A Third of the rivers and waters turn bitter	Blood in the rivers and springs of water
4	Pale Horse (named Death) to kill by sword, famine, and plague. Power over a Fourth of earth.	A Third of the sun, a Third of moon and a Third of stars were struck, a third less light. Woe, woe, woe	Sun scorches men with fire
5	Martyrs are slain for their testimony "How long—to avenge our blood"	Star falls from heaven, the key to the bottom-less pit; Abyss (Abaddon). Do not harm grass, plants or trees or those with the seal of God. Men will suffer agony for five months.	Beast's kingdom turns to darkness
6	Great Earthquake. Sun turns black and the sky recedes as a scroll	A Third of mankind killed by the four angels of the Euphrates. Plagues of fire smoke and sulfur. (9:13–21)	The Euphrates dries up—preparation for Armageddon. The three evil spirits come out of the mouths of the dragon, the beast, and the false prophet.
	First Interval	Second Interval	
	7:1 The Four angels standing at the four corners of the earth. Do not harm until the 144,000 servants of God are sealed.	Angel with the little book. (10:1–2) The two witnesses. (11) The vision of the two olive trees and lampstands Ark of the Covenant revealed (11:19)	

7	Silence in heaven for a half-hour, censer of incense filled with fire hurled to the earth. Thunder, lightning, and earthquakes. (8:1)	The Kingdoms of this world have become the kingdoms of our Lord (11:15)	"It is done" a great earthquake like no other. The great city is split into three parts.
	12:10 Textual midpoint (Eng or Gk)		
		Third Interval	
	Note: In chapters 1–3 there are 16 sevens' No fours until chapter four No threes until chapter four	The woman and the red dragon (Ch 12) (10 horns, 7 heads, 7 crowns) The beast out of the sea (10 horns, 7 heads, 10 crowns) The beast of the earth (2 horns, 666) The Lamb and the 144,000 (14:1) The three angels The harvest of the earth (14:14) Patient endurance of the saints	The woman on the beast (10 horns, 7 heads) The fall of Babylon (Ch. 18)
	4s 13x: (four, fourth, quart(er)) 3x: (seven, (s)). 3x: (three, third)	3s 19x: (third(s), three) 8x: (seven, (s)) 5x: (four, fourth)	7s 10x: (seven (s, th)) 59 sevens (in all of Revelation) 2x: (four, fourth) 3x: (third, three)

11. THE END

Chapters seventeen and eighteen describe the downfall of Babylon the Great.

Chapters nineteen to twenty-two describe the return of the Messiah, the establishment of the New Jerusalem and the tree of life which is on either side of the river of life and to which we have access because the Seed born to the woman prevailed, as well as to those who have kept the words of the Book.

The object of this chapter is to show that the tree of life is operative within the dynamics of the outpouring of wrath as symbolized by the seven seals, trumpets, and bowls. The tree provides the hope of a way of life through the pattern of destruction. The Book of Revelation, which is a symbolically constructed book, seems to reflect the symbolism of the menorah which, in itself, is a stylized tree of life.

THE APOCALYPSE AND THE TREE

The Book of Revelation is troubling because of its apocalyptic nature. However, if we can see through the visions of devastation and understand that there may be a symbolic order to the book, it helps to appreciate that there is a plan within the redemptive purpose.

Chapter 21

Relationship between the Books of Daniel and Revelation

There are many similarities between the books of Daniel and Revelation. The phrase; time, times, and half times is used both by and only by Daniel and John to describe several centuries and possibly millennial periods during which secular and sacred realms wield authority. The dream of King Nebuchadnezzar, which was interpreted by Daniel as a huge statue having a "head of fine gold, its chest and arms of silver, its middle and thighs of bronze, its legs of iron, its feet partly of iron and partly of clay" (Daniel 2), is an example of long-term historic prophecy. The book of Revelation has a similar prophetic view of future events.

There has been some suggestion that Revelation is a continuation of Daniel. Of the approximately 72 instances of the term seal or sealed found in the Bible, 32 are found in Revelation and four in Daniel, half the total number of the whole book. Four times Daniel is told to "seal up the vision," "to seal the words" until the time of the end (8:26, 9:24, 12:4, 12:9). In the reverse, in Revelation the seven seals are opened in chapter six, the 144,000 are sealed and in 22:10 John is told "not to seal the words" because the time is at hand. The book of Revelation is an opening up of the original sealing by Daniel. After the admonition to "shut up the words" in 12:4, Daniel "looked; and there stood two others, one on this riverbank and the other on that riverbank" (12:5) which appears to mirror the tree on either side of the river in Rev. 22:2.

The expression "time, times and half a time" is in Daniel and Revelation. The element of time is unusually specific in both books but remains somewhat of a mystery because of its symbolic nature. The expression in Daniel refers to the beast who will subjugate the saints (7:25) for "time, times and half a time" and the "man clothed in linen" (12:7) who prophesies that the vision will be released after "time, times and half a time." The expression "one thousand two hundred and sixty days" is also found only in Daniel (as 1,290)[1] and Revelation (as 1,260) and is also related as indicated previously showing that $1 + 2 + \frac{1}{2} = 3\frac{1}{2}$ equals 1260/360. In Daniel 12:11 "from the time that the daily sacrifice is taken away, and the abomination of desolation is set up, there shall be one thousand two hundred and ninety days." In Revelation, the two witnesses will prophesy, and the woman will hide in the desert for one thousand two hundred and sixty days or for a time, times and half a time.

In Daniel chapter eight, the ram with two horns is mentioned several times and is said to be the "kings of Medea and Persia." In Revelation 13:11 it speaks of a "beast coming up out of the earth, who had two horns like a lamb and spoke like a dragon possibly relating to the vision of the ram in Daniel.

In Daniel chapter seven, there are four great beasts that came up from the sea, a lion, a bear, a leopard, and one difficult to describe but which had ten horns and a little horn, with "eyes like the eyes of a man, and a mouth speaking pompous words." In contrast and diametrically opposed to the four beasts of Daniel are the "four living creatures" in Revelation. They are a lion, a calf, a man, and an eagle, each having six wings, they are full of eyes and proclaim before the throne "Holy, holy, holy, Lord God Almighty, Who was and is and is to come!" (4:8) The "four living creatures" are mentioned eleven times in Revelation. The only other mention in the Bible are "four living creatures" in Ezekiel (1:5–14) the heads of which have four faces; a man, a lion, an ox, and an eagle like the four living creatures in Revelation. The four great beasts in Daniel are probably an anti-type of the four living creatures in Revelation.

Ezekiel	Man	Lion	Ox	Eagle
Daniel	Man	Lion	Bear	Leopard
Revelation	Man	Lion	Calf	Eagle

1. Whatever the meaning of the 30-day difference, the symbolic times are related because both parties identify with the time, times, and half time which is a form of the 1,260. The added 30 days, or month of Daniel could imply a difference of time between then and the time of Revelation.

> They had the likeness of a man. Each one had four faces, and
> each one had four wings. Their legs were straight, and the soles
> of their feet were like the soles of calves' feet. They sparkled like
> the color of burnished bronze. The hands of a man were under
> their wings on their four sides; and each of the four had faces
> and wings. Their wings touched one another. The creatures did
> not turn when they went, but each one went straight forward. As
> for the likeness of their faces, each had the face of a man; each of
> the four had the face of a lion on the right side, each of the four
> had the face of an ox on the left side, and each of the four had
> the face of an eagle. Thus were their faces. Their wings stretched
> upward; two wings of each one touched one another, and two
> covered their bodies. And each one went straight forward; they
> went wherever the spirit wanted to go, and they did not turn
> when they went. As for the likeness of the living creatures, their
> appearance was like burning coals of fire, like the appearance
> of torches going back and forth among the living creatures. The
> fire was bright, and out of the fire went lightning. And the liv-
> ing creatures ran back and forth, in appearance like a flash of
> lightning. (Ezek 1:5–14) NKJV.

Some would argue that the book of Daniel is written at a later date.
However, Josephus, as a first century witness, describes the fulfillment of
Daniel's prophecies.

> There should arise a certain king that should overcome our na-
> tion and their laws, and should take away their political govern-
> ment, and should spoil the temple, and forbid the sacrifices to be
> offered for three years' time. And indeed, it so came to pass, that
> our nation suffered these things under Antiochus Epiphanes,
> according to Daniel's vision, and what he wrote many years
> before they came to pass. In the very same manner Daniel also
> wrote concerning the Roman government, and that our country
> should be made desolate by them. All these things did this man
> leave in writing, as God had showed them to him, insomuch
> that such as read his prophecies, and see how they have been
> fulfilled, would wonder at the honor wherewith God honored
> Daniel; and may thence discover how the Epicureans are in an
> error, who cast Providence out of human life.[2]

The books of Daniel and Revelation reveal that, in as much as we
have symbolic signs, we also have symbolic times. The symbolic signs are
easier to imagine within our present circumstance, however symbolic times

---

2. Josephus, *Antiquities*. X.11.7

require a very dispassionate and impartial view of history. It is a view that can appreciate the circumstances of the time and understand the movement that is humanity's desire for a better life as well as to identify the circumstances that have caused evil and bloodshed. The purpose of Revelation is to understand the time. "Blessed is the one who reads the words of this prophecy and blessed are those who hear it and take to heart what is written in it because the time is near." (Rev 1:3 NIV)

In the following chapter, I included a quotation from the work of Henry Grattan Guinness who describes periods of very long-term sacred cycles and cycles of tyranny based on Daniel's times and weeks of years. These chronological patterns compare to the pattern of the menorah, the number seven and a midpoint of 3½ cycles. Secondly, I suggest Bernard Lonergan's notion of cosmopolis as an outline of the movement towards compassionate humanity.

Chapter 22

Moving Forward

SACRED TIMES, HUMAN PROCESS

As much as there are sacred signs, there are also sacred times. Do some events have a qualitative unity wherein very many occurrences combine to form an integrated whole? Many have experienced time slowing down as in accidents, or also in what I might call comic convergence, where thousands of people instantly perceive some idiosyncrasy, or in times of war or extreme crisis where some good has prevailed which could only be explained by a supernatural occurrence. In retrospect, history has rationalized these events or relegated them to their anecdotal files. However, what is rational is what is relevant at the level of what is understood. Beyond our understanding, there exists a transcendent realm with its own operative conditions. "The heart has its reasons which reason does not understand." (Blaise Pascal, *Pensées*). "Le cœur a ses raisons, que la raison ne connaît point. On le sent en mille choses. C'est le cœur qui sent Dieu, et non la raison. Voilà ce que c'est que la foi parfaite, Dieu sensible au cœur."

Grattan Guinness (1835–1910) in *Light for the Last Days* (1886) has suggested that there are long-term cycles of sacred prophecy. Early Biblical scholars have always equated Daniel's "seventy weeks" or 490 years (7 x 70) to the anointing of "the Most Holy" after which "Messiah shall be cut off" and in another instance the "prince who is to come Shall destroy the city and the sanctuary" (Daniel 9). Guinness has suggested that there are further periods of 2,520 years (7 x 360) or variations thereof depending on lunar, solar, or sacred cycles. These periods may correspond to a "time of the gentiles" and a completion of a sacred cycle. Writing in 1886 Guinness suggested:

> The secret things belong to God. It is not for us to say. But there can be no question that those who live to see this year 1917 will have reached one of the most important, perhaps the most momentous, of these terminal years of crisis.[1]

Apparently, Arthur Balfour was aware of the prophetic importance of this date leading up to the Balfour Declaration. General De Lisle also encouraged a reluctant Allenby (who had been discouraged by previous attempts to take Palestine) to accept the mandate to take Jerusalem suggesting that the cycle of oppression against a Jewish remnant had reached its conclusion. In the film documentary, *The Destiny of Britain,* Guinness' grandson critiques the current notion that we are in the final days, (as described in *Remnant* or *Left Behind*) suggesting that that was not indicated by the book title.[2] The documentary is hosted by Kelvin Crombie.

The quotation from Guinness is included to suggest that there is a symbolic order to time outside of our very mundane perception.

A more rational approach to human process might be Lonergan's notion of cosmopolis.

LONERGAN COSMOPOLIS

> Practical intelligence necessitates classes and states, and no dialectic can promise their permanent disappearance. What is both unnecessary and disastrous is the exaltation of the practical, the supremacy of the state, the cult of the class. What is necessary is a cosmopolis that is neither class nor state, that stands above all their claims, that cuts them down to size, that is founded on the native detachment and disinterestedness of every intelligence, that commands man's first allegiance, that implements itself primarily through that allegiance, that is too universal to be bribed, too impalpable to be forced, too effective to be ignored.[3]

1. Guinness, *Light for the Last Days.* 255. Henry Grattan is a descendant of Arthur Grattan Guinness who founded the brewery.

2. Youtube: https://www.youtube.com/watch?v=n7fVkgwQwtw (accessed 2016 April) conversation with Rev. Peter and Michele Guinness, the grandson of Henry Grattan Guinness. Discussing the environment at the time of the late 1800s and the liberation of Jerusalem in 1917. The segment is part of a documentary titled *The Destiny of Britain,* by Hatikva Films.

3. Lonergan, *Insight,* 238.

Chapter 23

The Function of the Eternal in the Temporal

According to Lonergan's theory of cognitive operations, we approach transcendence as we move from experience to understanding and by understanding to judgment and eventually to making decisions that move us beyond our immanent reality. Our desire is that eventually, we become a part of a larger whole wherein we arc vitally connected. We hope that "swords will be turned into plowshares" and that the "wolf will dwell with the lamb"—two examples where a former reality has been radically transformed and opposing viewpoints are reconciled.

From what I understand of Lonergan, the cognitive operations, from experience to judgment are mirrored in the metaphysical being which I understand to be the soul of the individual. Experience is mirrored in potency, understanding reflects the form of things, and judgment is reflected in act. The cognitive and sequential order of understanding, our understanding that one and one is two or that day follows night, is mirrored in a part of us which is not as determined by process but by being.

Right next door to our sequential life is a life of timelessness, a life where we are at home with the totality of the universe. Our typical Western lifestyle demands that we get things done and that we have a purpose for everything. Is it possible that we have unlearned and deprived ourselves of being? In Isaiah 11:6 it says, "the calf and the lion. . . and the little child shall lead them." What does the little child have over the experienced, decisive, knowledgeable adult? If the function of experience, understanding, and judgment is mirrored in potency, form and act, then there is another innate part of being human that can respond to life in all its forms and act to engage, respond, and go beyond our present disconnected reality. We will have transcended the limitations of our present state and we will be able to participate fully with all of creation.

I believe that this is the notion of the Tree of Life. On the one hand, it acts as a symbolic frame of reference that helps us to grasp the known unknown. On the other hand, it appears to be a very present, but elusive, reality. It does not appear present in the concrete sense, but it is traceable through its various elements. How else can we explain the fact that two separate authors, separated by millennia, describe the existence of the same tree, a tree that has the unusual qualities of Life? The tree is subsumed within the entire Bible. It is not referred to as present, but only by inference until the author of Revelation has a vision of its future import towards the very end of the book. The nature of the tree of life is contained within creation but hidden from our natural perspective.

According to Genesis 1:26, man was made in God's image and likeness. We are made in the image of the I AM. We have the inherent capacity to understand what eternity means. From our ponderous insight by insight development, we have an opportunity to grasp the unknown through our transcendent understanding, that intrinsic to our makeup is a quality of the eternal. We have the capacity to transcend from our chronological state to a state of unity in infinity. Presumably, that is the goal of most religions, that is the desire to understand the sacred.

Chapter 24

Conclusion

I hope to have shown that the tree of life is an underlying, but primary form which is represented throughout the Bible. It is present as a beginning and an end and is singular in nature. There is only one tree of life. In its apparent absence, it reveals itself through multiple elements as the Seed, the menorah, the burning bush, the oil of anointing and in the person of the Anointed One. The tree reveals that there is an organic consistency to the Bible. The book is understood in its relationship to eternal life as symbolized on an elementary level by the tree. It has a fundamental form that corresponds to our own understanding of life and our self-appropriation of transcendent consciousness.

Although the notion of a tree of life is difficult to grasp, we know that it represents a known unknown which we can intelligently approach through understanding. As mankind, we can hope that, as we move through our process of awareness, a process of evolved consciousness, we will approach a new reality that is infinitely more life-affirming and inclusive of creation in its totality. In Romans 11, Paul suggests that as foreigners, we are grafted in as wild branches to the cultivated olive of the patriarchs. The activity of being grafted into the tree points to our historical redemption as much as the tree in Revelation points to a future redemption of the species.

I also hope to have illustrated that, through a conscious attentive process, mankind can approach a transcendent consciousness which signals a new relationship, beyond our personal, tribal, and national concerns, to an understanding that we are a unique organism, in heartfelt relationship to a very real, concrete, and yet supra-conscious God.

I would like to have written a book, so that in some distant future, whether in this world or the next, I will be able to read what I had written and say to myself, yes that makes sense, now I can continue from where I had left off.

Notes on Drawing

The green tree of life represents the continuity of the tree throughout creation, albeit in other forms. It shows up as Noah's olive leaf which is a token of universal peace for all mankind. It is also represented in Isaiah. The anointed One is described as a "Rod from the stem of Jesse, and a Branch shall grow out of his roots." We are ultimately redeemed from the curse of separation by the cross of Christ. Paul attests to this when he says, "cursed is everyone who hangs on a tree" (Gal 3:13b) and that Christ has redeemed us from the curse of the law.

The ochre represents the continuity which originates from the Seed of the woman in Genesis 3:15, to its completion in Revelation 22:16, "the root and offspring of David." The ochre links the Seed to the Oil of Anointing in Exodus 30, the promise of a Messiah (Dan 9), the two olive trees which are the two anointed ones (Zech 4), to the Christ, the anointed, and finally the seven lampstands which are the seven churches and the two witnesses of Revelation chapters one and eleven.

The red represents disastrous events in the life of Israel. These events are described by Judges, Samuel, and Habakkuk and are contrary to the slow, but prosperous, work of the olive. The Red also symbolizes the four horsemen, described in Zechariah and Revelation as harbingers of disaster. It also represents the bloodline of the Messiah.

The dimensions of the drawing follow the ratio of the Ark of the Covenant which was 1½ x 2½ cubits or approximately 27" x 45," the ratio being 1.6:1. The leaves of the tree which symbolize the "healing of the nations" (Rev 22:2), also represent the wings of the cherubim guarding the ark as well as the door to the Garden of Eden. Each wing has 36 leaves for a total of 144 (4 x 36). The leaves could be taken to mean the 12 fruits of the 12 months (Rev 22:2), the 12 tribes of 12,000 (Rev 7), or the 144,000 virgins (Rev 14). Lastly, the Hebrew for "life," חי is equal to 18 in gematria (2 x 18 = 36), in the

Hebrew letter—numbering system. These dimensions are mostly symbolic using artistic license to convey the design.

The dark blue represents the river of life.

In a comment to Sara Terreault, an associate professor at Concordia, I suggested that my conception was my *Mondrian* (1872–1944) design for the Bible. Professor Terreault had recently given a lecture showing the development of Piet Mondrian's art form from very realistic tree forms to his more widely known elementary squares, which I was not aware of.

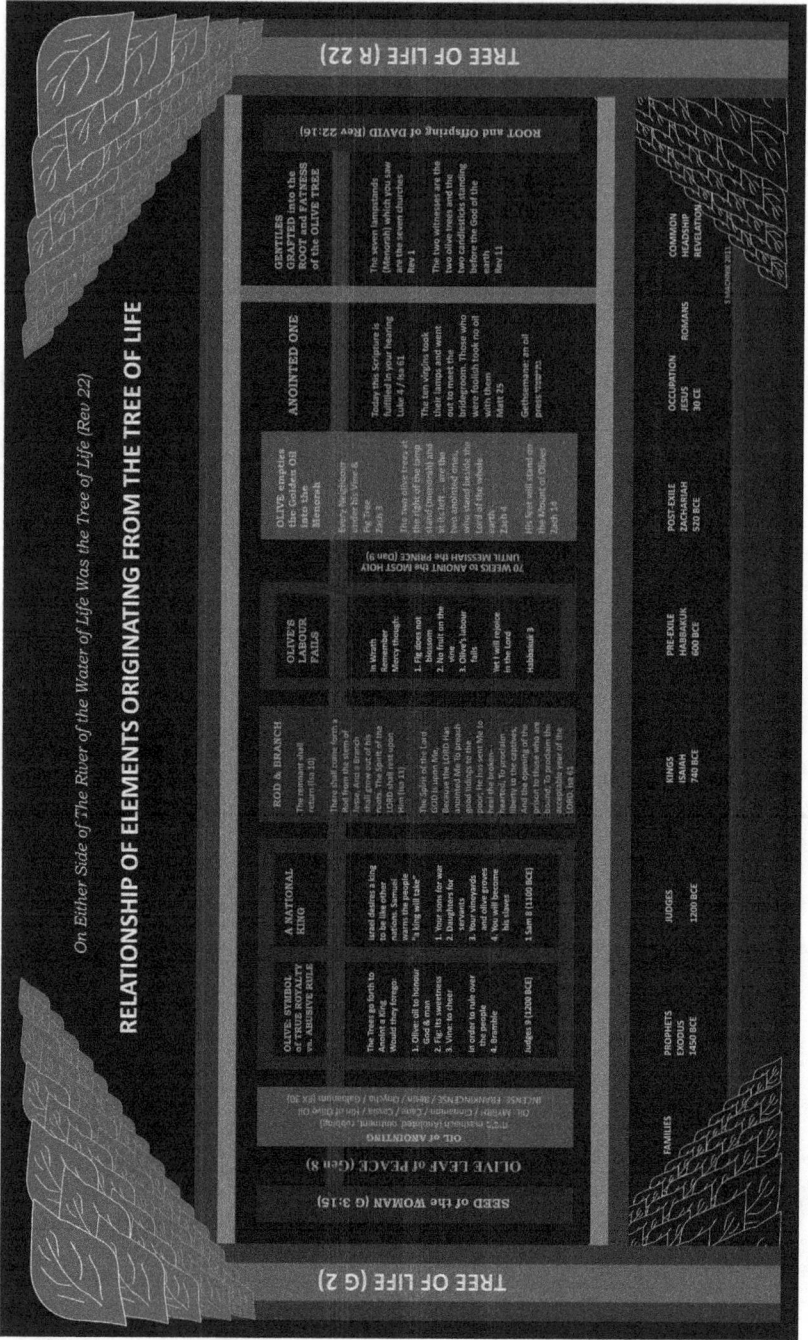

On Either Side of The River of the Water of Life Was the Tree of Life (Rev 22)

RELATIONSHIP OF ELEMENTS ORIGINATING FROM THE TREE OF LIFE

Figure 25: The River of Life; design by author

Appendix Overview

The appendices are a reference system to support the historical or etymological basis of the main text. They are not intended as part of the main book but are given as background material for further research. Most of the reference texts predate the 20th century. The biographies are generally derived from the Dictionary of National Biography edited by Leslie Stephen and published between 1885 to 1900, as well as the Encyclopaedia Britannica from a similar period. I used the first paragraph of the biography to situate the place of origin of the writer and the last paragraph which contained his or her major works. Some biographies are available from Wikisource and can be accessed at that location as in: https://en.wikisource.org/wiki/Author:William_Shakespeare and further referenced at https://en.wikisource.org/wiki/Shakespeare,_William_(DNB00), which is the listing from the Dictionary of National Biography. The Shakespeare file contains approximately 50 pages of text as accessed on May 21, 2020. And see for a complete listing: https://en.wikisource.org/wiki/Dictionary_of_National_Biography,_1885–1900

Appendix 1

The Rosary-Cross

The Rosary is a Catholic tradition and prayer beads existed long before the Reformation. Many Christians are averse to the saying of repetitious prayers. However, I sense that there is a strategic intent on the part of heaven, to the implementation of the rosary. The veneration of Mary is not the same as the worship of Christ. In Luke 1:28 the angel addresses Mary as "Rejoice, highly favored one, the Lord is with you; blessed are you among women!" Mary later says to Elizabeth, "henceforth all generations will call me blessed." (Luke 1:48b NKJV). In my Baptist Hymnal (Convention, 1956) which has many of my favorite songs, of the 554 hymns only one, number 73, is dedicated to Mary. As a Christian, I try to walk a fine line between doctrines.

The origin of the word *bead* in the OED is identified as ME. *bede*, OE. *bedu*, OFris. *bede*, OS. *bede*, Du. *bede*, mod.G. *bitte*, Goth. *bida*, OHG. *beta*, f. Goth. *bidjan*, in OE. *biddan*, to pray, see Bid. And, the first description is: 1. Prayer, and connected senses. c 885. K Aelfred, *Baeda*. 1b. In later usage (after sense 2 became the popular one) there was almost always a reference direct or indirect to the use of the rosary. The origin of the word *bead* in the Hebrew appears to be variously translated as *bead* (Song 1:10,11), *turn* (Esth 2:12,15), *form, shape,* (Gen 29:17), *turtledove* (Gen, Lev), תור *tor*.

A well-known thoroughfare in London, which housed publishing houses was called Paternoster Row and next to it were Ave Maria Lane and Amen Corner. It is thought that prayer beads were made there. There is also the legend attributed to the monk Nennius in his *History of the Britons* (c.830) that during the battle near Guinnion castle, "Arthur bore the image of the Holy Virgin, mother of God, upon his shoulders, and through the power of our Lord Jesus Christ, and the holy Mary, put the Saxons to flight."[1]

In the Jewish tradition, the LORD spoke to Moses, saying that the tassel was used to remind us of God's presence. "Speak to the people of Israel, and bid them to make tassels on the corners of their garments throughout their generations, and to put upon the tassel of each corner a cord of blue; and it shall be to you a tassel to look upon and remember all the commandments of the LORD." (Numbers 15:38–39a) RSV.

I had originally wanted to make an abacus for my granddaughter to help her understand numbers. In the end, it developed into a Rosary, which had ten indentations with a blue bead for the Hail Mary's and five indentations with a white bead for the Lord's Prayer. One green bead represented the completion of five decades, one of the three mysteries, and the saying of the Apostles Creed.

I only recently started praying the Rosary and later came to understand the history behind it. A friend of my parents, Jim Shaw, who had worked with Dorothy Day in New York and who had stayed with us for a few months, wrote a book on the Rosary and the history of Cap de la Madeleine near Trois Rivieres. This gave me some insight into its history.

Also, Gilbert Durand's psychological dynamics appeared to correspond to the three mysteries. This was an important insight for me because it provided a psychological understanding of the events. We are made in the image of the I Am, we partake in His suffering for the reconciliation of humanity and we believe in the glory to come. The mystery of the Incarnation, that is God becoming man, is the first of the three mysteries, and could be described as the beginnings of human consciousness. That is, that we are not just flesh and blood but that we have a spirit that can identify with God's Holy Spirit which is here to connect us with the divine, our primordial identity. The second and third mysteries are the Sufferings of Jesus and the Resurrection.

There is also a sense of sacred history underlying human history and the history of the Rosary illustrates part of that dynamic. There is a historical development that underlies the evolution of consciousness. Consciousness has a form and at different periods, a more refined level of consciousness manifests itself as mankind develops. Examples would be: 1. The Magna Carta (1215): 2. the trials at Nuremberg after WWII which addressed our system of justice (1945–1946). A government should be held accountable for genocide: 3. Mahatma Gandhi's principle of non-violence (early 1900s): 4. the United Nations; The Universal Declaration of Human Rights (1948),

---

1. Nennius, *History of the Britons*, 29.

and; 5. Martin Luther King's, "I have a dream,—all men are created equal
. . ." (1963). The 1960s were also a time of spiritual awakening.

St. Dominic (8 August 1170—6 August 1221) is usually associated
with the beginnings of the rosary. An early development occurred in 1571,
1000 years after the birth of Mohammed, the Ottoman Empire tried to
conquer Italy and the Vatican. Christianity was outnumbered by the naval
forces that threatened them. The Pope asked for help from Christian nations
but in the end, only a few nation-states responded. He asked laypersons
and soldiers and sailors alike to pray the Rosary and a decisive victory was
achieved against the larger Ottoman force. It was known as the Battle of
Lepanto, October 7, 1571. The Ottoman casualty rate was four times that of
the Christian. Miguel de Cervantes (1547–1616), the author of Don Quix-
ote, was in the Spanish naval infantry at the time. The victory was attributed
to the praying of the Rosary and the Pope later founded the feast of Our
Lady of Victory on October 7th. The name of a Quebec City Church probably originates from the Pope's commemoration. The following is a copy of
the plaque commemorating the defeat of the English in 1688. General Wolfe
later conquered Quebec in 1759.

> NOTRE-DAME-DES-VICTOIRES
> CONSTRUITE EN 1688
> NOMMÉE AINSI A LA SUITE
> DU SIÈGE DE PHIPPS ET DU
> DÉSASTRE DE LA FLOTTE DE WALKER
> ELLE EST LA PLUS ANCIENNE
> EGLISE DE PIERRE DU QUEBEC

Figure 26: Notre Dame des Victoires Church in Quebec City 1688 AD

The Battle of the city of Vienna also played an important role where
Christians were compelled to defend their civilization against Moslem
forces. The battle began on September 11, 1683. Victory was attributed to
the saying of the rosary by the Polish, German, and Austrian troops. According to the activist Brigitte Gabriel, Osama Bin Laden's 9/11 attack on
New York was perpetrated in part to exact revenge for this Moslem defeat.
After WWII, parts of Austria were still under Soviet control. Fr. Petrus Pav-
licek, after making a pilgrimage to Mariazell, the principle Marian shrine in
Austria, was told by an interior voice: "Do as I say and there will be peace."
He encouraged Austrians to publicly pray the Rosary and after ten years in
1955, the Russian army quietly left Austria, unlike what happened to Hun-
gary (1956) and Poland. The town of Mariazell has an interesting history.
In 2007 Pope Benedict XVI visited to celebrate the 850th anniversary of

the Shrine of Mariazell, which was founded in 1157 AD. Following WWII, 5,000 Soviet troops were billeted in the town.

Sister Lucia, one of the three children present at Fatima, writes, that the apparition of Our Lady ended her initial message with the direction, "Pray the Rosary every day, in order to obtain peace for the world, and the end of the war." (May 13, 1917) Sister Lucia continues, "To pray the Rosary is something everybody can do, rich and poor, wise and ignorant, great and small." She continues, it is "a prayer which is within our reach." "We need to count, in order to have a clear and vivid idea of what we are doing." "God, ... chose to stoop to the simple ordinary level of all of us."[2]

In Randall Sullivan's *The Miracle Detective*, an account of the apparition of Mary at Medugorje in Bosnia and Herzegovina, the Madonna tearfully "pleads for peace" and repeatedly warns that "religious divisions were the work of evil."[3] The apparitions began in 1981. The eventual conflict from 1992–1995 in the former Yugoslavia, involved the Orthodox Serbs, the Catholic Croats, and the Muslims. In an unusual development, on September 4, 2020 Kosovo is the first Muslim majority country to establish diplomatic ties with Israel. Serbia and Kosovo will set up their embassies in Jerusalem.[4]

It is sometimes difficult to appreciate the level of historical disinformation. The Vietnamese history teacher and poet Nguyen Chi Thien (d. 2012) was jailed for 27 years for suggesting that the United States and not the Soviet Union had bombed Hiroshima and had conquered Japan. Why would anti-nuclear activists protest against the United States government and not the Russian government for the bombing? While in prison Thien memorized his 700 poems and later was able to put them to paper. In the Message of Fatima in 1917 Mary asked Christians to pray for the consecration of Russia. The following is a patent application for a Rosary-cross.

2. https://www.ncregister.com/blog/joseph-pronechen/fatimas-sister-lucia-explains-why-the-daily-rosary-is-a-must attributed to Sister Lucia's book *Calls from the Message of Fatima*.

3. Sullivan, *Miracle Detective*, 246.

4. https://www.nytimes.com/aponline/2020/09/04/us/politics/ap-us-united-states-balkans.html accessed September 13, 2020

ROSARY—PRAYER BEAD COUNTER[5]

This is a device to keep track of prayers. It is made of a material, most commonly of wood, in which there are indentations to accommodate prayer beads which are held in line by a string or wire.

Typically, and there can be other variations, there are three beads which represent the most common prayers in the Christian tradition. That is, the Apostle's Creed, the Lord's Prayer and the Hail Mary.

The device can be of any shape, but it is usually a rectangular bar with indentations on one side for the Apostle's Creed and the Lord's Prayer and indentations on the opposite side for the Hail Mary's. The wire/string element is held in place at the end of the bar which maintains tension on the wire.

The advantage and claim:

The advantage of the Prayer Bead Counter is that it keeps track of the position of the last prayer. There is a long-standing and worthwhile tradition of prayer beads held in place by a string. The claim of the following device is that it is more compact and has the advantage of a 'memory' in the sense that the bead records the last position of the last prayer.

The following is one example of the device.

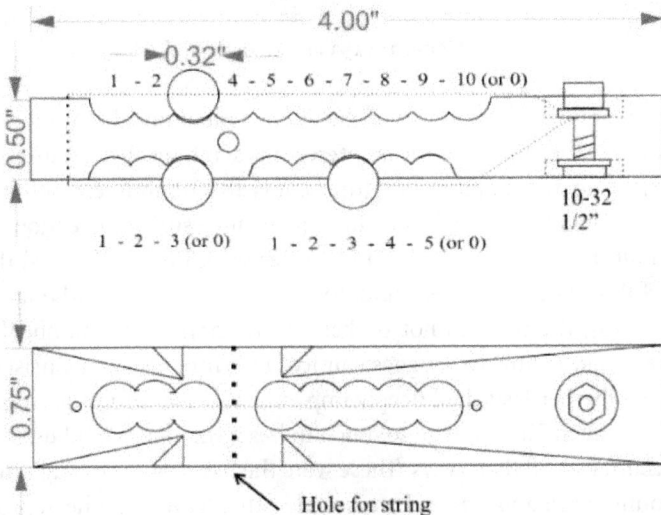

Rosary-Prayer Bead Counter
Designed by Stephen Machnik, January 2019

Figure 27: Prayer bead counter

5. Canada patent application 3,077,788.

Number 153 and the Rosary

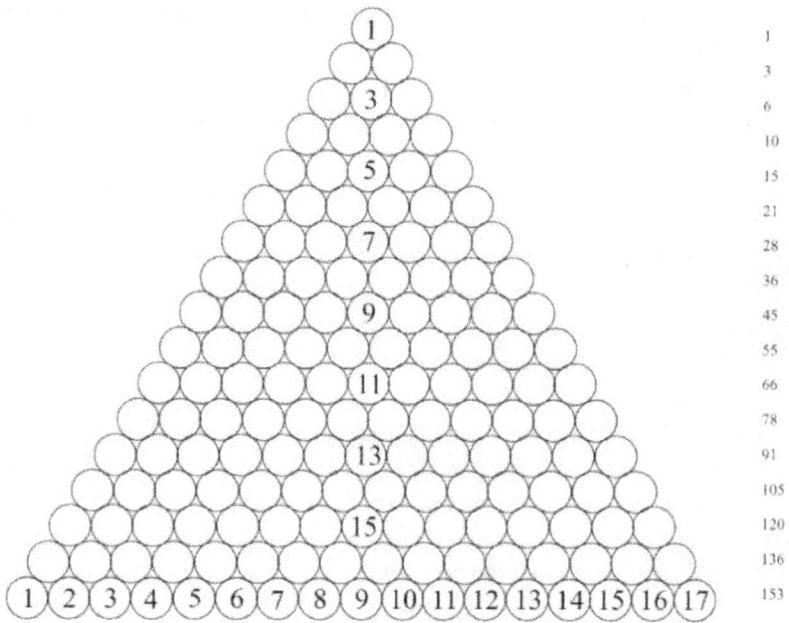

Figure 28: 153 as a triangle

Louis de Montfort in his Secret of the Rosary mentions the number—153 Hail Mary's.[6] The number 153 is interesting symbolically because it corresponds to the decades, fives and threes. It is also reminiscent of the number of fish caught in an episode subsequent to Jesus' resurrection which makes it all the more unusual. "Simon Peter went up and dragged the net to land, full of large fish, one hundred and fifty-three; and although there were so many, the net was not broken." (John 21:11) The number 153— ἑκατόν πεντήκοντατριῶν—suggests unity (1), trinity (3), and Christ (5).[7] I wondered whether Jesus had deeply impacted the lives of 153 persons who would have taken His message so much to heart that they could do nothing but proclaim it in all their ways. These were the fish that were caught up. We can account for 12 apostles and 70 disciples, that leaves 71 others, probably many known and unknown women such as Mary Magdalene.

6. Montfort, Secret of the Rosary, 26.

7. The one's are all representative of unity and the threes of the trinity. If you want a 'rational' explanation for the symbolism of the number five, the units of anointing oil (the word origin for the name of the messiah/Christ) are all multiples of five (Exod 30:23)

In the world of numbers, 153 is also interesting for the following properties:

Table 13: Number 153

```
1+2+3+4+5+6+7+8+. . . 17      = 153
1! +2! +3! +4! + (5x4x3x2x1)   = 153
9 x 17                         = 153
```

The Jewish Encyclopedia says that there are 153 occurrences of the Tetragrammaton in the book of Genesis. However, I only counted 141. I'm not sure why there is a discrepancy.

Appendix 2

Genealogy of Jesus

In Haggai 2:23 Zerubbabel (gen #56 in Table 14) is prophesied to be a "signet" as is evident in the line of David. "In that day, saith the LORD of hosts, will I take thee, O Zerubbabel, my servant, the son of Shealtiel, saith the LORD, and will make thee as a signet: for I have chosen thee, saith the LORD of hosts." Zerubbabel recombines the descendants of Nathan and Solomon in the line of Christ as in the chart. Zerubbabel reverses the curse of Jeconiah. "*As* I live," says the LORD, "though Coniah the son of Jehoiakim, king of Judah, were the signet on My right hand, yet I would pluck you off." (Jer 22:24)

In Lionel Smithett Lewis' *St. Joseph of Arimathea at Glastonbury*[1] He records the existence of manuscripts giving the genealogy of Jesus, His family, and His relationship to Joseph of Arimathea. Lewis was the Vicar of Glastonbury for more than three decades and wrote extensively on the legend and its basis in history. He references the following MSS.

1. English College of Arms, Heralds Office: Roll 33, Box 26

2. *Annales Cambriae*, Harlean MSS, British Museum, 3859, f. 193b

3. MS 20, Jesus College

---

1. Lewis, *Joseph of Arimathea*, 155–9.

Table 14. Genealogy of Jesus

	Luke 3:34–38			Luke 3:23–38		Matt 1:1–17
	Adam	21			Abraham	
2	Seth	22			Isaac	
3	Enos	23			Jacob	
4	Cainan	24			Judah	
5	Mahalalel	25			Perez	
6	Jared	26			Hezron	
7	Enoch	27			Ram	
8	Methuselah	28			Amminadab	
9	Lamech	29			Nashon	
10	Noah	30			Salmon	
11	Shem	31			Boaz	
12	Arphaxad	32			Obed	
13	Cainan	33			Jesse	
14	Shelah	34			David	
15	Eber	35		Nathan		Solomon
16	Peleg	36		Mattathah		Rehoboam
17	Reu	37		Menan		Abijah
18	Serug	38		Melea		Asa
19	Nahor	39		Eliakim		Jehoshaphat
20	Terah	40		Jonan		Joram
		41		Joseph		Uzziah
		42		Judah		Jotham
		43		Simeon		Ahaz
		44		Levi		Hezekiah
		45		Matthat		Manasseh
		46		Jorim		Amon
		47		Eliezer		Josiah
		48		Jose		Jeconiah
		49		Er		
		50		Elmodam		
		51		Cosam		
		52		Addi		
		53		Melchi		
		54		Neri		
		55			Shealtiel	
		56			Zerubbabel	
		57		Rhesa		
		58		Joannas		
		59		Judah		
		60		Joseph		
		61		Semei		
		62		Mattathiah		
		63		Maath		
		64		Naggai		
		65		Esli		
		66		Nahum		Abiud
		67		Amos		Eliakim
		68		Mattathiah		Azor
		69		Joseph		Zadok
		70		Janna		Achim
		71		Melchi		Eliud
		72		Levi		Eleazar
		73		Matthat		Matthan
		74		Heli		Jacob
		75		Joseph		Joseph
		76			Jesus Christ	

In the publication *Y Cymmrodor, The Magazine of the Honourable Society of the Cymmrodorion*. It contains the text of *The Annales Cambriae and Old Welsh Genealogies*, from Harleian MS. 3859.[2]

However imperfect the record, I have set it out in the table following to serve as a reference point. Ann, the maternal grandmother of Jesus is shown to have had three husbands, Joachim, Cleopas and Salome (a male). Mary the daughter of Cleopas and wife of Alphaeus has four sons who become the half-brothers of Jesus. Later the monk, John of Glastonbury (in the 14th century), records descendants of Joseph of Arimathea (through Josephes and Helaius) to the ninth generation showing a female descendent Ygerna who is said to be the mother of Uther Pendragon and grandmother of King Arthur. However, these records are difficult to confirm.

> The kingdom of Wessex began about the year of grace 495 under Cerdic and his son Cynric. In the eleventh year of Cerdic, when Utherpendragon, the brother of Aurelius Ambrosius, had been killed with poison, his son Arthur, a youth of fifteen years, began to reign over the Britons. He was born of his mother Igerna in Cornwall, in a castle called Tintagel. Thus through his mother he was descended from the noble decurion Joseph of Arimathaea, who buried the Lord Jesus. Helains[3], Joseph's nephew, begat Josue. Josue begat Aminadab. Aminadab begat Castellors. Castellors begat Manael. Manael begat Lambord and Urlard. Lambord begat a son who begat Igerna, of whom Utherpendragon begat the noble and famous King Arthur.[456]

Pedigrees from Jesus College MS 20[7]
[IV. Fo. 34b]

2. *Y Cymmrodor*, Vol. IX, 141–183.

3. Aka: Alain le Gros, see *The Chronicle of Glastonbury*, 1985 fn. 83

4. Glastonbury, *Chronicle of Glastonbury*, 73.

5. Carley, James P. *John of Glastonbury. Cronica sive Antiquitates.* (British Archeological Reports 47i 1978) p.89

6. Regnum Westsaxonum incepit Cerdico et Kynrico filio suo circa annum gracie quadringentesimum nonagesimum quintum. Huius Cerdici anno decimo Uterpendragun, fratre Aurelii Ambrosii, ueneno extincto, incepit regnare super Britones filius suus Arthurus, quindecim annorum iuunis. Natus quippe est matrem Igerna in Cornubia in quodam castro Tintagel uocitato. Traxit utique originem per matrem ab illo nobili decurione Ioseph ab Armathia qui Dominum Ihesum sepeliuit. Helains enim nepos Ioseph genuit Iosue. Iosue genuit Aminadab. Aminadab genuit Castellors. Castellors genuit Manael. Manael genuit Lambord et Urlard. Lambord genuit filium qui genuit Igernam, ex qua rex Uterpendragon genuit nobilem et famosum Arthurum. Hiis diebus floruit Sanctus Gildas doctor eximius et Britonum historiographus.

7. *Y Cymmrodor*, Vol. VIII, 83–97

M. Kasswallawn. yn amser y kasswallawn hwnw y kymellawd y rufeinwyr treth o ynys prydein. Kaswallawn M. beli mawr M. Anna. yr anna hon oed verch y amherawdyr rufein. yr anna hono a dywedei wyr yr eifft y bot yn gyfynnithderw y veir vorwyn.

[V]

Eweint m tepwyll m Vrban m Grad m Kwnedyl m Kudeern m Tegant m Kyndeern weldic m elud m eudos m eudolen m auallach m aphlech m Beli mawr vab. anna val y mae vchot.

[VI. Fo. 35a.]

Cuneda. M. Edern. M. Padarn beisrud. M. tegyth M. Iago. M. genedawc. M Cein. M. Gorein. M Doli. M. Gwrdoli. M. Dwfyn. M. Gordofyn. M. Anuueret. M. eimet. M. Dibun. M. Prydein. M. Ewein. M. Auallach. M. Amalech. M. Beli. M. Anna. val y dewetpwyt vchot.

An entry from the Harleian MS. 3859: 193b Col. I,[8] possibly from the 11th century gives the following:

Amalech qui fuit beli magni filiuf. et anna mater eiuf quam dicunt effe confobrina mariae uirginif matrif.d'ni n'ri ih'u xp'i.
Amalek, who was the son of Beli the great and his mother Anna, who they say is a cousin of the Virgin Mary mother of Our Lord Jesus Christ.

The following table is difficult to develop from sources and I hope I haven't added to the confusion. According to the Protoevangelium of James, Joachim and Anna were without child until visited by an angel. Their daughter Mary was therefore an anointed child and was dedicated to the temple at the age of three for a period of twelve years.

---

8. *Y Cymmrodor*, Vol. IX. Art. The Annales Cambria and Old-Welsh Genealogies from Harleian Ms. 3859. Edited by Egerton Phillimore pp.141–183, p.170 of the review. In Phillimore's footnote he suggests: Sometimes the contractions for "Iesus Christus" (ih's xpc or the like), and for "Dominus noster" (dn's n'r). 151.

Table 15: Family of Jesus

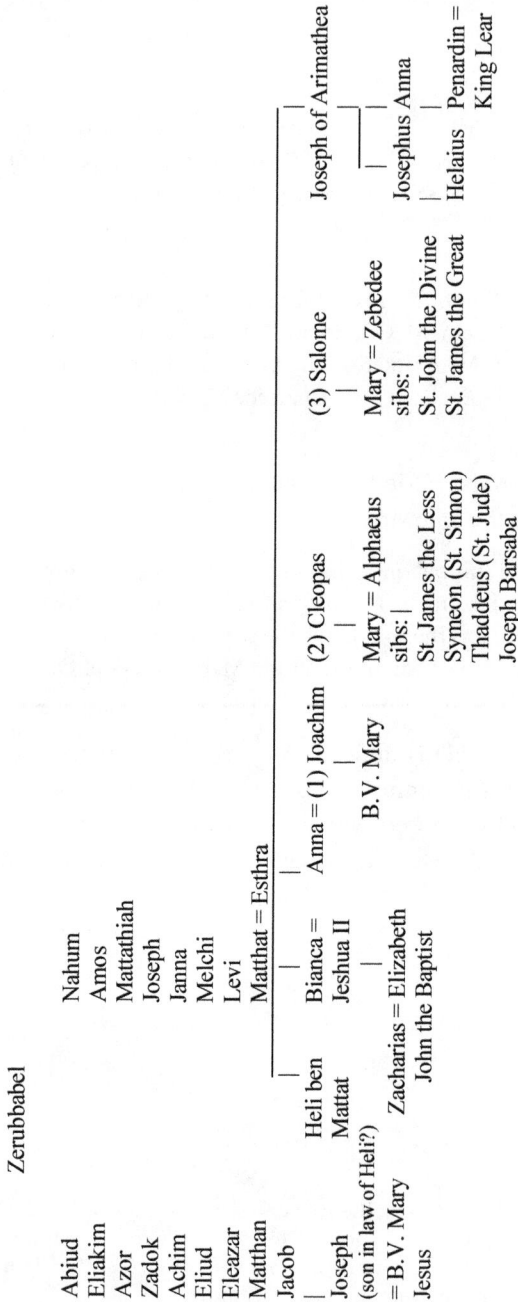

Zerubbabel

Abiud
Eliakim
Azor
Zadok
Achim
Eliud
Eleazar
Matthan
Jacob

Nahum
Amos
Mattathiah
Joseph
Janna
Melchi
Levi
Matthat = Esthra

Heli ben Mattat

Joseph
(son in law of Heli?)
= B.V. Mary

Jesus

Bianca = Jeshua II

Zacharias = Elizabeth
John the Baptist

Anna = (1) Joachim

B.V. Mary

(2) Cleopas

Mary = Alphaeus
sibs: |
St. James the Less
Symeon (St. Simon)
Thaddeus (St. Jude)
Joseph Barsaba

(3) Salome

Mary = Zebedee
sibs: |
St. John the Divine
St. James the Great

Joseph of Arimathea

Josephus Anna

Helaius   Penardin =
King Lear

Data from: English College of Arms, Heralds Office: Roll 33, Box 26; Jesus College MS 20; Harleian MS. 3859: 193b Col. I.; Lewis, St. Joseph, 155–58.

Appendix 3

Sacred history and its relationship to Glastonbury

Table 16. Chronology of legends and events related to Glastonbury Abbey (G.A.)

CENTURY	Kings. Legendary and recorded	Abbot Disciple	Chronicler or Author	Pope	Events Glastonbury Abbey (G.A.)
	BRITISH				For ref. code: AC, AU, EH, etc. see the end of the chart.
	Brutus 1050 BC.		E. O. Gordon, The founding of London 1050 BC. HB P4		
			Sir Edward Creasy, 1000 BC. British tin mines supplied Solomon's temple		
	Beli Mawr 130 BC.		Herodotus, 484–25 BC, British tin trade. 400 BC.		
	Llyr (or King Lear)		Diodorus Siculus, British tin trade. 60 BC.		
	Kymbelinus (or Cymbeline) as in Shakespeare				

#				
1	Arviragus	Joseph of Arimathea / Cornish tradition	Peter 30–67 / Linus 67–76	Joseph quarried his own tomb. Jerome's Vulgate refers to him as *"nobilus decurio"*

The possible relationship of Beli Mawr/Anna, who is a cousin of the Virgin Mary AC Fol. 193b
Joseph was a "tin-man", he exported tin from Cornwall to the Middle East
Disciples to France CH BkII-IX; HB BkIV; CH XII-XVI; CH P3,39,51;
Joseph of Arimathea comes to England 36 AD. Befriended by King Arviragus.
C P6–10; CH Bk I Ch VIII S 8; CG P3–17 etc.
Maria Magdalena mortua est. Tigernachi Annales. AD 54.
2nd arrival of J of A after a commission by St. Philip 63 AD. The Glastonbury Thorn

			Anacletus 76–88 / Clement 88–99 / Evaristus 99–105	
		Juvenal the poet	"The proud Arviragus come tumbling down." The poet Juvenal to Emperor Domitian (51-96 AD).	
	Marius CH BkII ChX / Also: CG P53 (d. 125)	Sir Henry Spelman	Alexander I 105–115 / Sixtus I 115–125	Brass plate testifying to Joseph's arrival. C P9 (Spelman 1562-1641)
	Coel CH BkII ChXI / "Old King Cole"	R.F.S. Cressy	Telesphorus 125–136	Death of Joseph. July 27, 82 AD. CH Bk2 Ch12
2	Lucius c. 136–181 AD. and his dau. Gwladys of Britain (Silures tribe) Wife of Cadfan of Britain of Cambria and dau. Helena merch Cadfan. Wife of Constantius I Chlorus 250–306		Hyginus 136–140 / Pius I 140–155 / Anicetus 155–166 / Soterius 166–174 / Eleutherius 175–189 / Victor I 189–199	King Lucius requests the support of Pope Eleutherius. C P31; EH, 167 AD, P307. Sts. Fagan and Damian sent to England. GR P21; CH BkIII ChIX aka: Phaganus and Diruvianus CG P3, 59–63. 166 AD.

Note: Bede has Pope E. at 167 AD. B. V, C. 24
Construction of Glastonbury Abbey by Lucius 163 AD.

		Tertullian 155–240	Zephyrinus 199–217 / Natali 199–200	The British Isles are subject to Christ. (Tertullian)
3			Callistus 217–22 / Hippolytus 217–35 / Urban I 222–30 / Pontain 230–35 / Anterus 235–36 / Fabian 236–50 / Cornelius 251–53 / Novatian 251–58 / Lucius I 253–54 / Stephen I 254–57 / Sixtus II 257–58	Constantine the Great 272–337 AD. Said to be the first Christian emperor of Rome, converted at the Battle of the Milvian Bridge on October 28, 312 after adopting the sign of Christ: ☧. His mother St. Helena (Flavia Iulia Helena Augusta "of the Cross.") A.k.a. Helena of Colchester is said to have found the Holy Sepulcher and the Cross of Christ.
		Eusebius 260–340	Dionysius 259–68 / Felix I 269–74 / Eutychian 275–83	*The Ecclesiastical History of Eusebius Pamphilus. pp. 5, 22* "(The apostles) visited ... the distant shores of Britain"
			Caius 283–96 / Marcellinus 296–304	
4			Marcellus I 308–9 / Eusebius 309 / Miltiades 311–14 / Sylvester I 314–35 / Marcus 336 / Julius I 337–52 / Liberius 352–366 / Felix II 355–365 / Damasus I 366–84 / Ursicinus 366–67 / Siricius 384–99	St. Helena. Possible ancestral relations to Coel II King of Colchester de Camulod (de Bretagne) a descendant of Beli Mawr. Another alleged relation is Helena merch Cadfan, wife of Constantius I Chlorus, Roman Emperor (250–306). Daughter of Cadfan of Britain of Cambria, III and Gwladys Princess of Britain (Silures tribe) AC Fol. 193b. See: https://www.geni.com/people
5	Welsh Kings Padarn Beisrudd c. 400 Cunedda ap Edern Einion Yrth ap Cunedda c. 470–500 Cadwallon Lawhir ap Einion c. 500–534		Anastasius I 399–401 / Innocent I 401–17 / Zosimus 417–18 / Eulalius 418–19 / Boniface I 418–22	

Patrick arrived in Ireland in the ninth year of the reign of Theodosius the Less and in the first year of the episcopate of Xistus, (Sixtus–432?) 42nd bishop of the Roman Church. So, Bede, Maxcellinus and Isidore compute in their chronicles. (Annals of Ulster 432.1) multiple records of d.o.d. St. Patrick d. 493 AU 492 and 493. St. Patrick (361–473) at Glastonbury. CG P59–67, Patrick's mother is the sister of St. Martin of Tours CG P59. The vision of Patrick CG P65

	Welsh Kings cont'd. Maelgwn Gwynedd 534–547 Rhun Hir ap Maelgwn 547–586 Beli ap Rhun 586–599 Iago ap Beli 599–616		Celestin I 422–32 Sixtus III 432–40 Leo I 440–61 Hilarius 461–8 Simplicius 468–83	Christianity in England 439 AD. AU 439–524 The Angles come to England in 464 AD. AU 469
	U496.1	An eclipse of the sun was visible.		
	U & AU represent *The Annals of Ulster*			
	Vortigern Vortimer Aurelius Ambrosius Uther Pendragon	St. Benignus d.467 CG P3, 69–71, d. 468 AC St. Brigid of Kildare 453–524 (b. 454, AC) Maelgwyn of Llandaff 450	Felix III 483–92 Gelasius I 492–6 Anastasius II 496–8 Symmachus 498–514 Laurentius 498–501	Vortigern invites the Saxons Hengist and Horsa to fight the Picts. EH, AD 449 P. 309. Uther P. is the brother of Aurelius Ambrosius CG P73 467 AD. Death of Uter Pendragon, king of England, to whom succeeded his son, King Arthur, who instituted the Round Table. AU 467
6	U512.2	There was an eclipse of the sun.		
	Invasion of Anglo–Saxons	St. Columba 521–597		Hormisdas 514–23 John I 523–6 Felix IV 526–30 Boniface II 530–32	Maelgwn Gwynedd 534–547 AD, said to have died during the Justinian Plaque Columba AC, (AD 521–595); AU 519 or 523–601. Repose of Colum Cille (Columba) on the fifth of the Ides of June in the 76th year of his age. AU 595
			Time of the prophet Melkin who preceded Merlin CG P55. "Merlin prophetically foretold Arthur" HB P212		
	Arthur Followed by SAXON Reign			Dioscorus 530 John II 533–5 Agapetus 535–6	Arthur's reign: d. 542 AD (Geoffrey of Monmouth). HB P193 Battle of Mount Badon AD 516: CH Bk X Ch XII; AC, AD 516; GR Bk I Ch I
	Is Bede not clear: EH Bk I Ch 16–17 450 AD? Arthurs Dream HB P 179. Arthur changes his coat of arms from three red lions with heads turned backward, (from Brutus) to green, with a silver cross with the image of the Virgin and Child. CG P 79 Arthur fights Cerdic CG P3, 75 Arthur dies in battle with Mordred. AC, AD 537; HR, AD 542 P193; CG, 542 AD P31; 81 HB P193 542 AD.			
	Battle of Baedon 516	"The Battle of Badon, in which Arthur carried the Cross of our Lord Jesus Christ for three days and three nights upon his shoulders [or shield] and the Britons were the victors" A.C.			
	Death of Arthur 537				"The Strife of Camlann in which Arthur and Medraut perished". A.C.
	Cerdic 1st king of Saxon Wessex, 519–534	Saint David 500–589		Silverius 536–7	*Life* (of David) by Geraldis Cambrensis. Son of Sant and his mother St. Non born in Cardigan CG P81 Cerdic & (son) Cynric CG, (AD 495), P73
	540 U554.2	Baillie. Comet strikes southwest Britain A pestilence i.e. leprosy called the sámthrosc			
	Cynric 534–560		Saint Gildas 516–570	Vigilius 537–55	*De Excidio et Conquestu Britanniae* (G.B.) Gildas son of Kau Gildas CG, P 75; AU 570, (AD 512)
	Ceawlin 560–592	St. Augustine d.604		Pelagius I 556–61 John III 561–74	Augustine to England. AU 598 (AD 597); EH 597.
	Ceol 592–597			Benedict I 575–9 Pelagius II 579–90 Gregory I 590–604	Augustine meets King Ethelbert of Kent and British bishops EH Bk II Ch II, 603
	U591.1	An eclipse of the sun, i.e. a dark morning.			
7	Ceolwulf 597–611	Worgret		Sabinian 604–6 Boniface III 607	Battle of Caer Legion (Chester) in which 1200 monks are killed. AU 613.
	Cynegils 611–642	Lademund		Boniface IV 608–15 Adeodatus 615–8	EH Bk II Ch II, (603 AD)
	U614.2	A star was seen at the eighth hour of the day.			
	Cwichelm 626–636	Bregored	CG P73	Boniface V 619–25 Honorius I 625–38	The battle of Cadwallon, king of the Britons and Ainfrith AU 632
	MERCIAN Dynasty	Beorhtwald		Severinus 640 John IV 640–2	
	Penda 645–648			Theodore I 642–9	
	U664–668	The Plague reached Ireland on the 1st of August. "the buide Chonaill"			

		In Mag Itha of Fotharta, the plague first raged in Ireland. From the death of Patrick 203 years, and from the first mortality 112 years.			
	U665.3	The falling asleep—from the same pestilence i.e. the buide Chonaill—of Féichéne of Fobar, and Ailerán the learned, and Crónán son of Silne.			
	U670.1	A great snowfall occurred. A great famine.			
	U672.4	An abundance of mast.			
	CERDICING Dynasty			Martin I 649–55	
	Cenwalh 642–5 and 648–674			Eugene I 654–7; Vitalian 657–72	Cenwalh. *Chronicle of the Kings of England* (pub.1125 AD). pp. 21–25
	Seaxburh 672–674			Adeodatus II 672–6	
	Cenfus 674			Donus 676–8	
	U677.1	A bright comet was seen in the months of Sept. and October.			
	Æscwine 674–676			Agatho 678–81	
		Adamnán the abbott of Iona		Leo II 682–3; Benedict II 684–5; John V 685–6	Adamnán proceeded to Ireland and gave the Lex Innocentium to the people. AU 697
	Centwine 676–685; Cædwalla 685–688			Conon 686–7; Sergius I 687–701; John VI 701–5	Adamnán, abbot of Í, rests in the 77th year of his age. AU 704. Ina. Reconstructs G.A.
	Start of 8th C.			John VII 705–7	EH, (688 AD), P 330
	Ina 688–726	St. Cuthbert	Bede 673–735	Sisinnius 708; Constantine 708–15; Gregory II 715–31	Ina. Charter to G.A. 725 AD. St. Cuthbert (c. 634– 20 March 687) monasteries of Melrose and Lindisfarne
	Æthelheard 726–740	St. Indract 688–726; St. Æthelwold of Lindisfarne (d.740)		Gregory III 731–41; Zachary 741–52; Stephen II 752–7; Paul I 757–67; Stephen III 767–72; Adrian I 772–95	Birth of Bede? AU 650 or 654. The slaying of Indrechtach son of Dúnchad of Muirisc AU 707. Bede composed a great book this year. AU 712. Bede rested, AU 735. The date of Easter is changed in the monastery of Í. AU 716.
	Cuthred 740–756; Sigeberht 756–757				Cuthred: Charter to G.A. April 30, 745. Bishops of G.A. CG P37
	U689.8	Part of the sun was obscured.			
8	U700.6; U709.5	Famine and pestilence prevailed in Ireland for three years, so that man ate man.			
	U718.8	A pestilence called bacach with dysentery in Ireland.			
	U734.2	An eclipse of the moon at its full. A lunar eclipse on the eleventh of the Kalends of February.			
	U745.1	A horrible and wonderful sign was seen in the stars at night.			
	U746.2	Dragons were seen in the sky.			
	U753.1	A dark sun.			
	U760.6	Famine and a great mast-crop.			
	U762.1	A great snowfall and a dark moon.			
	U763.5	A dark sun at the third hour of day.			
	U764.1; U764.4	A great snowfall which lasted almost three months. A great scarcity, and famine. An abnormally great drought.			
	U765.9	A great scarcity and famine.			
	U769.6	A shortage of bread.			
	U773.4; U773.7	An earthquake and famine; and a leprous disease attacked many. An abundance of oak-mast.			
	U786.9; U788.4	Unaccustomed drought and heat of the sun. Nearly all bread-grain failed. An abundance of oak-mast afterwards.			
	U794.7	A dark moon on the second of the nones 4th of December. A pestilence called scamach. The moon became red like blood on the twelfth of the Kalends of March. The devastation of all the islands of Britain by heathens.			
	Cynewulf 757–786	Geoffrey d.782		Leo III 795–816	
9	Beorhtric 786–802	Aethelwine		Stephen IV 816–7	
	U802.9	Coluim Chille was burned by the heathens.			
	U806.1; U806.6	In which a great pestilence broke out in the island of Ireland. A great crop of mast.			
	U807.6	The moon was turned to the colour of blood.			
	Egbert 802–839	Wigbeorht d.800		Paschal I 817–24	

U825.7	A great pestilence in the island of Ireland affected the old, the children and the weak; there was great famine and shortage of bread.			
U826.6	Great terror in all Ireland, i.e. from a warning of plague given by Iellán's son of Mumu.			
U836.8 U840.8	A great crop of mast, both nuts and acorns, and as a result the streams became blocked up and stopped running. In this year below the Norsemen first came to Ireland			
Æthelwulf 839–858	Wigthegn d.836		Eugene II 824–7 Valentine 827 Gregory IV 827–44	Cinaed son of Ailpín, king of the Picts, and Ethelwulf, king of the Saxons, d. AU 858
Æthelbald 858–860	Alfstan d.842		Sergius II 844–7 Leo IV 847–55	
Æthelberht 860–865	Tunbeorht d.876		Benedict III 855–8 Nicholas I 858–67	
U858.2 U864.4 U865.1	Cinaed son of Ailpín, king of the Picts, and Ethelwulf, king of the Saxons, died. Muiredach son of Niall, abbot of Lugbad, dies. A solar eclipse on the Kalends 1st of January, and a lunar eclipse in the same month.			
Æthelred I 865–871			Adrian II 867–72	
Alfred the Great 871–899			John VIII 872–82 Marinus I 882–4 Adrian III 884–5 Stephen V 885–91 Formosus 891–6 Boniface VI 896 Stephen VI 896–7	Born at Wantage, Berkshire, in 849, Alfred was the fifth son of Aethelwulf, king of the West Saxons. https://www.royal.uk/alfred-great-r-871-899 Alfred appears to be the first royal listed on royal.uk as accessed May 2020.
U878.8	There was a lunar eclipse on the Ides 15th of October, the fourteenth of the moon, on the fourth feria about the third watch; and a solar eclipse on the fourth of the Kalends of November 29 October, the twenty-eighth of the moon, on the fourth feria, about the seventh hour of daylight, fifteen solar days having intervened.			
U885.5 U891.9	A solar eclipse and stars were seen in the heavens. The sea cast up a woman in Scotland, whose length was 195 feet; the length of her plaits 17 feet; the finger of her hand 7 feet; the length of her nose 7 feet; and altogether she was as white as a swan.			
	St. Neot d.870?		Romanus 897 Theodore II 897 John IX 898–900	
1 0	U911.3 U912.8 U917.1	Two suns ran together on the same day, i.e. on the day before the Nones of May 6. A dark and rainy year. A comet appeared. Snow and extreme cold and unnatural ice this year, so that the chief lakes and rivers of Ireland were passable and causing death to cattle, birds and salmon. Horrible portents also: the heavens seemed to glow with comets; and a mass of fire appeared with thunder in the west beyond Ireland, and it went eastwards over the sea.		
U921.9 U935.5 U950.6	A lunar eclipse on the third feria, the fifteenth of the Kalends of January at the first hour of night. An abundance of oak-mast. An abnormally great mast-crop.			
Invasion of the Danes	Daniel d. 956 Aelfric d. 988		Benedict IV 900–3 Leo V 903 Sergius III 904–11	Many Saxons fell but Athelstan, king of the Saxons, enjoyed a great victory. AU 937
Edward The Elder 899–924 Æthelstan 924–939 Edmund I 939–946 Eadred 946–955 Eadwig 955–959 Edgar I (the Peaceful) 959–975			Anastasius III 911–3 Lando 913–4 John X 914–28 Leo VI 928 Stephen VIII 929–31 John XI 931–5 Leo VII 936–9 Stephen IX 939–42 Marinus II 942–6 Agapetus II 946–55	Edmund I: Charter to Glastonbury. St. Edmund is killed by the Vikings for defending his Christianity. "When Athelstan died without immediate successors, his half brother Edmund successfully suppressed rebellions by the Mercian Danes. Edmund I was murdered at a feast in his own hall, at the age of 25 in 946, after only seven years on the

				John XII 955–63 Leo VIII 963–4 Benedict V 964	throne, and his brother Edred succeeded him." https://www.royal.uk/edmund-i-r-939-946
		St. Dunstan 909–988		Leo VIII 964–5 John XIII 965–72 Benedict VI 973–4	
	Edward the Martyr 975–978 Æthelred II 978–1016			Benedict VII 974–83 John XIV 983–4 John XV 985–96 Gregory V 996–9	
	U965.1	Great and intolerable famine in Ireland, so that the father was wont to sell his son and daughter for food.			
	U981.3	An abnormal mast-crop in the above year.			
1 1	U1018.7 U1023.1	A comet appeared this year for the space of a fortnight in the autumn season. A lunar eclipse on the fourteenth day of the January moon, that is, on Thursday the fourth of the Ides 10 of January. A solar eclipse, moreover, a fortnight afterwards on the twenty-seventh of the same moon, Thursday the ninth of the Kalends of Feb. 24 Jan.			
	U1066.3 U1087.8 U1093.7 U1094.8	A great harvest of nuts in all Ireland, so that it hindered the rivers. A great harvest of mast in this year. A great harvest of mast in this year. Extremely bad weather throughout Ireland, which gave rise to want.			
	Edmund II (Ironside) 1016 Cnut the Great 1016–35 Harthacnut 1035–42 Edward the Confessor r.1042–1066			Sylvester II 999–1003 John XVII 1003 John XVIII 1003–9 Sergius IV 1009–12 Benedict VIII 1012–24 John XIX 1024–32 Benedict IX 1032–45 Sylvester III 1045 Benedict IX 1045 Gregory VI 1045–6 Clement II 1046–7 Benedict IX 1047–8 Damasus II 1048 Leo IX 1049–54 Victor II 1055–7 Stephen X 1057–8	"In 1042 Edward 'the Confessor' became King. As the surviving son of Ethelred and his second wife, Emma, he was a half-brother of Hardicanute, through their mother. With few rivals (Canute's line was extinct, and Edward's only male relatives were two nephews in exile), Edward was undisputed king; the threat of usurpation by the King of Norway rallied the English and Danes in allegiance to Edward." https://www.royal.uk/edward-iii-confessor-r-1042-1066
	Harold II 1066 William I of Normandy 1066–87 William II 1087–1100		Domesday Book 1086 AD	Nicholas II 1058–61 Alexander II 1061–73 Gregory VII 1073–85 Victor III 1086–7 Urban II 1088–99	Domesday book: Glastonbury recorded as XII hides of land which are called "The Secret of the Lord" CG P3 The 12 hides were originally donated by Arviragus, Marius and Coel. CG P57 W of N "ravaged the church of Glastonbury" CG P39
1 2	Henry I 1100–35	Herlewinus 1102		Paschal II 1099–1118 Gelasius II 1118–9 Callistus II 1119–24 Honorius II 1124–30	
	U1108.8 U1108.9 U1115.1	A great harvest of oakmast throughout all Ireland. A fruitful year with good weather and plenty of corn and mast this year. Extremely bad weather in the form of frost and snow from the fifth of the Kalends of January 28 Dec. to the fifteenth of the Kalends of March 15 Feb., or a little longer, and it inflicted slaughter on birds and beasts and men, and from this great want arose throughout all Ireland, and particularly in Laigin.			
	U1116.5	There was a great pestilence; hunger was so widespread in Leth Moga, both among Laigin and Munstermen that it emptied churches and forts and states, and spread through Ireland and over sea, and inflicted destruction of staggering extent.			
		Henry de Blois	Chrétien de Troyes	Innocent II 1130–43 Celestine II 1143–4	*Perceval, the Story of the Grail*, (CT) 1169–1181
	Stephen 1135–54	Henry de Saliaco	Mr. Willis	The finding of Arthur's tomb AD 1170 (or 1191) or 1278 see Gerald of Wales De Principis Instructione	

	Henry II 1154–89		Walter Map (1140 – c. 1210) chronicler for Henry II. *De nugis curialium*. William of Malmesbury 1095–1143 CG P7. Malmesbury: *Gesta pontificum Anglorum* (Deeds of the English Bishops), *Gesta regum Anglorum* (Chronicle of the Kings of England) *De Antiquitate Glastonie Ecclesie Vita Sancti Dunstani*. 1184: Destruction of abbey records by fire		
	Richard I 1189–99 John 1199–1216		Lucius II 1144–5 Eugene III 1145–53	*The Life of Gildas* (c.1130–1150)	
			Anastasius IV 1153–4 Adrian IV 1154–9 Alexander III 1159–81 Lucius III 1181–5 Urban III 1185–7 Gregory VIII 1187 Clemen III 1187–91		
		Caradoc of Llancarfan	Celestine III 1191–8 Innocent III 1198–1216		
			Geffrei Gaimar. *Estoire des Engleis* (1130?)		
			Henry of Huntingdon 1088–1157 *Historia Anglorum*		
			Geoffrey of Monmouth 1100–1155. *Historia regum Britanniae* 1136 AD *Life of Merlin, Aurora*		
13	Henry III 1216–72	Petrus Riga 1140–1209	Honorius III 1216–27 Gregory IX 1227–41		
		Savaricus d.1205	Giraldus Cambrensis 1146–1223	Celestine IV 1241 Innocent IV 1243–54	*De instructione principis* (Arthur's tomb) *Giraldi Cambrensis Opera* de Boron *Joseph d'Arimathe* (1200)
		Robert de Boron	Alexander IV 1254–61 Urban IV 1261–4 Clement IV 1265–8		
	Sept 11, 1276 Earthquake – St. Michael's on Tor				
	Edward I 1272–1307	John of Taunton d. 1291 CG P7	Adam of Domerham d.1291	Gregory X 1271–6 Innocent V 1276 Adrian V 1276 John XXI 1276–7 Nicholas III 1277–80 Martin IV 1281–5 Honorius IV 1285–7 Nicholas IV 1288–92 Celestine V 1294	*Perlesvaus* 13th C French Arthurian romance, also called *Li Hauz Livres du Graal* (The High Book of the Grail). *Historia de rebus gestis Glastoniensibus* (A of Domerham) CG P7
14	Edward II 1307–27	Geoffrey Fromont 1303		Boniface VIII 1294–1303 Benedict XI 1303–4 Clement V 1305–14	
	Edward III 1327–1377	Adam de Sodbury (abbot of G.A. 1323–1334)	John of Glaston-bury 14th C	John XXII 1316–34 Benedict XII 1334–42 Clement VI 1342–52 Innocent VI 1352–62	*The Chronicle of Glastonbury Abbey*. 1342 Edward III visits G.A. 1331. On June 10, 1345, Edward III authorizes John Blome to search for Joseph of Arimathea's grave.
	Richard II 1377–99	John of Breyton 1334–42	Urban V 1362–70 Gregory XI 1370–8		
	House of Lancaster:	Walter de Monington 1342–75	Urban VI 1378–89 Boniface IX 1389–1404		
	Henry IV 1399–1413	John Chinook 1375–1420	Innocent VII 1404–6		
15	Henry V 1413–22 Henry VI 1422–1461 Henry VI (2nd r.) 1470–71	John Capgrave 1393–1464	Martin V 1417–31 Eugene IV 1431–47 Nicholas V 1447–55		
	Jeanne d'Arc (6 January c. 1412 – 30 May 1431) "The Maid of Orléans" (French: La Pucelle d'Orléans)				
	House of York: Edward IV 1461–70 Edward V 1483 Richard III 1483–85 House of Tudor: Henry VII 1485–1509	Callistus III 1455–8 Pius II 1458–64 Paul II 1464–71 Sixtus IV 1471–84 Innocent VIII 1484–92 Alexander VI 1492–1503			

	Monarchs	Authors	Popes	References
		Richard Pynson	Pius III 1503 Julius II 1503–13	*Lyfe of Joseph of Armathia* 1520. Printed by Pynson.
16	Henry VIII 1509–47 Edward VI 1547–53 Mary I 1553–58 Elizabeth I 1558–1603 James VI/I 1567–1625 Of Scot. VI: 1567–1625	John Leland 1503–1552	Pius III 1503 Julius II 1503–13 Leo X 1513–21 Adrian VI 1522–3 Clement VII 1523–34 Paul III 1534–49 Julius III 1550–5 Marcellus II 1555 Paul IV 1555–59 Pius IV 1559–65	*Collectanea*. Joseph of Arimathea and disciples land at Marseilles (35 AD). Cardinal Cesare Baronio (1538 –1607)
	The Battle of Lepanto, October 7, 1571		Pius V 1566–72	
			Gregory XIII 1572–85 Sixtus V 1585–90 Urban VII 1590 Gregor XIV 1590–1 Innocent IX 1591 Clement VIII 1592–1605	
17	James I of Eng. 1603–25 Charles I 1625–49 Cromwell Interregnum 1649–60	R.F.S. Cressy 1605–1674	Leo XI 1605 Paul V 1605–21 Gregory XV 1621–23 Urban VIII 1623–44	
	Charles II 1660–85 James II 1685–8 William III 1689–1702	William Dugdale 1605–1686	Innocent X 1644–55 Alexander VII 1655–67	Dugdale. *Monasticon Anglicanum*. 1693 Cressy. *The church–history of Brittany*. 1668
			Clement IX 1667–9 Clement X 1670–6	
	The Battle of the City of Vienna September 11, 1683		Innocent XI 1676–89 Alexander VIII 1689–91 Innocent XII 1691–1700	
	Thomas Hearne, 1678–1735, *The History and Antiquities of Glastonbury* 1722			
18	Anne 1702–7 George I 1714–27 George II 1727–60 George III 1760–1820		Clement XI 1700–21 Innocent XIII 1721–4 Benedict XIII 1724–30 Clement XII 1730–40 Benedict XIV 1740–58 Clement XIV 1769–74 Pius VI 1775–99	
19	George IV 1820–30 William IV 1830–7 Victoria 1837–1901		Pius VII 1800–23 Leo XII 1823–29 Pius VIII 1829–30 Grego XVI 1831–46 Pius IX 1846–78 Leo XIII 1878–1903	
	1928. Rev. Lionel Smithett Lewis rediscovers tomb of Joseph of Arimathea. Capt. p. 93, Eedle p. 219			
20	Edward VII 1901–10 George V 1911–36 Edward VIII 1936 George VI 1937–1952 Elizabeth II, b. April 21, 1926, r. June 2, 1953		Pius X 1903–14 Benedict XV 1914–22 Pius XI 1922–39 Pius XII 1939–58 John XXIII 1958–63 Paul VI 1963–78 John Paul I 1978 John Paul II 1978–2005	
21			Benedict XVI 2005–13 Francis 2013	

LIST OF REFERENCE LETTERS

AC *Annales Cambriae*, Harlean MSS, British Museum, 3859

AU *The Annals of Ulster*. *http://www.ucc.ie/celt/published/T100001A/index.html*
Accessed April 7, 2017 (Note: typically, the year is -1 from the entry number)

C Spelman, Henry. *Concilia*. (1639. Early English Books Online)

CG Glastonbury, John of. *The Chronicle of Glastonbury Abbey*. Ed. James P. Carley.
Trans. David Townsend (1342. Reprint, Suffolk UK: The Boydell Press, 1985.)

CH Cressy, Serenus. *The church-history of Brittany* (1668. Early English Books Online)

EH Bede, The Venerable. *Ecclesiastical history of England. Also, the Anglo-Saxon
chronicle*. (7th C). (1887. London, George Bell)

GR Malmesbury, William of. *Gesta regum Anglorum. The history of the English kings*.
Trans. J. A. Giles (1090–1143. Reprint, Covent Garden UK, 1847)

HB Geoffrey of Monmouth, *History of the Kings of Britain*. Trans. Aaron Thompson. (c.
1150. Reprint, Cambridge, Ontario 1999) 1100–1155

List of Popes: *The Catholic Encyclopedia* http://www.newadvent.org/cathen/12272b.
htm

History of earth comet strikes: http://www.barry.warmkessel.com/4related.html

The reference for King Lucius, the first Christian king of Britain, is taken from geni.
com.[1]

MANUSCRIPTS WHICH ATTEST TO THE ORIGINS OF BRITAIN AND GLASTONBURY

This appendix might seem excessively long. The basic idea, as well as the relationship to symbolic form, is described in the chapter titled Glastonbury.
At the same time, the historical evidence illustrates quite conclusively a historical trajectory that has not been properly corroborated. This evidentiary
trail will inevitably lead to many more unusual streams of history.

Ancient British Tin Trade

E. O. Gordon. *Prehistoric London*.[2] (Llandn)
London Founded 1050 BC.
Sir Edward Cressy. *History of England*[3]

"The British tin mines mainly supplied the glorious adornment of Solomon's
Temple."

1. https://www.geni.com/people/St-Lucius-Lleuver-Mawr-King-of-the-Silures/
6000000000396294595

2. Gordon, *Prehistoric London*, Covenant, (1946).

3. Cressy, *History of Britanny*, Vol. 1, 18.

The history of the tin industry is an important reference point showing that the sea-going tribes of Israel (Asher and Zebulon) and the Phoenicians who bordered on the same, carried on an extensive metal trade between the south-west of Britain and the Middle East. This trade at the time of Jesus was the source of Joseph of Arimathea's wealth and position in the land of Judah. The whereabouts of Jesus is unknown between age 12 and the beginning of His ministry. It appears that even the townspeople did not recognize Him when He first preached, suggesting that He was living elsewhere. Legend suggests that he accompanied His great-uncle Arimathea on his voyages and that He built a house of wattle and clay to honor His mother.

Roman and Greek Historians and the Tin Trade with Britain

The Greeks and Romans had some idea that tin was being imported from Britain but were unable to ascertain the location since the Phoenician traders would run their ships aground rather than have their source of revenue discovered. In the *American Journal of Archaeology, Sources of Tin and the Beginnings of Bronze Metallurgy*, James D. Muhly argues for the origins of the tin trade. He suggested that the "on-the-ground evidence for tin smelting" in the Bronze Age was "exceedingly rare" and the evidence for this process could only be found at St. Austell in Cornwall. Further that, the Aegean world was making extensive use of the tin found in "Cornwall and Devon, and Brittany, (the Massif Central)." That the mining had begun by "the beginning of the British Early Bronze Age, ca. 2000 BC."[4]

Herodotus (484–425 BC.)[5]

> (N)or do I know of the real existence of "Tin Islands" (Kassiteridas) from which tin (kassiteros) comes to us: for first the name Eridanos itself declares that it is Hellenic and that it does not belong to a Barbarian speech, but was invented by some poet; and secondly I am not able to hear from anyone who has been an eye-witness, though I took pains to discover this, that there is a sea on the other side of Europe. However that may be, tin and amber certainly come to us from the extremity of Europe.

Four hundred years later Strabo seems to have a better idea of the location of Britain and the Cassiterides. Strabo, Geography (64 BC to 24 AD)

> Northward and opposite to this are the western coasts of Britain. Northward and opposite to the Artabri are the islands denominated Cassiterides, situated in the high seas, but under nearly the same latitude as Britain. Strabo, Geography 2.5.15

---

4. Muhly, *American Journal of Archaeology*, Vol. 89, No. 2, 278–87.

5. Herodotus, 3.115. 221.

He (Posedonius) says that tin is not found upon the sur-
face, as authors commonly relate, but that it is dug up; and that
it is produced both in places among the barbarians who dwell
beyond the Lusitanians and in the islands Cassiterides; and that
from the Britannic islands it is carried to Marseilles. Strabo.
Geography, 3.2.9

The Cassiterides are ten in number and lie near each other
in the ocean towards the north from the haven of the Artabri.
One of them is desert, but the others are inhabited by men in
black cloaks, clad in tunics reaching to the feet, girt about the
breast, and walking with staves, thus resembling the Furies we
see in tragic representations. They subsist by their cattle, leading
for the most part a wandering life. Of the metals they have tin
and lead; which with skins they barter with the merchants for
earthenware, salt and brazen vessels. Formerly the Phoenicians
alone carried on this traffic from Gades (Cadiz), concealing the
passage from everyone.[6](Note: there may have been a confusion between the description of the Scillies, the 'ten islands' and
Cornwall as the origin of the tin trade).

Tacitus describes the appearance of the Druids. (56–120 AD)

On the shore stood the opposing army with its dense array of
armed warriors, while between the ranks dashed women, in
black attire like the Furies, with hair dishevelled, waving brands.
All around, the Druids, lifting up their hands to heaven, and
pouring forth dreadful imprecations, scared our soldiers by the
unfamiliar sight, so that, as if their limbs were paralysed, they
stood motionless, and exposed to wounds. Then urged by their
general's appeals and mutual encouragements not to quail before
a troop of frenzied women, they bore the standards onwards,
smote down all resistance, and wrapped the foe in the flames of
his own brands. A force was next set over the conquered, and
their groves, devoted to inhuman superstitions, were destroyed.
They deemed it indeed a duty to cover their altars with the blood
of captives and to consult their deities through human entrails.
Tacitus. Annals. 14.32[7]

Pliny the Elder, Natural History (23–79 AD)

Opposite to Celtiberia are a number of islands called by the
Greeks the Tin Islands in consequence of their abundance of
that metal; and facing Cape Finisterre are the six Islands of the
Gods, which some people have designated the Isles of Bliss. But
immediately at the beginning of Baetica comes Cadiz, 25 miles

6. Strabo, *Geography*, 3.5.11.

7. Tacitus, *Complete Works of Tacitus*, Annals, 14.32.

from the mouth of the Strait, an island according to Polybius's account measuring 12 miles in length and 3 miles in breadth. (The area of the Scillies is approximately nine by three miles).[8]
Tin was first imported by Midacritus from the island of Cassiterides. Natural History VII. 119 See also XXXIV. 156–158 for a description of tin mining

Diodorus Siculus. *Library of History* B.v C.22 (written between 60–30 BC.)

But we shall give a detailed account of the customs of Britain and of the other features which are peculiar to the island when we come to the campaign which Caesar undertook against it, and at this time we shall discuss the tin which the island produces. The inhabitants of Britain who dwell about the promontory known as Belerium are especially hospitable to strangers and have adopted a civilized manner of life because of their intercourse with merchants of other peoples. They it is who work the tin, treating the bed which bears it in an ingenious manner. This bed, being like rock, contains earthy seams and in them the workers quarry the ore, which they then melt down and cleanse of its impurities. Then they work the tin into pieces the size of knuckle-bones and convey it to an island which lies off Britain and is called Ictis; for at the time of ebb-tide the space between this island and the mainland becomes dry and they can take the tin in large quantities over to the island on their wagons. (And a peculiar thing happens in the case of the neighbouring islands which lie between Europe and Britain, for at flood-tide the passages between them and the mainland run full and they have the appearance of islands, but at ebb-tide the sea recedes and leaves dry a large space, and at that time they look like peninsulas.) On the island of Ictis the merchants purchase the tin of the natives and carry it from there across the Strait to Galatia or Gaul; and finally, making their way on foot through Gaul for some thirty days, they bring their wares on horseback to the mouth of the river Rhone.[9]

Etymology: Turner, Sharon. *The History of the Anglo-Saxons*[10]

Κασσίτερον is the word used by the Greeks for tin. Bochart has founded an ingenious etymology of the "Britannic islands" on the Hebrew ברת אנך, Baratanac, which, he says, means the Land of Tin. He says Strabo calls Britain, βγετταvιχη. Boch. Canaan, lib. i. c. 39. p. 720. He also intimates, what is more probable, that the word Κασσίτερον may have been of Phenician origin. The Chaldean

8. Pliny, *Natural History,* IV. 119. N. 211.
9. Siculus, *Library of History* B.v C.22.
10. Sharon, *Anglo-Saxons,* 54.

> Targums, of Jonathan and Jerusalem, certainly call tin kastira and
> kistara, as the Arabs name it kasdar. See Numbers, xxxi. 22.

Tin in the Hebrew is בדיל *bdil*. The Arabic *kazdir* and Sanscript *kastir*
reveals the origin of *kassiteros*. The term אנך *anik* translates as plumbline.
Brown Driver Briggs: אֲנָךְ n.[m.] plummet (cf. words in cogn. lang. for lead,
tin, etym. dub., perh. foreign; As. anaku Lyons (sargon texte 92) Amos 7:8
plummet. The Hebrew terms covenant + plumb line (and by association;
lead, tin) would be more in keeping with the phonetic appellation of Britannic, אֲנָךְ + בְּרִית, *britanik*. The phrase suggests a covenant between Israel
(possibly the tribes of Zebulon or Asher living on the Mediterranean), the
Phoenicians, and the distant isle of Britain based on the metal trade. In the
17th century BC, Jacob blesses Zebulon saying: "Zebulun shall dwell by the
haven of the sea; He shall become a haven for ships, and his border shall
adjoin Sidon." (Gen 49:13) Of course, these word origin associations are
only speculation.

The origin of the name Britain is also said to be derived from Brutus,
the great-grandson of Aeneas:

> At this time Julius Caesar, the Roman emperor, carried on a victo-
> rious war against various countries, and having conquered Gaul,
> and from thence, "when he was on the coast of the sea of Ruten,"
> seen Britain, "towards the west," he made enquiries as to the op-
> posite country and its inhabitants. And when he received the in-
> formation as to both; this nation, said he, is of the same origin as
> we Romans; both are of the Trojan race; for we are derived from
> Aeneas, who settled in Rome, and whose great grandson Brutus,
> settled in Britain. As Brutus subdued the country, I imagine it
> will not be a hard task to me to make it subject to the Senate of
> Rome, since they inhabit an island arid, know nothing of war or
> arms. Accordingly he then sent a message to Caswallon requiring
> a peaceable submission of Britain to Rome, and the payment of a
> tribute, to prevent the shedding of the blood of those who were
> allied by the descents from their common ancestor Priam[11][12]

Sharon Turner. The History of the Anglo-Saxons[13]

> But though the Kimmerii, and their kindred the Kelts, may
> have peopled Britain, a more celebrated people are also stated
> to have visited it. The Phenicians, in their extensive commercial

11. Tysilio, *Chronicle of the Kings of Britain*, 73–4.

12. *The Chronicle of the Early Britons*, 26.

13. Turner. *History of the Anglo-Saxons*. 53–4.

navigations, colonized many of the islands, and some of the coasts of the Aegean and Mediterranean Seas. Inscriptions in their language have been found in Malta. They occupied Spain and founded Cadiz; and it was probably in pursuit of them that Nebuchadnezzar, the celebrated King of Babylon, became the conqueror of Spain. They had also an established intercourse with islands, which the Greeks called "the Islands of Tin," or Cassiterides. This, being a descriptive name, was probably the translation of the Phenician appellation. As Herodotus intimates that the Cassiterides were, with respect to Greece, in the farthest parts of Europe; (Herod. Thalia, c. 115) as Aristotle talks of Keltic tin ; (Aristot. lib. Mirabilium; and Mela places the Cassiterides in Celticis, or among the Keltae, lib. iii. c. 6, p. 262); and Strabo describes both these islands and Britain to be opposite to the Artabri, or Gallicia in Spain, but northward, and places them within the British climate; (Strabo, Geog. lib. ii. p. 181); as in another passage he states them to be as to Rome, without, or on our side of the columns of Hercules; (lb. lib. ii. p. 191); as he mentions them to be productive of tin, obviously connecting them at the same time with the British islands; (lb. lib. iii. p. 219. Here he says, that tin is produced among the barbarians above Lusitania, and in the islands Cassiterides, and from Britain is brought to Marseilles.and in another part, as being in the open sea, north from the port of the Artabri, (lb. lib. iii. p.265. In this passage Strabo says likewise, they are ten in number, adjoining each other): or Gallicia: the most learned, both at home and abroad, have believed the Cassiterides to have been some of the British islands. This opinion is warranted by there being no other islands famous for tin near the parts designated by Strabo; and by the fact that British tin was so celebrated in antiquity, that Polybius intended to write on the British islands and the preparation of tin. (Polyb. Hist. lib. iii. c. 5. Festus Avienus describes islands under the name of Aestrymnides, which are thought to be the same with Strabo's Cassiterides. He says they were frequented by the merchants of Tartessus and Carthage and were rich in tin and lead. De oris Marit.).

William Camden (1551–1623) The Location of the Sillies[14]

Quoting Sestus Avienus:

14. Camden, *Britannia*, 1519–22. N.504.

Where the wide Ifles Oefirynrnides are feen,
Enrich'd with deepeft: veins of Lead and Tin.
Stout are the Natives, and untam'd in war,
Gain is their ftudy, Trade their only care.
Yet not in Ships they try the watry road,
And rouze the fhapelefs Monfters of the flood:
For neither Gallies of the lofty pine
They know to frame, nor weaker maple join
In fhallow barks : but skins to skins they few ;
Secure in thefe to fartheft: parts they go,
And pathefs Seas with keels of leather plow.

Such alfo were us'd in this Sea in the year 914, For we read of
certain pious men tranfported from Ireland into Cornwal, in
a Carab or Caroch, which was made of two hides and an half.
Thus alfo the fame Avienus fpeaks of thefe Iflands, afterwards:

Oft the Tarteffians, thro' the well known Seas,
Would fail for traffick to th' Oeftrymnides;
And Carthaginians too.

Other Greek writers call'd thefe the Caffiterides, from their Tinne
.- as Strabo calls a certain place among the Drangi in Afia, Caf-
fiteron, for the fame reafon ; and Stephanus in his Book de Urbi-
bus obferves from Dionyfius, that a certain Ifland in the Indian
Sea was call'd Caffitera, from Tinne. As for Mictis, which Pliny
(upon the authority of Timaeus) fays is fix days fail, inward, from
Britain, and produces white Lead ; I dare not fay it was one of
thefe. Yet I am aware, that the learned Hermolaus Barbarus found
fome Manufcripts that have it Mitteris for Mictis, and thereupon
would read it Cartiteris. However, I may (from the authority of
the Ancients, from the fituation, and from their veins of Tinn)
warrant thefe to be the very Caffiterides, fo much fought for.
Over-againft the Artabri, who are oppofite to the weft parts of
Britain, fays Strabo, and north of them, lie thofe Iflands which
they call Caffiterides, fituate in effect in the fame Climate with
Britain. Thus alfo in another place. "The Sea is much wider between Spain and the Caffiterides, than between the Caffiterides
and Britain. The Caffiterides face the coaft of Celtiberia, faith Soli-
nus. Diodorus Siculus, In thofe Iflands next the Iberian Sea, call'd
from the Tinn, Caffiterides. Euftathius, The Caffiterides are Ten
Iflands lying clofe to one another, in the north. Now, confidering
that thefe Ifles of Silly are oppofite to the Artabri, i. e. Gallitia, in
Spain ; that they ftand directly north of them ; that they lie in the

fame Climate with Britain ; that they face Celtiberia ; that the Sea is much broader between them and Spain than between them and Britain ; that they lie juft upon the Iberian Sea, and clofe to one another, northward ; that there are only ten of any note, viz. St. Maries, Annoth, Agnes, Sampfon, Silly, Brefar, Rufco or Trefcaw, St. Helens, St, Martins, and Arthur ; again, considering, what is far more material, that they have veins of Tinn as no other Ifle in thefe parts has ; and laftly, that two of the lefler fort, Minan-Witham and Minuififand, feem to derive their names from Mines: From fo many concurring teflimonies, I fhould rather conclude thefe to be the Caffiterides, than either the Azores which lie too far weftward, or Cifarga (with Olivarius) which in a manner joins to Spain ; or even Britain it felt, with Ortelius ; fince there were many of the Caffiterides; and Dionyfius Alexandrinus, after he has treated of the Caffiterides, gives a feparate account of Britain. If any deny thefe to be the Caffiterides, becaufe there are more than ten ; let him alfo reckon the Habudes, and the Orcades : and if at the foot of his account he find the number of the Habudes * more or lefs than five ; and of Orcades, than thirty, as Ptolemy reckons them ; let him inquire for them in fome other place, than where they are generally fuppos'd to be, and I am pretty fure he will never find them by going this way to work. For the truth is, the ancient writers had no more certainty concerning thefe remote Parts and Iflands, than we have or the Iflands in the Streights of Magellan, and the Country of New Guiney. (*f.n. neither more)

THE EARLY CHRISTIAN DISPERSION

Joseph of Arimathea

Joseph quarried his own tomb. Was Joseph also an expert in quarrying and rock cutting and therefore experienced in metal mining? "When Joseph had taken the body, he wrapped it in a clean linen cloth, and laid it in his new tomb which he had hewn out of the rock; and he rolled a large stone against the door of the tomb and departed." (Mt 27:59–60) As suggested by Dennis Price, *The Missing Years of Jesus*. It can be translated as: "as having been cut in the rock by Joseph's own hand."[15] Specifically, Joseph, (λατομέω, *latomeo*), cut stones. That "he had hewn out of the rock." (AV, Darby, NAS, NKJV, RSV).[16]

---

15. https://www.youtube.com/watch?v=fU7uCGgVWMw
16. Price, *The Missing years Of Jesus.*

In the account from Nicodemus or the Acts of Pilate, the following very touching story is told of Joseph's imprisonment by the Sanhedrine and his escape.

> On the day of the Preparation, about the tenth hour, you shut me in, and I remained there the whole Sabbath in full. And when midnight came, as I was standing and praying, the house where you shut me in was hung up by the four corners, and there was a flashing of light in mine eyes. And I fell to the ground trembling. Then some one lifted me up from the place where I had fallen, and poured over me an abundance of water from the head even to the feet, and put round my nostrils the odour of a wonderful ointment, and rubbed my face with the water itself, as if washing me, and kissed me, and said to me, Joseph, fear not; but open thine eyes, and see who it is that speaks to thee. And looking, I saw Jesus; and being terrified, I thought it was a phantom. And with prayer and the commandments I spoke to him, and he spoke with me. And I said to him: Art thou Rabbi Elias? And he said to me: I am not Elias. And I said: Who art thou, my Lord? And he said to me: I am Jesus, whose body thou didst beg from Pilate, and wrap in clean linen; and thou didst lay a napkin on my face, and didst lay me in thy new tomb, and roll a stone to the door of the tomb. Then I said to him that was speaking to me: Show me, Lord, where I laid thee. And he led me, and showed me the place where I laid him, and the linen which I had put on him, and the napkin which I had wrapped upon his face; and I knew that it was Jesus. And he took hold of me with his hand, and put me in the midst of my house though the gates were shut, and put me in my bed, and said to me: Peace to thee! And he kissed me, and said to me: For forty days go not out of thy house; for, lo, I go to my brethren into Galilee. (Gospel of Nicodemus. Chapter 11. Translated by Alexander Walker)

The Two Josephs

In William John Lyons, *Joseph of Arimathea: A Study in Reception History*, the author suggests two personalities of Joseph. One is an active Joseph who boldly approaches Pilate as illustrated in Mark and Luke. And secondly, a passive Joseph as in John, who operates in secret, and who acquires the help of Nicodemus.[17]

---

17. Lyons, *Joseph of Arimathea*, 159.

Table 17: Joseph of Arimathea in the New Testament

Mark 15.42–47	Matthew 27.57–61	Luke 23.50–56a	John 19.38–42
Now when evening had come, because it was the Preparation Day, that is, the day before the Sabbath, Joseph of Arimathea, a prominent council member, who was himself waiting for the kingdom of God, coming and taking courage, went in to Pilate and asked for the body of Jesus. Pilate marveled that He was already dead; and summoning the centurion, he asked him if He had been dead for some time. So when he found out from the centurion, he granted the body to Joseph. Then he bought fine linen, took Him down, and wrapped Him in the linen. And he laid Him in a tomb which had been hewn out of the rock, and rolled a stone against the door of the tomb. And Mary Magdalene and Mary the mother of Joses observed where He was laid.	Now when evening had come, there came a rich man from Arimathea, named Joseph, who himself had also become a disciple of Jesus. This man went to Pilate and asked for the body of Jesus. Then Pilate commanded the body to be given to him. When Joseph had taken the body, he wrapped it in a clean linen cloth, and laid it in his new tomb which he had hewn out of the rock; and he rolled a large stone against the door of the tomb, and departed. And Mary Magdalene was there, and the other Mary, sitting opposite the tomb.	Now behold, there was a man named Joseph, a council member, a good and just man. He had not consented to their decision and deed. He was from Arimathea, a city of the Jews, who himself was also waiting for the kingdom of God. This man went to Pilate and asked for the body of Jesus. Then he took it down, wrapped it in linen, and laid it in a tomb that was hewn out of the rock, where no one had ever lain before. That day was the Preparation, and the Sabbath drew near. And the women who had come with Him from Galilee followed after, and they observed the tomb and how His body was laid. Then they returned and prepared spices and fragrant oils.	After this, Joseph of Arimathea, being a disciple of Jesus, but secretly, for fear of the Jews, asked Pilate that he might take away the body of Jesus; and Pilate gave him permission. So he came and took the body of Jesus. And Nicodemus, who at first came to Jesus by night, also came, bringing a mixture of myrrh and aloes, about a hundred pounds. Then they took the body of Jesus, and bound it in strips of linen with the spices, as the custom of the Jews is to bury. Now in the place where He was crucified there was a garden, and in the garden a new tomb in which no one had yet been laid. So there they laid Jesus, because of the Jews' Preparation Day, for the tomb was nearby. (NKJV)

The Glastonbury Thorn: Crataegus monogyna Biflora

In Withering's *British Plants*, vol. iii. p. 596, article "Crataegus," we read: "In a lane beyond the churchyard, on the opposite side of the street, near a pit, grows a very old tree [of the Glastonburiensis species]. A woman ninety years of age never remembers it otherwise than as it now appears.

"Another tree of the same kind may be seen two or three miles from Glastonbury. It has been reported to have no thorns, but that I found to be a mistake; it has thorns, like other hawthorns, but, as in other aged trees, they are few in number.

"There is also a full-sized tree of this kind in the garden at Piper's Inn. This variety blossoms twice a year: the winter blossoms, which are about the size of a sixpence, appear about Christmas-time; it may occasionally happen on Christmas Day, but it is sometimes sooner. This variety produces no fruit. The berries contain only one seed, and there seems to be only one pistil, but it was late in the season when I examined it (Oct. 1702). I was informed that the berries when sown produce plants nowise differing from the common hawthorn."

Probably the tree which gave birth to the tradition of its having sprung from the staff of Joseph of Arimathaea grew within the abbey, and may have died from age, or been destroyed in the Reformation. However that may be, the existence of this *lusus naturae* is unquestionable, and is not, as Dr. Hunter asserts, 'a sanctified deceit, sunk into discredit even with the meanest of the vulgar.'—*Sylvia*, vol. i. p. 178.

The following is from the Rev. R. Warner, F.A.S. (*History of the Abbey of Glaston*, 4to, 1826):—"The Holy Thorn has been introduced into many parts, and is now found in various gardens of Glastonbury and its vicinity. Pilgrimages continued to be made to this wonderful tree even in Mr. Eyston's time (died 1721), and its scions were sought for with the greatest avidity both by the pious of the Romish Church, and the superstitious of other systems of faith, till within these eighty years."

In the Evening Post, London, Jan. 1753, we read: "A vast concourse of people attended the noted thorn on Christmas Day (new style) ; but, to their great disappointment, there was no appearance of its blowing, which made them watch it narrowly till Jan. 5 (Christmas Day, old style), when it blowed as usual."

Strype records that one of Henry VIII.'s "visitors" sent up, with various relics, "two flowers (wrapped in white and black sarcenet), which on Christenmass even, 1536, *hora ipsa qua Christus natus fuerat* will spring, and burgen, and bare blossomes."

We are furthermore told that the spot on which St. Joseph planted his staff was on the south ridge of Weary-all-hill, now called Werrall Park. The *Avalonian Guide* states that "about the year 1740 the stump of the original thorn was seen, but that nothing now remains except grafts from it, growing in different places. The oldest of these grafts stands near St. John's church-yard at Glastonbury, and is a large tree, which still blossoms twice a year."[18]

The Dispersion of the Disciples to France, Spain, and Britain

There are many records, public and otherwise recounting the fate of the Jewish followers of Jesus shortly after His Crucifixion. It appears that some were put adrift to sea without oars and others like Joseph, probably had the means to navigate their own passage. Cardinal Cesare Baronio, an Italian cardinal and ecclesiastical historian of the Roman Catholic Church attests to records indicating that Joseph of Arimathea and initially at least fourteen others came to southern France to continue the witness of Christ.

Cardinal Cesare Baronio 1538–1607, Annales Ecclesiastici.[19]

> During this scattering, the disciple Ananius having proceeded to Damascus, gathered together a Church. Moreover we can conclude that at this time also Lazarus, Mary Magdalene,1 Martha and Marcella the waiting-woman, against whom most of the Jews were inflamed by hatred, not only had been driven out of Jerusalem but together with the disciple Maximinus, were placed in a boat without oars. It was believed (by the Jews) that that they were sure to die at sea, whom they say divine providence caused to land at Massilia (Marseilles)2 and being friends they bore the same dangers. Joseph of Arimathea the well-known Decurion whom they report sailed out of Gaul into Briton, and there according to the prophecy of the Gospels, ended his last days. But what does it avail to review journeys one at a time and to count the fruits gathered from prophecies? For even if the revelation of the Gospels had not yet been revealed to the Jews, nevertheless whence Luke says: "Therefore who had been scattered, were transformed into preachers of the Gospel of God." 3 4

18. Brewer, *Dictionary of Miracles*, 155–56.

19. Baronio, *Annales Ecclesiastici*, Vol. 1 208.

Ref: 1. Act. Magd. et soc. / 2. Manuscript. hist. Angl. qui hab. in Vatic. biblioth. (the Vatican library) / 3. Acts 8:4 *Therefore they that were scattered abroad went everywhere preaching the word.* / 4. With thanks to Mike Moody from Toronto for the translation.

The flight to the south of France documents the beginnings of Christian history to that region. It also records the arrival of Joseph and the not unlikely development that he would have continued across the English Channel to where he had been previously and hospitably received by King Arviragus.

Arles, Trophimus

In Rev. Lionel Smithett Lewis' book *Joseph of Arimathea at Glastonbury*,[20] he confirms a mission to Arles by Trophimus ("Trophimus have I left at Miletum sick" 2 Tim 4:20b). Arles is 90 kms north of Marseilles:

> The Abbe Maxime Latour referring to Trophimus being in Gaul says, "In 417 the Pope Zozimus recognized in the church of Arles the right of being Metropolitain over all the district of Narbonne because Trophimus its first Bishop had been for the Gauls the source of life whence flowed the stream of faith."[21]

The *Jewish Encyclopedia* has an entry that corresponds with the Christian account.

> Arles (Latin Arelas or Arelate, Hebrew ארליט & other spellings):

> City of France, in the department of Bouches du Rhone; ancient capital of Provence. The date of the settlement of the Jews in Arles is lost in antiquity. According to a legend, the emperor Vespasian placed Jews on three vessels, which were abandoned by their captains in the open sea. One of these came to Arles, another landed at Bordeaux, and the third reached Lyons. From *Siddur*, Roedelheim, 1868, ed. Baer, p. 112.[22]

Both the Jewish Encyclopedia and the Vatican texts agree that a boatload of Jews was cast adrift. The Encyclopedia suggests that it was by the emperor Vespasian and the latter because of the hatred of the Jews.

From the *Revue des Sciences Ecclesiastiques*,[23]

---

20. Lewis, *Joseph of Arimathea*, 115.

21. Lewis' quote is taken from *Revue des Sciences Ecclesiastiques*, July 1861.

22. Jewish Encyclopedia: *Arles* Vol. 2, 115.

23. *Revue des Sciences Ecclesiastiques*, Juillet 1860, 55.

Les historiens sont d'accord sur ce point avec les Pères et les Martyrologes. Adon de Vienne dit formellement dans sa chronique, que « saint Paul mis en liberté par Néron, se rendit en Espagne, et qu'il laissa pour prêcher saint Trophime à Arles » et saint « Crescent à Vienne »*

*Quo tempore credilur Paulus ad Hispanias pervenisse el Arelate Trophimum, Viennee crescenlem, discipulos suos, ad praedicandum reliquisse (Adon. chronic. ad annum Chr., lix)

Aout 1861[24]

Et, chose qu'il ne faut pas oublier, en 440, dix-neuf Évêques de la province d'Arles écrivent au pape saint Léon, comme chose *connue de toutes les provinces de la Gaule*, que saint Trophime a été envoyé à Arles par saint Pierre (Ep. S. Léon., Lxv. Ed. Migne). Dans cette lettre extrêmement précieuse, ces Évêques s'attachent à établir que l'église d'Arles est plus ancienne que celle de Vienne, qui dès 177, pourtant, envoyait des lettres aux chrétientés d'Asie. Quelques années auparavant, le pape Zozime (417) avait affirmé le même fait, et reconnaissait au siège d'Arles la puissance métropolitaine, parce qu'il avait été fondé par saint Trophime. Telle est la gravité de ces documents qu'ils ont entraîné l'assentiment de plusieurs savants opposés, du reste, à l'origine apostolique de nos églises.

Saintes Maries De La Mer, France.[25]

The Church of Saintes Maries De La Mer. Approximately 127 kms west of Marseille. First Christian witnesses: Mary (Marie) Jacobé, Mary Salomé, Lazarus (Lazare), Mary Magdalene (Madeleine), Martha (Marthe), Maximi, and Sara. The church is also the focus of an annual gathering of the Romani people (Gypsies) who venerate the black Sara, who is reputedly a servant of one of the Mary's. In the *Rolling Thunder Revue: A Bob Dylan Story* by Martin Scorsese, Bob Dylan visits the Romani flamenco guitarist, Manitas de Plata in St. Maries de la Mer, May 1975. For some background history of the church see footnote[26]

Legends and beliefs of the church:

24. *Revue des Sciences Ecclesiastiques*, Aout 1861, 165, n.743.
25. Note that the 'Marys of the Sea' is plural
26. http://www.saintesmaries.com/eng/the-church.html

Victims of pursuits in Palestine, the Saints were arrested, embarked on a vessel and then abandoned on a boat with neither sails nor oars. Guided by Providence, they approached the Provençal shore. The legend says that Mary Jacobé and Mary Salomé, persons who were close to Jesus and Mary, landed at this place accompanied by Lazarus, Mary Madeleine, Martha and Maximin. Whereas the disciples left to evangelise far off, the Saints, mature women as they were mothers of apostles, lived on this shore which bear their name. As regards Sara, one question remains unanswered: was Sara their handmaid or did she welcome them on our coast?

Aix-en-Provence, France. Saint Maximinus and Mary Magdalene

Saint Maximinus of Aix. Aix-en-Provence approximately 32 Kms north of Marseille. (French: Maximin d'Aix) was the first bishop of Aix-en-Provence in the 1st century. Saint-Maximin-la-Sainte-Baume 40 kms east of Aix venerates the memory of Mary Magdalene.

> According to his legend, he was the steward of the family at Bethany and one of the seventy-two disciples of Jesus. He accompanied Lazarus, Martha and Mary on their flight. He began the evangelisation of Aix-en-Provence together with Mary Magdalene. He is traditionally named as the builder of the first church on the site of the present Aix Cathedral. Mary Magdalene later left him to continue his apostolate alone when she withdrew to the solitude of a cave, which later became a Christian pilgrimage site Sainte-Baume. On the day she knew she was to die she descended into the plain so that Maximinus could give her communion and arrange her burial. Her sarcophagus is now at the Basilica of St Mary Magdalene at Saint-Maximin-la-Sainte-Baume, along with that of Sidonius, Marcelle, Suzanne and Maximinus, after whom the place was subsequently named. He died on 7 June, now the day of his feast. In the 3rd or 4th century his remains were placed in a sarcophagus. Sidonius (Saint Sidoine) succeeded him as bishop of Aix.[27]

27. French website with some information on the church: http://www.mariemadeleine.fr/index.php/entree.html

Catedral de Santiago, Spain. James the Elder

From the church web page:[28]

> The Apostle Saint James the Elder is one of the twelve disciples of Jesus Christ. Brother of John, the Evangelist, he is the son of Zebedee and Mary Salome. Along with Peter and John he belongs to the group of three privileged disciples who were admitted by Jesus into the important moments of his life, such as his agony in the Garden of Gethsemane and during his Transfiguration. According to the Acts of the Apostles, Saint James was the first Apostle to become a martyr by being beheaded by Herod Agrippa in the year 43 in Jerusalem. The tradition narrates how his body was taken by sea to Galicia, and was buried in a forest, today the site of the Cathedral.

In an address by Benedict XVI June 21, 2006 he says:

> A later tradition, dating back at least to Isidore of Seville (560–636), speaks of a visit he (James) made to Spain to evangelize that important region of the Roman Empire. According to another tradition, it was his body instead that had been taken to Spain, to the city of Santiago de Compostela.[29]
>
> Ref.: Le Livre de Saint Jacques ou Codex Calixtinus de Compostelle and, Isadore of Seville Etymologies.

Tarascon, France. Martha the sister of Lazarus

Approximately 100 kms north-west of Marseille. From Brewers, *A Dictionary of Miracles*[30]. The following history can be taken as fanciful or plausible but hopefully more credible than a Dan Brown novel. The story serves to place the major characters.

Apparitions of Christ and of Mary Magdalene to Martha (AD 84).

> Martha was the sister of Mary and Lazarus. Mgr. Guerin says she was the daughter of Theophilus the Syrian, a wealthy seigneur, and that her mother was Eucharis, a Jewish noble of the blood royal. "Elle avait pour soeur uterine Ste. Marie Madeleine, et pour frere uterin St. Lazarus." By this account Mary the sister of

---

28. http://www.catedraldesantiago.es/en/node/488

29. From the Vatican website: http://www.vatican.va/content/benedict-xvi/en/audiences/2006/documents/hf_ben-xvi_aud_20060621.html

30. Brewer, *Dictionary of Miracles*, 482–483.

Lazarus was Mary Magdalene. The pope's chamberlain says, after the Ascension, the Jews seized Martha, and placed her in a boat without sails, oars, or provisions, and set her adrift. That the boat carried her to Marseilles, where she introduced the Christian faith, and then went to Aix, Avignon, and other neighbouring parts. She ultimately took up her abode at Tarascon, where she lived in great austerity; went about barefooted, dressed in a coarse woollen robe, and wore a "tiare blanche en poil de chameau" for head-dress. "Son corps portait une ceinture de crins de cheval, remplie de noeuds, et un cilice qui lui dechirait les chairs (!!). One day St. Maximin quitted Aix to visit Martha, and at the same time Trophimus bishop of Arles, and Eutropius bishop of Orange, without concert, started on the same errand. So the three bishops met at Tarascon, and consecrated Martha's house for a Christian church (! !). As Martha had no wine to give her guests, Jesus Christ Himself came and changed some water into wine, which the bishops greatly commended. When the bishops left Tarascon, Martha asked Maximin to request her sister Mary to call and see her before she died. This he promised to do. Soon afterwards, "Notre Seigneur, pour la purifier davantage, et lui donner le moyen de meriter une couronne plus glorieuse," sent on her a fever which lasted for twelve months; and during this time her sister Mary died. "Les historiens racontent," that Jesus Christ Himself, accompanied with angels, visited Martha in her illness, and during this visit Martha saw angels carrying her sister's soul to heaven. "Dear sister," she cried, "why did you not give me a parting visit according to my request?"As her end drew nearer a vast number of Christians encamped around, and Mgr. Guerin says the following miracles are established on the highest possible authority : "ces prodiges que les historiens des premiers siecles nous racontent, ont done eu pour temoins non pas trois on quatre fideles privilegies, mais tout un people" (!!). At nightfall Martha had seven candles and three lamps lighted, "ce nombre avait-il I quelque chose de symbolique." Forthwith a great gust of wind filled all the house. It was not the descent of the Holy Ghost, as on the day of Pentecost, but the devil who had come to blow out the lights. Martha armed herself with the sign of the cross, and waking her guardians, who were asleep, she told them to light the candles and lamps again. As they went out to seek for a light, the chamber was filled with celestial light, and Mary her sister appeared, relighted the lamps and candles miraculously, and coming to the bed, said to Martha, "Dear sister, I am come to see you before your death, as you wished me to do. But see here; Christ Himself is come to fetch you home. Come, sister, and tarry not." Then Christ came to the dying saint, and said to her, "Here am I, Martha; as you served Me with so much devotion, and showed Me such hospitality in Bethany, I am now come to redeem you from exile, that where I am thou mayest be also. He then added, "Farewell, Martha, for a little time, while I go and prepare a place for you." Then Christ disappeared, and Mary, with a loving smile, disappeared also. The companions of Martha, on their return, found all the candles and lamps burning, and Martha requested to be carried into the open air. She was laid under a tree, "et on y traca une croix avec de la cendre." At sunrise, by her command, a crucifix was held before her (!!). "Come, Lord Jesus, come quickly!" she cried, and yielded up the ghost. Seven bishops (Parmenas, Germanus, Sosthenes, Epaphras, Marcellus, Evodius, and Synticus) led the multitude in singing the dirge, and celebrating the funeral rites, which lasted three days. "Ils chantaient nuit et jour autour de ce saint corps, allumant des cierges dans l'eglise, des lampes dans les maisons, et des feux dans les bois." She was buried on Sunday, and St. Front, the first bishop of Perigueux, was in his church, and waited in his chair for the people who were to join him in the sacrifice of the mass. Jesus Christ came to him, and said, "My son, come with Me to celebrate the obsequies of Martha, My host." "Il dit, et sur-le-champ, tous deux en un clin d'ceil apparurent à Tarascon dans l'eglise, tenant des livres dans leurs mains:" Christ at the head and the bishop at the feet," et eux sculs placerent le corps dans le tombeau, au grand etonnement de ceux qui etaient la presents." When the funeral was over, and the assembly dispersed, one of the clerks asked Christ who He was, and whence He came. Christ made no reply but handed the book He held in His hands to the clerk. On opening the book, he found on every page these words, "The memory of Martha, the hostess of Jesus, will be everlasting." The book contained nothing else. Meantime the deacon at Perigueux came and reminded St. Font that the congregation was waiting for him to begin mass ; and the bishop said he had been to Tarascon to assist in the funeral obsequies of Martha, whether in the body or out of the body he did not know—God knows ; he then added, "Send some one for my ring and gloves which I left in the church, when I lifted the body into the grave." A messenger was sent at once to Tarascon, and brought back the ring and gloves. These gloves were carefully preserved in the church at Tarascon till 1793.—Mgr. Guerin (chamberlain of pope Leo XIII.), Lives of the Saints, vol. ix. pp. 101, 102 (7th edit. 1880). Faillon, Monuments inedits sur l'Apostolat de St,

Marie-Magdeleine (1858). The chamberlain refers us to Peter de Natalibus, Raban Maur, Vincent de Beauvais, and others, and assures us that the above are facts beyond question, witnessed to not by three or four faithful witnesses, but by "tout un peuple."

In the footnote by Brewer he critiques the identities of the Mary's:

A tale so full of anachronisms can scarcely be matched; but be it remembered that this biography is recorded in the nineteenth century as a history worthy of all men to be received and believed. There is no Scripture proof that Mary the sister of Lazarus was Mary Magdalene, and the general opinion of Protestants is that they were different persons. Without doubt Mary the sister of Lazarus anointed the Lord, with ointment, and wiped His feet with her hair (John xi. 2; xii. 3). Luke (vii. 37, 39) also tells us of a woman who did the same, and in the heading of the chapter this woman is called "Mary Magdalene," but upon what authority I know not. The next chapter (viii.) introduces Mary Magdalene by name, not as the woman referred to at the close of the previous chapter, but as a new subject. Look at the last verse of chap. vii. "And Jesus said to the woman, Thy faith hath saved thee; go in peace." And the next chapter opens thus: "And certain women which had been healed of evil spirits and infirmities [viz.] Mary Magdalene, Joanna wife of Chuza, Susanna, and many others . . . were with Him." There seems no connection between the woman, without a name, who anointed the feet of Jesus, and the women mentioned by name who ministered to Him. Matthew (xxvi. 7) and Mark (xiv. 3) mention another woman, who anointed the head, not the "feet," of Jesus. It seems probable that Mary, Martha, and Lazarus were natives of Bethany, a suburb of Jerusalem. Certainly they lived there, and certainly Lazarus died and was buried there, but Mary the Magdalene was probably a native of Magdala in Gadara, near the Lake of Tiberias, quite another place. On the whole, there seems to be three anointings: (1) The woman mentioned by Matthew and Mark, who anointed the head of Jesus; (2) the woman "who was a sinner," mentioned by Luke, and called in the heading "Mary Magdalene:" and (3) Mary of Bethany, the sister of Lazarus and Martha, mentioned by John.

Britain. Aristobulus

Cressy, R. F. S. (1605–1674) of the Holy Order of S. Benedict. The Church-History of Brittany from the Beginning of Christianity to the Norman Conquest 1668. Cressy records the ministry of Aristobulus (Rom 16:10) to Britain before the arrival of Joseph of Arimathea. Different authors have claimed that Joseph arrived initially in 36 AD, with Mary the mother of Jesus. When Mary died, Joseph apparently returned to southern France and was later re-commissioned by St. Philip to return to Britain in 63 AD. Although Cressy is a Catholic Benedictine monk, he considers both Protestant and Catholic historical sources.

Book. 1 The Chvrch-History of Brittany Vnder Roman Governovrs. Chap VIII Section 1–8 Testimonies of the Acts of S. Aristobulus a Disciple of S. Peter, and an Apostle to the Brittains.

1. There is moreover still extant in *Ecclesiasticall Records* the Memory of an illustrious Disciple of S. *Peter* or S. *Paul,* who probably accompanied one of them into *Brittany,* & who after many years labour in our Lords vineyard was consummated here: and that is the *Blessed Apostolicall Saint Aristobulus.* Concerning whom we read this passage in the *Greek Menology: Aristobulus was one of the Seaventy Disciples, who was a follower of S. Paul, preaching the Gospell, and ministring to him in all places where he travelled: By whom likewise he was ordain'd a Bishop for the Region of the Brittains.* But in another Edition of the same *Menology,* translated formerly by one *William* a *Cardinal,* and inserted by *Canisius* in his second Volume of *Antiquities,* we read that this S. *Aristobulus* was ordained not by S. *Paul,* but S. *Barnabas:* for this is the tenour of that Passage: *The commemoration of S. Aristobulus a Bishop of Brittany, and Brother of the Blessed Apostle S. Barnabas, by whom being ordained a Bishop he was sent into Brittany, and there preaching the Faith of Christ, and constituting a Church, he attaind the glory of Martyrdome.*

2. Moreover a *Fragment* published lately by B. *Vsher* under the name of *Haleca* B. of *Caesar Augusta* (Sarragoçe) S. *Aristobulus* is declared to be the Disciple of S. *Peter:* These are the words, *Among the Brittains is celebrated the Memory of many Martyrs, and principally of S. Aristobulus one of the seaventy Disciples, who was also call'd Zebedaeus, the Father of Iames and Iohn, Husband of Maria Salome: who together with S. Peter went to Rome: And there leaving his family, he was sent a Bishop into England, where he dyed a Martyr, in the second yeare of the raign of the most cruell Emperour Nero.*

3. Now wheras *S. Aristobulus* is every where named *Bishop of the Brittains,* without any particular Citty assigned for his Sea, this doth argue that in those times of zeale and simplicity, *Apostolicall* men did not confine themselves to any determinate place, but like clouds hoverd up and down, being in a sort present to all, and dispensing showres seasonably every where. Thus *S. Augustin* our Apostle, at first was ordain *Bishop of the English Nation, as Bede* calls him, till more Provinces being converted, he confind himselfe to a particular Seat.

4. *Arnoldus Mirmannus,* with other Authours likewise, extend the life of this *Brittish Apostle* to the ninety ninth yeare of our Lord: affirming that he dyed in *Brittany.* And wheras both in the *Greek Menology,* and the *Fragment* of *Haleca,* as likewise in the *Roman Martyrologe* he is sayd, *after performing the course of his preaching to have been consummated by Martyrdome:* this is to be interpreted according to the expression of the Primitive times, in which those were called *Martyrs,* who for the propagation of the Gospell went into forraign parts, there exposing themselves to all dangers, and dying in such an Employment: though their death was not violent.

5. And such was the condition of *S. Aristobulus,* concerning whom this is further added in the *Greek Menology: Aristobulus having been ordained Bishop by S. Paul, was sent into Brittany, a region of most cruell and savage men: By whom he was sometimes tormented with stripes, and sometimes also dragg'd up and down the common Market-place. He perswaded many to adioyn themselves to Christ. And having constituted Churches, and ordaind Preists and Deacons there, he happily ended his life.*

6. In the *English Martyrologe* this is added, *That he dyed at Glastonbury,* a place far enough removed from the *Trinobantes,* where the *Romans* exercised their power. Probable it is, that having spent so many years in the laborious exercise of his *Apostolick Office,* he in his old age retired himself into that place of solitude and Recollection, there quietly disposing himself for his leaving the world. This was indeed a practise very familiar to like *Saints.* For thus in the following Age *Fugatius* and *Damianus* sent hither by *Pope Eleutherius* to convert *King Lucius* and his subjects, retired at last to the same place. And afterward the like was done by *S. Patrick,* who being a Native of *Brittany,* after having spent many years in propagating the Gospell in *Ireland,* at last returned back, and took up his finall rest at *Glastenbury.*

7. This is that *Aristobulus* mention'd by *S. Paul* in his *Epistle* to the *Romans,* saying, *Salute those which are of the household of Aristobulus.*

And the reason why he did not salute him by name, doubtles was the same for which he omitted the saluting of S. *Peter*: because he was at this time departed from *Rome* into, or towards *Brittany*.

8. Thus far did the Gospell make a progresse in *Brittany* in the very infancy of Christianity before the death of S. *Peter* and S. *Paul,* as may be gathered out of the few Relicks of *Ecclesiasticall Records* not wholly extinguish'd. A great accesse to which felicity of this Island accrew'd by the coming hither of S. *Ioseph* of *Arimathea* and his companions: which though hapning toward the end of *Nero's raign,* yet because most of the occurents pertaining to their *Gests* belong to the times of severall *Emperours* succeeding, we will refer them to the following Book: And for the present it will suffise that we have demonstrated that some of the *Apostles* penetrated as far as into *Brittany* to plant the Gospell here. A Truth testified expressly by *Theodoret,* as B. *Vsher* hath well observed: For he comparing the Apostles of *Christ* with the most famous of the *Grecian* and *Roman Lawgivers,* shews how much they were to be prefer'd. *For all that those Heathen Lawgivers could doe was to induce some particular Provinces or Commonweales to accept of their Laws, which all other Countreys reiected: Whereas, says he, our Galilaean fishermen, Publicans and Tent makers carried the Evangelicall Law to all Nations: inducing not the Romans only, or those which lived under their Empire to accept the Laws of our crucified Lord, but the Scythians also, and Sarmatians, Indians, Ethiopians and Persians, together with the Seres, Hyrcanians, Brittains, Cimmerians and Germans. And this they did not making use of arms or armies, but by perswasion of words, and demonstrating the great utility of the Laws which they preached: and for the preaching of them exposed themselves to great danger. Finis Libri primi.*[31]

Britain. Arimathea

Book 2. of *The Chvrch-History of Brittany*. Chap. 1. Sections: 1.2. S. Ioseph of Arimathea and his Companions principall Apostles of Brittany. 3.4.5. &c. This confirmed out of Authentick Records by English Embassadours in the Councils of Pisa, Siena and Constance, &c. 9. Likewise by an Ancient Charter of King Henry the second. (Note: Cressy affirms the hospitality of the "British princes" compared to "any country under the Romans" and suggests they are "better prepared for entertaining the Gospel of Peace).

31. Cressy, *Chvrch-History of Brittany*.

1. UPON that precious foundation of Faith and Piety which had been layd by the Holy *Apostles* in *Brittany,* their *Disciples* and Successours rais'd up a Temple to our Lord, a Temple though of no such amplitude as we find in the following age, yet not so unconsiderable, but that the fame thereof reached into forraign Countreys, as *Arnobius* who wrote above thirteen hundred years since, and *Tertullian* likewise observe.

2. Now the most eminent of the *Primitive Disciples,* and who contributed most to this heavenly building, was *S. Ioseph of Arimathea,* and eleaven of his companions with him, among whom is reckoned his *Son,* of his own name. These toward the latter end of *Nero's* raign,[32] and before *S. Peter* and *S. Paul* were consummated by a glorious Martyrdom, are by the Testimony of ancient *Records* sayd to have entred this Island, as a place for the retiredness of it, the benignity of the *Brittish Princes,* and the freedom from *Roman Tyranny,* more opportune, and better prepar'd for entertaining the Gospell of Peace, then almost any Countrey under the *Romans.*

3. But before we enquire into the occasion of the arrivall of these *Sons of Light,* or relate any of their particular *Gests,* the prejudice which in these later times has possess'd many minds against *Tradition,* obliges me in preparation to the *History* following, firmly to assert this Truth in generall; that such *Apostolicall* persons did indeed by their zeale and industry cultivate this barbarous *Island,* and this with better successe then perhaps any other Nation addicted to *Idolatry.*

4. Now a more efficacious *Proof* hereof cannot reasonably be desired then the testimony of a person eminently conversant in our Ecclesiasticall Monuments, and whose aversion from the *Roman Church* will cleare him from all suspicion of partiality: And this is the late *Protestant Archbishop of Armagh,* Doctour *Vsher,* who in a Collection of Antiquities regarding the Primitive Churches of *Brittany,* treating of this very argument hath this passage:

5. We must not omit to take notice that in the Generall Synods assembled by our Europaans, whensoever the Controversy was agitated touching the dignity and preeminence of the Brittish Kingdom in opposition to the French and Spaniards, the Oratours of the English Nation did usually appeale to this Tradition concerning S. Ioseph of Arimathea. This question was discuss'd first in the year one thousand four hundred and nine in the Councill of Pisa: and again eight years after in the Councill of Constance: out of which there is an extract of a most

32. 37–68 AD.

famous Disputation concerning the dignity and magnitude of the Kingdoms of Brittany and France, between the Embassadours of both in the Councill; which was printed at Lovain in the yeare one thousand five hundred and seaventeen. The said Extract taken out of Originall Acts of that Councill, and preserv'd in the Citty of Constance, was published by the care of Sir Robert Wingfeild Knight and Embassadour from King Henry the eighth to the Emperour Maximilian: and which is still extant in two Manuscripts of the same Councill. It was in the thirtieth Session that this Question was moved, Whether it be agreable to reason and iustice that the Kingdom of England should enioy equall Priviledges with that of France? And for the dignity of the English Church, it was among other things alledg'd, that presently after the suffring of our Saviour, Ioseph of Arimathea an honourable Counsellor, who took down from the Crosse Christs body, together with twelve companions, betimes in the morning entred into our Lords Vineyard, to wit, England, and converted the inhabitants to the Faith: To whom the King then raigning assigned for their sustenance twelve Hides of Land in the Diocese of Bath: All which twelve Preachers, as ancient Records witnes, were buried in the Monastery of Glastenbury, situate in the same Diocese. And with those twelve Hides of Land afore mention'd, the sayd Monastery was anciently endow'd and founded. *This was alledged by the* English *Oratours for their Kingdome: Whereas* France *received not the Faith till the time of* S. Dionysius, *by whose Ministery it was converted.*

6. Likewise in the Councill of Siena, in the year one thousand four hundred twenty four, the same Allegations were propos'd by Richard Fleming Bishop of Lincoln, and founder of Lincoln-Colledge in Oxford, when this Controversy was renew'd by the English in the presence of Pope Martin the fifth, against the Spaniards, Scots and French. But principally in the Councill of Basile, in the year one thousand four hundred thirty four, this contention came to great heat. For then the Embassadours of the King of England, as well in the publick Council before the Bishops, and in the Congregation deputed for Reformation, protested that they were to be prefer'd by reason of their more ancient reception of the Christian Faith: for they affirm'd, that the Noble Counsellor Ioseph of Arimathea together with others, in the fifteenth year after the Assumption of the glorious Virgin Mary came into England, and converted a great part of it to the Faith of Christ. And no long time after the Passion of our Lord Pope Eleutherius converted the whole

Kingdom entirely to the Faith. *This account gives* Alphonsus Garzias *who was Advocat for the right of* Spain *in that Council.*

7. And though he endeavours to enervate the reasons alledged by the *English Oratours,* yet his objections are so weak, that they rather establish them. For all that he opposes to the story of S. *Ioseph* is an old trifling *Legend* reporting, that when *Titus entred Ierusalem, he saw a certain very thick wall, which he commanded to be peirced through: and within they found a certain old man who call'd himself Ioseph of Arimathea, and sayd that he was clos'd up there by the Iews, because he had buried Christ: and that till that time he had been nourished with heavenly food.*

8. But common reason will shew how little force such a particular ungrounded story ought to have against the Tradition of a whole Nation: Therefore the *English Oratours* in opposition hereto *gave full assurance that in our most Ancient Books and Archives, especially in the Records of the most famous Abbey of Glastonbury, it is expressly declared that Ioseph with his companions, being persecuted either by Herod or the Roman President, were brought into this Island: where he preached the things which he had seen and heard of Christ, and by his preaching converted many. who being converted bestowed on him a world of rich gifts: all which he left to the Church erected by him in the honour of Christ. The which Church built by S. Ioseph was afterward transfer'd into a Religious Monastery and Abbatiall dignity: and by that famous Monastery the praises of our Lord have been continued to that present day.*

9. Thus publickly, and with so great Authority was this Tradition concerning S. *Ioseph's* preaching and converting the *Brittains,* confirm'd in severall *Generall Councils.* And more particularly as touching the Ancient Records testifying the Truth of this story, we find them with great advantage mention'd in an illustrious *Charter* extant to this day, which was given by our King *Henry* the *second* at *westminster* to the *Abbay* of *Glastonbury:* In which Charter the sayd King signifying *his intention to rebuild that Monastery not long before consum'd by fire: And to renew all the Priviledges confer'd on it by his Predecessours, King william the first, and second, and his Grandfather King Henry the first: as likewise by more Ancient Kings, S. Edgar the Father of S. Edward, King Edmond and his Father Edward, and his Grandfather King Alfred, King Bringwalth, Hentwyn, Baldred, Ina, the famous King Arthur, Candred, and many other Christian Kings: yea, moreover by Kenewalla in former times a Pagan King of Brittany: For this purpose he affirms that he caused a diligent inquisition to be made of the sayd Priviledges and*

Charters, which were presented and read in his presence: all which he confirmed and rene'wd to the same Church anciently call'd by some the Mother of Saints, and by others the Tomb of Saints: because it had been built by the very immediat Disciples of our Lord, and in the beginning dedicated by our Lord himselfe, as Venerable Antiquity doth testify. This testimony is given by King Henry the Second in his sayd Charter. All which considered, to deny so great a blessing conferd on our Nation, as the arrivall here of S. Ioseph, can only be an act of passion and unexcusable partiality.

Cressy continues the detailed story of Joseph throughout most of Book two. In chapter III, section 2, he describes a meeting with King Arviragus.

His name was Arviragus: (the same no doubt who in an ancient coyn is called Arivog:) but from what Ancestours he was descended, is not clearly enough reported in History: Certain Modern Writers will needs make him the same with Caractacus before spoken of, suppos'd likewise by them to be the same with Cogidunus the youngest son of Cunobelin: from whom also they are willing to deduce King Lucius in a direct line, who raigned in the following Age: By which art they indeed give some grace to their Histories, by a distinct sorting of actions and occurrents to the precise years of Kings then suppos'd to raign in this Island.

EARLY ESTABLISHMENT OF CHRISTIANITY IN BRITAIN

Tertullian (155–240): *Ante-Nicene Fathers: Latin Christianity*: The Writings of the Fathers down to 325 AD.[33]

For whom have the nations believed,—Parthians, Medes, Elamites, and they who inhabit Mesopotamia, Armenia, Phrygia, Cappadocia, and they who dwell in Pontus, and Asia, and Pamphylia, tarriers in Egypt, and inhabiters of the region of Africa which is beyond Cyrene, Romans and sojourners, yes, and in Jerusalem Jews, and all other nations; as, for instance, by this time, the varied races of the Gætulians, and manifold confines of the Moors, all the limits of the Spains, and the diverse nations of the Gauls, and the haunts of the Britons—inaccessible to the Romans, but subjugated to Christ, and of the Sarmatians, and Dacians, and Germans, and Scythians, and of many remote

33. Tertullian, *Ante-Nicene Fathers*, v.3. 251.

nations, and of provinces and islands many, to us unknown, and which we can scarce enumerate?

Eusebius. 260–340 Christianity in England. *The Ecclesiastical History of Eusebius Pamphilus.*[34]

> They (the apostles) visited the burning climes of Africa, and the various regions of Asia, to proclaim the glad tidings of salvation; and a great part of Europe, from the countries bordering on the Mediterranean to the distant shores of Britain, received the light of Christian truth.
>
> It appears that the churches of Syria and Mesopotamia continued to follow the custom of the Jews, and celebrated Easter on the fourteenth day of the moon, whether falling on Sunday or not. All the other churches observed that solemnity on Sunday only, viz. those of Rome, Italy, Africa, Libya, Egypt, Spain, Gaul and Britain; and all Greece, Asia, and Pontus.

Death of Joseph of Arimathea. (July 27, 82 AD)

R.F.S. Cressy. *Church History of Brittany, from the Beginning of Christianity to the Norman Conquest.*

> Epitaph: "After I had buried Christ, I came to the Brittains: Here I taught them, and here I was buried."[35]

King Lucius requests support from Pope Eleutherius

Venerable Bede. *Ecclesiastical History of the English People.*

> In the year of our Lord's incarnation 156, Marcus Antoninus Verus, the fourteenth from Augustus, was made emperor, together with his brother, Aurelius Commodus. In their time, whilst Eleutherus, a holy man, presided over the Roman church, Lucius, king of the Britons, Sent a letter to him, entreating that by his command he might be made a Christian.[36]

Capgrave, John. *Chronicles and Memorials of Great Britain and Ireland.*

---

34. Eusebius, *Ecclesiastical History,* 5, 22.
35. Cressy, *Church History,* Book II, Chap XII.
36. Bede, *Ecclesiastical History,* p.10 b.1 c.4.

In the XIX. yere of Antoni was Eleutheri Pope, a Grek of nacion. He receyved a letter fro the Kyng of Grete Britayn, cleped Lucius, that he schuld send summe prestes to this lond to baptize him, and his puple. And the Pope sent hedir Fugan and Damian, which performed this dede. Summe Chronicles sey this was in yere of oure Lord 165.[37]

Construction of Glastonbury Abbey

Memorials of St. Edmund's Abbey.

Prima constructio monasterii Glastoniae propter monachos ibi habitantes, tempore Lucii regis Britanniae, qui misit epistolam ad Elutherium papam propter Christianitatem, clxiii. (163 AD)

The construction of the monastery of Glastonbury by the monks who lived there during the time of Lucius King of England who had sent a letter to pope Elutherium for the sake of Christianity, clxiii.[38]

St. Augustine. *Letter to Pope Gregory.* This letter though widely quoted cannot be substantiated. Does it exist in the Vatican library?

In the Western confines of Britain there is a certain royal island of large extent, surrounded by water, abounding in all the beauties of nature and necessaries of life. In it the first neophytes of catholic law, God before acquainting them, found a church constructed by no human art, but divinely constructed for the salvation of His people. The Almighty has made it manifest by many miracles and mysterious visitations that He cotinues to watch over it as sacred to Himself, and to Mary the mother of God.

The Catholic Cardinal Reginald Pole who had been in exile under the reign of Henry VIII returned during the short reign of Mary I (Bloody Mary 1516–1558). Mary I and Cardinal Pole both die on November 17, 1558 during an influenza epidemic. Pole addresses parliament in November of 1554 and acknowledges Britain's position as the first to convert to Christ. It is interesting to compare Pole's appreciation of Catholicism with the account of John Foxe who chronicled the event. Says Pole: "I will not rehearse the manifold benefit that this realm hath received from the apostolic see, nor how ready the same hath been to relieve us in all our necessities." To which

---

37. Capgrave, *Chronicle of England*, 67.
38. *Memorials of St. Edmund's Abbey*, Vol. III.

Foxe replies in his footnote: "Nay rather what riches and treasures the see of Rome hath sucked out of England, it is incredible." However, the testimony to Britain's history is what is important.

> I signify unto you all, that my principal travail is, for the restitution of this noble realm to the ancient nobility, and to declare unto you, that the see apostolic, from whence I come, hath a special respect to this realm above all others; and not without cause, seeing that God himself, as it were by providence, hath given this realm prerogative of nobility above others ; which to make more plain unto you, it is to be considered that this island, first of all islands, received the light of Christ's religion. For as stories testify, it was "prima provinciarum quae amplexa est fidem Christi."[39]

William Camden. (1551–1623) Glastonbury Abbey[40]

> In this Ifland Itood the monaftery of Glaftenbury which is very ancient; deriving its original from Jofeph of Arimathea, the fame who bury'd Chrift's body, and whom Philip the Apoftle of the Gauls fent into Britain to preach the Gofpel. For this is attefted by the moft ancient Hiftories of this Monaftery, and alfo by an Epiftle of S. Patrick the Irifh Apoftle, who led a monaftick life here for 30 years together if it be indeed true that he wrote the account of Avalonia afcrib'd to him, which Dr. Ryves, in his difcourfe relating to that Saint, denies. From hence, this place was by our Anceftors call'd, The firft ground of God, The firft ground of the Saints in England, The rife and fountain of all Religion in England, The burying-place of the Saints, The mother of the Saints; and they faid of it, that it was built by the very Difciples of our Lord. Nor is there any reafon why we fhould call this in queftion, fince I have before fhewn, that the Chriftian Religion, in the very infancy of the Church, was preach'd in this Ifland; and fince Freculphus Lexovienfis has told us, that this Philip brought barbarous nations bordering upon darknefs, and living upon the Ocean, to the light of knowledge, and haven of faith.

William Camden (description of pyramids over Arthur's grave)

> Take alfo, if you pleafe, fome other monuments of this place, tho' not altogether fo ancient, out of William of Malmsbury. What is a mystery to all mankind I would willingly fet down, if the truth might poffibly be fifted out; i. e. what thofe Pyramids mean,

39. Foxe, *Acts and Monuments*, Vol. VI, 569.
40. Camden, *Britannia*. 78, N. 292.

fome feet diftant from the old Church, and facing the Monks Church-yard. The higher, and that nearer the Church, has five ftories, and is 26 foot high. This, tho' it is ready to fall for age, has yet some monuments of antiquity plainly legible but not fo plainly intelligible. For in the upper moft fiories, there is an image of an Epifecopal figure. In the fecond, an image flowing fomething of a King-like pomp, and thefe letters, HER. SEXI. and BLISWERH. In the third too are thefe names, WEMCHESTE. BANTOMP. WINEWEGN. In the fourth, HATE. WVLFREDE. and EANFLEDE. In the fifth (which is the lower moft,) an Image, and this writing, LOGWOR. WESLIELAS, and BREGDENE. SWELWES. HWINGENDES. BERNE. The other pyramid is 18 foot high, and has four ftories, in which are written HEDDE bifhop, and BREGORRED, and BEORWALDE. What thefe may fignifie, I dare not rafhly determin; but only make a probable conjecture, that the bones of thofe men whofe names are written on the outfide may be laid in hollow ftones within. As for LOGWOR, he is pofitively adffirm'd to be the perfon from whom the place now call'd Montacute' was formerly nam'd LOGWERESBEORH. From BREGDEN, is BRENTAKNOLLE, now called Brentemers: And BEORWALDE too was Abbot after HEMGISELUS.[41]

William Camden

The Saxons indeed about the 44th year after their landing in Britain, by a breach of Articles renewing the war, laid fiege to this city, but being furpriz'd by the warlike Arthur, they betook themfelves to Badon-hill, where (tho' in a defperate condition,) they fought it out to the laft, and were flain in great numbers. This feems to be the fame hill with that we now call Lannefdown, hanging over a little village near the city, nam'd Bathfton, and fhowing at this day its bulwarks, and a rampire. I know there are fome who feek for it in Yorkfhire; but let Gildas himfelf reftore it to this place. For in an old Manufcript-Copy of his Hiftory, in the Cambridge-Library, where he treats of the victory of Aurelius Ambrofius, he fays, To the year of Badon-hill fiege, which is not far from the mouth of Severn. But if this will not convince them, let them underftand farther, that the adjoyning vale lying along the river Avon for a great way together, is call'd in Britifh Nant-Badon, i. e. the vale of Badon; and where to feek Badon-hill but near Badon-valley I cannot tell.[42]

41. Camden. *Britannia, Somersetshire*, 81, N. 294.
42. Camden. *Britannia, Somersetshire*, 89, N. 298.

William of Malmesbury. *Chronicle of the Kings of England* 1125 AD.[43]

But since we have arrived at the times of Kenwalk, (642 AD) and the proper place occurs for mentioning the monastery of Glastonbury, I shall trace from its very origin the rise and progress of that church as far as I am able to discover it from the mass of evidences. It is related in annals of good credit that Lucius, king of the Britons, sent to Pope Eleutherius, thirteenth in succession from St. Peter, to entreat, that he would dispel the darkness of Britain by the splendour of Christian instruction. This surely was the commendable deed of a magnanimous prince, eagerly to seek that faith, the mention of which had barely reached him, at a time when it was an object of persecution to almost every king and people to whom it was offered. In consequence, preachers, sent by Eleutherius, came into Britain, the effects of whose labours will remain forever, although the rust of antiquity may have obliterated their names. By these was built the ancient church of St. Mary of Glastonbury, as faithful tradition has handed down through decaying time. Moreover there are documents of no small credit, which have been discovered in certain places to the following effect: "No other hands than those of the disciples of Christ erected the church of Glastonbury." Nor is it dissonant from probability: for if Philip, the Apostle, preached to the Gauls, as Freculphus relates in the fourth chapter of his second book, it may be believed that he also planted the word on this side of the channel also. But that I may not seem to balk the expectation of my readers by vain imaginations, leaving all doubtful matter, I shall proceed to the relation of substantial truths.

The church of which we are speaking, from its antiquity called by the Angles, by way of distinction, "Ealde Chirche," that is, the "Old Church," of wattle-work, at first, savoured somewhat of heavenly sanctity even from its very foundation, and exhaled it over the whole country ; claiming superior reverence, though the structure was mean. Hence, here arrived whole tribes of the lower orders, thronging every path; here assembled the opulent divested of their pomp; and it became the crowded residence of the religious and the literary. For, as we have heard from men of old time, here Gildas, an historian neither unlearned nor inelegant, to whom the Britons are indebted for whatever notice they obtain among other nations, captivated by the sanctity of the

43. Malmesbury, *Chronicle*, 21–25.

place, took up his abode for a series of years.[44] This church, then, is certainly the oldest I am acquainted with in England, and from this circumstance derives its name. In it are preserved the mortal remains of many saints, some of whom we shall notice in our progress, nor is any corner of the church destitute of the ashes of the holy. The very floor, inlaid with polished stone, and the sides of the altar, and even the altar itself above and beneath are laden with the multitude of relics. Moreover in the pavement may be remarked on every side stones designedly interlaid in triangles and squares, and figured with lead, under which if I believe some sacred enigma to be contained, I do no injustice to religion. The antiquity, and multitude of its saints, have endued the place with so much sanctity, that, at night, scarcely any one presumes to keep vigil there, or, during the day, to spit upon its floor : he who is conscious of pollution shudders throughout his whole frame : no one ever brought hawk or horses within the confines of the neighbouring cemetery, who did not depart injured either in them or in himself. Within the memory of man, all persons who, before undergoing the ordeal of fire or water, there put up their petitions, exulted in their escape, one only excepted : if any person erected a building in its vicinity, which by its shade obstructed the light of the church, it forthwith became a ruin. And it is sufficiently evident, that, the men of that province had no oath more frequent, or more sacred, than to swear by the Old Church, fearing the swiftest vengeance on their perjury in this respect. The truth of what I have asserted, if it be dubious, will be supported by testimony in the book which I have written, on the antiquity of the said church, according to the series of years. In the meantime it is clear, that the depository of so many saints may be deservedly styled an heavenly sanctuary upon earth. There are numbers of documents, though I abstain from mentioning them for fear of causing weariness, to prove how extremely venerable this place was held by the chief persons of the country, who there more especially chose to await the day of resurrection under the protection of the mother of God. Willingly would I declare the meaning of those pyramids, which are almost incomprehensible to all, could I but ascertain the truth. These, situated some few feet from the church, border on the cemetery of the monks. That which is the loftiest and

---

44. There is a Life of Gildas, written not long after this history, by Caradoc of Lancarvon, in which we are told, that, while he was residing at Glastonbury, a prince of that country carried off Arthur's queen and lodged her there ; that Arthur immediately besieged it, but, through the mediation of the abbat, and of Gildas, consented, at length, to receive his wife again and to depart peaceably.

nearest the church, is twenty eight feet high and has five stories: this, though threatening rain from its extreme age, possesses nevertheless some traces of antiquity, which may be clearly read though not perfectly understood. In the highest story is an image in a pontifical habit. In the next a statue of regal dignity, and the letters, Her Sexi, and Blisperh. In the third, too, are the names, Pencrest, Bantomp, Pinepegn. In the fourth, Bate, Pulfred, and Eanfled. In the fifth, which is the lowest, there is an image, and the words as follow, Logor, Peslicas, and Bregden, Spelpes, Highingendes Beam. The other pyramid is twenty-six feet high and has four stories, in which are read, Kentwin, Hedda the bishop, and Bregored and Beorward. The meaning of these I do not hastily decide, but I shrewdly conjecture that within, in stone coffins, are contained the bones of those persons whose names are inscribed without. At least Logor is said to imply the person from whom Logperesbeorh formerly took its name, which is now called Montacute; Bregden, from whom is derived Brentknolle and Brentmarsh; Bregored and Beorward were abbats of that place in the time of the Britons; of whom, and of others which occur, I shall henceforward speak more circumstantially. For my history will now proceed to disclose the succession of abbats, and what was bestowed on each, or on the monastery, and by what particular king. And first, I shall briefly mention St. Patrick, from whom the series of our records dawns. When the Saxons were disturbing the peace of the Britons, and the Pelagians assaulting their faith, St. Germanus of Auxerre assisted them against both ; routing the one by the chorus of Hallelujah, and hurling down the other by the thunder of the Evangelists and Apostles.[45] Thence returning to his own country, he summoned Patrick to become his inmate, and after a few years, sent him, at the instance of Pope Celestine, to preach to the Irish. Whence it is written in the Chronicles, "In the year of our Lord's incarnation 425, St. Patrick is ordained to Ireland by Pope Celestine." Also, "In the year 433 Ireland is converted to the faith of Christ by the preaching of St. Patrick, accompanied by many miracles." In consequence executing his appointed office with diligence, and in his latter days returning to his own country, he landed in Cornwall, from his altar, which even to this time is held in high veneration by the inhabitants for its sanctity and efficacy in restoring the infirm. Proceeding to Glastonbury, and there becoming monk, and abbat, after some years he paid the debt of nature. All doubt of the truth of

45. Bede, *Ecclesiastical History*, b, i. c. 20.

this assertion is removed by the vision of a certain brother, who, after the saint's death, when it had frequently become a question, through decay of evidence, whether he really was monk and abbat there, had the fact confirmed by the following oracle. When asleep he seemed to hear some person reading, after many of his miracles, the words which follow —"this man then was adorned by the sanctity of the metropolitan pall, but afterwards was here made monk and abbat." He added, moreover, as the brother did not give implicit credit to him, that he could show what he had said inscribed in golden letters. Patrick died in the year of his age 111, of our Lord's incarnation 472, being the forty-seventh year after he was sent into Ireland. He lies on the right side of the altar in the old church: indeed the care of posterity has enshrined his body in silver. Hence the Irish have an ancient usage of frequenting the place to kiss the relics of their patron. Wherefore the report is extremely prevalent that both St. Indract and St. Briget, no mean inhabitants of Ireland, formerly came over to this spot. Whether Briget returned home or died at Glastonbury is not sufficiently ascertained, though she left here some of her ornaments; that is to say, her necklace, scrip, and implements for embroidering, which are yet shown in memory of her sanctity, and are efficacious in curing divers diseases. In the course of my narrative it will appear that St. Indract, with seven companions, was martyred near Glastonbury, and afterwards interred in the old church.

St. Patrick's Chart or Epistle, Charta Sancti Patricii

(This document is said to be of dubious origin but is widely quoted). The consecration of St. Michael's church, Glastonbury

> But on a certain Night, when I had laid down to fleep, the Lord Jefus Chrify appeared to me in a Vifion, faying, PATRICK, my Servant , know that I have chofen this Place to the Honour of my Name, that here Men may reverently invoke my Archangel Michael, and this fhall be a Sign to thee and thy Brethren, that they alfo may believe; thy Left Arm fhall be dried up, until thou haft told what thou haft feen to thy Brethren, which are in the Cell below, and thou fhalt return here again.

King Arthur

William of Malmesbury. *Chronicle of the Kings of England*, 520 AD.

> It is of this Arthur that the Britons fondly tell so many fables, even to the present day; a man worthy to be celebrated, not by idle fictions, but by authentic history. He long upheld the sinking state, and roused the broken spirit of his countrymen to war. Finally, at the siege of Mount Badon* relying on an image of the Virgin, which he had affixed to his armour, he engaged nine hundred of the enemy, single-handed, and dispersed them with incredible slaughter.[46]
>
> *Said to be Bannesdown, near Bath. Giraldus Cambrensis says, the image of the Virgin was fixed on the inside of Arthur's shield, that he might kiss it in battle.

King Ina establishes Glastonbury Abbey, 688 AD

Bede's *Ecclesiastical History of England and the Anglo-Saxon Chronicle.*

> This year (688) Ina succeeded to the kingdom of the West-Saxons, and held it thirty-seven years ; and he built the minster at Glastonbury ; and he afterwards went to Rome, and there dwelt to the end of his days : and the same year Caedwalla went to Rome, and received baptism from the pope, (Sergius) and the pope named him Peter ; and in about seven days he died. Now Ina was the son of Cenred, Cenred of Ceolwald, Ceolwald was Cynegil's brother, and they were sons of Cuthwine the son of Ceawlin, Ceawlin of Cynric, Cynric of Cerdic.
>
> This year (688) king Caedwalla went to Rome, and received baptism of Pope Sergius, and he gave him the name of Peter, and in about seven days afterwards, on the twelfth before the Kalends of May, while he was yet in his baptismal garments, he died ; and he was buried in St. Peter's church. And Ina succeeded to the kingdom of the West-Saxons afte him, and he reigned twenty-seven years.[47]

46. Malmesbury, *Chronicle*, b1c1, 11.
47. Bede, *Ecclesiastical History*, 330.

Charter of King Ina to Glastonbury, 725 AD

William of Malmesbury, *Chronicle of the Kings of England.*

In the name of our Lord Jesus Christ : I, Ina, supported in my royal dignity by God, with the advice of my queen, Sexburga, and the permission of Berthwald, archbishop of Canterbury, and of all his suffragans ; and also at the instance of the princes Baltred and Athelard, to the ancient church, situate in the place called Glastonbury (which church the great high-priest and chiefest minister formerly through his own ministry, and that of angels, sanctified by many and unheard-of miracles to himself and the eternal Virgin Mary, as was formerly revealed to St. David,) do grant out of those places, which I possess by paternal inheritance, and hold in my demesne, they being adjacent and fitting for the purpose, for the maintenance of the monastic institution, and the use of the monks, Brente ten hides, Sowy ten hides, Pilton twenty hides, Dulting twenty hides, Bledenhida one hide, together with whatever my predecessors have contributed to the same church :* to wit, Kenwalk, who, at the instance of archbishop Theodore, gave Ferramere, Bregarai, Coneneie, Martineseie, Etheredseie ; Kentwin, who used to call Glastonbury, "the mother of saints," and liberated it from every secular and ecclesiastical service, and granted it this dignified privilege, that the brethren of that place should have the power of electing and appointing their ruler according to the rule of St. Benedict : Hedda the bishop, with permission of Caedwalla, who, though a heathen, confirmed it with his own hand, gave Lantokay : Baltred, who gave Pennard, six hides : Athelard who contributed Poelt, sixty hides ; I, Ina, permitting and confirming it. To the piety and affectionate entreaty of these people I assent, and I guard by the security of my royal grant against the designs of malignant men and snarling curs, in order that the church of our Lord Jesus Christ and the eternal Virgin Mary, as it is the first in the kingdom of Britain and the source and the fountain of all religion, may obtain surpassing dignity and privilege, and, as she rules over choirs of angels in heaven, it may never pay servile obedience to men on earth. Wherefore the chief pontiff, Gregory, assenting, and taking the mother of his Lord, and me, however unworthy, together with her, into the bosom and protection of the holy Roman church ; and all the princes, archbishops, bishops, dukes, and abbats of Britain consenting, I appoint and establish, that, all lands, places, and possessions of St. Mary of Glastonbury be free, quiet, and undisturbed, from all royal taxes and works, which are wont to be appointed, that is to say, expeditions, the building of bridges or forts, and from the edicts or molestations of all archbishops or bishops, as is found to be confirmed and granted by my predecessors, Kenwalk, Kentwin, Caedwalla, Baltred, in the ancient charters of the same church. And whatsoever questions shall arise, whether of homicide, sacrilege, poison, theft, rapine, the disposal and limits of churches, the ordination of clerks, ecclesiastical synods, and all judicial inquiries, they shall be determined by the decision of the abbat and convent, without the interference of any person whatsoever. Moreover, I command all princes, archbishops, bishops, dukes, and governors of my kingdom, as they tender my honour and regard, and all dependants, mine as well as theirs, as they value their personal safety, never to dare enter the island of our Lord Jesus Christ and of the eternal Virgin, at Glastonbury, nor the possessions of the said church, for the purpose of holding ever to the offence of the servants of God there residing : moreover I particularly inhibit, by the curse of Almighty God, of the eternal Virgin Mary, and of the holy apostles Peter and Paul, and of the rest of the saints, any bishop on any account whatever from presuming to take his episcopal seat or celebrate divine service or consecrate altars, or dedicate churches, or ordain, or do anything whatever, either in the church of Glastonbury itself, or its dependent churches, that is to say—Sowy, Brente, Merlinch, Sapewie, Stret, Sbudeclalech, Pilton, or in their chapels, or islands, unless he be specially invited by the abbat or brethren of that place. But if he come upon such invitation, he shall take nothing to himself of the things of the church, nor of the offerings ; knowing that he has two mansions appointed him in two several places out of this church's possessions, one in Pilton, the other in the village called Poelt, that, when coming or going, he may have a place of entertainment, Nor even shall it be lawful for him to pass the night here unless he shall be detained by stress of weather or bodily sickness, or invited by the abbat or monks, and then with not more than three or four clerks. Moreover let the aforesaid bishop be mindful every year, with his clerks that are at Wells, to acknowledge his mother church of Glastonbury with litanies on the second day after our Lord's ascension ; and should he haughtily defer it, or fail in the things which are above recited and confirmed, he shall forfeit his mansions above mentioned. The abbat or monks shall direct whom they please, celebrating Easter canonically, to perform service in the church of Glastonbury, its dependent churches, and in their chapels. Whosoever, be he of what dignity, profession, or degree, he may, shall hereafter, on any occasion whatsoever, attempt to pervert, or nullify this, the witness of my munificence and liberality, let him be aware that, with the traitor Judas, he shall perish, to his eternal confusion, in the devouring flames of unspeakable torments. The charter of this donation was written in the year of our Lord's incarnation 725, the fourteenth of the indiction, in the presence of the king Ina, and of Berthwald, archbishop of Canterbury.[48]

* Kemble's Charters, vol. i. p. 85

- Saxons in England, Vol.1, London Bernard Quaritch, 15 Piccadilly. 1876

Cuthred, Charter of Glastonbury, 745 AD

William of Malmesbury. *Chronicle of the Kings of England* 1125 AD.

In the name of our Lord Jesus Christ, I, Cuthred, king of the West Saxons, do hereby declare that all the gifts of former kings—Kentwin, Baldred, Kedwall, Ina, Ethelard, and Ethbald king of the Mercians, in country houses, and in villages and lands, and farms, and mansions, according to the confirmations made to the ancient city of Glastonbury, and confirmed by autograph and by the sign of the cross, I do, as was before said, hereby decree that this grant of former kings shall remain firm and inviolate, as long as the revolution of the pole shall carry the lands and seas with regular movement round the starry heavens. But if any one, confiding in tyrannical pride shall endeavour on any occasion to disturb and nullify this testamentary grant, may he be separated by the fan of the last judgment from the congregation of the righteous, and joined to the assembly of the wicked for ever, paying the penalty of his violence. But whoever with benevolent intention shall strive to approve, confirm, and defend this my grant, may he be allowed to enjoy un failing immortality before the glory of Him that sitteth on the throne, together with the happy companies of angels and of all the saints. A copy of this grant was set forth in presence of king Cuthred, in the aforesaid monastery, and dedicated to the holy altar by the munificence of his own hand, in the wooden church, where the brethren placed the coffin of abbat Hemgils, the 30th of April, in the year of our Lord 745.[49]

48. Malmesbury, *Chronicle*, 32–35.
49. Malmesbury, *Chronicle*, 37.

Edmund I, Charter of Glastonbury, 944 AD

William of Malmesbury. *Chronicle of the Kings of England* 1125 AD.

In the name of our Lord Jesus Christ, I Edmund, king of the Angles, and governor and ruler of the other surrounding nations, with the advice and consent of my nobility, for the hope of eternal retribution, and remission of my transgressions, do grant to the church of the holy mother of God, Mary of Glastonbury, and the venerable Dunstan, whom I have there constituted abbat, the franchise and jurisdiction, rights, customs, and all the forfeitures of all their possessions ; that is to say,[50] burhgeritha, and hundred-setena. athas and ordelas, and infangenetheofas, hamsocne, and fridebrice, and forestel and toll, and team, throughout my kingdom, and their lands shall be free to them, and released from all exactions, as my own are. But more especially shall the town of Glastonbury, in which is situated that most ancient church of the holy mother of God, together with its bounds, be more free than other places. The abbat of this place, alone, shall have power, as well in causes known as unknown ; in small and in great ; and even in those which are above, and under the earth ; on dry land, and in the water ; in woods and in plains ; and he shall have the same authority of punishing or remitting the crimes of delinquents perpetrated within it, as my court has ; in the same manner as my predecessors have granted and confirmed by charter ; to wit, Edward my father, and Elfred his father, and Kentwin, Ina, and Cuthred, and many others, who more peculiarly honoured and esteemed that noble place. And that anyone, either bishop, or duke or prince, or any of their servants, should dare to enter it for the purpose of holding courts, or distraining, or doing anything contrary to the will of the servants of God there, I inhibit under God's curse. Whsoever therefore shall benevolently augment my donation, may his life be prosperous in this present world; long may he enjoy his happiness: but whosoever shall presume to invade it through his own rashness, let him know for certain that he shall

---

50. The exact meaning of some of these terms is not easily attainable, but they are generally understood to imply—jurisdiction over the burgh, or town—hundred court—oaths and ordeals—thieves taken within the jurisdiction—housebreakers—breach of peace—offences committed on the highways, or forestalling—tolls—warranty, or a right of reclaiming villains who had absconded. The charter therefore conveys a right to hold various courts, and consequently to try, and receive all mulcts arising from the several offences enumerated, which being generally redeemable by fine, produced considerable sums; besides, what was perhaps of more importance, exemption from the vexations of the king's officers. (footnote: B ii, C VII)

be compelled with fear and trembling to give account before the tribunal of a rigorous judge, unless he shall first atone for his offence by proper satisfaction." The aforesaid donation was granted in the year of our Lord Jesus Christ's incarnation 944, in the first of the indiction, and was written in letters of gold in the book of the Gospels, which he presented to the same church elegantly adorned.[51]

Domesday Book 1086 AD, Somerset

The Domesday record is an important document because it confirms the status of Glastonbury in the 11th century as an entity not subject to the policies of the king and which had a sacred jurisdiction that was known as the "Secret of the Lord."[52]

> The Domus Dei, in the Great Monastery at Glastonbury called the Secret of the Lord: The Glastonbury church hath its own villa XII hides of land which have never paid tax

As mentioned previously the first three kings of the Common Era, Arviragus, Marius and Coel collectively bequeathed the first 12 hides of land. Many subsequent kings later donated land which was requisitioned by the Saxons, the Normans, and Henry VIII. The hide represented an amount said to be tillable by oxen in one year, approximately 160 acres. Four hides or 640 acres equals one square mile. A section is usually one square mile containing 640 acres and 36 sections make up one township or 23,040 acres. Twelve hides would represent 1,920 acres. The entry in the Doomsday Book in 1086, is a significant witness testifying to the worth that previous realms had placed on the land.

Finding of King Arthur's Tomb, 1170 AD

Gerald of Wales 1146–1223. Latin: Giraldus Cambrensis; Welsh: Gerallt Gymro; French: Gerald de Barri. The Discovery of the Tomb of King Arthur from *Liber de Principis Instructione* [On the Instruction of Princes]

---

51. Malmesbury, *Chronicle*, 141–43.

52. http://opendomesday.org/book/somerset/09/ http://opendomesday.org/place/ST5038/glastonbury/ Domesday Book images kindly made available by Professor J.J.N. Palmer. Images may be reused under a Creative Commons BY-SA licence. Professor J.J.N. Palmer and George Slater.

The memory of Arthur, the celebrated king of the Britons, should not be concealed. In his age, he was a distinguished patron, generous donor, and a splendid supporter of the renowned monastery of Glastonbury; they praise him greatly in their annals. Indeed, more than all other churches of his realm he prized the Glastonbury church of Holy Mary, mother of God, and sponsored it with greater devotion by far than he did for the rest. When that man went forth for war, depicted on the inside part of his shield was the image of the Blessed Virgin, so that he would always have her before his eyes in battle, and whenever he found himself in a dangerous encounter he was accustomed to kiss her feet with the greatest devotion.

Although legends had fabricated something fantastical about his demise (that he had not suffered death, and was conveyed, as if by a spirit, to a distant place), his body was discovered at Glastonbury, in our own times, hidden very deep in the earth in an oak-hollow, between two stone pyramids that were erected long ago in that holy place. The tomb was sealed up with astonishing tokens, like some sort of miracle. The body was then conveyed into the church with honor, and properly committed to a marble tomb. A lead cross was placed under the stone, not above as is usual in our times, but instead fastened to the underside. I have seen this cross and have traced the engraved letters — not visible and facing outward, but rather turned inwardly toward the stone. It read: "Here lies entombed King Arthur, with Guenevere his second wife, on the Isle of Avalon."

Many remarkable things come to mind regarding this. For instance, he had two wives, of whom the last was buried with him. Her bones were discovered with her husband's, though separated in such a way that two-thirds of the sepulcher, namely the part nearer the top, was believed to contain the bones of the husband, and then one-third, toward the bottom, separately contained the bones of his wife — wherein was also discovered a yellow lock of feminine hair, entirely intact and pristine in color, which a certain monk eagerly seized in hand and lifted out; immediately the whole thing crumbled to dust.

Indeed, there had been some evidence from the records that the body might be found there, and some from the lettering carved on the pyramids (although that was mostly obliterated by excessive antiquity), and also some that came from the visions and revelations made by good men and the devout. But the clearest evidence came when King Henry II of England explained the whole matter to the monks (as he had heard it from an aged British poet): how they would find the body deep down, namely more than 16 feet into the earth, and not in a stone tomb but in an oak-hollow. The body had been placed so deep, and was so well concealed, that it could not be found by the Saxons who conquered the island after the king's death — those whom he had battled with so much exertion while he was alive, and whom he had nearly annihilated. And so because of this the lettering on the cross — the confirmation of the truth — had been inscribed on the reverse side, turned toward the stone, so that it would conceal the tomb at that time and yet at some moment or occasion could ultimately divulge what it contained.

What is now called Glastonbury was, in antiquity, called the Isle of Avalon; it is like an island because it is entirely hemmed in by swamps. In British it is called Inis Avallon, that is, insula pomifera [Latin: "The Island of Apples"]. This is because the apple, which is called aval in the British tongue, was once abundant in that place. Morgan, a noble matron, mistress and patroness of those regions, and also King Arthur's kinswoman by blood, brought Arthur to the island now called Glastonbury for the healing of his wounds after the Battle of Camlann. Moreover, the island had once been called in British Inis Gutrin, that is, insula vitrea [Latin: "The Island of Glass"]; from this name, the invading Saxons afterwards called this place Glastingeburi, for glas in their language means vitrum [Latin: "glass"], and buri stands for castrum [Latin: "castle"] or civitas [Latin: "city"]. It should be noted also that the bones of Arthur's body that they discovered were so large that the poet's verse seems to ring true: "Bones excavated from tombs are reckoned enormous. "Indeed, his shin-bone, which the abbot showed to us, was placed near the shin of the tallest man of the region; then it was fixed to the ground against the man's foot, and it extended substantially more than three inches above his knee. And the skull was broad and huge, as if he were a monster or prodigy, to the extent that the space between the eyebrows and the eye-sockets amply encompassed the breadth of one's palm. Moreover, ten or more wounds were visible on that skull, all of which had healed into scars except one, greater than the rest, which had made a large cleft — this seems to have been the lethal one.[53][54]

53. Cambrensis, Vol. VIII, *De Principis Instructione Liber*, 126–29.

54. http://d.lib.rochester.edu/camelot/text/gerald-of-wales-arthurs-tomb John William Sutton (Translator) from: The Camelot Project 2001.

The King Arthur Cross

The leaden plate in the form of a Cross
found in King Arthur's grave at Glastonbury
Abbey in the reign of King Henry II.

The inscription reads: Hic jacet sepultus
inclytus Rex Arthurus in Insula Avalonia
(" Here lies interred in the Isle of Avalon
the renowned King Arthur.")

Figure 29: King Arthur's Inscription

Appendix 4

Origins of Kings

Table 18: Genealogy of Welsh Kings and associated tables
BC—1100 AD

Bran, King of Siluria
Caradog ap Bran, King of Siluria c.5
= Eurgain of Britain, bro. of Penarddun
Coellyn ap Caradog c.35
Owain ap Cyllin c.65
Meirchion Fawr Filwr ab Owain c.100
Cwrrig Goruc Mawr ap Meirchion
(130–215)
Gwrddwfin ap Cwrrig c.160 = N.N. De
Bretagne
Einudd ap Gwrddwfyn c.190 = Husband of (1) Gwrddwfn and (2) De
Bretagne
Arthfael ab Einudd c.230
Gwrgan Frych ap Arthfael c.260
Meirchion ap Gwrgan Frych c.295 =
Enynny verch Erbic
Meurig ap Merchion c.320

Euddolen ab Afallach (b.–35) bro. of
Owain ab Afallach
Eudos ab Euddolen (c.5–54)
Eneid ap Eudos, Brenin Powys
(c.25–83)
Endeyrn ab Eneid (c.60–154)
Endigant ap Endeyrn (c.90–184)
Rhydeyrn ap Endigant (c.120–200)
Rhyfedel ap Rhydeyrn (c.155–220)
Gradd ap Rhyfedel (c.185–250) =
Gwenllian verch Ieuaf
Urban ap Gradd (c.215–300) = Tangwystl verch Seysildyc
Telpwyl ap Urban, of Britain
(c.250–320)
Deheuvraint ap Tudbwyll (280–350) =
Wladysus verch Edenowen)
Tegfan Tasciovanus ap Deheuwaint
c.320–57

Crierwy ap Meurig c.355
Edric ap Crierwy c.385
Erb ap Edric c.415
Ninniaw ab Erb c.445 = bro. of Pebiau
ap Erb King of Ergyng
Llywarch Teithfall ap Ninniaw c.475
Tewdrig ap Llywarch, Saint c.505 =
Enynny verch Cynfarch
Athrwys ap Tewdrig is the possible
King Arthur
1. Athrwys ap Tewdrig, King of Gly. &
Gwent b.540
Morgan Mawr ab Athrwys c.570–665
Ithel ap Morgan c.600
= Cenedlon verch Briafel
Rhys ap Ithel, King of Gly & Gwent
c.635 = Ceingar Ferch Maredudd
Arthfael Hen ap Rhys c.665
Meurig ap Arthfael Hen b.695
Brochfael ap Meurig c.730
Arthfael ap Brochfael c.765
Rhys ap Arthfael b.795
Hywel ap Rhys 825–86
Owain ap Hywel (850–930)
= Nest verch Rhodri Mawr
Morgan Hen Mawr ab Owain 885–974
Idwallon ap Morgan Mawr 930–1021
Ithel ab Idwallon 970–1042
Gwrgan ab Ithel c.1005
Iestyn ap Gwrgan (1040–1093)
Iestyn = (1) Denis and progeny Rhydd-
erch/Meredith/Cadwagn/Griffith (+4
others)
Iestyn = (2) Angharad and progeny
Caradog/Madog/Morgan/Rhys/Nest
Nest verch Iestyn (1070) = Einnion ap
Collwyn

Ancestor to Sts. David and Teilo
Coel Hen ap Tegfan c.340–Nov.19.420
= Ystradwel verch Gadeon, of Rheged
Ceneu ap Coel Hen Saint-King
c.380–470
Gwrwst Ledlwm ap Ceneu (c.415–500)
Meirchion Gul ap Gwrwst (450–535)
Elidir Lydanwyn ap Meirchion (c.485–
560) = St. Gwawr ferch Brychan
Llywarch Hen ab Elidir (c.520) = He-
ledd verch Elidyr (+others)
Dwg ap Llywarch Hen (c.560)
Gwair ap Dwg (c.595–681)
Tegid ap Gwair c.630) = Anne of Brit-
ain (620–70)
Alcwn ap Tegid (c.660)
Sandde ap Alcwn (c.690) = Celeinion
verch Tudwal
Elidir ap Sandde (c.720–801)
Gwriad ap Elidir c.755 = Esyllt verch
Cynan (760–831)
Merfyn Frych ap Gwriad (c.790–844) =
Nest ferch Cynan and Nest ferch Cadell
Rhodri Mawr ap Merfyn c.820–78 =
Angharad verch Meurig
Cadell ap Rhodri Mawr (850–910)
bro. of Nest verch Rhodri Mawr
Owain ap Hywel of Glywysing
Hywel Dda ap Cadell (880–950) = Elen
verch Llywarch
Owain ap Hywel Dda (910–88) = Ang-
harad verch Llewelyn
Einion ap Owain (940–84) = Nest verch
Gwerystan of Devon

Saints David and Teilo of Wales (320–750)

Coel Hen ap Tegfan c.340–Nov.19.420
Gwawl verch Coel (Dau. of Coel) =
Edern Aeturnus ap Padarn
Cunedda Wledig ap Edern (386–460)
Son 1 of Cunneda:
Ceredig ap Cunedda (c.415) bro. of
Einion Yrth
Cedig Draws ap Ceredig (c.445) and
bro.
Hydwn Dwn ap Ceredig and son En-
sych ap Hydwn and son Saint Teilo ab
Ensych (c.500–60)
and:
Sandde ap Cedig (b.480) and son Saint
Dewi (David) Brevi ap Sandde (510–
Mar.1.589) Archbishop of Wales

Son 2 of Cunneda:
Einion Yrth ap Cunedda = Prawst verch
Tidlet
Owain Danwyn ab Einion (446–520)
Einion ab Owain, Saint (475)
Beli ab Einion (510)
Iago ap Beli (540–August 08, 613)
Cadfan ap Iago (570–625)
Cadwallon ap Cadfan (600–34)
St. Cadwaladr Fendigaid ap Cadwallon
(615–82)
Idwal Ywrch ap Cadwaladr (665–712) =
Angharad verch Alain
Rhodri Molwynog ap Idwal Ywrch
(700–54)
Hywel of Anglesey ap Rhodri Mol-
wynog (725–825) and bro. Cyan Dyn-
daethwy ap Rhodri (735–816)
Esyllt verch Cynan dau. of Cyan
(760–831) = Gwriad ap Elidir c.755

Welsh Kings (1100–1200)

Meyrig son of Griffith son of Iestyn
Morgan
Assar = Pain de Turbeville (1140–1207)
of Coety
Simmont de Turbeville
Pain II de Turbeville = Mathilde
Gilbert de Turbeville
Pain III de Turbeville
bro. Gilbert II de Turbeville = Meiwen
Gilbert III de Turbeville (son of G.II)
Richard de Turbeville
G. Pain IV de Turbeville

Cadell ap Einion (c.980–93) = Elinor
verch Gwerystan
Tudur Mawr ap Cadell c.1015 = Gwenl-
lian verch Gwyn
Rhys ap Tudur of Deheubarth
d.Apr.30.1093 = Gwladys verch
Rhiwallon
Nest verch Rhys (c.1085–1136)
Nest = Gerald FitzWalter of Pembroke
(1070–1136) and partner of Henry I
"Beauclerc"
Robert de Caen Earl of Glou.
(1090–1147)

House of de Turbeville / Spencer / Gamage (1200–1600)

Gamage of Coity (1200–1300)
Payne de Gamage c.1211
Robert de Gamage I c.1241
Robert de Gamage II of Coity
(1271–1306)
de Turbeville:
Payn IV de Turbeville and sis. Sarah de
Turbeville (1300–59) = William Gamage (1297–1325)
Catherine de T. sis. of Sarah de T. =
Roger de Berkrolles
Gilbert Gamage (1328–82) son of S.
William Gamage of Coety (1358–1419)
Thomas Gamage (1384–1429)
John Gamage (1413–87) = Margred
verch Morgan of Coity
Morgan Gamage (1447–88)
John Gamage (1413–87) = Lady Margred verch Morgan Baroness of Coity
Morgan Gamage (ap Sion) (1447–88)
Thomas Gamage (1484–1513)
Robert Gamage of Coity d.1553
John Gamage d.1584

Barbara Gamage (1) (1563–1621) =
Robert Sidney of Leicester (1563–1626)
= and (2) Sarah Blount.
Philip Sidney bro. of Rob. (1554–86) =
Frances Walsingham.

From previous col.
Nest verch Rhys = partner Henry I
Robert de Caen Earl of Glou. (1090–
1147) = Maud de Creully
William FitzRobert 2nd Earl of Glou.
(1112–83) = (1) Hawise de Beaumont
and (2) Mistress
Isabel Avise FitzWilliam FitzRobert
(1166–1217) = John King of England
Joan Plantagenet = Llewelyn Fawr ab
Iorwerth of Gwy. (1172–1240)
House of Despencer (1265–1307)

Gilbert de Clare = Joan of Acre (c.1265)
dau. of Edward I
Hugh le Despencer = Eleanor de Clare
Edward le Despencer = Anne de Ferrers
Edward le Despencer = Elizabeth de
Burghersh
Thomas le Despencer = Constance of
York
dau's. Mathilde and Isabel le Despencer

French origins of English Kings (1000–1400)

Geoffrey II Foulques d'Anjou (1043–1109)
Foulques d'Anjou V, Roi de Jérusalem (1089–1143) = (1) Ermengarde, (2) Mélisende d'Édesse Reine de Jerusalem
Geoffrey V of Anjou (1113–1151)
Henry II (1133–89)
Sons: Henry, Geoffrey, Richard Coeur de Lion (r.1189/99) and John of England (r.1199–1216)
Henry III (1207–r.1216/72)
Edward I (1239–1307) = Eleanor of Castile
Edward II (1284–1327)
Edward III (1312–77)
Richard II (r.1377/99)

House of Lancaster Red Rose (1340–1500)
Edward III
John of Gaunt founder of the House of Lancaster (1340–99)
Henry IV (1367–1413) = Mary de Bohun
Henry V (1387–1422) = Catherine of Valois
Henry VI (1421–71) = Marguerite d'Anjou
Henry VII (1457–r.1485/1509) = Elizabeth of York
House of York White Rose
Edward IV Plantagenet (1442–83)
Edward Plantagenet V (1470–85)
Richard III (r.1483/85)

House of Tudor English (1000–1600)

Henry Tudor VIII (1491–1547) and wife (1) Anne Boleyn + 7.
Edward VI (1537–r.1547/53)
Mary I (Bloody Mary) Stuart (1513–r.1553/58)
Elizabeth I Tudor (1533–r.1558/1603)
James VI/I (1566–r.03/25) = Anne of Denmark
Charles I Stuart (1600–r.25/49) = Henrietta Maria of France
Charles II (1630–r.60/85)
James II/VII (1633–r.85/88)
William + Mary (r.1689–1702)
Anne (1665–r.1702–14) = George of Denmark

House of Tudor Welsh
Rhys ap Tudur (1045–93)
Gruffyd ap Rhys, bro. of Nest (1081–1137)
Rhys ap Gruffyd b.1132
Gwenllian ferch Rhys = Ednyfed Fychan
Gronwy ap Ednyfed Fychan (1195–1268)
Tudur Hen ap Gronwy (1235–1311)
Gronwy ap Tudur Hen (1265–1331)
Tudur ap Gronwy (1310–67)
Maredudd ap Tudur (1370–1406) = Margaret ferch Dafydd
(2) Owen Tudur (d.1461) = Catherine of Valois = (1) Henry V
Edmund Tudur (1430–56) = Margaret Beaufort bro. of Jasper Tudur (1429–95)
Edmund Tudur is a father to Henry VII

House of Hanover (1700–1900)

George I (1660–r.1714/27) = Sophia Dorothea of Celle (1667–1726)
George II Augustus of Great Britain (1683–r.1727/60) = Caroline of Ansbach.
Heir apparent: Frederick Louis Hanover of Wales (1707–51)
George III William Frederick of Hanover (1738–r.1760/1820) = Charlotte of
Mecklenburg-Strelitz
George IV (1762–r.1820/30)
William IV (1765–r.1830/37)
Queen Victoria (1819–r.1837/1901) = Francis Albert Augustus Charles Em-
manuel (1819–61)

Norman Kings and Welsh House of Mortimer (1000–1460)

William the Conqueror (1024–87) =
Matilda of Flanders
Henry I (1068–1135) = Matilda of
Scotland, Adelicia, and others
Stephen (r.1135/54)
Henry II (1133–r.1154/89) = Eleanor
d'Aquitaine
Richard the Lionheart K. of England
(1157–99) + bro.:
John Plantagenet K. of England
(1166–1216)
Llewellyn the Great = Joan Plantagenet
(1188–1237)
Ralph Mortimer = Gwladus Ddu verch
Llewelyn or alt. = Gwenllian verch
Llewelyn

Mortimer Cont'd
Roger Mortimer (1231–1282)
Edmund Mortimer (1252–1304)
Roger Mortimer (1287–1330)
Edmund Mortimer II (1306–31)
Roger Mortimer (1328–60)
Edmund Mortimer (1351–81) = Phil-
lipa Plantagenet
Roger Mortimer (1374–98) = Eleanor
Holland
Richard Earl of Cambridge (1385–
1415) = Anne Mortimer
Richard 3rd Duke of York (1411–60) =
Cecily Neville

House of Stuart (1500–1788)

James IV Stewart (1473–r.88/1513) = Margaret Tudor (1489–1541) dau. of Henry
VII
James V Stewart K. of Scots (1512–42) = Mary of Guise
Mary Queen of Scots (1542–87) = Henry Stuart
Reign in England:
Elizabeth I Tudur (1533–r.58–1603) dau. of Henry VIII
James VI/I (1566–r.03/25) = Anne of Denmark, son of Mary Queen of Scots
Charles I Stuart (1600–r.25/49)
Interregnum: Oliver Cromwell and son Richard (r.1649/60)
Charles II (1630–r.60/85)
James II/VII Stuart (1633–r.85/88–d.1701)
James Francis Edward Stuart (1688–1766)
Charles Edward Stuart "Bonnie Prince Charlie" (1720–1788)

House of Hanover (1800–1917)

Queen Victoria (1819–r.1837/1901) = Francis Albert Augustus Charles Emmanuel (1819–61)
House of Saxe-Coburg and Gotha.
Edward VII (1841–r.1901/10)
House of Windsor
George V (1865–r.1910/36) = Mary of Teck
George VI (1895–r.1936/52) = Queen Elizabeth Queen Mother
Elizabeth II (Apr.21.1926–r.1952) = Prince Philip Duke of Edinburgh
(Jun.10.1921)

House of Spencer and Sidney to the modern era

Henry Sidney = Mary Dudley and son Philip Sidney (1554–86) poet, soldier (emissary for Elizabeth I) = Frances Walsingham and bro.: Robert Sidney
Robert Sidney of Leicester (1563–1626) = Barbara Gamage (1) (1563–1621) = and (2) Sarah Blount (1582–1655).
Dorothy Sidney = Henry Spencer (1620–43)
Robert Spencer Sunderland = Anne Churchill Marlborough (Ancestors of Winston Churchill)
Charles Spencer Sunderland = Anne
John Spencer (1708–46) = Georgiana Caroline Cowper
John Spencer (1734–83) = Margaret Georgiana Poyntz
George John Spencer = Lavinia of Lucan (+sis. Georgiana (b.1757) = Cavendish)
Frederick Spencer (1798–1857) = Georgiana (Poyntz) and Adelaide Spencer (d.1877)
Charles Robert Spencer = Margaret
Albert Edward Spencer (1892–1975) = Cynthia Eleanor of Abercorn
Edward John Spencer (1924–92) = (1) Frances Ruth of Formoy = (2) Raine McCorquodale, dau. of Barbara Cartland.
Diana Frances Spencer (Jul.1.1961–Aug.31.1997) = Prince Charles (Nov.14.1948)
+ sibs of D.S. incl. Charles Spencer (b.1964) = Karen Gordon
William Arthur Phillip Louis Mountbatten (Jun.21.1982) = Catherine Elizabeth Middleton (Jan.9.1982)
Henry (Harry) Charles Albert David of Wales (Sep.15.1984) = Rachel Meghan Markle (Aug.4.1981)

In appendix 5 following, a significant representation of English and foreign literary giants testify to the actual and imaginative influence of the Arthurian legends. These legends represent the broken link between the origins of Christian settlements in the British Isles and the more formal establishment of Christian institutions. They cannot be discounted as myth.

Appendix 5

Literary Origins of the Arthurian Legend

GILDAS (C. 490–570)[1]

(T)hat they (the Britons) might not be brought to utter destruction, took arms under the conduct of Ambrosius Aurelianus, a modest man, who of all the Roman nation was then alone in the confusion of this troubled period by chance left alive. His parents, who for their merit were adorned with the purple, had been slain in these same broils, and now his progeny in these our days, although shamefully degenerated from the worthiness of their ancestors, provoke to battle their cruel conquerors, and by the goodness of our Lord obtain the victory. (§.25)

After this, sometimes our countrymen, sometimes the enemy, won the field, to the end that our Lord might in this land try

---

1. GILDAS (516?—570?), British historian, tells us that he was born in the year of the battle of Mount Badon (Mons Badonicus), but gives no indication of the date of the battle. The tenth–century Latin chronicle, which is our next best authority after him for early Welsh history, puts this battle seventy–two years after the point at which its own record begins (Harl. MS 3859, generally quoted as 'Annales Cambriae MS. A'). The editors of 'Monumenta Historica Britannica' make the chronicle begin 444, which would give 516 for the date of both the battle and Gildas's birth. Dictionary of National Biography, edited by Leslie Stephen, and Sidney Lee, Macmillan, London, Vol. VII, 1908, T. F. T. 1224.

after his accustomed manner these his Israelites, whether they loved him or not, until the year of the siege of Bath-hill, when took place also the last almost, though not the least slaughter of our cruel foes, which was (as I am sure) forty-four years and one month after the landing of the Saxons, and also the time of my own nativity. And yet neither to this day are the cities of our country inhabited as before, but being forsaken and overthrown, still lie desolate; our foreign wars having ceased, but our civil troubles still remaining. (§.26)[2]

BEDE (C. 673–MAY 25, 735)[3]

(A)nd unanimously imploring the Divine assistance, that they might not utterly be destroyed. They had at that time for their leader, Ambrosius Aurelius, a modest man, who alone, by chance, of the Roman nation had survived the storm, in which his parents, who were of the royal race, had perished. Under him the Britons revived, and offering battle to the victors, by the help of God, came off victorious. From that day, sometimes the natives, and sometimes their enemies prevailed, till the year of the siege of Baddesdown-hill, when they made no small slaughter of those invaders, about forty-four years after their arrival in England.[4]

---

2. Gildas, *The Ruin of Britain*, 22.

3. BEDE, or more accurately BAEDA (673–735), was born in the district which was the next year given for the foundation of the monastery of St. Peter's, at Wearmouth, in what is now the county of Durham. The exact date of his birth has been disputed. It depends on the short account which he gives of himself at the end of the 'Historia Ecclesiastica.' He brings that work down to 731 –for the notice of the defeat of the Saracens in the following year is probably an insertion made later, either by himself or by some other hand–and he says that he had then reached his fifty–ninth year. Mabillon (Acta SS. O. B. iii. 505) is therefore probably right in fixing his birth in 673. Some, however (PAGI, Critic, in Ann. Baron. p. 141, followed by Stevenson), place it in 674, and others (GEHLE, Disput. Hist. Theol. and Mon. Hist. Brit.} in 672. Besides the short account which Baeda gives of himself, and what we can glean from his writings and from incidental notices of him by others, we have no trustworthy materials for his life until we come to his last hours; for the two anonymous biographies of him (H. E. ed. Smith, App., and MABILLON, saec. iii. 501) are one of the eleventh and the other of the twelfth century. [Baedae Hist. Eccl. et Opera Historica, Stevenson; other works in Opera Omnia, ed. Giles; Gehle's Disputatio Hist.–Theol. de Baedae vita, &c.; Wright's Biog. Lit.; Ebert's Bibliog. Dict.; and authorities quoted in text.] W. H. Dictionary of National Biography, edited by Leslie Stephen, Macmillan, London, Vol. IV, 1885, 98–105

4. Bede, *Ecclesiastical History*, 26.

NENNIUS THE HISTORY OF THE BRITONS. C.830 AD[5]

The eighth (battle) was near Guinnion castle where Arthur bore the image of the Holy Virgin, mother of God, upon his shoulders, and through the power of our Lord Jesus Christ, and the holy Mary, put the Saxons to flight.[67]

CARADOC OF LLANCARVAN 12TH C[8]

Cadwalader had no sooner received this vision, but immediately he relates the whole to his friend Alan, who presently consulted

5. NENNIUS (*fl.* 796), historian, is the traditional author of the 'Historia Britonum.' From incidental allusions in the body of the work it would appear that the time of writing was the end of the eighth century, and that the counties of Brecknock and Radnor formed the district in which the writer lived. In § 49 the author gives a genealogy of Fernmail, 'qui regit modo in regionibus duabus Buelt et Guorthigornaun.' Builth was a 'cantref' of Powys and Gwrtheyrnion a 'cwmwd'of Radnor, while Fernmail's date can be fixed by a genealogy given in 'Y Cymmrodor,' x. 110, and by other evidence, between 785 and 815 (Zimmer, pp. 66–71). In § 35 a reference to Catell, king of Powys, points to the date of writing having been previous to 808 (*ib.* pp. 71–3). The genealogies given in §§ 57–65 favour the same period as the date of the final composition of the 'Historia,' for the 'Genealogia Merciorum' in § 60 ends with Ecgfrith, the son of Offa, who reigned for a few months in 796; it is therefore probable that the work was originally completed in that year (*ib.* pp. 81– 82). That the writer lived on the borders of Mercia in Brecknock or Radnor is further probable from the inclusion in the 'Mirabilia' in § 73 of two wonders in Buelt and Ereing (Erchenfield in Herefordshire), of the latter of which he remarks, 'ego solus probavi.' C. L. K. Dictionary of National Biography, edited by Sidney Lee. Vol. XIV, 1909, 217–21

6. Nennius. *The History of the Britons.* 29.

7. Henry of Huntingdon, who likewise gives this account, says the image was upon his shield; and it has been well remarked that the Welsh ysgwyd is a shoulder and ysgwydd a shield, and that a Welsh original had been differently translated. The Four Ancient Books of Wales, William F. Skene, 55.

8. CARADOG of LLANCARVAN (d.1147?) Welsh ecclesiastic and chronicler was as his name indicates, probably either born at or a monk at the famous abbey of Llancarvan in the vale of Glamorgan. He was apparently one of the brilliant band of men of letters that gathered round Earl Robert of Gloucester, the bastard son of Henry I. Caradog was a friend of Geoffrey of Monmouth, who at the end of his famous 'British History,' which ends with Cadwaladr Vendigaid, says: 'The princes who afterwards ruled in Wales I committed to Caradog of Llancarvan, for he was my contemporary. And to him I gave the materieals to write that book.' (Hist. Brit. bk. xii. Ch. xx.) [Bale's Script. Brit. Cat. pp. 195–6; Pits, De Angliae Scriptoribus, p. 215; Owen's Introduction to the Gwentian Brut (Cambrian Archaeological Assc.); Wright's Biog. Brit. Lit. Anglo–Saxon period, p. 199, Anglo–Norman period, p. 166–7; Stevenson's Gildas (Eng. Hist. Soc.), Preface, pp. xxvii–xxx.] T. F. T. Dictionary of National Biography, edited by Leslie Stephen. Vol. 9, 30.

all his prophetical books, chiefly the famous works of the two Merlins, Ambrosius and Sylvestris : the first is said to have been begotten on a spirit, and born in the town of Carmarthen, whence he received the name of Merlin, and to have flourished in the reign of King Vortigern. The latter, called Caledonius, from the forest Caledon in Scotland, and Sylvestris or Merlin Wyllt, because he fell mad and lived desolately after he had seen a monstrous shape in the air, prophesied in the time of King Arthur, and far more full and intelligible than the former.[9]

GEOFFREY OF MONMOUTH (C. 1100–C. 1155)[10]

Arthur succeeds Uther his father in the kingdom of Britain and besieges Colgrin. p.149

> For on Modred's side fell Cheldric, Elasius, Egbrict, and Bunignus, Saxons; Gillapatric, Gillamor, Gistafel, and Gillarius, Irish; also the Scots and Picts, with almost all their leaders: on Arthur's side, Olbrict, king of Norway; Aschillius, king of Dacia; Cador Limenic Cassibellaun, with many thousands of others, as well Britons as foreigners, that he had brought with him. And even the renowned king Arthur himself was mortally wounded; and being carried thence to the isle of Avallon to be cured of his wounds, he gave up the crown of Britain to his kinsman Constantine, the son

9. Caradoc, *The History of Wales*, 9.

10. GEOFFREY of MONMOUTH (1100?–1154), otherwise Galfridus or Gaufridus Arturus, Galfridus Monemutensis, styled by Welsh writers Galffrai or Gruffyd ab Arthur, bishop of St. Asaph and chronicler, was either born or bred at Monmouth about the commencement of the twelfth century, and may have been at one time a monk of the Benedictine abbey there. He was the son of Arthur, who, according to Welsh authorities, was family priest of William, earl of Gloucester, an apocryphal personage. Geoffrey was brought up as 'foster son' by his paternal uncle Uchtryd, archdeacon and subsequently bishop of Llandaff (*Archæologia Cambrensis*, 3rd ser. 1864, x. 124). He went to Oxford and made the acquaintance of Archdeacon Walter [see Calenius, Walter] as early as 1129, when the two witnessed the Oseney charter subscribed by Geoffrey as Gaufridus Arturus (see *Journ. Arch. Instit.* 1858, p. 305). It was from Walter that Geoffrey professed to have obtained the foundation of his great work. He begins and ends his 'Historia Regum Britanniæ' with an acknowledgment that it was based upon a certain 'librum vetustissimum' 'Britannici sermonis, quem Gualterus Oxenfordensis archidiaconus ex Britannia advexit.' Before the book was half completed, however, Alexander, bishop of Lincoln [q. v.], desired Geoffrey to make a Latin version of the 'Prophecies of Merlin' from the Cymric. Wright (*Biog. Lit.* 1846, p. 144) and Hardy (*Catalogue*, i. 350) agree in referring the final edition of the 'Historia Regum Britanniæ,' as we now possess it, to the autumn of 1147.

of Cador, duke of Cornwall, in the five hundred and forty-second year of our Lord's incarnation. 192–3[11]

WACE 1100[12]

Arthur desired to hold his court at Caerleon, and to bid his barons to attend him everyone. He commanded, therefore, to the feast, kings and earls, dukes and viscounts, knights and barons, bishops and abbots. Nor did Arthur bid Englishmen alone, but Frenchman and Burgundian, Auvergnat and Gascon, Norman and Poitivin, Angevin and Fleming, together with him of Brabant, Hainault, and Lorraine, the king bade to his dinner. Frisian and Teuton, Dane and Norwegian, Scot, Irish, and Icelander, him of Cathness and of Gothland, the lords of Galway and of the furthest islands of the Hebrides, Arthur summoned them all.[13]

11. Monmouth, *History of the Kings of Britain*, 192–3.

12. WACE (*fl.* 1170), chronicler, was born in Jersey, probably about 1100. His parents' names are unknown; his mother was a daughter of Toustein, chamberlain to Robert I, duke of Normandy (*Romania*, ix. 526). When a child, Wace was 'put to letters' at Caen; later he 'studied long in France;' before 1136 he was settled at Caen as a 'clerc lisant' and a man of letters. Of his 'many romances' (narrative poems in the Romance tongue, i.e. old French) only five remain. His 'Life of S. Nicolas' has been edited by Monmerqué (*Mélanges publiés par la Société des Bibliophiles Français*, vol. vii.) and by Delius (Bonn, 1850); his poem on the 'Conception of the Virgin' by Mancel and Trébutien (Caen, 1842), and by Luzarche (Tours, 1859); the fragments of his 'Life of St. Margaret' by Joly (Paris, 1879); and his 'Brut' by Le Roux de Lincy (Rouen, 1836–8). The last-named, interesting chiefly as having served as the basis of Layamon's, was 'made' in 1155, and presented, according to Layamon [q. v.], to Eleanor of Aquitaine [q. v.] In 1160 Wace 'set to work on the history of Rou (Hrolf) and his race' for Henry II. In March 1162 he was with the court at Fécamp, and in or before 1169 the king gave him a prebend at Bayeux. If we may identify him with the 'Wascius' mentioned in a Bayeux charter of 1174 (Du Méril, p. 221), he was still living in that year. [The best account of Wace and his work is by M, Gaston Paris in Romania, 1880, ix. 594 et seq. The sole original authorities are Wace himself and four charters cited by Du Méril, Essais sur quelques points d'Archéolgie, pp. 220, 221. See also Körtubg's essay, Ueber die Quellen des Roman de Rou (Leipzig, 1867); Mr. J. H. Round's article on Wace and his Authorities, in Engl. Hist. Rev. October 1893 (reprinted in Feudal England, pp. 409–18); and pp. 31–37 of Mr. T. A. Archer's article on the Battle of Hastings, in Engl. Hist. Rev. January 1894.] K. N. Dictionary of National Biography, edited by Leslie Stephen. 1890, Vol. 58, 404–5

13. Wace. *Arthurian Chronicles*, 64.

WALTER MAP (C.1140–1210)[14]

R. Silvestris Merlin
Tolde prophecie well and fyn,
And prophecied well sure
Under Kyng Arthure,
Openly, and not so cloos
As Merlin Ambros.
Ther ben hilles in Snowdonye
That ben wonderly hye,
With heyght as grete alwaye
As a man may goo a daye;
And heet Eriri on Walssh,
Snowy-hilles in Englissh.
In these hilles ther is
Leese ynouh for al bestis of Walis;
These hilles on coppe beres

14. MAP or MAPES, WALTER (fl. 1200) mediæval author and wit, was from his name of Welsh descent, and he speaks of the Welsh as his fellow-countrymen (De Nugis, ii. 20). Map, which is Welsh for 'son,' and which has been shortened to Ap in forming modern patronymics, seems to have been used by the Saxons as a nickname for a Welshman. Walter himself was almost, certainly a native of Herefordshire; he calls himself 'a marcher of Wales' (ib. ii. 23), and his De Nugis Curialium' abounds in legends relating to 'that county; moreover, he was throughout his life more or less closely connected with the city of Hereford. It is known that there was a succession of Walter Maps at Wormsley, about eight miles north of that city, between 1150 and 1240 (cf. citations from Hist. MSS. 3586 and 6726, ap. Ward, Cat. of Romanca, i. 736–8). Walter may have been a member of this family, but there is no certain evidence, although he is known to have held land at Ullingswick, at no great distance (Cart. S. Peter Gloucester, ii. 156, Rolls Ser.) It has, however, been argued, though on very insufficient grounds, that Map was a native of Pembrokeshire (Notes and Queries, 3rd ser. xi. 386; Hardy, Cat. Brit. Hist. ii. 487). All that we know of his parents is that they were of sufficient station to have been of service to Henry II, before and after he became king (De Nugis, v. 6). Map was probably born about 1140, and went to study at Paris soon after 1154, for Louis VII had lately married Constance of Castile, and he was there at least as late as 1160, for he studied under Girard la Pucelle, who began to teach in or about that year (ib. v. 5, ii. 7). He was, however, back in England before 1162, for he was present at the court of Henry II, while Thomas Becket was still chancellor (ib. ii. 23). Map says that he had earned Henry's favour and affection through his parent's merits (ib. v. 6). He was one of the clerks of the royal household, and thus was frequently employed justice itinerant (Giraldus Cambrennis, Opera, iv. 219); his name occurs in this capacity at Gloucester in 1173 (Madox, Hist. Exhequer, i. 701), and as a justice in eyre for Herefordshire and the neighbouring counties in 1185 (Eyton, Itinerary of Henry II, pp. 176, 265). Giraldus says that Map always excepted the Jews and Cistercians from his oath to do justice to all men, since 'it was absurd to do justice to those who were just to none.' Map was with Henry at Limoges in 1173, when he had care of Peter of Tarentaise. Dictionary of National Biography, 1885–1900, Volume 36, by Charles Lethbridge Kingsford, p. 109

Two grete fissh weres;
Conteyned in that one ponde
Meveth with the wynde an ilond,
As though it dyde swymme,
And neyheth to the brymme,
So that heerdes have grete wonder
And wene that the world meveth under.[15]

LAYAMON (C. 1185–1225)[16]

Then was it accomplished that Merlin whilom said, that mickle care should be of Arthur's departure. The Britons believe yet that he is alive, and dwelleth in Avalun with the fairest of all elves; and the Britons ever yet expect when Arthur shall return. Was never the man born, of ever any lady chosen, that knoweth of the sooth, to say more of Arthur. But whilom was a sage hight Merlin; he said with words—his sayings were sooth—that an Arthur should yet come to help the English.[17]

15. Mapes, *Latin Poems*, 354.

16. LAYAMON, early English poet, was the author of a chronicle of Britain entitled *Brut*, a paraphrase of the *Brut d' Angleterre* by Wace, a native of Jersey, who is also known as the author of the *Roman de Rou*. The excellent edition of Layamon by Sir F. Madden (Society of Antiquaries, London, 1847) should be consulted. All that is known concerning Layamon is derived from two extant MSS., which present texts that often vary considerably, and it is necessary to understand their comparative value before any conclusions can be drawn. The older text (here called the A–text) lies very near the original text, which is unfortunately lost, though it now and then omits lines which are absolutely necessary to the sense. The later text (here called the B–text) represents a later recension of the original version by another writer who frequently omits couplets, and alters the language by the substitution of better–known words for such as seemed to be obsolescent; e.g. *harme* (harm) in place of *balewe* (bale), and *dead* in place of *feie* (fated to die, or dead). Hence little reliance can be placed on the B–text, its chief merit being that it sometimes preserves couplets which seem to have been accidentally omitted in A; besides which, it affords a valuable commentary on the original version. See *Layamon's Brut, or a Chronicle of Britain; a Poetical Semi-Saxon Paraphrase of the Brut of Wace*; . . . by Sir F. Madden (1847); B. ten Brink, *Early English Literature*, trans, by H.M.Kennedy (in Bohn's Standard Library, 1885); H Morley, *English Writers*, vol. iii. (1888); J. Schipper, *Englische Metrik*, i. (Bonn, 1882), E. Guest, *A History of English Rhythms* (new ed. by W. W. Skeat, 1882), Article "Layamon," in the *Dict. Nat. Biog.*; *Six Old English Chronicles*, including Gildas, Nennius and Geoffrey of Monmouth (in Bohn's Antiquarian Library); *Le Roux de Lincy, Le Roman de Brut, par Wace, avec un commentaire et des notes* (Rouen, 1836—1838), E. Matzner, *Altenglische Sprachproben* (Berlin, 1867), (J. W. H.) Dictionary of National Biography, edited by Leslie Stephen. 1892, Vol. 32, 301–2

17. Layamon, *Arthurian Chronicles*, 264.

LAYAMON, TALIESIN'S PROPHECY

In Kinbelins days, who was king in Britain, came on this middle-earth a maidens son; born [he] was in Bethlehem, of the best of all maidens [a sweet maiden]. He is named Jhesu Christ, through the Holy Ghost, 'of all worlds the treasure, lord of angels'! Father he is in heaven, 'and' 'mankinds [each man his] saviour; 'Son he is on earth, of the good maiden;' and the Holy Ghost he holdeth with himself.[18]

GERALD OF WALES (C. 12TH C), DE INSTRUCTIONE PRINCIPIUM, 1216[1920]

Here in The Isle of Avalon Lies Buried the Renowned King Arthur, With Guinevere, His Second Wife." Hic jacet seculptus inclytus Rex Arthurus cum Wennevereia uxore sua secunda in insula Avalonia."

The tomb of king Arthur and Guinevere

Arthuri quoque Britonum regis inclyti memoria est non supprimenda, quem monasterii Glastoniensis egregii, cujus et ipse patronus suis diebus fuerat praecipuus et largitor ac sublevator magnificus, historiae multum extollunt. Prae cunctis enim

---

18. *Layamon's Brut*, 386 [9064].

19. Geraldi Cambrensis, *De Instructione Principium*, Vol 8 126.

20. GIRALDUS CAMBRENSIS (1146–1220), medieval historian, also called Gerald de Barri, was born in Pembrokeshire. He was the son of William de Barri and Augharat, a daughter of Gerald, the ancestors of the Fitzgeralds and the Welsh princess, Nesta, formerly mistress of King Henry I. Falling under the influence of his uncle, David Fitzgerald, bishop of St David's, he determined to enter the church. He studied at Paris, and his works show that he had applied himself closely to the study of the Latin poets. In 1172 he was appointed to collect tithe in Wales and showed such vigour that he was made archdeacon. In 1176 an attempt was made to elect him bishop of St David's, but Henry II. was unwilling to see any one with powerful native connexions a bishop in Wales. In 1180, after another visit to Paris, he was appointed commissiary to the bishop of St David's, who had ceased to reside. But Giraldus threw up his post, indignant at the indifference of the bishop to the welfare of his see. In 1184 he was made one of the king's chaplains and was elected to accompany Prince John on his voyage to Ireland. While there he wrote a Topographia Hibernica, which is full of information, and a strongly prejudiced history of the conquest, the Expugnatio Hibernica. In 1186 he read his work with great applause before the masters and scholars of Oxford. In 1188 he was sent into Wales with the primate Baldwin to preach the Third Crusade. 1911 Encyclopædia Britannica, Volume 12.

ecclesiis regni sui sanctae Dei genitricis Mariae Glastoniensem
ecclesiam plus dilexit et prae caeteris longe majori evotione pro-
movit. Unde cum vir bellator exstiterit, in anteriori parte clipei
sui Beatae Virginis imaginem interius, ut eam in conflictu prae
oculis semper haberet, depingi fecerat; cujus et pedes, quoties
positus in congressionis articulo fuerat, deosculari cum plurima
devotione consueverat.

MONKS OF ST. ALBANS, CHRONICA MAJORA,
MID- TO LATE-13TH CENTURY

Here lies the renowned King Arthur, buried in the isle of Avalon

ADAM OF DOMERHAM, HISTORIA DE
REBUS GLASTONIENSIBUS, 1291[21]

Here lies interred in the isle of Avalon, the renowned King Arthur

21. ADAM of Domerham (d. after 1291), monk of Glastonbury, was a native of
Domerham, a village in Wiltshire belonging to Glastonbury Abbey. He wrote a history of his house, entitled 'Historia de Rebus gestis Glastoniensibus,' which exists in a
manuscript in the library of Trinity College, Cambridge, possibly the author's own copy.
It has been published by Thomas Hearne in two volumes. The first volume, however,
does not contain any part of the work of Adam. The history forms a continuation of the
treatise of William of Malmesbury, 'De Antiquitate Glastoniæ.' It begins at 1126, when
Henry of Blois, afterwards bishop of Winchester, became abbot, and ends with the death
of Abbot John of Taunton in 1291. A large part of the history is taken up with papal
bulls, charters, and other documents. From some expressions used by Adam about the
character of Abbot Michael (1235–1252) it may be supposed that he entered the convent
in his time. He was, therefore, a member of the fraternity during part of that period of
difficulty and discord which followed the annexation of the abbey to the see of Wells by
Bishop Savaric, a proceeding which brought on Glastonbury heavy expense and loss
of property, and which endangered its independence. He relates the history of these
troubles at considerable length, and says in his preface that his object in writing his book
was to incite his readers to protect or to increase the prosperity of his church, which once
enjoyed privileges above all others, but was then bereft of her liberties and possessions.
Adam, who was an eyewitness of the proceedings, gives an interesting account of the
visit of Edward I and his queen to Glastonbury in April 1278, when the tomb of King
Arthur was opened, and his bones and the bones of Guinevere were borne by the English
king and his queen to a new resting–place before the high altar. Adam appears to have
followed the example of his abbot, John of Taunton, in doing his best to recover for the
monastery some of the treasures which it had lost. His history is generally said to end at
1290, the date assigned by him to the death of John of Taunton, with which he concludes

WOLFRAM VON ESCHENBACH (C. 1200-D. C. 1216)[22]

Parzival enters the palace of the Fisher King

> And last of those maids a maiden, o'er the others was she the
> queen,

---

his work. This date seems, however, to be incorrect, for he records the burial of Eleanor, queen of Edward I, as taking place 27 Dec. 1290. He says that after that event Abbot John was summoned by the king to the funeral of his mother, Eleanor of Provence, which was performed at Ambresbury on the festival of the Nativity of the B. V. Mary, 8 Sept. 1291. Abbot John was sick at the time but did not like to fail in obedience to the king's command. His death on the festival of St. Michael is the last event recorded by Adam of Domerham, who therefore brings down his story to 1291. [Adam de Domerham, Historia de Rebus gestis Glastoniensibus, ed. Hearne, Oxford, 1727; John of Glaston. Chronicon, ed. Hearne, 1726; Dugdale, Monasticon, i. 6; Willis, Architectural History of Glastonbury; Jas. Parker in Somerset Archæol. Society's volume for 1880.] W. H.

22. WOLFRAM VON ESCHENBACH, the most important and individual poet of medieval Germany, flourished during the end of the 12th and beginning of the 13th century. He was one of the brilliant group of Minnesingers whom the Landgrave Herrmann of Thuringia gathered round him at the historic castle of the Wartburg. We know by his own statement that he was a Bavarian, and came of a knightly race, counting his achievements with spear and shield far above his poetical gifts. The Eschenbach from which he derived his name was most probably Ober-Eschenbach, not far from Pleinfeld and Nuremberg; there is no doubt that this was the place of his burial, and so late as the 17th century his tomb was to be seen in the church of Ober-Eschenbach, which was then the burial place of the Teutonic knights.

The problem of the source of the Parzival is the crux of medieval literary criticism (see Perceval), These are the leading points. The poem is divided into sixteen books. From iii. to xii., inclusive, the story marches *pari passu* with the Perceval of Chretien de Troyes, at one moment agreeing almost literally with the French text, at the next introducing details quite unknown to it. Books i. and ii., unrepresented in Chretien, relate the fortunes of the hero's father, and connect the story closely with the house of Anjou; the four concluding books agree with the commencement, and further connect the Grail story with that of the Swan Knight, for the first time identifying that hero with Parzival's son, a version followed by the later German romance of Lohengrin. At the conclusion Wolfram definitely blames Chretien for having mistold the tale, while a certain Kiot, the Provencal (whom he has before named as his source), had told it aright from beginning to end. Other peculiarities of this version are the representation of the Grail itself as a stone, and of the inhabitants of the castle as an ordered knighthood, Templeisen; the numerous allusions to, and evident familiarity with, Oriental learning in its various branches; and above all, the connecting thread of ethical interpretation which runs through the whole poem. The Parzival is a soul-drama; the conflict between light and darkness, faith and doubt, is its theme, and the evolution of the hero's character is steadily and consistently worked out.

Wolfram was, above all, a man of deeply religious character (witness his introduction to Willehalm), and it seems to have been this which specially impressed the mind of his compatriots; in the 13th century poem of Der Wartburg-Krieg it is Wolfram who is chosen as the representative of Christianity, to oppose the enchanter Klingsor von Ungerland. (J. L. W.) *The Encyclopaedia Brittanica* Vol. XXVIII, 1911, New York, 775-6

So fair her face that they thought them 'twas the morning's
    dawn, I ween!
And they saw her clad in raiment of Pfellel of Araby,
And she bare aloft on a cushion of verdant Achmardi
Root and blossom of Paradise garden, that thing which men call
    'The Grail,'
The crown of all earthly wishes, fair fulness that ne'er shall fail!
Repanse de Schoie did they call her, in whose hands the Grail
    might lie,
By the Grail Itself elected was she to this office high.
And they who would here do service, those maids must be pure
    of heart,
And true in life, nor falsehood shall have in their dealings part.[23]

The peculiar presentment of the Knights of the Grail as Templars
(Templeisen), having their residence in a castle surrounded by
a forest, recalls the fact that a close connection between the Order of Templars and the House of Anjou had existed for some
time previous to the date of this poem, a tax for the benefit of
the Order having been imposed on all his dominions by Fulk v.
on his return from his first pilgrimage to Jerusalem in 1120. A
community of Knights Templars was founded by Henry Fitz-
Empress fifty years later at Vaubourg, in the forest of Roumare
which became very famous. (The location of Monsalvasch in
the Pyrenees hardly seems to accord with the indications of the
poem, which make it only thirty-six hours' ride from Nantes)
... Finally, the name of the poet claimed by Wolfram as his authority, Kiot = Guiot = Guy, is distinctly Angevin, the hereditary
Angevin princely names being Fulk, Geoffrey, and Guy.[24] (From
Jessie Weston)

RALPH OF COGGESHALL C.1225[25]

This year was found in Glastonbury the bones of the famous
Arthur, the former king of England; in an ancient sarcophagus

23. Von Eschenbach, *Parzival*, 135.

24. Von Eschenbach, *Parzival*, 294.

25. COGGESHALL, RALPH of (*fl.* 1207), chronicler, a native of Bernewell, Cam-
bridgeshire, and a monk of the Cistercian abbey at Coggeshall, was chosen abbot in 1207,
and about midsummer 1218, contrary to the wish of the convent, resigned the abbacy on
account of ill-health. He took up the chronicle of Ralph Niger (edited by Colonel Robert

stored near two ancient erect pyramids in which words were inscribed but because of their extreme wear the information could not be read.

Hoc autem anno inventa, sunt Glastingeberiam ossa famosissimi Arturi, quondam regis Britanniae, in quodam vetustissimo sarcophago recondita, circa quod duae antiquae pyramides stabant erectae, in quibus litterae quaedam exaratae erant, sed ob nimiam barbariem et deformationem legi non poterant.[26]

MARGAM ABBEY (WALES) CHRONICLE

Here lies the famous King Arthur, buried in the isle of Avalon.
Some date it early 1190s, others 14th century

DANTE ALIGHIERI (C. 1265–SEPTEMBER 14, 1321)[27]

If thou art bent to know the primal root.

Anstruther for the Caxton Society, 1851), who ended his work at 1161, corrected the expressions of indignation against Henry II with which the earlier writer concludes, and carried the chronicle down to 1178. The 'Chronicon Anglicanum' that bears the abbot's name begins at 1066. It contains several references to the affairs of the Cistercian order and to local events, such as those which concerned the monastery itself or its neighbourhood, and a large number of matters which were either told to the writer by visitors to the abbey, or which in various ways came under his notice and struck him as especially important or curious. Up to 1187 the entries are generally brief. After that date, when Ralph undertook the work, they become full, and are often of considerable importance. Although from an entry under 1207 it would seem as though the work was carried down to 1227, none of the copies of it extend beyond 1224. Manuscripts of the 'Chronicon' exist in the Cottonian collection in the British Museum, in the College of Arms, and in the National Library at Paris. From the imperfect Paris thirteenth–century manuscript, formerly belonging to the church of St. Victor, Martene printed the 'Chronicon' down to 1200, and from 1213–16 as distinct works in his 'Veterum Scriptorum . . . collectio,' v. 801–69, and nearly the whole is reprinted in 'Dom. Bouquet,' vol. xviii. The Cottonian MS., the author's autograph copy, has been followed by Mr. J. Stevenson in the edition he prepared for the Rolls Series in 1875. The 'Chronicon Terræ Sanctæ,' which has been ascribed to the author of the 'Coggeshall Chronicle,' is by another hand. Both the 'Chronicon Anglicanum' and the 'Chronicon Terræ Sanctæ' were printed by Mr. A. J. Donkin in 1856. [R. de Coggeshall's Chronicon Anglicanum, preface, and 162, 163, 187, ed. Stevenson, Rolls Series; Hardy's Descriptive Catalogue, ii. 415, 541, iii. 65, Rolls Series.] W. H. Dictionary of National Biography, edited by Leslie Stephen. 1887, Vol. XI, 223

26. Coggeshall, *Chronicon Anglicanum*, 36.

27. DANTE, Dante (or Durante) Alighieri (1265–1321), the greatest of Italian

From whence our love gat being, I will do
As one, who weeps and tells his tale. One day,
For our delight we read of Lancelot,
How him love thrall 'd. Alone we were, and no
Suspicion near us. Hell, Canto V (121–126)

Not him (Mordred), whose breast and shadow Arthur's hand
At that one blow dissevered. Hell, Canto XXXII (59–60)

And Beatrice, that a little space
Was severed, smiled; reminding me of her,
Whose cough emboldened (as the story holds)
To first offence the doubting Guenever. Paradise, Canto XVI
(12–15)

L'autorite de Dante suffirait pour nous convaincre qu' Arnaud
Daniel avait compose plusieurs romans. Mais il reste une preuve
positive de l'existence d'un roman d'Arnaud Daniel; c'est celui
de *Lancelot du Lac*, dont la traduction fut faite, vers la fin du
treizieme siecle, en allemand, par Ulrich de Zatchitschoven, qui
nomme Arnaud Daniel comme l'auteur original.[28]

poets, was born at Florence about the middle of May 1265. He was descended from an
ancient family, but from one which at any rate for several generations had belonged
to the burgher and not to the knightly class. His biographers have attempted on very
slight grounds to deduce his origin from the Frangipani, one of the oldest senatorial
families of Rome. We can affirm with greater certainty that he was connected with the
Elisei who took part in the building of Florence under Charles the Great. Dante himself
does not, with the exception of a few obscure and scattered allusions, carry his ancestry
beyond the warrior Cacciaguida, whom he met in the sphere of Mars (Par. xv. 87, foil.).

Bibliography. —The first attempt at a bibliography of editions of Dante was made
in Pasquali's edition of his collected works (Venice, 1739); but the first really adequate
work on the subject is that of the viscount Colomb de Batines (1846–1848). A supplement by Dr Guido Biagi appeared in 1888. Julius Petzholdt had already covered some
of the same ground in Bibliographia Dantea, extending from 1865 to 1880. The period
from 1891 to 1900 has been dealt with by SS. Passerini and Mazzi in Un Decennio di
bibliografia Dantesca (1905). The catalogues of the two libraries already named, and
that of Harvard University, are worth consulting. For the MSS. Dr E. Moore's Textual
Criticism (1889) is the most complete guide. (A. J. B.*) The Encyclopaedia Brittanica
Vol. VII, 1911, New York, 810–7.

28. Dante Alighieri, *The Vision*, 483.

GIOVANNI BOCCACCIO (C. JUNE 1313–DECEMBER 21, 1375)[29]

In Boccacio's Decameron, the story of Prencipe Galeotto (Prince Galehaut), is a fictional king who is a close friend of Lancelot and an enemy of King Arthur.

JOHN CAPGRAVE ~1400[30]

In these dayes was Arthures body founde in the cherch yerd at Glaskinbury in a hol hok, a crosse of led leyd to a ston, and the

29. BOCCACCIO. A complete edition of Boccaccio's Italian writings, in 17 vols., was published by Moutier (Florence, 1834). The life of Boccaccio has been written by Tiraboschi, Mazzuchelli, Count Baldelli (*Vita di Boccaccio*, Florence, 1806), and others. In English the best biography is Edward Hutton (1909.) The first printed edition of the *Decameron* is without date, place or printer's name; but it is believed to belong to the year 1469 or 1470, and to have been printed at Florence. Besides this, Baldelli mentions eleven editions during the 15th century. The entire number of editions by far exceeds a hundred. A curious expurgated edition, authorized by the pope, appeared at Florence, 1573. Here, however, the grossest indecencies remain, the chief alteration being the change of the improper personages from priests and monks into laymen. The best old edition is that of Florence, 1527. Of modern reprints, that by Forfoni (Florence, 1857) deserves mention. Manni has written a *Storia del Decamerone* (1742), and a German scholar, M. Landau, who published (Vienna, 1869) a valuable investigation of the sources of the *Decameron*, subsequently brought out in 1877 a general study of Boccaccio's life and works. An interesting English translation of the *Decameron* appeared in 1624, under the title *The Model of Mirth, Wit, Eloquence and Conversation.*—(F. H.) The *Encyclopaedia Brittanica* Vol. IV, 1911, New York, 102–5.

30. CAPGRAVE, JOHN, (1393–1464), Augustinian friar, theologian, and historian, was born, as he has himself noted in his chronicle (p. 259), on 21 April 1393. He was a native of Lynn in Norfolk— 'my cuntre is Northfolk, of the toun of Lynne' (*Prologue to the Life of St. Katharine*)—where he passed nearly all his days. Bale and others wrongly name Kent as his county. Studious in youth, and 'sticking to his books like a limpet to its rocks,' he was sent to one of the universities, but to which one is uncertain; Leland names Cambridge, but only on conjecture. Tanner, however, adduces evidence for this university from Capgrave's own words in a manuscript now destroyed (*Cotton. MS.* Vitellius D. xv, *Life of St. Gilbert*). On the other hand, Bale and others state that Capgrave took the degree of Doctor of Divinity at Oxford; and Pamphilus (f. 139) adds that he lectured there. It has been suggested (introd. to Capgrave's *Chronicle*, Rolls Series, p. x) that he may have received his early education at Cambridge, that place being more conveniently near to Lynn, and afterwards migrated to the sister university. He was ordained priest in 1417 or 1418, four or five years, he tells us (*De illustr. Henricis*, p. 127), before the birth of Henry VI. At an early age he had elected to enter the order of Augustine Friars; but we do not know when he first became an inmate of the house of the friars at Lynn. It may not, however, be too much to infer that he was connected with it from youth, and that he

letteris hid betwyx the ston and the led. This was the wryting, as
Giraldus seith, which red it:—"Here lith the nobil Kyng Arthure,
with his seconde wyf, Veneraca, in the ylde cleped Avallone."
His bones, whan thei were founde, passed the mesure of other
men. (1170 AD).[31]

JEHAN FROISSART (C. 1337–C. 1410)[32]

In 1369 Froissart's patron, Wenceslaus of Bohemia, Duke of Luxembourg
and Brabant, commissions Meliador, an Arthurian romance.

may have received a part of his education within its walls. Soon after taking his doctor's
degree he was promoted to be provincial of his order in England. An official document
dated 1456 is quoted by White Kennet (Parochial Antiquities, 1818, ii. 399) in which
Capgrave, as provincial, recognises a claim to the patronage of the convent of Austin
Friars at Oxford, then existing near the site of Wadham College.

[Bale's Script. Brit. Cat.; Leland's Commentarii de Scriptoribus Brit. (1709); Jos.
Pamphili Chronica Ordinis fratrum Erem. S. Augustini (1581); Tanner's Bibl. Brit.;
Rolls editions of Capgrave's Chronicle and Liber de illustr. Henricis (1858).] E.M.T.
Dictionary of National Biography, edited by Leslie Stephen. 1887, Vol. IX, 20–2.

31. Capgrave, The Chronicle of England, 140.

32. FROISSART, JEAN (1338–1410?), French chronicler and raconteur, historian
of his own times. The personal history of Froissart, the circumstances of his birth and
education, the incidents of his life, must all be sought in his own verses and chronicles.
He possessed in his own lifetime no such fame as that which attended the steps of
Petrarch; when he died it did not occur to his successors that a chapter might well be
added to his Chronicle setting forth what manner of man he was who wrote it. The
village of Lestines, where he was cure, has long forgotten that a great writer ever lived
there. They cannot point to any house in Valenciennes as the lodging in which he put
together his notes and made history out of personal reminiscences. It is not certain
when or where he died, or where he was buried. One church, it is true, doubtfully
claims the honour of holding his bones. It is that of St Monegunda of Chimay.

"Gallorum sublimis honos et fama tuorum, Hie Froissarde, jaces, si modo forte jaces."

The first edition of Froissart's Chronicles was published in Paris. It bears no date; the
next editions are those of the years 1505, 1514, 1518 and 1520. The edition of Buchon,
1824, was a continuation of one commenced by Dacier. The best modern editions are
those of Kervyn de Lettenhove (Brussels, 1863–1877) and Simeon Luce (Paris, 1869–
1888); for bibliography see Potthast, Bibliotheca hist. medii aevi, i. (Berlin, 1896). An
abridgment was made in Latin by Belleforest, and published in 1672. An English translation was made by Bouchier, Lord Berners, and published in London, 1525. See the "Tudor Translations" edition of Berners (Nutt, 1901), with introduction by W. P. Ker; and
the " Globe " edition, with introduction by G. C. Macaulay. The translation by Thomas
Johnes was originally published in 1802–1805. For Froissart's poems see Scheler's text
in K. de Lettenhove's complete edition; Meliador has been edited by Longnon for the
Societe des Anciens Textes (1895–1899). See also Madame Darmesteter (Duclaux),
Froissart (1894). (W. Be.) Encyclopaedia Brittanica, Vol. XI, New York 1911, 242–6.

Car en Escoce on entendi 2015
Que li rois Artus court tenroit
A Carlion, et la venroit
En devant de le Pentecouste.
Ceste nouvelle bien agouste
Au roy Hermont et a ses gens, 2020
Car il dient que tant est gens
Li rois Artus, et de grant nom,
C'au jour nommé, a Carlion,
Sera fleur de chevalerie.[33]

GEOFFREY CHAUCER (C. 1340–1400) THE WIFE OF BATH[34]

In the olden days of King Arthúr,
Of which that Britons speaken great honoúr,
All was this land fulfillèd of faèrie;
The Elf-Queen, with her jolly company,

33. Froissart, *Méliador,* 59.

34. CHAUCER, GEOFFREY (1340?–1400), poet, was born, according to the date accepted until recent years, in 1328. This date, now rejected, seems to have been first given by Speght, who published an edition of Chaucer's works in 1508. Of Speght's authority nothing is known; but it is plausibly conjectured that the assertion was merely a guess of his own, founded on the statement, no doubt correct, that Chaucer died in 1400, and on the tradition that he died an old man. But there can be no doubt that in the middle ages and after a man of about sixty was held to be an old man. The date 1328, moreover, makes Chaucer's artistic life most difficult to understand, if not quite unintelligible. If he was born in 1328, then when he wrote the 'Boke of the Duchesse' he was forty-one, which is scarcely credible, the comparative crudity of that work considered. Mr. Walter Rye has lately shown that Chaucer's father was not fourteen years old in December 1324, and so not eighteen at the close of 1328. This appears from the record of certain legal proceedings taken against one Agnes de Westhale and three persons of the name of Stace for carrying of the said young Chaucer (see *Academy,* 29 Jan. 1881). Some twenty years ago Mr. E. A. Bond discovered the name of Geoffrey Chaucer on two parchment leaves, which proved to be fragments of the household account of the Lady Elizabeth, wife of Prince Lionel, third son of Edward III (see *Fortnightly Review,* 15 Aug. 1866). [The Chaucer Society publications; Tyrwhitt's Introductory Discourse to the Canterbury Tales, &c., in his edition of the Canterbury Tales, 1775–8; Godwin's Life of Chaucer, 4 vols. 2nd ed. 1804; Nicolas's Life of Chaucer in the Aldine edition; Todd's Illustrations of Gower and Chaucer, 1810; Matthew Browne's 'Chaucer's England', 2 vols. 1869; John Saunders's Cabinet Pictures of English Life; Chaucer, 1846; Bernhard ten Brin's Chaucer Studien, 1870, and his Chaucer's Sprache und Verkunst, 1884; Morris's Chaucer's Prologue, &c.; Skeat's Man of Lawes Tale, &c.; and also the Prioresses Tale, &c., in the Clarendon Press Series; Henry Morley's English Writers; Ward's Chaucer, in the Men of Letters Series; Warton's Hist, of English Poetry; Lowell's My Study Windows.] J. W. H. *Dictionary of National Biography,* 1885–1900, Volume 10 154–67.

Dancèd full oft in many a greenè mead.
This was the old opinion as I read.
I speak of many hundred years ago,
But now can no man see no elvès mo'[35]

The following commentary is by Richard Brathwait in 1665.

Prince *Arthur*, the Son of *Vther*, born in *Cornwal*, was Crowned
King of *Britain* in the Year 516. He was a Prince, for Spirit no
less Couragious, than in all his Attempts Victorious. His Courage proclaimed him a man, and his good Fortune an happy man.
He fought twelve several Battels against the *Saxons*, and alwaies
returned Conqueror. And having now to his succeeding memory reduced his Countrey to quietness, and planted the Peaceful
Olive in his Confines; to express his true Love to Chivalry, and
memorize such who were not only Associates, but Assistants
in his Victory; He constituted the Order of the Round Table, in
which Order, he only retained such of his Nobility, as were most
Renowned for Vertue and Chivalry. This Round Table he kept
in divers places, especially at *Carlion*, *Winchester*, and *Cama-
let* in *Somersetshire*. In memory of which Foundation, by the
Testimony of *Leyland*, there is yet to be seen in *Denbighshire*,
in the Parish of *Llansavan*, in the side of a Stony Hill, a place
artificially compos'd, wherein be four and twenty Seats for men
to sit in, some less, and some bigger, according to their several
Statures; cut out of the main Rock by man's Hand; where young
people coming to seek their Cattel, use to sit, play, and repose :
They commonly call it *Arthur's* Round Table. To insist on those
Fabulous Relations which former times have broached touching this Prince, I will not, but refer them, who take delight in
the Report of such Wonders, to our Old Wives Legends. Let it
suffice them, that in this King's daies (if they will take the word
of a good Old Wife of *Bath)*[36]

---

35. http://academic.brooklyn.cuny.edu/webcore/murphy/canterbury/7wife.pdf 37.
36. Chaucer, *Wife of Bath*, 75.

SIR THOMAS MALORY (C. 1400–MARCH 14, 1471)[37]

Chapter X: How Galahad Departed with the Shield, And How King Evelake Had Received the Shield of Joseph of Aramathie[38] Sir Galahad, said the squire, that knight that wounded Bagdemagus sendeth you greeting, and bad that ye should bear this shield, wherethrough great adventures should befall. Now blessed be God and fortune, said Galahad. And then he asked his arms, and mounted upon his horse, and hung the white shield about his neck, and commended them unto God. And Sir Uwaine said he would bear him fellowship if it pleased him.

37. MALORY, Sir THOMAS (fl. 1470), author of 'Le Morte Arthur' was, according to Bale, a Welshman. Bale, quoting Leland's 'Syllabus et Interpretatio Antiquarum Dictionum,' 1542, mentions a place called 'Mailoria, on the boundaries of Wales, near the River Dee.' The spot has not been identified. The theory of Malory's Welsh origin is doubtless due to his choice of subject. At least four families of the name were long connected with the English Midlands, but none of the pedigrees seem to include the writer. In the fifteenth century William Malore or Malory of Hutton Conyers acquired, by marriage with the daughter of Sir Richard Tempest, the estate of Studley Royal, near Ripon, and a member of the family is buried in Ripon Cathedral, but none of this family bore the name of Thomas. The manor of Kirkby Mallory, Leicestershire, belonged for at least two centuries to another family of the name. It was sold in 1377 by Sir Ankitell Malory. Sir Ankitell's son, Sir Thomas, was a large landowner in Leicestershire and Warwickshire, but is of too early a date to be identified with the writer; he left an only child, Elizabeth, wife of Sir Robert Ever, and she died in 1482 (Nichols, *Leicestershire*, iv. 761; Burton, *Leicestershire*).

In the preface to his edition of 'Le Morte Arthur,' Caxton writes that he 'emprised to imprint a book of the noble histories of the said King Arthur and of certain of his knights after a copy unto me delivered, which copy Sir Thomas Malory did take out of certain book of French, and reduced it into English.' Malory concludes his text with the words: 'all gentlemen and gentlewomen that read this book of Arthur and his knights from the beginning to the ending, pray for me while I am alive that God send me good deliverance, and when I am dead I pray you all pray for my soul; for this book was ended the ninth year of the reign of King Edward the Fourth by Sir Thomas Mallore, knight, as Jesu help him for his great might, as he is the servant of Jesus both day and night.' Malory's translation was therefore finished between 4 March 1469 and 4 March 1470. In the colophon Caxton again mentions Sir Thomas as the reducer of the work into English, but adds that it was by himself 'divided into xxi books chapitred, and enprinted and finished in the Abbey Westminster, the last day of July the year of our Lord mcccclxxxv.' Malory's description of himself as 'the servant of Jesu both day and night' has been assumed to imply that he was a priest, but his description of himself as 'knight' confutes the suggestion. Pious ejaculation at the conclusion of their labours is characteristic of mediæval authors.

[Dr. Sommer, in the edition noticed above, has collected the available information (see especially ii. 1–17, iii. 335 seq.); an Essay on the purely Literary Aspects of Malory's Work, by Mr. Andrew Lang, appears in vol. iii. pp. xiii seq., of Dr. Sommer's work. Bale vaguely notices Malory in his Scriptores, 1548.] S. L. *Dictionary of National Biography*, 1885–1900, Vol. XXXV by Sidney Lee 439–40.

38. Malory, Sir Thomas, *Le Morte D'Arthur*, Book XIII, Chap. X, 355–56.

Sir, said Galahad, that may ye not, for I must go alone, save this squire shall bear me fellowship: and so departed Uwaine. Then within a while came Galahad there as the white knight abode him by the hermitage, and every each saluted other courteously. Sir, said Galahad, by this shield be many marvels fallen? Sir, said the knight, it befell after the passion of our Lord Jesu Christ thirty-two year, that Joseph of Aramathie, the gentle knight, the which took down our Lord off the holy Cross, at that time he departed from Jerusalem with a great party of his kindred with him. And so he laboured till that they came to a city that hight Sarras. And at that same hour that Joseph came to Sarras there was a king that hight Evelake, that had great war against the Saracens, and in especial against one Saracen, the which was King Evelake's cousin, a rich king and a mighty, which marched nigh this land, and his name was called Tolleme la Feintes. So on a day these two met to do battle. Then Joseph, the son of Joseph of Aramathie, went to King Evelake and told him he should be discomfit and slain, but if he left his belief of the old law and believed upon the new law. And then there he shewed him the right belief of the Holy Trinity, to the which he agreed unto with all his heart; and there this shield was made for King Evelake, in the name of Him that died upon the Cross. And then through his good belief he had the better of King Tolleme. For when Evelake was in the battle there was a cloth set afore the shield, and when he was in the greatest peril he let put away the cloth, and then his enemies saw a figure of a man on the Cross, wherethrough they all were discomfit. And so it befell that a man of King Evelake's was smitten his hand off, and bare that hand in his other hand; and Joseph called that man unto him and bade him go with good devotion touch the Cross. And as soon as that man had touched the Cross with his hand it was as whole as ever it was tofore. Then soon after there fell a great marvel, that the cross of the shield at one time vanished away that no man wist where it became. And then King Evelake was baptised, and for the most part all the people of that city. So, soon after Joseph would depart, and King Evelake would go with him whether he would or nold. And so by fortune they came into this land, that at that time was called Great Britain; and there they found a great felon paynim, that put Joseph into prison. And so by fortune tidings came unto a worthy man that hight Mondrames, and he assembled all his people for the great renown he had heard of Joseph ; and so he came into the land of Great Britain and disinherited this felon paynim and consumed him, and therewith delivered Joseph out of prison. And after that all the people were turned to the Christian faith.

JOHN LELAND (1503-1552)[3940]

Here lies the famous King Arthur, buried in the isle of Avalon
In Presbyterio.
Edmundus Senior in bor. parte. / Edmundus Irenside in merid.
parte. / Arcturus in medio.
Epit. Arturii.
Hic jacet Arturus flos regum, gloria regni, Quem mores, probitas commendant laude perenni. / Versus Henrici Swansey Abbatis Glaston.
Infer, ad pedem ejusdem tumuli.

39. Leland, *Itinerary in England and Wales,* 316.

40. LELAND or LEYLAND, JOHN (1506?—1552), antiquary, born in London about 1506, probably belonged to a Lancashire family. He had a brother known as John Leland senior, and the distinguishing appellation of 'junior' sometimes applied to him is doubtless due to his bearing the same christian name as his brother. He was doubtless a collateral descendant of the older Latin writer called, like his brother, John Leland the elder [q. v.], and of Richard Leland or Leyland, treasurer of the Duke of Bedford›s household, who witnessed his master›s will in 1435 (Nicolas, *Testamenta Vetusta,* p. 243). When on his great tour about 1537 the antiquary visited Sir William Leyland, possibly a kinsman, at his house at Morley near Leigh in Lancashire (*Itinerary,* v. 89; Baines, *Lancashire,* iii. 601–2), and a John Leyland, who may have been the antiquary's brother, acted subsequently as Sir William's executor.

John was sent to St. Paul's School, London, under William Lily [q. v.] He found a patron in one Thomas Myles, whose generosity in paying all the expenses of his education he freely acknowledged in an 'encomium' inscribed 'ad Thomam Milonem' (Leland, *Encomia,* 1589). He removed in due course to Christ's College, Cambridge, and proceeded B.A. in 1522. Subsequently he studied at All Souls' College, Oxford, where he appears to have made the acquaintance of Thomas Caius. He ultimately completed his studies in Paris under Francis Sylvius, and became intimate with Budé (Budæus), Jacques le Febvre (Faber), Paolo Emilio (Paulus Emilius), and Jean Ruel (Ruellus) (*Notes and Queries,* 2nd ser. v. 492).

[Information kindly supplied by John Leyland, esq.; Huddesford's Lives of Leland, Wood, and Hearne, 1772; Bale's Script. Brit. Cat. (1557), pp. 671–2; Wood's Athenæ Oxon. ed. Bliss, i. 197; Letters of Eminent Lit. Men (Camd. Soc.), pp. 355–6; Tanner's Bibl. Brit.; Macray's Annals of Bodleian Libr.; Cooper's Athenæ Cantabr. i. 110, 542; Retrospective Review (1854), ii. 171 sq.; Tanner's Bibl. Brit.; Strype's Cranmer, iii. 325–328; Hazlitt's Bibliographical Collections and Notes; Maitland's Early Printed Books in the Lambeth Library; Bernard's Cat. MSS. Angliæ, 235 sq.; MS. Sloane, 885, f. 64 sq.; Saturday Review, 15 Feb. 1879, 5 Sept. 1885.] S.L. *Dictionary of National Biography,* by Sidney Lee, 1885–1900, Volume 33 13–17.

https://en.wikisource.org/wiki/Leland,_John_(1506%3F-1552)_(DNB00)

Arturi jacet hic conjux tumulata secunda, / Quae meruit coelos virtuturn prole secunda.
Inscript. in capite tumuli.
Henricus Abbas. / Crucifixi imago in capite tumuli. / Arturii imago ad pedes. / Crux super tumulum. (p.288)
Pons periculosus: Or ever this river cum to Glessenbyri by a mile it cummith to a bridge of stone of a 4. arches communely caullid Pontperlus, wher men fable that Arture cast in his swerd. (p.148)

The people can telle nothing ther but that they have hard say that Arture much resortid to Camalat. The old Lord Hungreford was owner of this Camallat. Now Hastinges the Erle of Huntendune by his mother. Diverse villages there about bere the name of Camalat by an addition, as Quene-Camallat, (Queen's Camel) and other. (p.151)

Also, abowt Camelford ar certen old mynes, wrought yn tymes past, but of what metalle yt ys now onknowen. Wyth yn a myle above that poore village sowth runneth the ryver that goyth ynto the Severn se at Paddistow; and yt is the greatest ryver on the north syde of Cornewale, and ys cawled yn the commune spech there Dunmere, and yn the Kyngges grawnt of privilege to the chanons of Bodmynne, and the burgeses of the same towne, Alan, yt may fortune for Alaune. * Sum historyes cawled Cablan. By this ryver Arture fowght his last feld, yn token wherof the people fynd there yn plowyng bones and harneys.

Wyth yn iiii. myles of the sayde Camylford apon the north clif ys Tintagel, the which castel had be lykehod iii. wardes, wherof ii. be woren away with gulfyng yn of the se, yn so much that yt hathe made ther almost an isle, and no way ys to enter ynto hyt now but by long elme trees layde for a bryge. So that now withowte the isle renneth alonly a gate howse, a walle, and a fals braye dyged and walled. p.316)

EDMUND SPENSER (C. 1552–JANUARY 13, 1599)[41]

Thither the great magicien Merlin came,

41. SPENSER, EDMUND (1552? –1599), poet, was a Londoner by birth. His father migrated to London from the neighbourhood of Burnley in north-east Lancashire, not far from the foot of Pendle Hill. As early as the close of the thirteenth century there was a freehold held by a Spenser at Hurstwood in the township of Worsthorne, some three miles to the south-east of Burnley. This seems to have been the original settlement of

As was his use, ofttimes to visitt mee;
For he had charge my discipline to frame,
And Tutors nouriture to oversee.
Him oft and oft I askt in privity,
Of what loines and what lignage I did spring;
Whose aunswere bad me still assured bee,
That I was sonne and heire unto a king,
As time in her just term the truth to light should bring.[42]

WILLIAM CAMDEN (1551–1623), BRITANNIA, 1607[43]

Here lies the famous King Arthur, buried in the isle of Avalon

---

the family, and its head in the reign of Elizabeth bore the Christian name of Edmund.

[Gabriel Harvey's Letter-book (Camden Soc.), 1884, and Harvey's Works, ed. Grosart, with the published Calendars of Irish State Papers, 1580–1599, and of the Carew Papers, are the chief contemporary authorities. Aubrey's Lives supplies some seventeenth-century gossip. Dr. Grosart's copious memoir forms vol. i. of his edition of Spenser's Works (1882–4, privately printed). The best biography is that by Dean Church in the Men of Letters series. Other useful memoirs are prefixed to Todd's edition of the Works (1805) and, by Professor J. W. Hales, to the Globe edition (1869, revised edit. 1897); Craik's somewhat diffuse Spenser and his Times (3 vols. 1845), Cooper's Athenæ Cantabrigiensis, and Professor Morley's English Writers (vol. ix. 1892). Collier's Bibliographical Account supplies many useful hints; see also paper by Professor Gollancz, read before British Academy 27 Nov. 1907 (The Times, 28 Nov. 1907). Among separately issued critical essays are John Jortin's Remarks on Spenser (1734); Thomas Warton's Observations on the Faerie Queene (1752 and 1762); William Huggins's comments on Warton in The Observer Observ'd (1756); Mrs. C. M. Kirkland's Spenser and the Fairy Queen (New York, 1847); and J. S. Hart's Essay on the Life and Writings (New York, 1847). A Spenser Society, founded at Manchester in 1866 by James Crossley [q. v.], has, with the object of illustrating Spenser's work, issued reprints of the works of his less-known contemporaries in some thirty-four volumes (1867–82). Of recent contributions to Spenserian criticism (not separately published) the most suggestive are Leigh Hunt's essay in his Imagination and Fancy; John Wilson's seven papers in Blackwood's Magazine, 1834–5; Mr. J. R. Lowell's essay in his volume on The English Poets; the essays by Aubrey de Vere and Professor Dowden in biography by Dr. Grosart; Mr. Ruskin's analysis of the first book of the Faerie Queene in The Stones of Venice; Mr. Roden Noel's preface to Spenser's Works in the Canterbury Poets; and Dean Church's Introduction to a selection from Spenser's poetry in Mr. Humphry Ward's English Poets.] J.W.H and S.L.

Dictionary of National Biography, John Wesley Hales and Sidney Lee 1885–1900, Vol. LIII, 384–98

42. Spenser, *The Faerie Queen*, Book I, Canto IX, 164.

43. CAMDEN, WILLIAM (1551–1623), antiquary and historian, was born in the Old Bailey in London on 2 May 1551. His father was Sampson Camden, a native of Lichfield, who in early life, came up to London to follow the profession of a painter, and was a member of the Guild of Painter-Stainers. In the inscription on a cup which his son bequeathed to the guild he was described as 'Pictor Londinensis,' which, as Gough

It hath alfo plenty of River-fifh, on one fide from Usk, and on
the other from Wy; both abounding with Salmon and Trout,
but the Wy with a better fort call'd Umbrae:. It is inclofed on
all parts, except the North, with high mountains: having on the
Weft, the mountains of Cantre-bychan; and towards the South,
the Southern-hills, whereof the chief is call'd Kader Arthur, or
Arthur's Chair, from two peaks on the top of it, fomewhat re-
fembling a Chair. Which, in regard it is a lofty feat, and a place of
ftrength, is afcribed in the vulgar appellation of it, to Arthur the
moft puiffant and abfolute Monarch of the Britains. A Fountain
fprings on the very top of this hill; which is as deep as a draw-
well, and four fquare; affording trouts, tho' no water runs out
of it. Being thus guarded on the South with high mountains, it
is defended from the heat of the Sun with cool breezes; which,
with an innate wholfomnefs of the air, renders the Country
exceeding temperate. On the Eaft, it hath the mountains of Tal-
garth and Ewias.[44]

observes, may apply either to his profession or his company. Camden's mother was Elizabeth, daughter of Giles Curwen of Poulton Hall, Lancashire, and came of the ancient
family of Curwen of Workington in Cumberland, a descent of which he speaks with
modest pride in his 'Britannia.' At an early age he was entered at Christ's Hospital, probably as a 'town child' or 'free scholar,' but the year is unknown. His biographer, Dr. Smith,
infers, from the fact of the hospital having been founded for the benefit of orphans,
that he had then already lost his father; and Bishop Gibson disregards the story of his
admission. But Degory Wheare, his contemporary, presumably had good authority for
stating the fact; and he also seems to imply that Camden's father had the care of his early
training. In the registers of St. Augustine's Church, London, is entered the marriage of
Sampson Camden and Avis Carter, 4 Sept. 1575. This might be a second marriage of
Camden's father, but more probably a brother is referred to (see Chester, Westm. Abbey
Registers, p. 122). In 1563, at the age of twelve, the boy was attacked by the plague at
Islington ('peste correptus Islingtoniæ,' Memorabilia), but there is no evidence for Anthony Wood's addition that there 'he remained for some time, to the great loss of his
learning.' On his recovery he was sent to St. Paul's School, where he remained until 1566,
when he went up to Oxford, being then in his fifteenth or sixteenth year.
    [Camden's Memorabilia de seipso, his Jac. I Annalium Apparatus, and his corre-
spondence, all in Smith's Camdeni Epistolæ (1691); his address ad Lectorem in the
1600 ed. of the Britannia; Degory Wheare's Parentatio Historica (1624); Camdoni Vita,
by Smith (1601); Life in Gibson's Britannia; Life in Gough's Britannia ; Life in Bayle's
Dictionary (1736); Life in the Biographia Britannica; Life in Wood's Athenæ Oxon. (ed.
Bliss), vol. ii.: Letters of Eminent Literary Men (Camd. Soc. 1843); Chester's Westminster Abbey Registers (1875)]. E. M. T. Dictionary of National Biography, 1885–1900,
Vol. VIII, by Edward Maunde Thompson, 277–85
    https://en.wikisource.org/wiki/Camden,_William_(DNB00)
    44. Camden, Britannia, Vol. ii.703.

CAMDEN'S CRITIQUE:

Monmouth alfo glories in the birth of Galfridus Arthurius Bifhop of St. Afaph, who compil'd the Britifh Hiftory; an Author
well skill'd in Antiquities, but, as it feems, not of entire credit:
fo many ridiculous Fables of his own invention hath he inferted
in that work. In fo much that he is now rank'd amongft thofe
writers that are prohibited by the Church of Rome. But altho'
this Jeffrey of Monmouth (as well as moft other Writers of the
Monkifh times) abounds with Fables, which is not deny'd by
fuch as contend for fome Authority to that Hiftory ; yet that
thofe Fables were of his own Invention, may feem too fevere
a cenfure, and fcarce a juft accufation : fince we find moft or
all of them, in that Britifh Hiftory he tranflated ; of which an
ancient copy may be feen in the Library of Jefus-College at
Oxford, which concludes to this effect : Walter Arch-deacon
of Oxford compos'd this Book in Latin, out of Britifh Records :
which he afterwards thus render'd into modern Britifh. We find
alfo many of the fame Fables in Ninnius, who writ his Eulogium
Britannia about three hundred years before this Galfridus Ar-
turius compos'd the Britifh Hiftory. As to the regard due to that
Hiftory in general, the judicious Reader may confult Doctor
Powel's Epiftle De Britannica Hiftoria recte intelligenda; and Dr.
Davies's Preface to his Britifh Lexicon; and ballance them with
the arguments and authority of thofe who wholly reject it.

Here Duglefs, a fmall brook, runs with a ftill gentle ftream;
near which our Arthur (as Ninnius tells us) defeated the Saxons
in a memorable battel. Near the rife of it, ftands Wiggin, a Town
(as they fay) formerly called Vibiggin.

(A large round entrenchment) goes by the name of King
Arthurs Round Table: and it is poffible enough, it might be a
Jufting-place. However, that it was never defign'd for a place of
ftrength, appears from the trenches, being on the infide. Near
this, is another great Fort of Stones, heap'd-up in form of a
horfe-fhoe and opening towards it call'd by fome King Arthur's
Caftle, and by others Mayburgh, or Maybrough.[45]

---

45. Camden, *Britannia*, Vol. ii.,712, 970, 998.

WILLIAM SHAKESPEARE (BAPTISED 26 APRIL 1564–23 APRIL 1616)[46]

Hotspur. I cannot choose. Sometimes he angers me

46. SHAKESPEARE, WILLIAM (1564–1616), dramatist and poet, came of a family whose surname was borne through the middle ages by residents in very many parts of England—at Penrith in Cumberland, at Kirkland and Doncaster in Yorkshire, as well as in nearly all the midland counties. Distribution of the name. The surname had originally a martial significance, implying capacity in the wielding of the spear (Camden, *Remains*, ed. 1605, p. 111; Verstegan, *Restitution*, 1605). Its first recorded holder is John Shakespeare, who in 1279 was living at 'Freyndon,' perhaps Frittenden, Kent (*Plac. Cor.* 7 Edw. I, Kanc.; cf. *Notes and Queries*, 1st ser. xi. 122). The great mediæval guild of St. Anne at Knowle, whose members included the leading inhabitants of Warwickshire, was joined by many Shakespeares in the fifteenth century (cf. *Reg.* ed. Bickley, 1894). In the sixteenth and seventeenth centuries the surname is found far more frequently in Warwickshire than elsewhere. The archives of no less than twenty-four towns and villages there contain notices of Shakespeare families in the sixteenth century, and as many as thirty-four Warwickshire towns or villages were inhabited by Shakespeare families in the seventeenth century. Among them all William was a common christian name. At Rowington, twelve miles to the north of Stratford, and in the same hundred of Barlichway, one of the most prolific Shakespeare families of Warwickshire resided in the sixteenth century, and no less than three Richard Shakespeares of Rowington, whose extant wills were proved respectively in 1560, 1591, and 1614, were fathers of sons called William. At least one other William Shakespeare was during the period a resident in Rowington. As a consequence, the poet has been more than once credited with achievements which rightly belong to one or other of his numerous contemporaries who were identically named.

The poet's ancestry cannot be traced with certainty beyond his grandfather. The Bacon theory of W.S.:

The most learned exponent of this strange theory was Nathaniel Holmes, an American lawyer, who published at New York in 1866 'The Authorship of the Plays attributed to Shakespeare,' a monument of misapplied ingenuity (4th edit. 1886, 2 vols.). Bacon's 'Promus of Formularies and Elegancies' (London, 1883), edited by Mrs. Henry Pott, a voluminous advocate of the Baconian theory, presses the argument of parallelisms between Bacon and Shakespeare. A Bacon Society was founded in London in 1885 to develop and promulgate the theory, and it inaugurated a magazine (named since May 1893 'Baconiana'). A quarterly periodical also called 'Baconiana,' and issued in the same interest, was established at Chicago in 1892. 'The Bibliography of the Shakespeare–Bacon Controversy' by W. H. Wyman, Cincinnati, 1884, gives the titles of 255 books or pamphlets on both sides of the subject, published since 1848; the list was continued during 1886 in 'Shakespeariana,' a monthly journal published at Philadelphia, and might now be extended to twice the original figure. The Baconian theory has found its widest acceptance in America. There it was pressed to most extravagant limits by Ignatius Donnelly of Hastings, Minnesota, in 'The Great Cryptogram: Francis Bacon's Cypher in the so-called Shakespeare Plays' (Chicago and London, 1887, 2 vols.), and by Mrs. Gallup, of Detroit, in 'The Bi-Literal Cypher of Francis Bacon,' 1900. Both writers thought to detect cipher-statements in the Shakespeare First Folio categorically stating that Bacon was author of the plays. Many refutations have been published of Donnelly's and Mrs. Gallup's baseless contention (cf. *Nineteenth Cent.* May 1887.] S. L. *Dictionary of National Biography*, 1885–1900, Volume 51, by Sidney Lee. https://en.wikisource.org/wiki/Shakespeare,_William_(DNB00)

With telling me of the moldwarp and the ant,
Of the dreamer Merlin and his prophecies,
And of a dragon and a finless fish,
A clip-wing'd griffin and a moulten raven,
A couching lion and a ramping cat,
And such a deal of skimble-skamble stuff
As puts me from my faith.[47]

Then comes the time, who lives to see't,
That going shall be us'd with feet.
This prophecy Merlin shall make, for I live before his time.[48]

THOMAS HEYWOOD (C. 1573–AUGUST 16, 1641)[49]

Woe's me for the red Dragon, for alach,

47. Shakespeare, *Henry IV*, Act III. Scene I.
48. Shakespeare, *King Lear*, Act III. Scene II.
49. HEYWOOD, THOMAS (*d.* 1650?), dramatist, was, according to his own account, a native of Lincolnshire (see his verses prefixed to James Yorke's *Book of Heraldry*, and his funeral elegy on Sir George St. Poole of Lincolnshire, his 'countreyman,' in *Pleasant Dialogues and Dramas*); but Mr. Symonds has found no Heywood pedigree in the 'Visitations' of the county. In the dedication of the 'English Traveller' Heywood speaks of a Sir William Elvish as his 'countreyman.' From his reference (*ib.*) to 'that good old Gentleman, mine vnkle (Master Edmund Heywood), whom you' (Sir Henry Appleton, bt.) 'pleased to grace by the Title of Father,' he may be concluded to have been of good family. He can hardly have been born much later than 1575. In the 'Apology for Actors' (bk. i.) he incidentally mentions 'his residence at Cambridge;' and William Cartwright (*d.* 1687) [q. v.], in the dedication to the 'Actor's Vindication,' 1658, says that Heywood was a fellow of Peterhouse. There is, however, no record of him at Cambridge.
[For general information concerning Thomas Heywood and his writings see the Introductions to an Apology for Actors (Shakespeare Society's Publications, 1841); The English Traveller in Old Plays, a continuation of Dodsley's Collection, 6 vols. 1816, vi. 101–5; Pearson's reprint of Heywood's Dramatic Works, 6 vols. 1874, vol. i.; J. A. Symonds and A. W. Verity's (select plays of) Thomas Heywood in the Mermaid Series, 1888; A Marriage Triumph in Percy Society's Publications, vol. vi. 1842; Henslowe's Diary, edited by J. P. Collier (Shakespeare Society's Publications, 1845); Halliwell's Dictionary of Old English Plays, 1860; Biographia Dramatica, 1812, vol. i. pt. i.; Collier's History of English Dramatic Poetry, &c., new edition, 1879; A. W. Ward's History of English Dramatic Literature, 1875, ii. 105–31; C. H. Herford's Studies in the Literary Relations of England and Germany in the Sixteenth Century, 1886. For criticism on Heywood as a dramatic poet see Charles Lamb's Specimens of Early Dramatic Poetry, 1808; Retrospective Review, xi. 126–54, 1825; Edinburgh Review for April 1841, art. 'Beaumont and Fletcher and their Contemporaries;' Symonds's Shakespeare's Predecessors; Ward's Hist. English Drama.] A. W. W. *Dictionary of National Biography*, 1885–1900, Vol. XXVI, by Adolphus William Ward 338–42.

The time is come, hee hasteth to his mach:
The bloudy Serpent, (yet whose souls are white)
Implys that Nation, on which thy delight
Was late sole-fixt, (the Saxons) who as friends
Came to thee first, but ayming at shrewd ends
They shall have power over the drooping red,
In which the British Nation's figured:
Drive shall he them into caves, holes, and dens,
To barren Mountains, and to moorish fens,
Hills shall remove to where the valleyes stood,
And all the baths and brooks shall flow with blood.
The worship of the holy God shall cease.
For in thilk dayes the Kirke shall have no peace:
The Panims (woe the while) shall get the day,
And with their Idols mawmetry beare sway,
And yet in fine shee that was so opprest,
Shal mount, & in the high rocks build her nest.
For out of Cornwall shall proceed a Bore,
Who shall the Kerk to pristine state restore,
Bow shall all Britaine to his kingly beck,
And tread he shall on the white Dragon's neck.[50]

JOHN DRYDEN (AUGUST 9, 1631–MAY 1, 1700)[51]

Enter Arthur, and Merlin at another Door.

50. Heywood, *The Life of Merlin,* 54.

51. DRYDEN, JOHN (1631–1700), poet, was born 9 Aug. 1631 at Aldwinkle All Saints, Northamptonshire (the precise day is doubtful: Malone, p. 5). His father was Erasmus, third son of Sir Erasmus Dryden, bart., of Canons Ashby, Northamptonshire; his mother was Mary, daughter of Henry Pickering, rector of Aldwinkle from 1597 to 1637, in which year he died, aged 75. Erasmus and Mary Dryden were married 21 Oct. 1630 at Pilton, near Aldwinkle (*Notes and Queries,* 2nd ser. xii. 207). The Drydens (or Dridens), originally settled in Cumberland, had moved into Northamptonshire about the middle of the sixteenth century. Erasmus Dryden after his marriage lived at Tichmarsh, where the Pickerings had a seat.

[Perfunctory lives of Dryden are in Cibber's Lives of the Poets (1753) and in Derrick's Collective Edition of Dryden's Poems (1760). The first important life was Johnson's admirable performance in the Lives of the Poets (1779–81). The editions by Peter Cunningham (1854) and by Birkbeck Hill (1905) contain some new facts. Malone's badly written but full life (1800) forms vol. i. of the Miscellaneous Prose Works. Scott prefixed an excellent life to the edition of Dryden's Complete Works (1808). The lives by Robert Bell prefixed to the Aldine edition (1854), and especially that by W. D. Christie prefixed to the Globe edition of Dryden's Poems (1870), are worth consulting. See also

Scene of the Wood continues.

Merl. Thus far it is permitted me to go;
But all beyond this Spot, is fenc'd with Charms;
I may no more; but only with advice.
Arth. My Sword fhall do the reft.
Merl. Remember well, that all is but Illufion;
Go on; good Stars attend thee.
Arth. Doubt me not.
Merl. Yet in prevention
Of what may come, I'll leave my *Philidel*
To watch thy Steps, and with him leave my Wand;
The touch of which, no Earthy Fiend can bear,
in whate'er Shape transform'd, but muft lay down
His borrow'd Figure, and confefs the Devil.
Once more Farewel, and profper. (Exit Merlin)
Arth. walking. No Danger yet, I fee no Walls of Fire,
No City of the Fiends, with Forms obfcene
To grin from far, on Flaming Battlements.
This is indeed the Grove I fhou'd deftroy;
But where's the Horrour? Sure the Prophet err'd
Hark! Mufick, and the warbling Notes of Birds.[52]

ALFRED LORD TENNYSON (AUGUST 6, 1809–OCTOBER 6, 1892)[53]

Idylls of the King: The Holy Grail (spoken by King Arthur)

Dryden by G. Saintsbury in the English Men of Letters Series, and a valuable study of Dryden and his contemporaries in Le Public et les Hommes de Lettres en Angleterre (1660–1744), by Alexandre Beljame (1881).] L. S. *Dictionary of National Biography*, 1885–1900, Vol. XVI, by Leslie Stephen 64–75.

52. Dryden, *King Arthur,* 36.

53. TENNYSON, ALFRED, first Baron Tennyson (1809–1892), poet, the fourth of twelve children of the Rev. Dr. George Clayton Tennyson, rector of Somersby, a village in North Lincolnshire, between Horncastle and Spilsby, was born at Somersby on 6 Aug. 1809. His mother was Elizabeth, daughter of the Rev. Stephen Fytche, vicar of Louth in the same county. Of the twelve children of this marriage, eight were sons, and of these, two besides Alfred became poets of distinction, Frederick Tennyson [q. v.] and Charles, who in later life adopted the name of an uncle, and became Charles Tennyson-Turner [q. v.] All of the children seem to have shared the poetic faculty in greater or less degree. [The only complete and authoritative life of Tennyson is that by his son, in two volumes, published in October 1897. A provisional memoir, careful and appreciative, by Mr. Arthur H. Waugh, appeared in 1892, and Mrs. Ritchie's interesting Records of Tennyson, Raskin, and

' "And spake I not too truly, O my knights?
Was I too dark a prophet when I said
To those who went upon the Holy Quest,
That most of them would follow wandering fires,
Lost in the quagmire? — lost to me and gone,
And left me gazing at a barren board,
And a lean Order — scarce returned a tithe —
And out of those to whom the vision came
My greatest hardly will believe he saw;
Another hath beheld it afar off,
And leaving human wrongs to right themselves,
Cares but to pass into the silent life.
And one hath had the vision face to face,
And now his chair desires him here in vain,
However they may crown him otherwhere.
' "And some among you held, that if the King
Had seen the sight he would have sworn the vow:
Not easily, seeing that the King must guard
That which he rules, and is but as the hind
To whom a space of land is given to plow.
Who may not wander from the allotted field
Before his work be done; but, being done,
Let visions of the night or of the day
Come, as they will; and many a time they come,
Until this earth he walks on seems not earth,
This light that strikes his eyeball is not light,
This air that smites his forehead is not air
But vision — yea, his very hand and foot —
In moments when he feels he cannot die,
And knows himself no vision to himself,
Nor the high God a vision, nor that One
Who rose again: ye have seen what ye have seen."
'So spake the King: I knew not all he meant.'[54]

the Brownings in 1892. Various primers, handbooks, and bibliographies have also from time to time been published.] *Dictionary of National Biography*, 1885–1900, Vol. LVI, by Alfred Ainger, 66–75. https://en.wikisource.org/wiki/Tennyson,_Alfred_(DNBoo)

54. Tennyson, *The Holy Grail*, 432–3

MATTHEW ARNOLD (DECEMBER 24, 1822—APRIL 15, 1888)[55]

Where Merlin by the enchanted thorn-tree sleeps.
For here he came with the fay Vivian,
One April, when the warm days first began;
He was on foot, and that false fay, his friend,
On her white palfrey: here he met his end,
In these lone sylvan glades, that April day.
This tale of Merlin and the lovely fay
Was the one Iseult chose, and she brought clear
Before the children's fancy him and her.[56]

GEORGE MACDONALD (1824–1906)[57]

I sat down opposite to it by the table, on which I laid the great
old volume, and read. It contained many wondrous tales of Fairy

55. ARNOLD, MATTHEW (1822–1888), poet and critic, the eldest son of Dr. Thomas Arnold [q. v.], afterwards famous as headmaster of Rugby, and his wife Mary (Penrose), was born on 24 Dec. 1822 at Laleham, near Staines, where his father then took pupils. Thomas Arnold [q. v. Suppl.] was his younger brother. Matthew migrated to Rugby with his family in 1828, but in 1830 returned to Laleham as pupil of his maternal uncle, the Rev. John Buckland. In August 1836 he was removed to Winchester, and in 1837 entered Rugby, which he left in 1841 for Balliol College, Oxford, where he had gained a classical scholarship.
[Arnold's correspondence is the only comprehensive authority for his life. Professor Saintsbury's monograph (1899) is admirable wherever it is not warped by hostility to Arnold's speculative ideas and some of his literary predilections. References to him in contemporary literature are endless, and he is the subject of innumerable critiques, including essays upon his poetry by Mr. A. C. Benson and the present writer, accompanying editions of his poems, and a remarkable article on the Poems of 1853 by Froude, in the Westminster Review (January 1854). The ethical aspects of Arnold's teaching are examined in John M. Robertson's Modern Humanists, 1891; in G. White's Matthew Arnold and the Spirit of the Age, 1898; and in W. H. Hudson's Studies in Interpretation, New York, 1896. An interesting sketch of Arnold as a teacher is given in Sir Joshua Fitch's Thomas and Matthew Arnold in the Great Educators Series, 1897. A few additional letters were printed with Arthur Galton's Two Essays upon Matthew Arnold, 1897. There is an interesting estimate of Arnold as a thinker in Crozier's My Inner Life, 1898, pp. 521–9.] R. G. Dictionary of National Biography, 1901 supplement, by Richard Garnett 70–5. https://en.wikisource.org/wiki/Arnold,_Matthew_(DNB01)

56. Arnold, Poems, 104.

57. MACDONALD, GEORGE (1824–1906), poet and novelist, born on 10 Dec. 1824 at Huntly, West Aberdeenshire, was descended from one of the 120 MacDonalds who made good their escape from the massacre of Glencoe in Feb. 1692. His Jacobite

Land, and olden times, and the Knights of King Arthur's table. I read on and on, till the shades of the afternoon began to deepen; for in the midst of the forest it gloomed earlier than in the open country. At length I came to this passage:— Here it chaunced, that upon their quest, Sir Galahad and Sir Percivale rencountered in the depths of a great forest.[58]

WILLIAM MORRIS (24 MARCH 1834—3 OCTOBER 1896)[59]

And every morn I scarce could pray at all,
For Launcelot's red-golden hair would play,
Instead of sunlight, on the painted wall,
Mingled with dreams of what the priest did say;

---

great-grandfather was born on 16 April 1746, the day of the battle of Culloden, in which his great-great-grandfather, a red-haired piper, lost his sight. From Portsoy in Banff-shire the family ultimately moved to Huntly, where George MacDonald's grandfather, who spoke Gaelic, was farmer and banker. The author's father, also George MacDonald, grew up on the farm, marrying as his first wife Helen, daughter of Captain MacKay, R.N., of Celtic lineage, and sister of the Gaelic scholar, Mackintosh MacKay [q. v.]. His parents were congregationalists. Already a poet who saw symbolic meanings in what others found commonplace, he was regarded by the students as something of a vision-ary. Of his university life he gave a graphic picture in his poem 'Hidden Life' (in *Poems*, 1857). He graduated M.A. in March 1845, and on 28 February 1868 his university made him hon. LL.D. https://en.wikisource.org/wiki/MacDonald,_George_(DNB12)

58. Macdonald, *Phantastes*, 21.

59. MORRIS, WILLIAM was known to be energetic, versatile, and industrious for he accomplished many projects throughout his career. He was a popular and prolific Victo-rian poet and translator of Northern mythology. As an artist-craftsman he invented and revived lost techniques for printing, and for creating textiles, embroidery and stained glass. By opening his own textile factory, he became a successful entrepreneur in the decorating and manufacturing business. During the last two decades of his life he became an ardent Socialist, giving hundreds of lectures on the topic throughout Britain. Despite various ventures, Morris had a lasting enthusiasm for medievalism and Arthuriana. Mor-ris's interest in the Arthurian legends first became apparent while he was a student at Oxford, from 1853–1855. At this time Arthuriana had been popularized by Tennyson and Southey's edition of Malory's *Morte d'Arthur*. One of Morris's favorite poems to read aloud dramatically to Edward Burne-Jones was Tennyson's "*The Lady of Shalott*." By this time Tennyson had also published "Sir Lancelot and Queen Guinevere," "*Morte d'Arthur*," and "*Sir Galahad*." Burne-Jones and Morris expanded their reading circle when, in 1855, they joined a literary brotherhood called the Set. In September of 1855 Morris and Burne-Jones bought a copy of Robert Southey's 1817 version of Malory's *Morte d'Arthur*. This Southey edition was popular among the Pre-Raphaelites; Rossetti declared in 1857 that the world's two greatest books were *The Bible* and *Morte d'Arthur*.

Grim curses out of Peter and of Paul;
Judging of strange sins in Leviticus;
Another sort of writing on the wall,
Scored deep across the painted heads of us.

Christ sitting with the woman at the well,
And Mary Magdalen repenting there,
Her dimmed eyes scorch'd and red at sight of hell
So hardly 'scaped, no gold light on her hair.

And if the priest said anything that seemed
To touch upon the sin they said we did,
(This in their teeth) they looked as if they deem'd
That I was spying what thoughts might be hid

Under green-cover'd bosoms, heaving quick
Beneath quick thoughts; while they grew red with shame,
And gazed down at their feet: while I felt sick,
And almost shriek'd if one should call my name.

The thrushes sang in the lone garden there:
But where you were the birds were scared I trow:
Clanging of arms about pavilions fair,
Mixed with the knights' laughs; there, as I well know,

Rode Launcelot, the king of all the band,
And scowling Gauwaine, like the night in day,
And handsome Gareth, with his great white hand
Curl'd round the helm-crest, ere he join'd the fray.[60]

MARK TWAIN (NOVEMBER 30, 1835 — APRIL 21, 1910)[61]

A Connecticut Yankee in King Arthur's Court

60. Morris, *Romances, King Arthur's Tomb*, 20–1.

61. TWAIN, MARK, the *nom de plume* of Samuel Langhorne Clemens (1835–1910),
American author, who was born on the 30th of November 1835, at Florida, Missouri.
His father was a country merchant from Tennessee, who moved soon after his son's
birth to Hannibal, Missouri, a little town on the Mississippi. When the boy was only
twelve his father died, and thereafter he had to get his education as best he could. Of actual schooling he had little. He learned how to set type, and as a journeyman printer he
wandered widely, going even as far east as New York. At seventeen he went back to the
Mississippi, determined to become a pilot on a river-steamboat. In his *Life on the Mississippi* he has recorded graphically his experiences while "learning the river." In 1875

ALGERNON CHARLES SWINBURNE (5 APRIL 1837—10 APRIL 1909)[62]

> With hope and life, came greeting from King Lot
> Out of his wind-worn islands oversea,
> And homage to my king and fealty
> Of those north seas wherein the strange shapes swim,

---

he published *The Adventures of Tom Sawyer*, the sequel to which, *Huckleberry Finn*, did not appear until 1884. The result of a second visit to Europe was humorously recorded in *A Tramp Abroad* (1880), followed in 1882 by a more or less historical romance, *The Prince and the Pauper*; and a year later came *Life on the Mississippi*. *The Adventures of Huckleberry Finn*, the next of his books, was published (in 1884) by a New York firm in which the author was chief partner. This firm prospered for a while, and issued in 1889 Mark Twain's own comic romance, *A Connecticut Yankee at King Arthur's Court*, and in 1892 a less successful novel, *The American Claimant*. But after a severe struggle the publishing house failed, leaving the author charged with its very heavy debts. After this disaster he issued a third Mississippi Valley novel, *The Tragedy of Pudd'nhead Wilson*, in 1894, and in 1896 another historical romance, *Personal Recollections of Joan of Arc*, wherein the maid is treated with the utmost sympathy and reverence. After Mark Twain's death, his intimate friend, W. D. Howells, published in 1910 a series of personal recollections in *Harper's Magazine*. B.M. *Encyclopædia Britannica*, Vol. 27, 490.

62. SWINBURNE, ALGERNON CHARLES (1837–1909), poet, born in Chester Street, Grosvenor Place, London, on 5 April 1837, was eldest child of Admiral Charles Henry Swinburne (1797–1877), by his wife Lady Jane Henrietta (1809–1896), daughter of George Ashburnham, third earl of Ashburnham. His father was second son of Sir John Edward Swinburne (1762–1860), sixth baronet of Capheaton, in Northumberland. This baronet, who exercised a strong influence over his grandson, the poet, had been born and brought up in France, and cultivated the memory of Mirabeau. In habits, dress, and modes of thought he was like a French nobleman of the ancien regime. From his father, a cut and dried unimaginative old 'salt,' the poet inherited little but a certain identity of colour and expression; his features and something of his mental character were his mothers. Lady Jane was a woman of exquisite accomplishment, and widely read in foreign literature. From his earliest years Algernon was trained, by his grandfather and by his mother, in the French and Italian languages. He was brought up, with the exception of long visits to Northumberland, in the Isle of Wight, his grandparents residing at The Orchard, Niton, Ventnor, and his parents at East Dene, Bonchurch.

His parents were high-church and he was brought up as 'a quasi-catholic' He recollected in after years the enthusiasm with which he welcomed the process of confirmation, and his 'ecstasies of adoration when receiving the Sacrament.'

The name of Swinburne, with an occasional anecdote, occurs in many recent biographies, such as The Autobiography of Elizabeth M. Sewell, the Recollections of Mr. A. G. C. Liddell, the lives of D. G. Rossetti, Edward Burne-Jones, Richard Burton, Whistler, John Churton Collins, and Ruskin. R. H. Shepherd's Bibliography of Swinburne (1887) possesses little value. Swinburne left behind him a considerable number of short MSS., principally in verse. The prose tales have been recorded above, and certain of the verse; his posthumous poems, none of which have yet been published, also include a series of fine Northumbrian ballads.] E. G. *Dictionary of National Biography*, 1912 supplement, 456–65. https://en.wikisource.org/wiki/Swinburne,_Algernon_Charles_(DNB12)

As from his man; and Arthur greeted him
As his good lord and courteously, and bade
To his high feast; who coming with him had
This Queen Morgause of Orkney, his fair wife,
In the green middle Maytime of her life,
And scarce in April was our king's as then,
And goodliest was he of all flowering men,
And of what graft as yet himself knew not;
But cold as rains in autumn was King Lot
And grey-grown out of season: so there sprang
Swift love between them, and all spring through sang
Light in their joyous hearing; for none knew
The bitter bond of blood between them two,
Twain fathers but one mother, till too late
The sacred mouth of Merlin set forth fate
And brake the secret seal on Arthur's birth,
And showed his ruin and his rule on earth
Inextricable, and light on lives to be.[63]

EDWIN ARLINGTON ROBINSON (DECEMBER 22, 1869—APRIL 6, 1935)[64]

The story is that Merlin warned the King
Of what's come now to pass; and I believe it
And Arthur, he being Arthur and a king,
Has made a more pernicious mess than one,
We're told, for being so great and amorous:
It's that unwholesome and inclement cub
Young Modred I'd see first in hell before
I'd hang too high the Queen or Lancelot.[65]

63. Swinburne, *Tristram of Lyonesse*, 24–5.

64. ROBINSON, EDWIN ARLINGTON (1869–), American poet, was born at Head Tide, Me., Dec. 22 1869. From the public schools of Gardiner, Me., he proceeded in 1891 to Harvard, but withdrew after two years to take a business position in New York City. From 1905 to 1910 he was connected with the N.Y. Customs House, and then returned to Gardiner to devote his time to literature, and especially to poetry. He became a member of the National Institute of Arts and Letters. His works include *The Torrent and the Night After* (1896); *The Children of the Night* (1897); *Captain Craig* (1902); *The Town down the River* (1910); *Van Zorn* (1914, a play); *The Porcupine* (1915, a play); *The Man against the Sky* (1916); *Merlin* (1917); *Lancelot* (1920); *The Three Taverns* (1920); *Avon's Harvest* (1921); *Collected Poems* (1921). *Encyclopædia Britannica*, 1922, Vol. 32

65. Robinson, *Merlin*, 18.

JESSIE LAIDLAY WESTON (DECEMBER 28, 1850—SEPTEMBER 29, 1928)

Every folk must have its national hero, and it is worthy of note that the Saxon or Teutonic heroic legends never took real root in this land. That they were introduced we know. Have we not the poem of Beowulf. But Beowulf and his fight with Grendel and the dragon, were less popular than the record of how Arthur slew the giant of Mont S. Michel and conquered the Demon Cat. The great Siegfried legend certainly came to these shores, and we find traces of its influence in Celtic romance; but the only Teutonic hero who seems to have gained firm footing on English ground was Wieland, who as Wayland Smith still survives in popular tradition.

Whatever the reasons may have been, the fact remains that as the various nationalities in this island slowly welded themselves into one people, and Briton, Saxon, Dane and Norman became English, the hero adopted as their national hero was the chief of the conquered, not of the conquering races. Thus when Geoffrey of Monmouth, drawing upon a work probably compiled by a continental Breton, gave to the world his *"Historia Britonum"* in which the pseudo-historical deeds of Arthur were solemnly related, the book was received with avidity, and Norman and Angevin Kings, without a drop of British blood in their veins, gloried in the renown of their predecessor. His history was bound up with the history of Great Britain, and the inhabitants of that land, recognising this, hailed him as their own.[66]

The Gawain and Perceval stories certainly came into connection with each other at a very early date, and probably before the latter, at least, was definitely united to the Arthurian cycle; Perceval's connection with King Arthur's court is, in both Chretien and Wolfram, extremely slight.[67]

GILBERT KEITH CHESTERTON (29 MAY 1874 – 14 JUNE 1936)[68] THE MYTH OF ARTHUR

O learned man who never learned to learn,

---

66. Weston, *King Arthur,* 7.
67. Weston, *Sir Gawain,* 64.
68. Chesterton, Gilbert Keith [G. K. C.] (1874–1936), writer, was born on 29 May

Save to deduce, by timid steps and small,
From towering smoke that fire can never burn
And from tall tales that men were never tall.
Say, have you thought what manner of man it is
Of who men say "He could strike giants down"?
Or what strong memories over time's abyss
Bore up the pomp of Camelot and the crown.
And why one banner all the background fills,
Beyond the pageants of so many spears,
And by what witchery in the western hills
A throne stands empty for a thousand years.
Who hold, unheeding this immense impact,
Immortal story for a mortal sin;
Lest human fable touch historic fact,
Chase myths like moths, and fight them with a pin.
Take comfort; rest—there needs not this ado.
You shall not be a myth, I promise you.[6970]

There are many more recent poems and stories probably too numerous to mention. There is T. S. Eliot's, *The Waste Land*, J.R.R. Tolkien's, *The
Fall of Arthur*.[71] There is C. S. Lewis' *That Hideous Strength*.[72] "That's just the

1874 at 32 Sheffield Terrace, Campden Hill, London, the elder son of Edward Chesterton
(d. 1922), estate agent, and his wife, Marie Louise, née Grosjean (d. 1933). His maternal
grandfather's family were of Swiss French origin, though they had been in England for
several generations; his maternal grandmother came from an Aberdeen family called
Keith—hence Chesterton's second name. From: https://www.oxforddnb.com/ # 32392.

69. http://www.gkc.org.uk/gkc/books/arthur.html and http://www.gkc.org.uk/gkc/
books /

70. Chesterton. Poems, 64.

71. TOLKIEN, J.R.R. in full John Ronald Reuel Tolkien, (born January 3, 1892,
Bloemfontein, South Africa—died September 2, 1973, Bournemouth, Hampshire,
England), English writer and scholar who achieved fame with his children's book The
Hobbit (1937) and his richly inventive epic fantasy The Lord of the Rings (1954–55).
At age four Tolkien, with his mother and younger brother, settled near Birmingham,
England, after his father, a bank manager, died in South Africa. In 1900 his mother
converted to Roman Catholicism, a faith her elder son also practiced devoutly. On her
death in 1904, her boys became wards of a Catholic priest. Four years later Tolkien
fell in love with another orphan, Edith Bratt, who would inspire his fictional character
Lúthien Tinúviel. His guardian, however, disapproved, and not until his 21st birthday
could Tolkien ask Edith to marry him. In the meantime, he attended King Edward's
School in Birmingham and Exeter College, Oxford (B.A., 1915; M.A., 1919). During
World War I he saw action in the Somme. After the Armistice he was briefly on the staff
of The Oxford English Dictionary (then called The New English Dictionary).https://
www.britannica.com/biography/J-R-R-Tolkien

72. LEWIS, CLIVE STAPLES (29 November 1898—22 November 1963) was a British writer and lay theologian. He held academic positions in English literature at both

point," said Mr. Drimble. "One can imagine a man of the old British Line, but also a Christian and a fully-trained general with Roman technique, trying to pull this whole society together and almost succeeding." . . . "Has it ever struck you what an odd creation Merlin is? He's not evil: yet he's a magician. He is obviously a Druid: yet he knows all about the Grail."[73] There is Arthur Owen Barfield's, *The Quest of the Sangreal*.[74] T. H. White[75] wrote *The Once and Future King*. (1958) There are multiple musicals and films

---

Oxford University (Magdalen College, 1925–1954) and Cambridge University (Magdalene College, 1954–1963). He is best known for his works of fiction, especially The Screwtape Letters, The Chronicles of Narnia, and The Space Trilogy, and for his non-fiction Christian apologetics, such as Mere Christianity, Miracles, and The Problem of Pain. Lewis and fellow novelist J. R. R. Tolkien were close friends. They both served on the English faculty at Oxford University and were active in the informal Oxford literary group known as the Inklings. According to Lewis's memoir Surprised by Joy, he was baptised in the Church of Ireland, but fell away from his faith during adolescence. Lewis returned to Anglicanism at the age of 32, owing to the influence of Tolkien and other friends, and he became an "ordinary layman of the Church of England." Lewis's faith profoundly affected his work, and his wartime radio broadcasts on the subject of Christianity brought him wide acclaim. Lewis wrote more than 30 books which have been translated into more than 30 languages and have sold millions of copies. The books that make up The Chronicles of Narnia have sold the most and have been popularised on stage, TV, radio, and cinema. His philosophical writings are widely cited by Christian apologists from many denominations. In 1956, Lewis married American writer Joy Davidman; she died of cancer four years later at the age of 45. Lewis died on 22 November 1963 from kidney failure, one week before his 65th birthday. In 2013, on the 50th anniversary of his death, Lewis was honoured with a memorial in Poets' Corner in Westminster Abbey. https://en.wikipedia.org/wiki/C._S._Lewis

73. Lewis, *That Hideous Strength*, 33.

74. https://owenbarfield.org/the-quest-of-the-sangreal/

75. WHITE, T. H. (born May 29, 1906, Bombay, India—died Jan. 17, 1964, Piraeus, Greece), English novelist, social historian, and satirist who was best known for his brilliant adaptation of Sir Thomas Malory's 15th-century romance, Morte Darthur, into a quartet of novels called The Once and Future King.

White was educated at Cheltenham College and at Cambridge. He taught at Stowe School (1930–36), and while there he attained his first real critical success with an autobiographical volume, England Have My Bones (1936). He afterward devoted himself exclusively to writing and to studying such recondite subjects as the Arthurian legends, which were to provide the material for his books. White was by nature a recluse, for long periods isolating himself from human society and spending his time hunting, fishing, and looking after his strange collection of pets.

The Once and Future King (1958) comprises The Sword in the Stone (1939), The Queen of Air and Darkness—first published as The Witch in the Wood (1940)—The Ill-Made Knight (1941), and The Candle in the Wind. The Once and Future King was adapted in 1960 into a highly successful musical play, Camelot; a motion picture, also called Camelot (1967), was based on the play. White's other works include The Goshawk (1951), a study of falconry, and two works of social history, The Age of Scandal (1950) and The Scandalmonger (1951). https://www.britannica.com/biography/T-H-White

such as Broadway's *Camelot*, (1960) a musical by Alan Jay Lerner (lyrics) and Frederick Loewe (music). It is based on the legend of King Arthur and adapted from the T. H. White novel *The Once and Future King*. The musical starred Richard Burton as King Arthur, and Julie Andrews as Guinevere. Elton John's *Candle in the Wind* was originally written for Norma Jean, otherwise known as Marilyn Monroe. When Princess Diana Spencer died in 1997 the artist, in cooperation with the lyricist, Bernie Taupin was asked to rewrite the song to commemorate Diana Spencer. Candle in the Wind is one of the books included within T.H. White's, *The Once and Future King*. Whether this was Taupin's original inspiration, I cannot say. However, the symbolism returns the Arthurian myth to the house of Spencer.

Appendix 6

Word Origins of the Menorah and Oil of Anointing

Table 19. Word Roots

A. WORD ROOTS

Exodus 25	Strongs # Hebrew	Strongs #1 Greek Septuagint Greek NT	Translations KJV
Lampstand	4501 מְנֹרָה menowrah	3087 λυχνια luchnia	OT: candlestick 40; 40
Bowls, basins	1375 גְּבִעִים gebiyim	2902.1 κρατηρες κρατέω krateo	OT: bowl 8, cup 5, pot 1; 14 NT: hold 12, take 9, lay hold 8 . . . etc. 47x
		5357 φιάλη phiale	The bowl of Revelation is written as φιάλη and is found only in Rev. (KJV: vial 12x)
Almond	8246(7) שָׁקֵד shaqad	2594.4 καρυισκους	Almond (from the root watch) 9, wake 1, remain 1, hasten 1; 12 (also nut-like)

1. The Strong's numbering system is indexed to the Brown Driver Briggs Lexicon

313

Exodus 25	Strongs # Hebrew	Strongs #1 Greek Septuagint Greek NT	Translations KJV
Branch	7070 קָנֶה qaneh	2562.2 καλαμισκω	OT: reed 28, branch 24, calamus 3, cane 2, stalk 2, balance 1, bone 1, spearmen 1; 62
		2798 κλάδος klados	Also: measuring rod Also: he bought הֲנָק NT: branch 11
Knob	3730 כַּפְתֹּר kaphtor	4968.1 σφαιρωτηρ	knop 16, lintel 2; 18
Flower	6525 פֶּרַח perach	2918 κρινον	flower 14, bud 2, blossom 1; 17 NT: lily 2.
Shaft	3409 יָרֵךְ yarek	2737.1 καυλος	thigh 21, side 7, shaft 3, loins 2, body 1; 34 Also: lowermost κατώτερος katoteros

Isaiah 11:1 There shall come forth a Rod from the stem of Jesse, and a Branch shall grow out of his roots. NKJV

Rod	2415 חֹטֶר choter	4464 ῥάβδος rhabdos	OT: branch, twig, rod (2) NT: rod 6, staff 4, sceptre 2; 12
Stem	1503 גֶּזַע geza	4491 ῥίζα rhiza	OT: stock 2, stem 1; 3 stem, trunk, stock (of trees) NT: root, 17
Branch	5342 נֵצֶר netser	2562.2 καλαμισκω	OT: branch, 4 sprout, shoot, branch (always fig) LXX: translates as flower
Roots	8328 שֹׁרֶשׁ sheresh	4491 ῥίζα rhiza	OT: root 30, bottom 1, deep 1, heels 1; 33 NT: root, 17

Ecclesiastes 12:5 uses the word amygdaline for almond in LXX
Numbers 17:8 and Jer. 1:11 translate almonds as walnuts

B. THE SEVEN SEALS, TRUMPETS AND BOWLS OF REVELATION

Lampstand	4501 מְנֹרָה menowrah	3087 λυχνια luchnia	OT: candlestick 40; 40 NT: candlestick; 12
Seal	2368 חֹתָם chothm	4973 σφραγις sphragis	OT: signet 9, seal 5; 14 NT: seal; 16
Trumpet	7782 שׁוֹפָר showphar	4536 σάλπιγξ salpigx	OT: trumpet 68, cornet 4; 72 NT: trumpet 9, trump 2; 11
Bowl	4219 מִזְרָק mizrq	5357 φιάλη phiale	OT: basins 11, bowl 21; 32 NT: vial 12; 12

C. THE SEED OF THE WOMAN AND THE REMNANT

Seed	2233 זרע zera	4690 σπέρμα sperma	OT: seed 221, child 2, carnally + 07902 2, carnally 1, fruitful 1, seedtime 1, sowing time 1; 229 NT: seed 43, issue 1; 44
Remnant	7611 שארית sheriyth	2640 κατάλειμμα kataleimma	OT: remnant 44, residue 13, rest 3, remainder 2, escaped 1, misc 3; 66 NT: remnant 1; 1
Branch	5342 נֵצֶר netser	2562.2 καλαμισκω	OT: branch, 4

D. THE OIL OF ANOINTING

Myrrh	4753 מֹר mor	3464 μύρον muron	OT: myrrh 12; 12 From מַר bitter (4843) NT: ointment 14; 14 (3464) NT: myrrh 2 (4666)
		4666 σμύρνα smurna	
Cinna- mon	7076 קִנָּמָן qinna- mown	2792 κινάμωμον kina- momon	OT: cinnamon 3 NT: cinnamon 1 cinnamon was a well-known aromatic substance, the rind of *Laurus cinnamonum* called *korunda-gauhah* in Ceylon (Sri Lanka)
Cane	7070 קָנֶה qaneh	2563 κάλαμος kalamos	OT: reed 28, branch 24, calamus 3, cane 2, stalk 2, balance 1, bone 1, spearmen 1; 62 NT: reed 11, pen 1; 12
Cassia	6916 קִדָּה qiddah		OT: cassia 2; 2 possible root: קדקד (qodqod) head
Olive Oil	2132 זַיִת zayith	1636 ἐλαία elaia	OT: olive 17, olive tree 14, oliveyard 6, olivet 1; 38 OT: oil 165, ointment 14, olive 4, oiled 2, fat 2, things 2, misc 4; 193
	8081 שֶׁמֶן shmn	1637 ἔλαιον elaion	NT: olives 11, olive tree 3, olive berries 1; 15 NT: oil 11 (1637)

E. THE INCENSE

Stacte	5198 נָטָף nataph		OT: stacte 1, drops 1; 2 storax-gum (drops of stacte)
Onycha	7827 שְׁחֵלֶת shacheleth		OT: onycha 1 Black murex-shell
Galbanum	2464 חֶלְבְּנָה chelbanah		OT: galbanum 1
Frankincense	3828 לְבֹנָה labownah	3030 λίβανος libanos	OT: frankincense 15, incense 6; 21 NT: frankincense 2; 2

Appendix 7

Myvyrian Archaiology

Table 20. An abridged copy of the list of kings[1]

1. Annyn of Troy (Einion) was the first king of Cambria. He was the son of Prydain the son of Aedd the Great, who was a king of the Cimbric nation before they came to the island of Britain, which before it was inhabited, was called the Sea-girt Country.

2. Selys the Aged, the son of Annyn, caused the woods to be burnt, that he might have open ground for corn and cattle.

3. Brwth, the son of Selys the Aged, was the first who made war in the island of Britain.

4. Cymryw, the son of Brwth, first instituted laws in Britain.

5. Ithon, the son of Cymryw, was a great improver of national government.

6. Gweirydd the Great, the son of Ithon, was a very wise prince.

7. Peredur, the son of Gweirydd.

8. Llyfeinydd the son of Peredur, was a mighty man.

9. Gorwst, the son of Llyfeinydd, was the swiftest man of foot.

10. Tewged the Dark, the son of Llyfeinydd, succeeded to the kingdom, after his brother Gorwst.

1. Williams, *Iolo Manuscripts*, 331.

317

11. Llarian the Gentle.

12. Ithel, the son of Llarian, was a very beneficent king, and the first who taught effectually the proper culture of wheat.

13. Enir, the son of Ithel, called Enir the Bard, was an exceedingly wise king, and a good bard. He reduced to fair order the maxims of wisdom and conferred high distinctions on bards and druids; so that he and they became supreme through the world for wisdom and knowledge. Druids was the appellation, in those days, given to persons of learning and faith.

14. Calchfynnydd the Aged, was the first who made lime,

15. Llywarch, the son of Calchfynnydd, was the first who constructed fortresses of stone and mortar.

16. Idwal the Proud, the son of Llywarch, was a man supreme in all great exploits, and lived in the time of Dyfnwal Moelmud.

17. Archwyn, the son of Idwal, was a deaf and dumb king, but a very wise and brave man.

18. Rhun Gamber, the son of Idwal, was a very valiant king. He enacted a law that no one should intermeddle with his neighbour's concerns.

19. Gorfyniaw, the son of Rhun Gamber, was a very wicked and cruel king.

20. Cynfarch, the son of Rhun, was killed for his cowardice.

21. Bleddyn, the son of Rhun, was an exceedingly good king.

22. Morgan, the son of Bleddyn, was a truly good king, who effected incalculable benefits1 for his country.

23. Berwyn, the son of Morgan, was a mighty king, who inflicted summary vengeance on his enemies.

24. Ceraint the Drunkard, the son of Berwyn, was the first who made malt liquor properly.

25. Brywlais, the son of Ceraint, was a good king, a melodious bard, and a sweet singer.

26. Alafon, the son of Brywlais, was a very kind king in word and action; and, also, a bard of transcendent compositions.

27. Annyn the Rugged, the son of Alafon, was a potent monarch.

28. Dingad, the son of Annyn, was the first who raised cavalry to repel hostile invasion.

29. Greidiol, the son of Dingad, fought against the Coranians, slew them, and drove them entirely out of Cambria.

30. Ceraint, the son of Greidiol, was a wise king; but having fallen in love with a young woman who did not requite his affection, he became deprived of memory and reason.

31. Meirion, the son of Dingad, Ceraint's uncle, succeeded him.

32. Arch, the son of Meirion, systematized the art of war.

33. Caid, the son of Arch, was the first who constructed bridges over rivers.

34. Caradog, the son of Arch, succeeded, because of the infancy of his nephew Ceri, the son of Caid. This Caradog (Caractacus) was the bravest and most renowned of any in the whole world; having evinced pre-eminent valour on all occasions. He vanquished the Romans in many battles; but was, at last, overcome through treachery, and carried captive to Rome. His daughter, Eurgain, married a Roman chieftain, who accompanied her to Cambria. This chieftain had been converted to Christianity, as well as his wife Eurgain, who first introduced the faith among the Cambro-britons and sent for Ilid (a native of the land of Israel) from Rome to Britain. This Ilid is called, in the service of his commemoration, St. Joseph of Arimathea.

35. Ceri, the son of Caid, was a remarkably wise man, and constructed many ships at the expense of the country and its lords; hence he was called Ceri of the extensive navy, having numerous fleets at sea. He lived at the place called Porth-Kery.

36. Baran, the son of Ceri, was a mighty king; far surpassing any of his predecessors in military courage; being deemed the most redoubtable of all princes. He lived to be 187 years of age, married eighteen wives, and had a hundred children.

37. Lleyn, the son of Baran, was a sagacious monarch of courageous might.

38. Tegid, the son of Baran, was a wise king and a good bard. He enacted excellent regulations for literature; restored ancient learning, which had nearly become lost; and instituted a council of bards and druids, as of old.

39. Llyr, (Lear,) the son of Baran, fought powerfully with many hostile nations.

40. Bran, the son of Llyr, was a valiant king.

41. Caradog, (Caractacus,) the son of Bran, was a very puissant king.

42. Cyllin, the son of Caradog, was an exceedingly wise and mild king. In his time a considerable number of Cambrians became converts to Christianity, through the ministry of the saints of Eurgain's congregation, and many other holy men from Greece and Rome, who were in Cambria at this time. This prince was the first in this country who gave proper names to infants; for previously, persons were not named before years of maturity, when the disposition became developed.

43. Owain, the son of Cyllin, did signal service to the Christians.

44. Eirchion, the son of Owain. In his time the infidels slew great numbers of the Christians; but he went against them.

45. Gorwg, the son of Eirchion, was an exceedingly wise and religious king. He caused wars to cease, procured skilful men from Rome, to instruct his subjects in the right systems of agriculture, raising corn, and architecture, contributed largely towards the support of learning and piety, and was a good bard.

46. Gorddyfwn, the son of Gorwg, was a turbulently mad king.

47. Rhun, the son of Gorwg, an exceedingly sagacious monarch, pursued the invariably beneficent course of his father. He instituted laws for learning and science.

48. Einydd, the son of Gorddyfwn, was a good king. He adhered to the faith of his uncle and grandfather and raised to exalted privileges all who professed Christianity.

49. Arthfael, the son of Einydd, called Arthfael the aged, erected, like his father, many churches, towns, and villages; but in his old age, he became an infidel.

50. Gwrgan the Freckled, the son of Arthfael, was a puissant sovereign.

51. Meirchion, the son of Gwrgan, built many towns, subdivided the country into cantreds, established literary and scientific regulations, and gave increased force to the privileges and degrees instituted for persons of approved learning and art.

52. Meyryg, the son of Mcirchion, was a brave far-famed king. In his time the Irish-Picts came to Cambria: he however marched against them, drove them away, and slew them.

53. Crair, the son of Meyryg; a very religious, wise, and merciful prince, who was slain by the unconverted.

54. Edric, the son of Crair, was an exceedingly unwise sovereign, and the cause of great ignorance and impiety in the country.

55. Bran, the son of Edric, was a frantic, wicked king, who died of anger and rage.

56. Tryhaearn, the son of Edric, succeeded, and was a haughty, impetuous sovereign.

57. Nyniaw, the son of Bran, who was a better king than his more immediate predecessors, cleared the country of enemies, and gave possessions to the churches; but in his latter period he became deprived of memory and reason.

58. Teithfallt, the son of Nyniaw, called, also, Teithfalch in some books, was a beneficent and religious, a wise and heroic monarch. He fought powerfully with the Saxons, and vanquished them; and he passed a law that made it imperative on all to contribute a portion of their wealth towards supporting religion, the clergy, learning, and the repairs of churches.

59. Tewdric, the son of Teithfallt, an eminently good king, who drove the infidel Saxons and Irish out of the country. He founded many churches and colleges, endowing them with possessions, built the Church of Llandaff, where formerly stood the church of Lucius, the son of Coel, which was burnt by the infidels, and endowed it amply with extensive lands. It was at his suggestion that this Iltutus brought Saint Germanus to Cambria; for the college of Eurgain was now extinct, having been entirely destroyed by the Saxons; but a new and contiguous one was established by Iltutus, through the gifts and affection of Tewdric; so that it became the principal college of all Britain, and the first in the world for learning and piety.

60. Meyryg the son of Tewdric, was a good king, who gave lands to the church of Teilo at Llandaff, and to the college of Iltutus, called now Llanilltud; (Llantwit Major).

61. Adras, the son of Meyryg, was a very heroic sovereign, who frequently put the Saxons to flight; killing and destroying them. He enacted many laws and ordinances for civil and ecclesiastical government; and was the first who instituted a class of Equestrians, for the maintenance of correct comportment in war, and due discipline at arms

62. Morgan, the son of Adras, called Morgan the Courteous, and Morgan of Glamorgan, was a renowned king, and an Equestrian of Arthur's court, and of the Round Table. He was Arthur's cousin.

Appendix 8

Maps of Southwest Britain

MAPS OF BRITAIN AND WALES 1600S.[1]

1. Camden, William. *Britannia*: or *a Chorographical Defcription of Great Britain and Ireland*. Translated from the edition published by the author in MDCVII. Enlarged by the latest discoveries, by Richard Gough, F. A. & R. SS. In three volumes. Illustrated with maps, and other copper-plates. John Nichols, for T. Payne and Son, Castle-Street, St. Martin's; and G. G. J. and J. Robinson, Pater-Noster-Row, MDCCI.XXXIX. [1789].

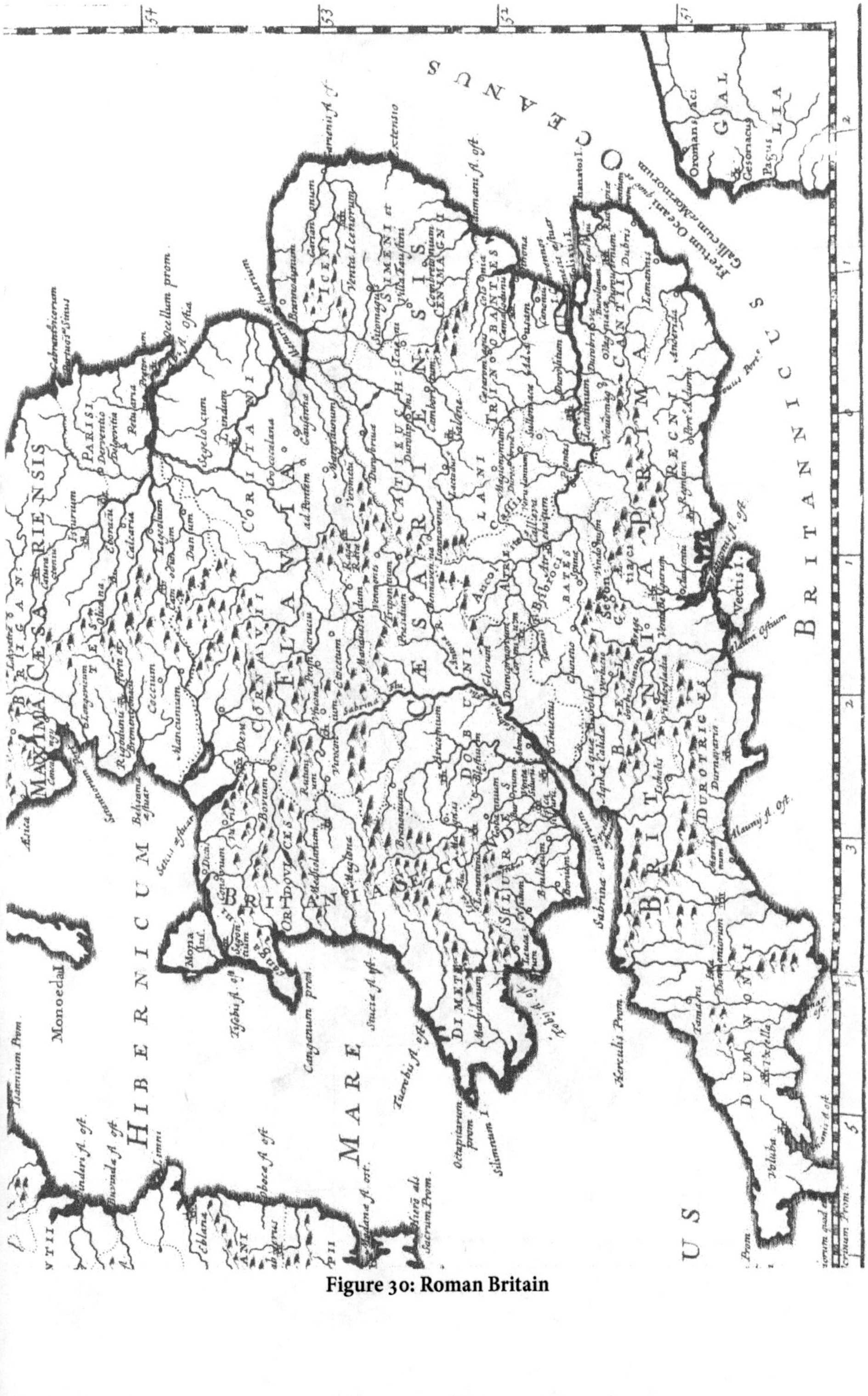

Figure 30: Roman Britain

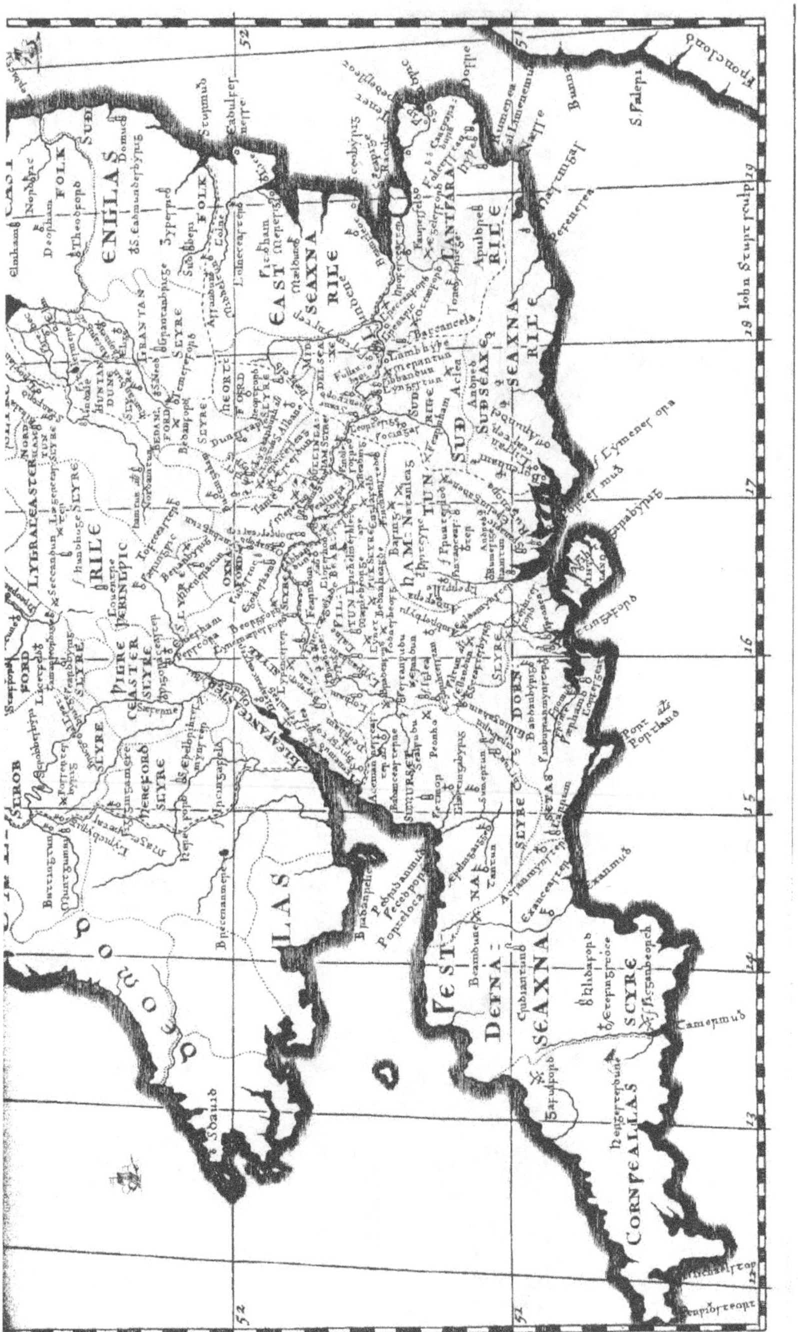

Figure 31: Saxon Britain

Figure 32: Somerset west

Figure 33: Somerset east

Figure 34: Monmouth Wales

Figure 35: Cornwall east

Figure 36: Cornwall west

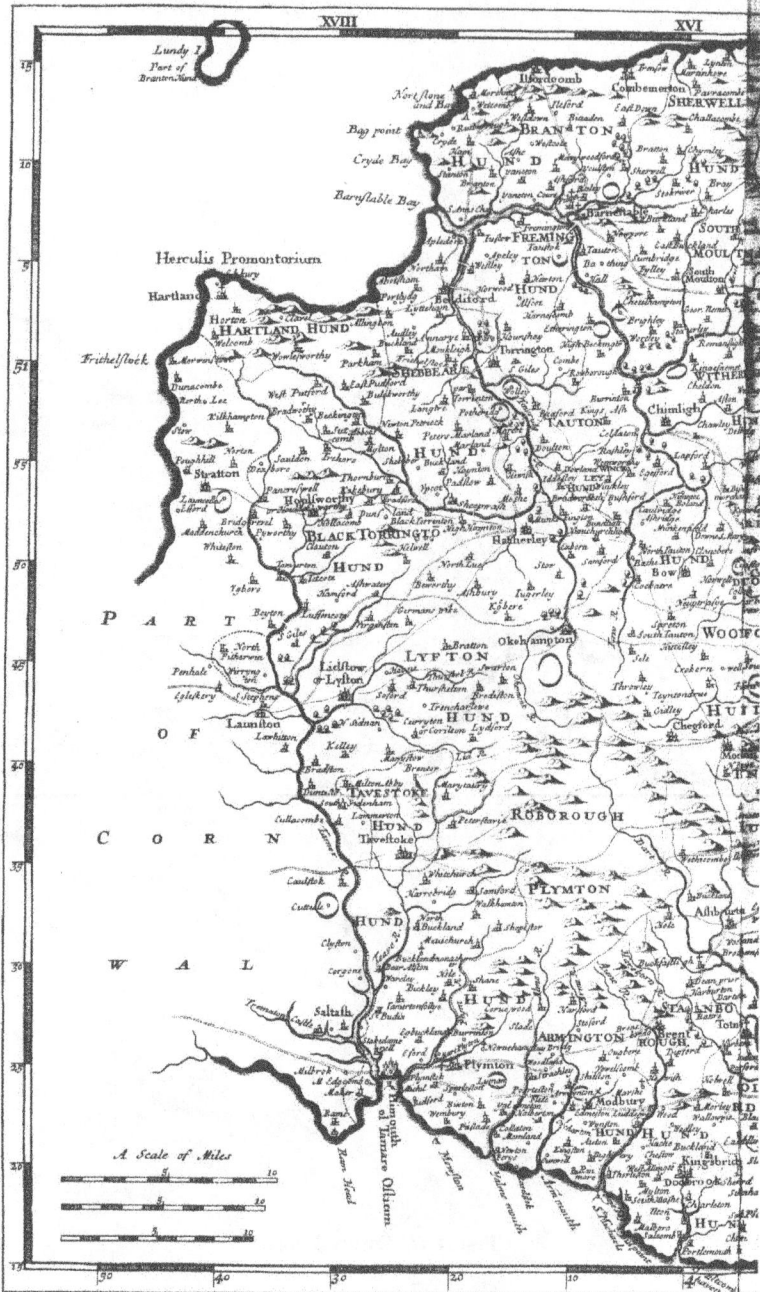

Figure 37: Devon west

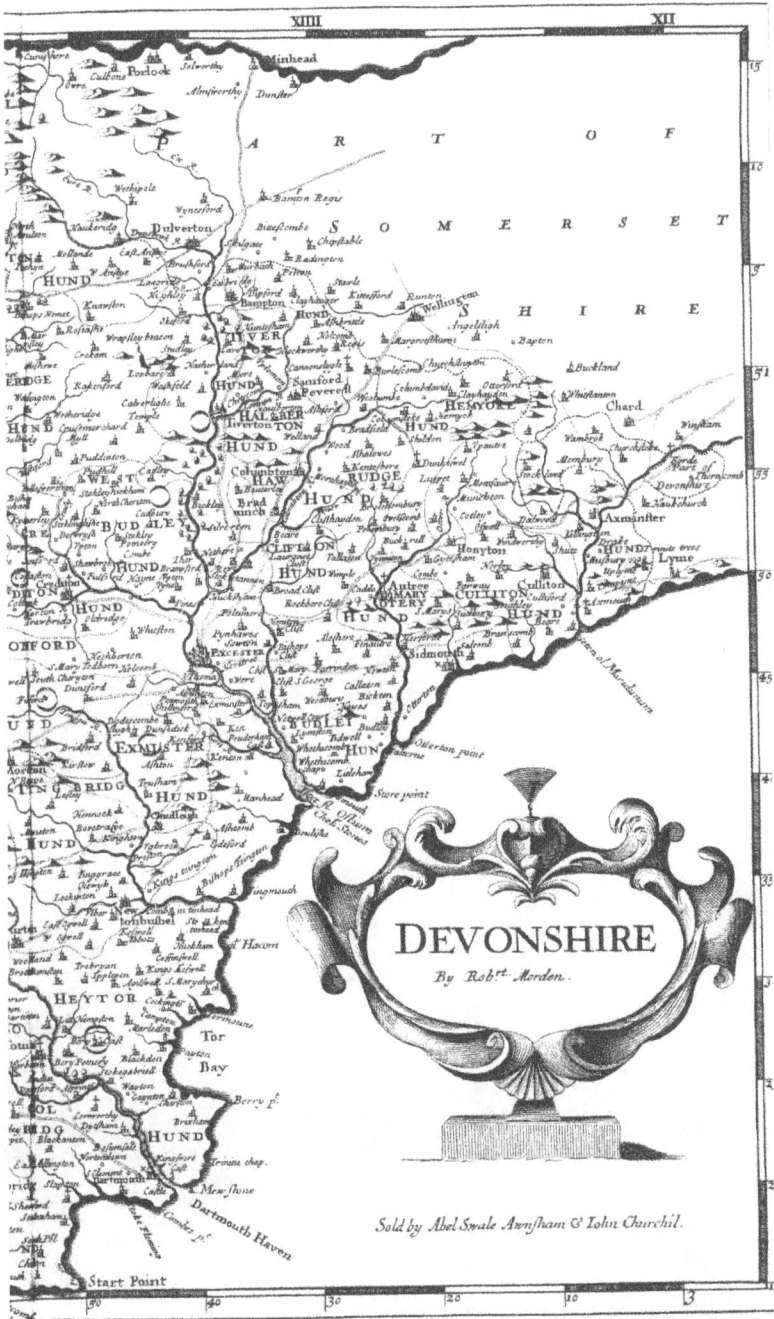

Figure 38: Devon east

Bibliography

Annales Cambriae, Harlean MSS, British Museum, 3859.

Ante Nicene Fathers, Vol 3. *Latin Christianity: Its Founder, Tertullian*. Edited by Philip Schaff and Allan Menzies. Grand Rapids, MI: Christian Classics Ethereal Library. 1885. Available at http://www.ccel.org/ccel/schaff/anf03.html

Aquinas, Thomas. *IX Metsphys.*, lect. 5, # 1828.

———. *Summa Theologica*. Vol. 1, Part 1, Question 97 Article 4.

Aristotle. *Metaphysics*, Theta, 6, 1048 a 25 ff

Arnold, Matthew. *Poems*. London: George Routledge & Sons, 1896.

Attenborough, Richard, dir. *Shadowlands*. C. S. Lewis biography. 1993.

Baillie, M.G.L. "The Belfast oak chronology to AD 1001." Tree-Ring Bulletin (1977) 37:1–12.

Baronio, Cardinal Cesare. *Annales Ecclesiastici*, Vol. 1, 208.

Bede, the Venerable. *Ecclesiastical History of England and the Anglo-Saxon Chronicle*. Edited by J. A. Giles. London: George Bell & Sons, 1887.

Biographia Britannica. Vol. I, No. 17. London, 1747.

Black's Guide to Cornwall. Edited by A. R. Hope Moncrieff, 22nd edition. London: A. & C. Black, 1919.

Blech, Benjamin. *The Secrets of Hebrew Words*. New Jersey: Jason Aronson, 1991.

Bosworth, Annette, MD. *Anyway You Can*. MeTone Life, 2018.

Braden, Gregg. *The Divine Matrix*. Hay House, 2006.

Brewer, Ebenezer Cobham. *A Dictionary of Miracles: The Glastonbury Thorn*. Philadelphia: J. B. Lippincott, 1894.

Brown, Francis, and S. R. Driver, and Charles A. Briggs, *Hebrew and English Lexicon*, 1906. Reprint, Peabody, Mass: Hendrickson, 2006.

Buber, Martin. *The Legend of the Baal Shem*. Translated by Maurice Friedman 1969. Reprint, Princeton, NJ: Princeton University Press, 1995.

Bucke, Richard Maurice. *Cosmic Consciousness*. E.P. Dutton, 1901, and Causeway, 1974.

Camden, William. *Britannia: or a Chorographical Defcription of Great Britain and Ireland*. Mary Matthews for Awnsham Churchill, William Taylor, in Pater-Nofter-Row. 2nd Ed. Vol. II, 1722.

Cambrensis. Giraldi. *De Principis Instructione Liber*. Opera, Vol. VIII, London, 1891.

Campbell, T.C., and Thomas M. Campbell. *The China Study: The Most Comprehensive Study of Nutrition Ever Conducted and the Startling Implications for Diet.* BenBella, 2006.

Campbell, Parpia, et al. "Diet, Lifestyle, and the Etiology of Coronary Artery Disease: The Cornell China Study." American Journal Cardiology (1998) 82:18T–21T.

Capgrave, John. *The Chronicle of England.* Edited by F. C. Hingeston. London: Longman, Brown, Green. 1858.

Caradoc. *The History of Wales*, Shrewsbury, Wales: John Eddowes, 1832.

Carley, James P. *John of Glastonbury. Cronica sive Antiquitates.* British Archeological Reports, 47i, 1978.

Casey, John L. Dr. *Dark Winter.* Boca Raton, FL: Humanix, 2014.

Cassuto, U. *A Commentary on the Book of Exodus.* Translated by Israel Abrahams. Jerusalem, Israel: Hebrew University Magnes Press, 1997.

———. *Biblical and Oriental Studies.* Translated from the Hebrew and Italian by Israel Abrahams. Skokie, Illinois: Varda, 5765/2005.

Catholic Encyclopedia: *Chalice.* Vol III, 1908.

Chaucer, Geoffrey. *Richard Brathwait's Comments in 1665 upon Chaucer's Tales of the Miller and the Wife of Bath.* Edited by C.F.E. Spurgeon for the Chaucer Society. Paternoster House, Charing-Cross Road, W.C.: Kegan Paul, Trench, Trubner & Co., 1901.

Chen J, Campbell T. C., Li J, et al. *Diet, Life Style and Mortality in China. A study of the characteristics of 65 Chinese counties.* Ithaca NY: Cornell University Press, 1990.

Chesterton Gilbert, Keith. *The Collected Poems of G. K. Chesterton.* New York: Dodd, Mead, 1961.

Christensen, Duane L., *Deuteronomy* V.2. Nashville, TN: Thomas Nelson, 2002.

Chopra, Deepak. *The Future of God.* PBS Special, 2014.

Chronicle of the Early Britons, Brut y Bryttaniait. Translated by Wm. Cooper. Jesus College, MS LXI. 2002.

Chronicle of the Kings of Britain, The. Translated by Rev. Peter Roberts, from the welsh copy attributed to Tysilio E. Williams. London: 1811.

Clarence, H. W. *Lessons from the Olive Tree, Mishpochah in Messiah.* Vol. 2. Issue 5 July 2003.

Coggeshall, Ralph of. *Chronicon Anglicanum.* London: Longman, Paternoster Row, 1875.

Crabb, Larry. *Understanding People.* Grand Rapids, Michigan: Zondervan, 1987.

Cressy, R. F. S. *The Church-History of Brittany from the Beginning of Christianity to the Norman Conquest.* Book 2, Chap VIII, 1668.

Crombie, Kelvin. *For the Love of Zion.* Hodder & Stoughton Religious, 1991.

Cronenberg, David, dir. *A Dangerous Method.* 2011.

Dante Alighieri. *The Vision, or Hell, Purgatory, and Paradise of Dante Alighieri.* Translated by Henry Francis Cary. London: Oxford University Press, 1916.

Davis, Garth, dir. *Mary Magdalene*, 2018.

de Bhaldraithe, Eoin. *The High Crosses of Moone and Castledermot, A Journey back to the Early Church.* Bolton Abbey Cistercian. Moone, Co. Kildare, Ireland: Data Print, 2009.

De Troyes, Chrétien. *The Story of the Grail.* Translated by Robert White Linker. University of North Carolina Press, 1960.

Dispenza, Dr. Joe. *Becoming Supernatural.* Hay House, 2017.

Doran, Robert, SJ. *Theology and the Dialectics of History*. University of Toronto Press, 1990.

Dryden, John. *King Arthur*. London: Jacob Tonfon, 1691.

Dunn, J. D. G. *Romans, Word Biblical Commentary*. Vol. 38b. Dallas TX: Word, 1988.

Durand, Gilbert. *The Anthropological Structures of the Imaginary*. Translated by Margaret Sankey and Judith Hatten. Brisbane, Australia: Boombana, 1999.

Eliot, T. S. *Four Quartets*. London: Faber & Faber, 1959.

———. *The Waste Land*. London: Faber & Faber, 1965.

Encyclopaedia Judaica: British Israelites. Ed. Michael Berenbaum and Fred Skolnik. Vol. 4. 2nd ed. Detroit, Michigan: 2007.

———. *Kabbala*. Keter Publishing House Ltd. Second Edition, Volume 11, 2007.

———. *Oil of Life*. Stone, Michael E. Editors, Michael Berenbaum and Fred Skolnik. Vol. 15. 2nd ed. Detroit, Michigan: 2007.

Eusebius. *Ecclesiastical History of Eusebius Pamphilus*, Bk I, Ch XIII. New York: Thomas N. Stanford, 1856.

Fitzmyer, J. A. *Romans: A New Translation with Introduction and Commentary*, B33. New York: Doubleday, 1993.

Foxe, John. *Acts and Monuments*. Vol. VI. London: R. B. Seeley and W. Burnside, 1841. orig. pub. 1563.

Froissart, Jean. *Meliador*. Published for Wenceslas de Boheme. Paris: Auguste Longnon, 1845.

Gildas. *The Works of Gildas and Nennius*. Translated by J.A. Giles. London: James Bohn, 1841.

Glastonbury, John of. *The Chronicle of Glastonbury Abbey*. Ed. James P. Carley. Translated by David Townsend. Reprint, Suffolk, UK: Boydell, 1985.

Goleman, Daniel. *Destructive Emotions, How Can We Overcome Them? A Scientific Dialogue with the Dalai Lama*. Bantam, 2003.

Goodman, Godfrey. *The Two Great Mysteries of Christian Religion*. J. Flesher 1653. Reprint, Hearne, Thomas. *The History and Antiquities of Glastonbury*. Oxford, 1722.

Gordon. *Prehistoric London*. London: Covenant, 1946.

Green, Glenda. *Love Without End*. Sedona, Arizona: Spiritis, 1999, 2006.

———. *The Keys of Jeshua*. 2nd Ed. Sedona, Arizona: Spiritis, 2007.

Guinness, Grattan and Mrs. Guinness. *Light for the Last Days*. London: Hodder & Stoughton, 1886.

———. *Light for the Last Days*. Edited and revised by Rev. E. P. Cachemaille. London: Morgan & Scott, 1917.

Guscin, Mark. *The Image of Edessa*. Leiden: Brill, 2009.

Harbison, Peter. *Irish High Crosses*. Drogheda, Ireland: Boyne Valley Honey.

Harris, R. Laird, and Gleason L. Archer, Jr., and Bruce K. Waltke. *Theological Wordbook of the Old Testament*. Moody, 2003.

Harris, Rachel. *Listening to Ayahuasca. New Hope for Depression, Addiction, PTSD, and Anxiety*. New World Library, 2017.

Harrison, John Kent, dir. *Beautiful Dreamers*. NFB, (National Film Board of Canada) 1990.

Hawthorne, G. F. et al. editors. *Dictionary of Paul and His Letters*. Downers Grove, ILL: Inter Varsity, 1993.

Hearne, Thomas. *The History and Antiquities of Glastonbury*. Oxford, 1722.

Herodotus, *The Histories*. 3.115. Translated by Aubrey de Selincourt. Edinburgh: Penguin, R & R Clark, 1954.

Heywood, Thomas. *The Life of Merlin Surnamed Ambrosius His Prophecies and Predictions*. London: Carmarthen, 1812.

Hill, Julia Butterfly. *The Legacy of Luna*. Harper Collins, 2000.

Hyatt, Andrew, dir. *Full of Grace*. 2015.

Jerome, *Vulgate*. Mark 15:43.

Jewish Encyclopedia: Arles. Vol. 2. New York: Funk and Wagnalls, 1902.

———. *Tetragrammaton*. Toy, C. H. and L. Blau, 1906.

Jones, Sidian Morning Star and Stanley Krippner, PhD. *The Voice of Rolling Thunder*. Rochester, Vermont: Bear & Company, 2012.

Josephus. *Antiquities of the Jews*. Book III Chapter 7.7

Jung, Carl. *Man and his Symbols*. With: M.-L. von Franz, Joseph L. Henderson, Jolande Jacobi, and Aniela Jaffe. New York: Anchor Doubleday, 1964.

Kalamian, Miriam and Dr. Thomas N. Seyfried, (foreward). *Keto for Cancer: Ketogenic Metabolic Therapy as a Targeted Nutritional Strategy*. Chelsea Green, 2017.

Kerr, John. *A Dangerous Method*. Vintage, 1994.

Kitson, Hugh, dir., and Kelvin Crombie, author. *The Destiny of Britain*. Hatikva Films, 2007.

Kjellgren, A., and A. Eriksson, and T. Norlander. *Experiences of Encounters with Ayahuasca—"the Vine of the Soul."* Journal of Psychoactive Drugs. 414, 309–15. 2009.

Klein, Naomi. *This Changes Every Thing*. Alfred A. Knopf, 2014.

Labuschagne, Casper. *The Blessing of Moses in Deuteronomy 33—Logotechnical Analysis*. http://www.labuschagne.nl/

Lambdin. *Arthurian Writers, A Biographical Encyclopedia*. Edited by Laura Cooner Lambdin and Robert Thomas Lambdin. Westport, CT: Greenwood, 2008.

Larson, D. W. and P. E. Kelly. "The extent of old-growth Thuja occidentalis on cliffs of the Niagara Escarpment." Canadian Journal of Botany (1991) 69 7: 1628–36. doi:10.1139/b91–206.

Layamon. *Arthurian Chronicles represented by Wace and Layamon*. London: J.M. Dent &Sons, 1912.

Leland, John. *Itinerary in England and Wales 1535–1543*. Edited by Lucy Toulmin Smith. London: George Bell and Sons, 1907.

Levenson, J. D. *Sinai and Zion*. Minneapolis, MN: Winston, 1985.

Levine, Etan. *The Evolving Symbolism of the Burning Bush*. Jerusalem, Israel: Dor le Dor, World Jewish Bible Society, 1980.

Lewis C. S. *Mere Christianity*. New York: Harper Collins, 2001.

———. *Till We Have Faces: A Myth Retold*. London: Geoffrey Bles, 1956.

———. *That Hideous Strength*. London: The Bodley Head, 1945.

Lewis, Lionel Smithett. *Joseph of Arimathea at Glastonbury*. Cambridge: Lutterworth, 1922, 2004.

Li Jun-Yao, Llu Be-Al, T Li Guang-Yi et al. *Atlas of Cancer Mortality in the People's Republic of China*. International Journal of Epidemiology. 10 (1981) 127–133.

Lipton, Dr. Bruce. *The Biology of Belief*. Hay House, 10th Anniversary Ed. 2015.

Llancarvan, Caradoc of. *The History of Wales*. Translated by Dr. Powell. Shrewsbury. 1832.

Lonergan, Bernard, SJ. *Collected works of Bernard Lonergan.* Vol. 4. Toronto: University of Toronto Press, 1988.

———. *Collected works of Bernard Lonergan. Topics in Education,* Vol. 10, 1993.

———. *Collected Works of Bernard Lonergan.* Vol. 18, *Phenomenology and Logic,* edited by Phil McShane. University of Toronto Press, 2001.

———. *Insight, A Study of Human Understanding.* New York: Philosophical Library, 1957.

———. *Insight, A Study of Human Understanding.* Edited by Frederick Crowe, SJ., and Robert Doran SJ. Vol. 3, University of Toronto Press, 1992.

———. *Method in Theology.* New York: Herder and Herder, 1972.

Luoma, Jon. *The Hidden Forest: The Biography of an Ecosystem.* Oregon State University Press, 2006.

Lupieri, E. F. *A Commentary on the Apocalypse of John.* Translated by M. Johnson and A. Kamesar. Mich: William B. Eerdmans, 2006.

Lyons, William, John. *Joseph of Arimathea: A Study in Reception History.* Oxford University Press, 2014.

Lucas, Alexander R. PhD, et al. *Mindfulness-Based Movement: A Polyvagal Perspective. Integrative Cancer Therapies.* Vol. 17(1) 5–15, 2018.

MacDonald, George. *Phantasies, A Faerie Romance.* London: Chatto & Windus, 1894.

Malmesbury, William of. *Gesta regum Anglorum. The history of the English kings.* Translated by J. A. Giles. Covent Garden, U.K.: Henry G. Bohn, 1847.

Malory, Sir Thomas, *Le Morte D'Arthur.* London: MacMillan, 1919.

Mapes, Walter. *The Latin Poems Commonly Attributed to Walter Mapes.* Edited by Thomas Wright. London: John Bowyer Nichols and Son, 1841.

McKusick, Eileen. *Tuning the Human Biofield.* Healing Arts, 2014.

Memorials of St. Edmund's Abbey. Edited by Thomas Arnold, University College, Oxford, Vol. III. Published 1896.

Meyers, Carol L. *The Tabernacle Menorah: A Synthetic Study of a Symbol from the Biblical Cult.* Montana: Scholars, 1976.

Monmouth, Geoffrey of. *History of the Kings of Britain.* Translated by Aaron Thompson. c. 1150. Reprint. Cambridge, Ontario: In parentheses, 1999.

Montfort, St. Louis de. *The Secret of the Rosary.* Translated by Mary Barbour. Bay Shore, New York: Montfort, 1965–91.

Morris, William. *Romances.* London: Dent and Sons, 1907.

Muhly, James D. *American Journal of Archaeology,* (Apr. 1985) Vol. 89, No. 2.

Munck, J. *Christ & Israel.* Philadelphia: Fortress, 1967.

Nennius. *The History of the Britons.* Translated by J. A. Giles. London: James Bohn, 1841.

Ober, Clinton, and Stephen T. Sinatra, and Martin Zucker. *Earthing: the most important health discovery ever!* Laguna Beach, CA: Basic Health, 2014.

Old Testament, The. Oxford, Clarendon, 1907.

Osmond, Louise, dir. *Arctic Passage, Prisoners of the Ice.* © 2006 WGBH Educational Foundation.

Patrick, Rev. Symon. *The Song of Solomon.* London: Dec 17, 1678.

Pearson, G. W., and Pilcher, J. R. et al. "High-Precision 14C Measurement of Irish Oaks to Show the Natural 14C Variations from Ad 1840 To 5210 Bc." Radiocarbon, Vol 28, No. 2b, (1986) 911–34.

Pentateuch with Targum Onkelos, haphtoroth and RaSHI's commentary. Vol. 2. Translated by M. Rosenbaum and A.M. Silbermann, 1934.

Pliny, *Natural History.* Translated by H. Rackham. London: William Heinemann, 1942.

Porges, Stephen W. *The Polyvagal Theory: Neurophysiological Foundations of Emotions, Attachment, Communication, and Self-regulation.* W. W. Norton, 2011.

Potkay, Monica Brzezinski. *Eternal Chalice.* Haights Cross Communications, 2006.

Price, Dennis. *The Missing Years of Jesus: The Extraordinary Evidence that Jesus Visited the British Isles.* UK: Hay House, 2010.

Purifoy, Thomas, dir. *Is Genesis History?* 2017.

Ramsay, William Mitchell, Sir. *Pauline and other studies in early Christian history.* A.C. Armstrong, 1906.

Rashi. *Commentary on Exodus.* Vol 2. 1221–1934.

Revue des Sciences Ecclesiastiques. Dirigée par M. L'Abbé D. Bouix. Paris. 1861.

Reynolds, Kevin, dir. *Risen,* 2016.

Richie, Chip, dir. *The Trail of Tears: Cherokee Legacy,* 2006.

Riggen, Patricia, dir. *Miracles from Heaven,* 2016.

Robbins, Jim. *The Man who Planted Trees; Lost Groves, Champion Trees, and an Urgent Plan to Save the Planet.* New York: Spiegel and Grau, 2012.

Robinson, Edwin, Arlington. *Merlin, A Poem.* New York: MacMillan, 1917.

Sanday, W. and A. C. Headlam. *The Epistle to the Romans ICC.* Edinburgh: T & T Clark, 1896, 1906, 1958.

Sauer, James B. and Christine Jamieson and Peter L. Monette. *A Commentary on Lonergan's Method in Theology.* LWS, 2001.

Scholem, Gershom G. *Major Trends in Jewish Mysticism.* New York: Schocken, 1941.

Scott, Donald E. *The Electric Sky.* Milwaukie, OR: Mikamar, 2006.

Seyfried, Thomas, Dr. *Cancer as a Metabolic Disease.* Wiley, 2012.

Schulze, Shelley, dir. *E.O. Wilson: Of Ants and Men.* Biodiversity Foundation, 2015.

Scorsese, Martin, dir. *Rolling Thunder Revue: A Bob Dylan Story.* 2019.

Shakespeare, William. *Henry IV.* New York: Houghton Mifflin, 1974.

———. *King Lear.* New York: Houghton Mifflin, 1974.

Siculus, Diodorus. *Library of History.* Translated by G. Booth. London: Military Chronicle Office, 1814.

Siegel,Taggart, and Jon Betz, dirs. *Seed: The Untold Story.* Collective Eye, 2016.

Simoneau, Yves, dir. *Bury My Heart at Wounded Knee,* 2007.

Skene, William F. *The Four Ancient Books of Wales,* Vols. 1. and 2. *The Cymric poems attributed to the Bards of The Sixth Century, containing the Book of Taliesin.* Edinburgh, Scotland: Edmonston and Douglas, 1868.

Slade, Renee and Ri Stewart, dirs. *The Quantum Activist,* 2009.

Smith's Revised Bible Dictionary: *Olive.*

Spelman, Henry, C. *Concilia.* 1639. Early English Books Online.

Spenser, Edmund. *The Faerie Queene.* London: William Ponfonbie. 1590.

Stegner, W. R. *Romans 9.6–29—A Midrash.* JSNT 22 (1984) 37–52.

Stephens, George, dir. *The Diary of Anne Frank,* 1959.

Strabo. *The Geography of Strabo.* Translated by H. C. Hamilton. New York: George Bell & Sons, 1892.

Sullivan, Randall. *The Miracle Detective.* New York: Grove, 2005.

Swinburne, Algernon Charles. *Tristram of Lyonesse.* London: William Heinemann, 1920.

Tacitus. *Complete Works of Tacitus.* Editors, Alfred John Church, William Jackson Brodribb, and Sara Bryant for Perseus. Reprinted, New York: Random, 1942.

Taylor, Dr. Jill. *My Stroke of Insight.* Penguin, 2009.

Tennyson, Alfred Lord. *The Works of Alfred Lord Tennyson.* London: MacMillan, 1890.

Tertullian. *Ante-Nicene Fathers.* Christian Classics Ethereal Library, 2006.

Theological Wordbook of the Old Testament. 1077b

Tillich, Paul. *Dynamics of Faith.* New York: Perennial Classics, 1957, 2001.

Turner, Sharon. *The History of the Anglo-Saxons.* Vol. I. Philadelphia: Carey and Hart. 1841.

———. *The Sacred History of the World.* Vol. II. London, Paternoster Row: Longman, Rees, Orme, Brown, Green and Longman,.1834.

Ullman, Montague, MD, and Stanley Krippner, PhD., with Alan Vaughan. *Dream Telepathy.* New York: Macmillan, 1973.

Unterman, Alan. *Dictionary of Jewish Lore and Legend.* London: Thames and Hudson, 1991.

Urban, Martina. *Aesthetics of Renewal: Martin Buber's Early Representation of Hasidism as Kulturkritik.* University of Chicago Press, 2009.

Von Eschenbach, Wolfram. *Parzival.* Translated by Jessie L. Weston. London, Strand: David Nutt, 1894.

Wace. *Arthurian Chronicles represented by Wace and Layamon.* London: J.M. Dent &Sons, 1912.

Wallace, Randall. dir. *Heaven Is for Real.* 2014.

Weston, Jessie. *King Arthur and his knights: a survey of Arthurian romance.* London: David Nutt, 1899.

———. *The Legend of Sir Gawain.* London: David Nutt, 1897.

Williams, Edward. *Iolo Manuscripts. The History, The Genealogy of Iestyn, the Son of Gwrgan.* Edited by Taliesin Williams (Ab Iolo) of Merthyr Tydfil. Llandovery, Wales: The Welsh MSS. Society, William Rees, 1847.

Wilson, Ian and Barrie Schwortz. *The Turin Shroud, The Illustrated Evidence.* London: Michael O'Mara, 2000.

Y Cymmrodor, The Magazine of the Honourable Society of the Cymmrodorion. Edited by Egerton Phillimore. Vol. VIII. & IX. Sardinia Street, W.C.: Whiting, 1887.

Yarden, Leon. *The Tree of Light.* Ithaca, N.Y.: Cornell University Press, 1971.

Yogananda, Paramahansa. *Autobiography of a Yogi.* Los Angeles, CA.: Self-Realization Fellowship, 1946.

Zinnemann, Fred, dir. *A Man for All Seasons.* Sir Thomas More. 1966.

Index

almond, xiv, 20, 52–53, 55, 57, 60–61, 119, 121, 123–24, 313–14.
Alpha and Omega, 69, 114, 170, 173.
Amor and Psyche, 13.
anoint(ed), xx, 61–62, 69, 104, 120–23, 126, 166–67, 179–80, 194, 198, 200, 210, 215, 243, 313–16.
apostles, saints, early Christians:
Aquinas, Thomas, 8, 15, 117–19.
Arimathea, Joseph of, 65–68, 71, 76, 81, 84, 98–103, 105–12, 212–18, 223–24, 226, 232–37, 244, 246–51, 253, 292–94, 319.
Aristobulus, 244–246, (Eubulus?), 71.
Anthony, of the desert, 94–96.
Augustine of Canterbury, 100, 102, 219, 245, 252, 288–89, 297.
Augustine of Hippo, 118.
Barnabas, 104, 244.
Bartholomew, 104.
Benedict, and order of St., 95, 106, 244, 260.
Briget, 258, Brigid, 219.
Claudia, (Gwladys), 71, 75, 77, 218.
David of Menevia, Wales, 100, 107, 219, 260, 269–70, 282.
Dominic, 82, 207.
Elizabeth, cousin of Mary, 13, 205, 216.
Eusebius, 72, 79, 218, 251.
Jacobe, Mary, 238–39.
Linus, 71, 77, 218.

Novatus, 77.
Patrick, 100, 149, 218, 220, 245, 253, 257–58.
Paul, 21, 43, 49, 58, 71, 75, 95–96, 111, 124, 159–66, 198, 200, 238, 244–47, 261, 306.
Penardim(n), 77, 216, Penarddun, 268.
Peter, 71, 94–95, 104–105, 144–45, 210, 218, 240, 244, 246–247, 255, 259, 261, 276, 306.
Praxedes, 77.
Pudentia, 77.
Rufus Pudens, 71, 75, 77.
Salome (male), 214, 216
Salomé (female), 216, 238–40, 244.
Sara(h) (and Mary Magdalene), 112, 238–39.
Sidonius, (Sidoine), 239.
Suzanne, Susanna, 239, 243.
Timotheus, 77.
Trophimus, (Trophime), 237, 238, 241.
Apostles Creed, 39, 206.
Aristotle, xix–xxi, 8, 10, 16, 35, 37, 185, 230.
Ark of the Covenant, 57–58, 60, 178, 187, 200, (ark of the Testimony), 62. (ark, Quran), 42, (Oviedo) 80.
art, 1, 23, 30, 51, 62, 96, 123, 201, 250, 252, 319–20.

aware(ness), 2, 35, 143, 163, 184, 195,
    198, 201, 231, 262, unaware,
    113.
ayahuasca, (PTSD), 143.
Baillie. Michael G. L., 73, 219.
Balfour, Sir Arthur, and Declaration,
    85, 195.
Baronio, Cardinal Cesare, 101, 224, 236.
beast(s), 168, 175, 181–82, 185–88,
    191, 222.
being, xiv, xxi, 1, 3–4, 7–11, 14–19,
    23–31, 34, 39, 41, 44, 50–51,
    53, 57, 63, 75–76, 103, 117–19,
    123, 128, 133, 140, 142, 148,
    153, 156, 160–61, 196–97, 237,
    240, 245, 287, 308.
Benedict XVI, 207, 224, 240.
Bible, xiii, xiv, xx, xxi, 3, 5, 8, 12,
    16–19, 21, 39, 47, 52, 56, 59,
    76, 93, 114–17, 119–20, 122,
    125, 127, 129, 144–45, 161–62,
    167, 169, 172–75, 183, 190–91,
    197–98, 201, 305.
Bible, books:
    Acts, (also of Pilate and Thomas
        etc.) 42, 72, 123, 233, 237, 240,
        244, 253.
    Chronicles, Chr. 121.
    Colossians, Col. 12.
    Daniel, Dan. 114, 119–21, 190–94,
        200.
    Enoch, 123, 165, 213.
    Ephesians, Eph. 161–62.
    Deuteronomy, Deut. 42, 46–49, 95,
        125, 127–28, 144, 165.
    Ecclesiastes, 314.
    Esther, Esth. 60, 205.
    Exodus, xiv, 14–15, 20–21, 31,
        34–35, 41–42, 49–50, 52–53,
        57–59, 62, 120–22, 124, 168,
        172, 176, 179, 182, 200, 210,
        313–14.
    Ezra, 123.
    Galatians, Gal. 127–28, 181, 200.
    Genesis, xiv, xx, 17, 41, 46, 48, 53,
        58, 114–15, 117, 119–21, 123,
        125, 128, 144–45, 148, 160,

165–67, 169, 173, 178, 180,
    197, 200, 205, 211, 229.
Habakkuk, Hab. 127, 200.
Haggai, Hag. 212.
Hebrews, Heb. 2, 50, 163, 174.
Hosea, 163.
Isaiah, Isa. 12, 15, 45–46, 49, 58–
    59, 98, 121, 159, 161, 163–66,
    196, 200, 314.
James, Protoevangelium of, 215.
James, 174.
Jeremiah, Jer. 148, 165, 212, 314.
Job, 57, 59, 172.
John, 31, 39, 44, 48, 67, 98, 111,
    183, 210, 233–34, 243.
Jonah, 34.
Josh. 15.
Jubilee, Jub. 165.
Jude, 165.
Judges, 124, 126, 183, 200.
Kings, Kgs. 60, 122.
Luke, 13, 42, 50, 98, 165, 183, 205,
    213, 233–34, 236, 243.
Mark, 42–44, 98–99, 104, 233–34,
    243.
Matthew, Matt. 12, 43–44, 98, 163,
    165, 183–84, 213, 234, 243.
Numbers, 57–58, 61, 123, 175, 184,
    206, 229, 314.
Peter, Pet. 165.
Proverbs, Prov. v, 114, 119, 125,
    174.
Psalms, Ps. 50, 148, 174.
Revelation, Rev. 17, 19, 50, 113–15,
    119–22, 127, 162, 165–66, 168,
    170, 173–75, 177, 182, 184,
    186, 190, 193, 200, 313.
Romans, Rom. 22, 49, 58, 71, 75,
    124–125, 129, 148, 159–66,
    176, 198, 244.
Ruth, 19.
Samuel, 124, 126–27, 200.
Song of Solomon, Song. 19, 43–44,
    176, 205.
Timothy, Tim. 71, 75, 104, 237.
Zechariah, Zech. 57–58, 66, 69,
    114–15, 121–22, 166, 173–74,
    176, 179–80, 184, 200.

Bible, persons:

Abraham, 18–19, 31, 42, 55, 58, 111, 120–21, 124, 166, 213.

Babylon, 127, 188, 230.

Barnabas, 104, 244.

David, 19, 39, 44, 159–60, 163, 166, 170–71, 176, 181, 200, 212–13.

Elijah, 38, 165.

Ephraim and Manasseh, 48, 94–95.

Ezekiel, 12, 50, 59, 114, 119, 165, 191–92.

Hebrew(s), xix, 5, 9, 15, 43, 46, 49, 52, 55, 57, 60, 114, 121, 124–25, 145, 164, 169, 172, 176, 179, 200–01, 205, 228–29, 237, 313–16.

Isaac, 19, 42, 120–21, 159, 163, 166, 213.

Jacob, xiv, 19, 42, 48, 120, 124, 182, 213, 216, 229.

James the great, the elder, 105, 216, 240.

James the less, 216.

Jesse, 52, 121, 166, 200, 213, 314.

Joachim and Anna, 214–16.

John the Divine, 19, 31, 39, 44, 48, 66–67, 98, 111, 113–14, 122, 162, 168–69, 174, 179, 183, 190, 210, 216, 233–34, 240, 243.

Jonah, 34.

Joseph son of Jacob, and blessings of, 46–48, 57, 95, 172, 182.

Lazarus, (Lazare), 236, 238–241, 243.

Magdalene, Mary, 92, 112, 210, 234, 236–43. Magdalen, 306, Magdalena, 218, Magdala, 243, Madeleine, 206, 238–40.

Martha, (Marthe), 92, 236, 238–43.

Mary, the Blessed Virgin, 13, 39, 67, 71, 75, 81, 100, 106, 108, 111–12, 128–29, 205–10, 215–16, 218–19, 234, 238–39, 244, 248, 252, 255, 259–61, 263, 265, 277, 279, 284. Madonna, 208.

Maximin(us), 236, 238–241.

Methuselah, 130–131, 213.

Moses, 14–15, 41–42, 47–48, 50, 58, 60–62, 95, 103, 121, 124, 175, 184, 206.

Nebuchadnezzar, 190, 230.

Noah, 200, 213.

Paul, 21, 43, 49, 58, 71, 75, 95–96, 111, 124, 159–66, 198, 200, 238, 244–47, 261, 306.

Peter, 71, 94–95, 104–105, 144–45, 210, 218, 240, 244, 246–247, 255, 261, 306.

Phoenicians, Phenicians, Sidon, 226–29.

Rahab, 46, 163.

Sarah and Abraham, 55.

Zacharias and Elizabeth, 216.

Zebedee, Zebedaeus, 216, 240, 244.

Zebulon, 48, 226, 229.

Zerubbabel, 212–13, 216.

Blake, William, 65.

Blech, Benjamin, 176.

bless(ed, ing), 31, 46–48, 74–75, 77, 95, 106, 108, 111, 124, 169, 172–74, 182, 193, 205, 229, 244, 250, 265, 292.

body, xxi, 58, 84, 100, 104, 117–19, 128, 140–41, 143, 160–62, 181, 183–84, 192, 208, 232–34, 240, 242, 248, 253, 258, 261, 265–66, 288, 314.

boy(hood), Kennedy, 65, Jesus, 112.

Bright, Dr. Pamela, xv, 93.

Bucke, Richard Maurice, 1–3, 50.

cancer, 138–39, 143, 181, 311.

catastrophic, comets, strikes, 73, 79, 144–45, 219–22, 225.

cause, 36, 43, 47, 103, 118–19, 135, 139, 144, 153, 155, 193, 221, 236, 249, 253, 256, 263, 317, 320. cause and effect, 67, 184.

Celtic cross, 93–97, 101.

Cervantes, Miguel de, 84, 207.

chalice, 57, 66–70.

child(ren), 3, 14, 37–38, 42, 60–61, 94, 110, 124, 129, 143, 156, 159, 161, 163, 172, 175–76, 180–82, 196, 208, 215, 219, 221, 279, 297, 302, 304, 307–08, 310, 315, 319.

China Study, the, 138.

Christ, and Jesus Christ, 13, 19, 39, 40, 42–44, 50–51, 58, 65, 67–69, 71–73, 76, 79–81, 83, 86, 94–96, 98, 100–04, 107, 110–12, 114, 128–29, 140, 142, 153–54, 157, 161–62, 168–69, 176, 180, 183–84, 186, 200, 205–06, 210, 212–16, 218–19, 226, 232–34, 236, 239–46, 248–53, 255, 257, 260–64, 277, 282, 292, 293, 306.

Christ, names of:
Alpha and Omega, 69, 114, 170, 173.
Faithful and True, 50, 171–76.
First and Last, 171, 173.
Lion of Judah, 181.
Messiah, messianic, 19, 38, 58, 69, 98, 114, 120–21, 124, 127, 159, 163, 166, 169–74, 176, 178, 182, 186, 188, 194, 200, 210.
Son of Man, 50, 160, 168–70, 172–76, 180–82.

Christian(s, ity), xix, 9, 19, 31–32, 39–40, 43, 67–68, 73–77, 79–81, 84, 92–93, 100, 102–06, 123, 129, 140–41, 145, 169, 178, 205, 207–09, 218–19, 221, 225, 232, 237–39, 241, 244, 246, 248–52, 255, 274, 284, 294, 299, 311, 319–20.

church(es), 21, 43, 66, 68, 71, 74–75, 80, 82–83, 86, 91, 93, 101–02 104–09, 111–12, 114, 122, 132, 162, 167–76, 180, 182–83, 185–86, 200, 207, 218, 222, 224–25, 235–42, 244–45, 247–65, 282–84, 286, 289, 297–98, 307, 311, 320–321.

churches, list of, 104–05.

cipher, 299.

Coelbren alphabet, 111.

cognitive, xix, xx, 2, 5, 8, 10, 24–28, 31, 37, 196.

cognitive operations:
decision, xxi, 6, 8, 9, 12, 18, 25, 27–28, 37, 39, 99, 177, 196, 207, 234, 257, 261.

experience(tial), xiii, xx, xxi, 1–4, 7–10, 12–13, 15, 23–34, 37–38, 40–42, 50, 68, 74, 112, 114, 117, 142, 153, 175, 194, 196, 232, 306.
judgment(s), xxi, 6–8, 10, 12, 15, 23–28, 37, 39, 62, 96, 103, 117, 124, 126, 129, 140, 154, 164–65, 176–77, 183, 185, 196–97, 200, 262, 264, 306.
know, known, xiii, xix–xxi, 5, 7–11, 14–15, 17, 19, 20, 25–30, 34, 38–39, 42, 44, 51, 65, 68–69, 72–73, 98–99, 103–04, 112, 115–16, 121, 138, 142, 145, 160, 196, 198, 210, 226, 229, 231, 242–43, 253–54, 258, 263–64, 281, 286, 303, 306, 309.
known unknown, xiv, 113, 115–17, 197–98, 210.
operation(s), xiii, xix–xxi, 2, 4, 7–10, 12, 14, 25, 27–28, 36–38, 40, 115–17, 139–40, 183–84, 189, 194, 196, 233.
understanding, xiii, xix, xx, xxi, 1, 5, 7–10, 12, 14–16, 18, 23–28, 30–31, 33, 37–40, 47, 51, 62–64, 66, 73, 76, 94, 98–99, 104, 114–15, 117–21, 125, 128–29, 131, 134, 141, 143–45, 167, 181, 184–85, 189, 193–94, 196–99, 206, 257, 281, 290.

condition(al, ed) see also unconditional, 14, 18, 21, 23–25, 49, 57, 135–36, 194, 245, 254.

conscious(ness), also sub, and super consciousness, xiii–xiv, xix–xxi, 1–3, 5, 7–11, 14, 24, 30, 34–35, 38, 51, 64, 66, 117, 125, 169, 175–76, 183–84, 198–99, 206, 256. (unconsciousness), xiii.

cosmic, 1–3, 39, 48, 62, micro, and/or macrocosmic, 48.

cosmology, 16–19.

cosmopolis, 193–95.

countries, place names, people groups:
Aix-en-Provence, France. 239, 241.

Arles, France, 237–238, 241.
Avalon(ia), Avallon, Avalun,
England, 67–68, 78, 100, 102,
105, 110, 236, 253, 265–66, 278,
281–83, 286, 289, 294, 296.
Badon, Baedon, battle of, 70, 75,
79, 219, 254, 259, 275.
Britain, 65, 71, 73–77, 79, 98–101,
105, 111, 195, 203, 218–20,
225–32, 236, 244, 246, 250–55,
260, 268–69, 273, 276, 278–79,
281–82, 286, 291, 293, 296–98,
301, 305, 307–11, 317, 319,
321, 322–31.
Britain, maps of, 322–31.
Caer Caradoc, 71.
Caerleon, 279, (KaerLheon), 327.
Catedral de Santiago, (or the El
Camino Trail), Spain. 105, 240.
Celtic, 68–69, 93–97, 101–02, 105,
227, 230–32, 305, 309.
China, 133, 138.
Coptic, 69, 93, 96–97.
Cornwall, England, 71, 100–101,
112, 214, 218, 226–27, 231,
257, 279, 291, 301, 328–29.
Druid(ic, s), 39, 110, 157, 227, 311,
318–19.
Edessa, Asia Minor, 72, 79–80,
88–91, 104, 186, 272.
Egypt, 17–18, 35, 42, 49, 59–60, 91,
93, 112, 250–51, (Aegypt) 103.
Egyptian, 18, 59–60, 93, 96–97,
111, 125.
Fatima, Portugal, 85, 208.
France, 82–84, 88, 90–91, 105, 218,
236–40, 244, 248, 272, 279, 307.
garden, Jesus' burial, 234–35.
Garden of Eden, 17, 19, 53, 68,
110, 114, 123, 128, 134, 200,
240, 285, 306.
Garden of Gethsemane, 92, 132,
148, 240.
Glastonbury, England, 71, 81, 84,
98–112, 186, 212, 214, 217–
267, 282–86, 294.
Hungary, 82, 86, 89, 91, 207.

Ireland, 94–96, 218–22, 231, 245,
251, 257–58 282, 311, 322.
Israel(ites), 14, 18–19, 35, 38,
42–44, 46, 49, 53, 57, 60–61,
66, 74, 112, 116, 121–22, 124,
126–27, 132, 159, 161–65, 176,
181, 200, 206, 208, 226, 229,
276, 319.
Jerusalem, 16, 18–19, 54, 65–66,
68, 72, 76, 80–92, 105, 112,
121–22, 124, 132, 162, 168,
171, 184, 188, 195, 208, 229,
236, 240, 243, 250, 272, 285,
293.
Jews, Jewish, xix, 17, 19, 21, 32,
43–44, 55, 62, 69, 92, 111–12,
125–27, 166, 195, 206, 211, 234,
236–37, 240–41, 250–51, 280.
Lepanto, battle of, 84, 207, 224.
Marseille(s), France, 101, 112, 224,
227, 230, 236–41.
Medugorje, Bosnia and
Herzegovina, 208.
Moriah, 53, 55.
Romani, 112, 238.
Rome, Romans, 54, 66, 71, 75, 82,
86, 88, 91, 100–02, 104–105,
124, 147–48, 192, 218, 226,
229–30, 236, 240, 244–47,
249–53, 259–60, 275–76, 287,
298, 310–11, 319–20, 323.
Saintes Maries De La Mer, France.
112, 238.
Sidon, Phoenicia, 229.
Tarascon, France. 240–42.
Tintagel castle, Cornwall, 295, 214.
Vienna, 85, 91, 207, 224, 288.
Wales, Welsh, 70–74, 80–81, 100,
110–111, 132, 150, 152, 158,
214–15, 218–19, 222, 264, 266,
268, 270, 272–73, 275, 277–78,
280, 282, 286, 292, 294, 322,
327.
Zion, 21, 121, 122, 181.
covenant, 12, 16–19, 21–22, 58, 60,
111–12, 125, 161, 178, 187,
200, 229.
Crabb, Larry, 129.

Creator, create, creation, creatures, xiii, xix, 9, 13, 16–21, 30, 39–40, 59, 62, 64, 69, 93, 114–15, 117, 125, 128–29, 131, 140, 143–45, 149, 153, 155, 159–61, 163, 171, 176–78, 183–86, 191–92, 197–98, 200, 207, 305, 311.

Cromwell, Oliver, 93, 102–03, 224, 273.

cross, 37, 46, 67, 69, 77, 81–82, 85, 93–97, 101–03, 105, 110–11, 126, 161, 186, 200, 205–11, 218–19, 241, 248, 262, 265–66, 288, 293.

crucifix(ion), 93–95, 98, 154, 157, 234, 236, 242, 246, 295.

cycle(s), 13, 16–18, 21–22, 130–46, 193–95, 309.

Day, Dorothy, 7, 206.

desire, xix, xx, 8, 15, 21, 26–27, 67, 73, 104, 112, 119, 125–27, 140, 193, 196–97, 247, 279, 303.

Dictionary of National Biography, 203, 275–307.

dimension, xix, xx, 12, 17, 33, 38, 59, 144, 200–01.

DNA, 112, 120, 125, 144.

Domesday Book, 222, 264.

Doran, Robert, S.J., 9, 11–12, 33.

Doyle, Sir Arthur Conan, 2.

dragon, 34, 37, 73, 180–81, 187–88, 191, 220, 300–01, 309.

Durand, Gilbert, 34–40, 206.

Dylan, Bob, 238, (son of the wave) 156.

earth, xiv, 5, 12–13, 17, 47–48, 57–58, 63, 73, 78, 122, 131, 135, 137, 141–42, 144–45, 149, 155–57, 164, 173–78, 181, 183–88, 191, 225, 228, 256, 260, 263, 265–66, 282, 285, 302–03, 308, (earthing), xxi, 183.

earthquake, 38, 177, 185, 187–88, 220, 223.

ecclesiastical, 104, 218, 225, 236–38, 244, 246–47, 251, 257, 259–61, 276–77, 321.

Ecclesiastical Councils, 71, 101.

electric energy, xxi, 140, 149, 183–84.

electrical components:

capacitance(tor), xxi, 183.

inductance(tor), xxi, 183.

magnetic, xxi, 13, 183–84.

resistance(tor), xxi, 183.

element(al, ary, s), xiii, xix–xxi, 2, 8–10, 12, 15–21, 25, 28, 30, 34–35, 37–38, 43–44, 48, 51–65, 67, 69, 115–17, 119, 125, 144, 153, 158–59, 163–64, 169, 174, 176, 183, 185, 191, 197–98, 201, 209.

emergent probability, 9, 139–40, 160.

enemy(ies), 13, 155, 259, 275–76, 288, 293, 318, 321.

energy(gic), xxi, 12, 27, 43, 137, 140, 158.

energy, divine, 43.

enlightenment, xiii, 2, 35, 63, 131.

evolution(ist), xix, xx, 2, 98, 133, 141, 144–45, 206, 284.

exist(ence), 2, 25, 27, 31, 39, 44, 49, 98, 102, 106, 115–16, 118, 129, 135, 155, 165, 194, 197, 205, 212, 226, 235, 252, 283, 285–87, 289.

faith, 18–19, 50, 65–66, 74, 78–79, 93, 103, 105, 125, 128, 159, 163, 171–76, 194, 235, 237, 241, 243–44, 247–49, 253, 255, 257, 284, 294, 300, 310–11, 318–20.

families (usually associated with the Shroud of Turin or Grail):

Battenberg, Alice of, 90, 92.

Charny, Geoffrey de, 83–84, 86–87, 90–92. (Porte Oriflamme), 84, 90.

Gamage of Coity, 71, 271, 274.

Henneberg, 86, 89, 91–92.

Hohenlohe, 86–87, 90–92.

Savoy, 84–85, 87–88, 90–91.

Spencer, 71, 271, 274, 312, Spenser, 295–96.

Family Tree DNA, 125.

feast days:

Christmas, 103, 235.

First Fruits, 18.

Passover, 18, 35, 38.

Pentecost, 18, 67, 241, Pentecouste, 290.

Rosh Hashanah, 18.
Sabbath(batical), 16, 18, 56, 180,
    233–34.
Shavuot, 18.
Succoth, 18, 42.
Unleavened Bread, 18, 35.
Year of Jubilee, 18, 56, 178.
Yom Kippur, 18, 56.
feel(ings), 2, 5, 10, 14, 23–31, 33–34,
    65–66, 184, 303.
female, feminine, 7, 42–47, 60, 153,
    178, 214, 265.
Fieldbrook stump, 132, 134.
food, 17, 34, 37–38, 118, 139, 222, 249.
force, 44, 50, 73, 84, 118, 142, 185, 195,
    207, 227, 249, 320.
Franklin, Capt. Sir John, 135.
Freud, Sigmund, xiii.
functional specialties, 31.
Gabriel, Brigitte, 207.
global warming, 134, 135, 139.
Global Coherence Initiative, 13.
God, xiii, xiv, 1, 13–17, 19, 21–22, 32,
    37–39, 41–47, 49–50, 55, 58,
    62–63, 67–68, 100, 103, 113,
    117, 120–23, 125–29, 145, 155,
    159, 161–63, 165, 168, 171–75,
    179, 181–82, 187, 191–92, 195,
    199, 206, 208, 234, 236, 242,
    252–53, 256, 260–61, 263, 265,
    276–77, 292, 301, 303.
God, names of:
    Elohim, 14–15, 178.
    Father, 13, 39, 47–48, 124, 161,
        184, 282.
    Holy Spirit, (see also spirit), 13, 47,
        66, 104, 122, 128, 160–61, 163,
        181, 206.
    image of God, xiii, 16–19, 67.
    image of the I AM, 197, 206.
    Shekhinah, 41–42, 46–47.
    YHWH, 14, 15, 47, 121.
good, 3, 11, 15, 17, 24, 31, 52, 82, 93,
    123, 126, 128, 144, 166, 194,
    222, 234, 255, 265, 275, 282,
    291–93, 297, 300, 302, 304,
    308, 318–21.
good, structures of the human, 31.

Gray, Dr. Leslie, (Rolling Thunder), 38.
Green, Glenda, 13, 50–51, 112, 128, 142.
Hail Mary, the, 13, 39, 205–11.
heal(th), 10, 17, 38, 40, 72–73, 114,
    123, 139, 141, 184, 200, 243,
    266, 285.
heart, xxi, 3, 13, 15, 30–31, 39–40,
    49–51, 95, 125–26, 144, 149,
    176, 193–94, 210, 285, 293.
Heart Math Institute, (Global
    Coherence Initiative), 13.
heaven(ly, s), xiv, 3, 19, 37–38, 42–44,
    48–49, 58, 62–63, 68, 120, 123,
    125, 128, 144–45, 155–56, 162,
    177–78, 183, 187–88, 205, 221,
    227, 241, 247, 249, 255–56,
    260, 262, 282.
Hill, Julia, 141.
history(ian, ical), 8, 11, 18–19, 21–23,
    32, 34–35, 42, 51, 55, 64–73,
    85–86, 93, 98–101, 104–12,
    115–16, 120–22, 129, 131, 135,
    144, 159, 163, 165, 183, 190,
    193–94, 198, 203, 205–08, 212,
    214, 217–67, 275–84, 288–90,
    292, 295–97, 300, 307, 309,
    310–11.
history, (functional specialties), 31–32.
historians:
    Bede, the Venerable, 71, 100–01,
        104, 218–20, 225, 245, 251,
        257, 259, 276.
    Camden, William, 101, 230–32,
        253–54, 296–98, 322–31.
    Capgrave, John, 223, 251–52,
        288–89.
    Cressy, R. F. S., 101, 106–08, 110–
        11, 218, 224–25, 244–51.
    Crombie, Kelvin, 195.
    Diodorus Siculus, 217, 228, 231.
    Gildas, 101, 214, 219, 223, 254–56,
        275–77, 281.
    Gilbert, Adrian, 71, 73.
    Goodman, Bishop of Gloucester,
        94, 102–03.
    Guinness, Henry Grattan, 193–95.
    Jerome, 99, 218.
    Josephus, 17, 55, 62–63, 192.

historians (continued):
    Malmesbury, William of, 186, 223,
        225, 255–64, 283.
    Monmouth, Geoffrey of, 101, 219,
        223, 225, 277–79, 281, 298, 309.
    Pliny the Elder, 227–228, 231.
    Spelman, Sir Henry, 101, 106–07,
        218, 225.
    Tacitus, 227.
    Taliesin, 150–158, 282.
    Tertullian, 218, 247, 250.
    Troyes, Chretien de, 67–68, 72, 81,
        88–89, 222, 284.
    Turner, Sharon, 129, 228–30.
    Ussher, James, 106, (Vsher), 244,
        246–47.
    Weston, Jessie, 67–68, 285, 309.
    Willis, Revd. R., 108–09, 222, 284.
    Wilson, Alan, 70–71, 73, 111.
hitlahavut, 49–50, 174.
Holmes, Sherlock, 2.
Holy Grail, (greil), 64–86, 222–23,
    284–85, 302–03, 311.
Hyman, Dr. Mark, 139.
illumination, 2–3.
immortal, 2–3, 118–19, 123, 156, 161,
    262, 310, (mortal), 73, 256, 310.
indigenous, 51.
infinite(ity), xv, xx, 1, 13, 118–19, 131,
    143–44, 197–98.
insight, xiii, xix–xxi, 2–3, 5, 7–11, 15,
    24, 26, 30, 116–17, 140, 195,
    197, 206.
integral(gration, grated, grity, grative), 9,
    12, 21, 25, 29, 31, 114, 142, 159,
    183, 194, (disintegrated), 33.
intent(ion, ionality), v, 5, 12, 14, 22, 50,
    55, 73, 107, 113, 141, 164–65,
    168, 186, 203, 205, 230, 249,
    262, (unintentionally), 72.
intercession, 13, 21, 160, 184.
interior(ity), 11, 15, 86, 129, 207, 283.
Jacobite, 105, 304.
Jobs, Steve, (Apple), 3.
John Paul II, 85, 87, 224.
joy(enjoy), 2–3, 27, 40, 60, 68, 102,
    128, 178, 221, 262–63, 283,
    308, 311.

Jung, Carl, xiii, 33–34.
just(ice), 12, 36, 44, 93, 128, 172, 206,
    234, 280, 296, (unjust), 62, 256.
King, Martin Luther, 65, 207.
Kennedy, John, F., 65.
Kings, queens, British, origins of:
    main table, 268–274.
    Afallach, 77, 268, Evelake? 292–93.
    Alfred the Great, 221, 249.
    Arthur, 66–68, 70–77, 79, 81, 98,
        100–01, 157, 205, 214, 219,
        222–23, 249, 253–54, 256, 259,
        264–67, 269, 275–312.
    Arviragus, 71, 77, 100, 105, 218,
        222, 237, 250, 264.
    Beli Mawr, 77, 215, 217–18,
    Brân the Blessed, 74, 75, 77, 268,
        319.
    Caradoc(g), 71, 77, 268, 319.
    Cuthred, 71, 220, 262–63.
    Edmund I, 71, 105, 221–22, 263.
    Elizabeth I, 224, 272–74.
    Elizabeth II, 103, 224, 274.
    Fisher King, 67–68, 284.
    Ina, 71, 104, 220, 249, 259–63.
    Llŷr Llediaith, (Lear), 74, 77, 217,
        319.
    Lucius (saint), 75, 77, 218, 225,
        245, 250–52, 255, 321.
    Penardim(n), 77, 216, Penarddun,
        268.
    Uther Pendragon, 214, 219, 278.
Kings, queens, other, origins of:
    Abgar V of Edessa, 72, 79, 186.
    Amalric I of Jerusalem, 72, 81, 86,
        88–91.
    Angelos, Isaac, Byzantine Emperor,
        82, 86, 89, 91.
    Árpád, Margaret Maria, of
        Hungary, 86, 89, 91.
    Brutus, 217, 219, 229.
    Caesar, Julius, 100, 228–29.
        (100BC–44BC)
    Caesar, Augustus, 244, (63BC–
        14AD)
    Constantine the Great, 77, 218.
    Pilate, 76, 95, 100, 112, 123,
        233–34.

Tiberius, emperor, 100. (42BC–AD37)

Knights of the Round Table, 65, 67, 219, 279, 285, 291–93, 298, 303, 305–306, 311, 321.

Knights Templar, 81–84, 86–87, 90–92, 285, (Templeisen), 82, 284–85.

Knights Teutonic, 81, 86, 90–92, 284, 309.

Krippner, Stanley, Dr. xv, 38, 184.

Labuschagne, Casper, 46–48, 172, 182.

Lama, Dalai, 30.

Lamb and the Lion, 51.

Last Supper, 66–69, 72, 76.

Lewis, C.S., 13, 140–41, 310–311.

Lewis, Rev. Lionel Smithett, 212, 216, 224, 237.

liturgical, xix, 21, (liturgies), 106.

Lonergan, Bernard, S.J., xiii, xix, xx, xxi, 2, 4–10, 15, 23–26, 29–34, 40, 115–17, 129, 140, 193, 195–96.

Lord's Prayer, the, 13, 39, 206, 209.

love, v, xv, 3, 12–13, 19, 21, 25, 43–44, 51, 68, 112, 145, 153, 171, 176, 183, 276, 287, 291, 304, 308, 310, 319.

Luther, Martin, 93.

Mandylion, 72, 79–80.

marriage, 19, 42–44, 71, 74, 84–87, 91, 162, 300, 301, 311, 319.

matter(ial), 3, 44, 99, 176, 255, 265, 286.

McGill University, 1, 32, 134.

Medicare, Canadian, 32.

meditation, 1, 13, 40.

menorah(ot), xiv, xix–xxi, 4, 17, 19–21, 24, 34, 37–38, 41, 47–48, 51–69, 113–16, 120–24, 167–89, 193, 198, 313–16.

menorah, elements of:

   bud(ded), xiv, xx, xxi, 17, 21–22, 34, 37–38, 55–61, 100–03, 123–24, 129, 168–69, 185, 314.

   bud, knob, calyx, xiv, 20–21, 52–53, 55–58, 69, 121, 124, 129, 314.

flame, xix, xxi, 3, 21–22, 37, 41, 49–50, 52–53, 61, 65, 157, 168, 173–74, 176, 227, 236, 262, 302, Oriflamme, 84, 90.

flower, xiv, xx, xxi, 17, 19–22, 34, 37, 52–57, 59–60, 93, 96, 123, 128, 156, 169, 178, 235, 308, 314.

lampstand(s), 20–21, 47–48, 50, 52–53, 57, 60, 62–63, 114–15, 122–23, 167–75, 179–82, 187, 200, 241–42, 313, 315.

light(enlightened), xiii, xix, 2–3, 14, 21, 35, 37–38, 43, 46, 49, 63, 69, 75, 80, 122–24, 128, 131, 145, 152, 156, 169, 174, 178, 187–88, 192, 194–95, 233, 241, 247, 251, 253, 256, 284, 296, 303, 305–06, 308.

mercy, 21, 33, 44, 57, 123, 127, 183.

Merlin, 81, 219, 223, 261, 278, 280–81, 295, 300–02, 304, 308, 311.

metaphor, xix, xx, 49, 56, 58, 124–25, 127, 159, 166.

metaphysical, xix–xxi, 8–10, 14, 16–18, 21, 27–28, 31, 37–38, 119, 140, 164, 196.

metaphysical elements:

   act, xiv, xx, xxi, 1, 5, 8, 9, 13–22, 24–25, 27–28, 35, 37, 39, 43–44, 51, 60, 66–67, 86, 100, 103, 114–16, 117–18, 120, 122, 131, 140–41, 144–45, 160–61, 164, 172–73, 177, 182–83, 196–97, 207, 233, 250, 253, 318.

   form, xiii–xiv, xix–xxi, 5, 8, 9, 14–21, 24–25, 28, 32, 34–38, 44–48, 50–53, 55–57, 59–60, 65–66, 76, 82, 93, 102, 113–114, 138, 140, 144, 152–56, 158–159, 162, 165–67, 169–170, 172–73 175, 182–83, 185, 191, 194, 196–98, 200–01, 205–206, 222, 225, 283, 298, 302.

   potency(tial), xxi, 8–9, 14–19, 21–22, 25, 28, 30, 35, 37–39, 76, 116–117, 120, 140, 164, 185, 196–197, 318.

Meyers, Carol, Dr., xx, 23–24, 53,
    57–59, 116, 122, 124, 162.
Midrash(im), 43, 123, 162–63.
Milarch, David, (Archangel Ancient
    Tree Archive), 134, 142.
Monasterboice, Ireland, 94–96.
monastery(ies) 93, 111, 220, 248–49,
    252, 255, 257, 262, 264–65,
    276, 282–83, 286.
Montfort, Louis de, 128–29, 210.
Moriah, (*salvia palaestina*), 53, Mt.
    Moriah, 55.
mystery, 21, 40, 43, 95, 102–03, 128–
    29, 162, 168, 182, 185, 191,
    206, 252–53.
mystic(al, ism) 1, 35–36, 38, 40, 43–44,
    49–50, 98, 101–102, 113, 122,
    128, 142.
Myvyrian Archaiology, 70, 74, 317–
    321.
National Ice Core Laboratory, 135,
    145–46.
nature(al), xiii–xiv, xix–xxi, 2, 5,
    13–16, 26, 39, 44, 46–47,
    50, 53, 63, 95, 98, 103, 113,
    115–19, 129, 134, 138, 141–43,
    154–55, 162, 164, 167, 183–85,
    189, 191, 194, 197–98, 221,
    227–28, 235, 252, 257, 311,
    supernatural, 115, 184, 194.
Novalis, 35.
number, 10, 53, 56, 59, 62–63, 83, 108,
    139, 157, 159, 163, 180–81,
    185, 190, 193, 201, 205–07,
    210–11, 225, 227, 230, 232,
    235, 241, 254, 256, 286, 288,
    307, 313–14, 320.
    three(s), xiv, xxi, 2, 5, 7, 20, 34–35,
        39–40, 44, 52–54, 57, 60, 62,
        68, 71, 74, 91, 94, 114, 126–27,
        147, 149, 152, 160–63, 168–69,
        172–77, 180, 183, 185, 187–88,
        192, 206, 208–10, 212, 214–15,
        219–20, 228, 235, 237, 240–43,
        261, 264, 266, 290, 298–99,
        308, 322.
    third(s), 2, 3, 17, 20, 62, 81, 141,
        145, 172, 174, 178–79, 185–88,

    206, 220–21, 237, 254, 257,
    265, 282, 290, 301, 307.
four(s, ty, etc.), 2, 14, 17, 20, 25,
    50, 60, 63, 66, 68–69, 81, 85,
    91, 112, 114, 126, 141, 144–45,
    150, 156–58, 169, 172–73,
    176–79, 184–88, 190–92, 200,
    207, 214, 221–22, 226, 233,
    236, 243, 247–48, 251, 254–55,
    257, 261–62, 264, 276–77, 279,
    284, 288, 290–92, 296–97, 299,
    302, 310–11.
seven(s, ty), 18, 21, 42, 47, 53,
    56, 60, 62–63, 66, 68, 82, 90,
    104, 121–23, 144–45, 167–70,
    173–191, 193–94, 200, 221,
    239, 241–42, 258–59, 275, 296,
    299, 306, 315.
object(ive) *see* also subjective, 2, 7, 11,
    14–15, 26–27, 30, 32–33, 36,
    53, 81, 86, 93, 98, 119, 142,
    154, 189, 249, 255, 283, 296.
olive (oil, tree), xx, 49, 58, 62, 66, 69,
    92, 114–115, 119–23, 125–27,
    132, 147–51, 159, 165–166,
    168, 177, 179–180 , 187, 198,
    200, 291, 316.
organic(ism), xiii, xix– xx, 10, 14,
    18–19, 41, 57, 114–15, 119–21,
    131–32, 140–41, 159–60, 165;
    198–99.
Oviedo, cloth of, 72, 80.
Pascal, Blaise, 194.
passion, 49, 78, 101–02, 107, 176, 248,
    250, 293.
Passover, *see* also feasts, 18, 35, 38.
pattern, xiii, xx, xxi, 3, 8, 13, 20, 34, 41,
    43, 47–48, 72, 93, 144, 159–65,
    167, 169, 175, 182, 185–186,
    189, 193.
perception, xiii, 2, 15, 30, 195.
person(al, ity), xx, 1, 3, 5–6, 8–9, 14,
    19, 23, 25, 27, 32–34, 38–39,
    42, 47, 69, 74, 86, 98, 100, 105,
    108, 116, 119, 128, 169, 176,
    198, 210, 233, 239, 243, 247,
    256–58, 261, 278, 288–90, 307,
    318, 320, depersonalized, 33.

Porges, Dr. Stephen, The Polyvagal
    Theory, 40.
power, 15, 23, 38–39, 43, 51, 67, 116,
    118, 120–21, 140, 142, 172,
    174, 182, 187, 206, 245, 260,
    263, 277, 282, 301, 319, 321.
pray(er, s), 13, 38–39, 51, 53, 85, 95,
    102, 126, 160, 183–84, 205–09,
    233, 292, 305.
primal(ary, ordial), xix, 12, 18, 21,
    31–34, 41, 49, 55, 59, 67, 104,
    116–18, 124–25, 127, 140,
    145, 155–56, 159–60, 163, 165,
    168–69, 179–80, 195, 198, 206,
    245–47, 252–53, 282, 286.
promise(d), xx, 18, 120, 123, 159–61,
    166, 169, 172, 195, 200, 241, 310.
prophecy(t), 38, 69, 104, 122, 124,
    157, 161, 168, 180–183, 187,
    190–195, 212, 219, 236, 278,
    280, 282, 300, 302–03.
psyche, 1, 10–13.
psychoanalysis, xiii.
psychological(gist), 5, 10–12, 15, 26,
    34–35, 38, 40, 64, 129, 206.
purpose, xxi, 8, 12, 14, 37, 40, 68, 73,
    118, 121, 168, 181, 189, 193,
    196, 249, 260–61, 263.
real(ity, ization), xix–xx, 2, 8–10, 14,
    22, 24, 31–32, 35, 40, 44, 46,
    73, 117, 135, 138, 140–42, 149,
    169, 176, 196–99, 201, 226,
    258, 309.
Reformation, 93, 100–02, 105, 205,
    235, 248.
relat(es, ions, ship), xiii, xiv, xix–xxi,
    1, 4–5, 8–10, 12–13, 15, 17,
    19–34, 38–39, 42, 47–48, 50,
    53, 56–59, 63, 66–67, 69, 71,
    74, 76, 86, 89, 99–100, 106,
    114–15, 119–21, 123, 125, 134,
    139–43, 158, 160–66, 168, 172,
    174, 176, 178–79, 181, 183–85,
    190–93, 198–99, 212, 217–66,
    277, 291, 300, 309.
remnant, 56, 159, 163–66, 195, 315.
represent(ation), xx, 18, 20–21, 23, 32,
    34, 36, 39–40, 43–44, 49, 59,

    62, 68–69, 73–74, 100, 113–15,
    117, 120–22, 126–27, 138, 149,
    159–60, 162, 164, 166–70, 172,
    175–76, 180–81, 183, 185–86,
    198, 200–01, 206, 209–10, 219,
    227, 264, 274, 281, 284.
response(ibility), 10, 13, 15–16, 18–19,
    21, 23, 33–34, 43, 86, 91–93,
    98, 100, 117, 126, 143, 165,
    175, 197, 207, corresponds,
    xiii, xix, xxi, 3, 8, 28, 32, 35,
    37, 38–40, 57–58, 101, 108,
    115–16, 179, 195, 198, 206,
    210, 237.
revelation(atory), v, xix–xxi, 14, 16–17,
    19, 21, 41, 48, 50, 52, 57, 59, 62,
    66–67, 76, 108, 113–17, 119,
    122, 124, 129, 167–93, 197–98,
    200, 236, 265, 313, 315.
Rosary, 13, 39, 82, 84–85, 128–29,
    205–11.
Sabbath(batical), 16, 18, 56, 180,
    233–34.
sacred, xx, 50–51, 55, 59, 62, 64–65,
    67, 71–73, 78, 81–82, 86, 91–
    93, 98, 102, 113, 122, 128–29,
    131, 144, 169, 180, 182, 186,
    190, 193–97, 206, 217–67, 308.
sacred times, 194–95.
Sampter, Jessie, 183.
seek(feek), 12, 180, 241, 254–55, 291.
Seyfried, Thomas N. Dr., 139.
Shavuot, Pentecost, 18, 67, 241, 290.
Shaw, Jim, 206.
Shroud of Turin, 64–65, 72, 74–76,
    79–92.
simultaneously, 115.
Sitting Bull, Chief, 125.
soul, 3, 11–16, 50, 96, 118, 128, 148,
    153, 196, 241, 284, 292, 301.
spirit(ual), see also Holy Spirit, xiii,
    3, 7, 9–15, 23, 26, 30, 33, 39,
    47, 50, 66–67, 104, 119, 122,
    128–29, 140, 143–44, 159–61,
    163, 168–69, 171, 173, 175–76,
    178, 181, 187, 192, 206–07,
    243, 259, 265, 278, 291, 304.

subject(ive), 5, 8–10, 14–15, 30, 32, 36,
        129, 143, 158, 218, 229, 243,
        245, 264, 287, 292, 299, 304,
        311, 320.
substance(tial), xx, 37–38, 66, 117, 252,
        255, 266, 316.
sustain(able), 10, 18, 33, 43, 95, 117,
        140, 142, 181.
sustenance, 143, 248, sustenazo, 160.
symbol(s, ism, ic), xiii–xiv, xix–xxi,
        3–5, 8–12, 16–21, 23–24, 30,
        33–35, 37–39, 44, 49–52, 55,
        57–59, 61–62, 64–69, 76, 98,
        100, 103, 105, 113–17, 119–25,
        127–29, 143, 158–62, 164–74,
        177–85, 189, 191–92, 195,
        197–98, 200–01, 210, 225, 241,
        305, 312.
symbols, elements:
    bowl(s), xiv, xx, xxi, 17, 20–22, 34,
        37–38, 52, 55, 57–58, 60–61,
        66–67, 69, 148, 157, 168–69,
        175–77, 179–80, 183–89, 313,
        315.
    bramble bush, (burning, thorn),
        14, 41–51, 53, 55, 81, 100–01,
        103, 110, 120–21, 126, 128,
        154–55, 169, 172, 174–75, 182,
        198, 218, 235–36, 304.
    branch(es), xiv, xix, 20–21, 49,
        52–53, 55, 58–59, 63, 69, 98,
        121–25, 128, 132, 155, 159,
        166–69, 172–77, 180, 182, 198,
        200, 284, 314–16.
    bud(ded, s), xiv, xx, xxi, 17, 21–22,
        34, 37–38, 55–61, 100, 102–03,
        123–24, 129, 168–69, 185, 314.
    bud, knob(p), calyx, xiv, 20–21,
        52–53, 55–58, 69, 314.
    candle(stick, labra, labrum),
        52, 55, 63, 67, 121, 241–42,
        311–13, 315.
    classification of images, 34, 36–40.
    coherence(t), 13, 183.
    cup, 21, 36–38, 52–53, 57, 61,
        65–69. 72–78, 100, 121, 141,
        184, 296, 313.

hawthorn stick, thorn, 100, 103,
        155, 235.
horse, 153, 176–77, 185–87, 200,
        228, 256, 292.
incense, 61–62, 177, 184, 188, 316.
lamp(s, stand), 20–21, 47–48, 50,
        52–53, 57, 60, 62–63, 114–115,
        122–123, 167–75, 179–82, 187,
        200, 241–42, 313, 315.
light(ning, enlightened), xiii, xix,
        2–3, 14, 21, 35, 37–38, 43, 46,
        49, 63, 75, 80, 122–24, 128,
        131, 145, 152, 156, 169, 174,
        178, 187–88, 192, 194–95, 233,
        241, 247, 251, 253, 256, 284,
        296, 303, 305–06, 308.
river, 17, 113–15, 178, 185, 187–88,
        190, 201–02, 221–22, 228, 254,
        292, 295, 297, 306, 308, 319.
river of life, 17, 113, 115, 188,
        201–02.
root, 21, 41–42, 44, 49, 52–53,
        56–57, 59–60, 69, 103, 121,
        125, 132–33, 141, 147, 149,
        153, 158–59, 166, 172, 178,
        181, 200, 285–86, 309, 313–16.
        (root of bitterness), 27.
seal(ed, s), 57–58, 168–69, 175–79,
        181, 183, 185–90, 265, 308,
        315.
seed, xix–xxi, 16–19, 37–40, 114,
        120–22, 124–25, 141–43,
        159–60 162–67, 180, 185, 188,
        198, 200, 235, 315.
Seed of the Woman, xx, 16, 19,
        114, 120–21, 124–25, 159, 163,
        166–67, 200, 315.
sefira(ot), 42, 44–45, 175.
shaft, 20, 55, 58, 172, 180, 182, 185,
        314.
singular(ity), 21, 113–15, 120, 159,
        162, 173, 183.
thorn of Glastonbury, 101, 103,
        110, 218, 235–36, 304.
time(s), xiii, xx, 9–10, 23, 34–36,
        39, 44, 57, 59, 65, 72–73,
        75–76, 91, 99, 101–03, 106,
        114, 116, 118, 120–21, 124,

134, 136–39, 141, 143–48, 157,
161–62, 164–66, 169, 172–85,
190–95, 207, 219, 226, 228–29,
234–36, 241–42, 245–49, 252,
255, 257, 265, 276, 278, 291,
293, 296, 298–301, 303, 305,
308, 310–11, 315, 318, 320.

time, times and half a time, 181,
185, 190–91, 193.

timelessness, 196.

trumpet(s), 168–69, 175–80, 183,
185–86, 189, 315.

water, 17, 35, 38, 46, 78, 118, 120,
127–28, 140, 145, 152, 156,
170, 178, 187, 233, 241, 252,
256, 263, 297.

woman clothed with the sun, 172,
175, 180–82.

temple, xix, 20, 41, 55, 59, 62, 66, 81,
113, 115, 122, 161, 169, 171,
176, 178, 181–82, 192, 215,
217, 225, 247.

Three Sisters, 149.

thought(s), 1, 3, 5, 26, 31, 44, 50, 99,
115, 141, 184, 205, 230, 233,
285, 299, 306–07, 310.

tin, (tinn, tinne, mining), 71, 98, 101,
112, 142, 217–18, 225–32.

transcendent(al, dence), xix, xxi, 3–4,
7–9, 28, 31, 35, 40, 49, 113, 115–
17, 119, 142, 194, 196–98, 318.

tree of life, (lower case without
headings), xiii, xiv, xx–xxi,
16–17, 19, 21, 41–42, 48, 50,
65, 69, 76, 93, 100, 113–127,
131, 135, 140, 144, 159–61,
166–69, 171, 173–75, 181,
188–89, 197–98, 200.

truth, 9, 11, 33, 39, 99, 232, 246–47,
249, 251, 253, 255–57, 266,
296.

unconditional(ed), 11, 22, 117. *see* also,
condition(al, ed).

unity (united), xiii, xxi, 9, 43–44, 102,
112, 124, 128, 176, 194, 197,
210, 309.

value(able), xxi, 8–11, 23–27, 31–33,
49, 51, 57, 64, 70, 101, 116–17,
138, 142, 176, 261, 281, 288,
302. valueless, 102.

Vignon markings, 85.

will, 8–9, 12–13, 18, 24–25, 30, 41, 44,
46, 48–49, 58, 60, 62–63, 99,
103, 114, 117, 124–29, 142,
144, 152, 156–59, 161, 163–64,
166, 168, 171–72, 175, 180,
182, 184–87, 191, 195–97, 199,
205, 207, 212, 232, 236, 242,
246–47, 249, 255–56, 263, 287,
291, 299.

witness(es), 48, 61, 66, 75–76, 85, 106,
114–15, 122, 135, 166, 168,
171–73, 179–82, 187, 191–92,
200, 226, 236, 238, 243, 248,
262, 264, 278, 283–84, 294.

worth(y), 99, 126, 142, 209, 243, 259,
264, 275–76, 287, 293, 301,
309, untrustworthy, 69.

Yogananda, 3, 39.

Note: some word references are found
in the footnotes.

www.ingramcontent.com/pod-product-compliance
Lightning Source LLC
Chambersburg PA
CBHW070909100426
42814CB00003B/109